Health and Wellbeing in Childhood

Second edition

The period from birth to 12 years is crucial in a child's development and can significantly impact future educational success, resilience and participation in society. The second edition of *Health and Wellbeing in Childhood* provides readers with a comprehensive foundation in health and wellbeing education across key priority areas, covering physical, social and emotional learning and development.

This edition has been thoroughly updated to include the latest research and resources, and incorporates expanded material on diversity, mental health and contemplative practice. A new instructor companion website, www.cambridge.edu .au/academic/healthandwellbeing, features a curated suite of reading materials, extension questions and sample responses designed to further readers' knowledge and skills for practice.

Each chapter features practical examples, case studies and links to curriculum documentation which illustrate the theory and draw connections to classroom practice, while key terms, reflective activities and end-of-chapter questions consolidate key concepts.

Written by an expert author team comprised of leading academics and practitioners, *Health and Wellbeing in Childhood* equips readers with the knowledge and skills to promote and implement effective practice in the field, making it essential reading for pre-service teachers, academics and practicing educators alike.

Susanne Garvis is Professor of Child and Youth Studies (Early Childhood) at the University of Gothenburg, Sweden.

Donna Pendergast is Professor and Dean of the School of Education and Professional Studies at Griffith University, Queensland.

Health and Wellbeing in Childhood

Second edition

Edited by

Susanne Garvis and Donna Pendergast

CAMBRIDGE
UNIVERSITY PRESS

University Printing House, Cambridge CB2 8BS, United Kingdom

One Liberty Plaza, 20th Floor, New York, NY 10006, USA

477 Williamstown Road, Port Melbourne, VIC 3207, Australia

4843/24, 2nd Floor, Ansari Road, Daryaganj, Delhi – 110002, India

79 Anson Road, #06–04/06, Singapore 079906

Cambridge University Press is part of the University of Cambridge.

It furthers the University's mission by disseminating knowledge in the pursuit of education, learning and research at the highest international levels of excellence.

www.cambridge.org
Information on this title: www.cambridge.org/9781316623008

First published 2014
Second edition 2017

Cover designed by Leigh Ashforth, watershed art + design
Typeset by Newgen Publishing and Data Services
Printed in Singapore by Markono Print Media Pte Ltd, May 2017

A catalogue record for this publication is available from the British Library

A Cataloguing-in-Publication entry is available from the catalogue of the National Library of Australia at www.nla.gov.au

ISBN 978-1-316-62300-8 Paperback

Additional resources for this publication at www.cambridge.edu.au/academic/healthandwellbeing

This book is dedicated to our families. We particularly dedicate this to the young people in our families.
Kyrra, Bess, Blyton, Zeke and Bader
and
James and Hamish

Contents

Part 2: Dimensions of health and wellbeing

Chapter 19: Fostering children's wellbeing through play opportunities   299
Marjory Ebbeck, Hoi Yin Bonnie Yim and Lai Wan Maria Lee

Chapter 20: Bullying and social emotional wellbeing in children   315
Cathrine Neilsen-Hewett and Kay Bussey

Chapter 21: Strengthening social and emotional learning
in children with special needs   333
Wendi Beamish and Beth Saggers

Kay Bussey is Associate Professor in Child and Adolescent Psychology at Macquarie University, Australia. She has been the recipient of numerous awards including a Fulbright Fellowship and an Award for Excellence in Higher Degree Research from Macquarie University. Kay's interests and publications span several areas of social development including moral development, gender development, bullying and aggression, and children's participation in the legal system. She has authored over 100 peer-reviewed articles and book chapters and has co-authored two books. The Australian Research Council and the National Health and Medical Research Council have funded her research.

Jennifer Cartmel is Senior Lecturer in the School of Human Services and Social Work, Griffith University, Australia. She is an experienced teacher, researcher and practitioner in the field of children and families, particularly in services such as school-age care, schools and integrated children's services. Jennifer's areas of expertise are in afterschool hours services, childhood studies, and workforce development in children's services. Her methodological expertise is in qualitative approaches. Her research examines the transformative changes in the thinking and practices of children and adults using a critical reflection model as they engage in schools and community services.

Siobhan Casey is an Occupational Therapist. She is currently undertaking her PhD studies where she is investigating the play and social skills of a group of resilient children aged four to seven years. Siobhan works as a Paediatric Occupational Therapist in a small rural town in Victoria, Australia.

Marilyn Casley is Lecturer in the Bachelor of Child and Family Studies, School of Human Services and Social Work, Griffith University, Australia. Marilyn has over 30 years' experience in children's and community services. Marilyn's research interests focus on using conversational processes to develop resilience and leadership skills in children, and the development of pedagogical leadership and integrated practice in children's and human services.

Sarah Cavanagh is Clinical Psychologist and Manager at the Australian Psychological Society (APS). She has over 15 years' experience in health promotion and prevention in both government and non-government sectors. Sarah has led the development of KidsMatter for the APS since 2008.

Jo Cole is a Clinical Psychologist with 20 years' experience in perinatal, infant, child and adolescent mental health, and mental health promotion, prevention and early intervention. From 2009 to 2015 she led the development of the KidsMatter Early Childhood initiative for the Australian Psychological Society. Jo is an experienced trainer, facilitator and clinical supervisor.

Susan Danby is Research Fellow and Professor in the School of Early Childhood, and Co-leader of the Childhoods in Changing Contexts Research Group, at Queensland

University of Technology, Australia. Her research investigates social interaction in children's peer groups, and adult–child communication in institutional contexts that include educational and family settings, helplines and clinical settings. Her recent projects investigate how young children engage with digital technologies in their everyday lives in home and school contexts. Susan is on the editorial boards of the *Journal of Early Childhood Literacy, Children & Society* (Wiley Online Library) and *Linguistics and Education.*

Galina Daraganova is Acting Executive Manger, Longitudinal Studies, Australian Institutue of Family Studies and Honorary Melbourne University Fellow specialising in survey methodology, social statistics, and statistical models for network-based social processes. She has significant experience working in academia and government in the field of epidemiology and health statistics with expertise in longitudinal data. Galina's work has broad application, from tracking the spread of infectious diseases to following the developmental trajectories of children from birth to adolescence. She has worked across different research teams in Australia, France and the USA and widely published on various topics including mental health and wellbeing; children's eating behaviour and body image; social and emotional wellbeing of children; and health and educational inequalities during childhood.

Elise Davis is Associate Director, Jack Brockhoff Child Health and Wellbeing Program at the University of Melbourne, Australia. Elise's research focuses on the promotion of children's health and wellbeing and quality of life for those experiencing health inequalities. She has also led the development and evaluation of a program that builds the capacity of child care educators to promote children's wellbeing. In addition, Elise has led the first qualitative studies assessing the knowledge and skills that child care educators (both in long day care and family day care) have in the area of mental health promotion.

Theresa Doherty is currently Advisor, Research Development for Public Health Services DHHS, Tasmania, Australia. She is also Research Fellow at the Institute for the Study of Social Change, University of Tasmania. She has held a range of health professional and policy positions in the public, private and academic sectors.

Janet Dyment is Senior Lecturer in the Faculty of Education at the University of Tasmania, Australia. Her research interests lie in whole-school approaches to sustainability as well as health and wellbeing. She teaches in the Outdoor and Sustainability Education program at the University of Tasmania and enjoys working with a number of environmental and educational community organisations.

Marjory Ebbeck is Emeritus Professor and a member of the University of South Australia's Professoriate. She supervises research degree students, many of them international. She also contributes as a Senior Academic Advisor to SEED Training Institute in Singapore. Marjory is an active researcher and scholar in the field of early childhood. She has been a consultant on development of early childhood teacher education programs to many countries including Brunei, Malaysia, Hong Kong, Singapore, the USA and the UK.

Mary Eckhardt currently manages the *Move Well Eat Well* – Early Childhood Award Program for the Health Settings Unit, DHHS, Tasmania, Australia. She has held a range of management, social marketing, policy and social research positions in the public, private and tertiary education sectors.

Sherridan Emery is Doctoral Candidate in the Faculty of Education at the University of Tasmania, Australia. Her research investigates the concept of cultural wellbeing in classroom communities where she engages teachers and educators in research conversations about supporting children's wellbeing in education. Sherridan is actively involved in international research collaborations in the field of Early Childhood Education for Sustainability and in postgraduate student wellbeing.

Lina Engelen is Research Fellow in the Faculty of Health Sciences, University of Sydney, Australia. She manages the Sydney Playground research project, aimed at increasing physical activity and social skills in primary school children by means of school playground intervention. Lina's research interests span children's health, physical activity, oral physiology, the interaction and perception of food, and nutrition. She is the author of journal articles and book chapters and her research has been presented at international conferences.

Kim-Michelle Gilson is Research Fellow within the Jack Brockhoff Child Health and Wellbeing Program at the University of Melbourne, Australia. She has a strong interest in mental health promotion, parental mental health and child disability. Kim is also a registered psychologist with experience in school settings.

Linda Harrison is Professor of Early Childhood Education and Associate Dean, Research, in the Faculty of Arts and Education, Charles Sturt University, Australia. Linda's research and writing focuses on very young children's experiences of child care/early education; transitions; child socio-emotional, cognitive and speech-language development; processes within services that underpin the provision of high-quality education and care; and new methodologies for researching these issues. She contributed to *Growing up in Australia: The Longitudinal Study of Australian Children* for the Australian Government Department of Social Services and draws on this very large dataset in much of her work.

Gavin Hazel is Program Leader at the Hunter Institute of Mental Health, Newcastle, Australia where he focuses on the development, implementation and evaluation of evidence-informed resources, practices, and professional education. Gavin is an experienced education and capability development professional, specialising in the area of child and youth mental health, wellbeing and resilience.

Judy Kynaston is General Manager of KidsMatter Early Childhood at Early Childhood Australia (ECA). Judy is an early childhood teacher with extensive experience in a variety of early childhood education and care services. Prior to commencing her role with ECA, she was involved in providing training to the early childhood education and care sector as well as advocating for children in the development of policy that improves the lives and wellbeing of young children.

Lai Wan Maria Lee is Vice-President of the Pacific Early Childhood Education Research Association (Hong Kong). Her research interests are Confucian values for young children, children's literature, creative art and music, child development, children in transition and teacher education. Maria is an advisor for the Hong Kong Intellectually Disabled Education and Advocacy League.

Narelle Lemon is Associate Professor in Education at Swinburne University of Technology, Melbourne, Australia. Narelle's research agenda is focused on engagement and participation in the area of building learner capacity to engage with cultural organisations and community arts programs; arts education; and social media for professional development including Twitter, Instagram, Pinterest and blogging. She is especially focused on social photography and the generation of visual narratives to shared lived experiences. Narelle blogs at *Chat with Rellypops*, Tweets as *@Rellypops*, and has recently begun a new project to promote stories of how creativity and mindfulness are applied to people's lives from various disciplines in the community. This *Explore and Create Stories* series is curated on Instagram through *@exploreandcreateco*.

Timothy Lynch is Primary Physical Education Teacher and Researcher at Plymouth University, UK. He is the current Vice-President (Oceania region) for the International Council for Health, Physical Education, Recreation, Sport and Dance (ICHPER-SD). ICHPER was founded as a non-government organisation (NGO) in 1958 and is officially recognised by UNESCO and the International Olympic Committee (IOC). Tim has been involved in primary (and early years), secondary and higher education for 22 years. He has 15 years' teaching experience as a primary classroom teacher, was Head Teacher for Foundation stage and Key Stage 1 (3–7 years), and is a Health and Physical Education (HPE) specialist. Timothy has worked in various school communities and education systems in Australia, Qatar and the UK.

Matthew Manning is Associate Professor and Applied Microeconomist in the Centre for Social Research and Methods at the Australian National University. Matthew's research focuses predominantly on the economics of crime and enforcement. He has published in areas such as juvenile justice, crime prevention, drug and alcohol prevention, police legitimacy and wellbeing/life satisfaction.

Jane McCormack is Adjunct Associate Professor at Charles Sturt University, Australia, and certified practising member of Speech Pathology Australia. She is a past winner of the Sir Robert Menzies Research Scholarship in the Allied

Health Sciences (2010), the SCOPUS Young Australian Researcher of the Year for Humanities and the Social Sciences (2011), and a runner-up in the Pursuit Award for international research into childhood disability (2013, Canada). Jane co-edited *Introduction to Speech, Language and Literacy* (Oxford University Press) and has co-authored chapters in *Measures for Children with Developmental Disabilities: An ICF Approach* (Mac Keith Press) and *Listening to Children and Young People with Speech, Language and Communication Needs* (J&R Press).

Sharynne McLeod is Professor of Speech and Language Acquisition at Charles Sturt University, Australia. She is an elected Life Member of Speech Pathology Australia, Fellow of the American Speech-Language-Hearing Association (ASHA) and has been an Australian Research Council Future Fellow. She is Vice-President of the International Clinical Linguistics and Phonetics Association (ICPLA) and was editor of the *International Journal of Speech-Language Pathology* (IJSLP; 2005–2014). Sharynne's books include *Children's Speech: An Evidence-Based Approach to Assessment and Intervention* (Pearson), *Introduction to Speech, Language and Literacy* (Oxford University Press), *The International Guide to Speech Acquisition* (Cengage), *Interventions for Speech Sound Disorders in Children* (Paul H. Brookes), *Children's Speech: An Evidence-Based Approach to Assessment and Intervention* (Pearson), *Speech Sounds* (Plural), *Listening to Children and Young People with Speech, Language, and Communication Needs* (J&R Press), *Multilingual Aspects of Speech Sound Disorders in Children* (Multilingual Matters) and *Working with Families in Speech-Language Pathology* (Plural).

Romana Morda is Senior Lecturer in Psychology at Victoria University, Melbourne, Australia. She is a registered psychologist with experience in working with children and their families. She completed a PhD that examined the development and enactment of leadership skills in young children's groups. Her research interests include the social and emotional development of children, leadership, workplace stress and bullying. She has also undertaken research examining student transition to university.

Geraldine Naughton is Professor in Paediatric Exercise Science in the School of Exercise Science, at the Melbourne campus of the Australian Catholic University. Her research focuses of improving health-related outcomes in young people through physical activity. She has researched with a range of young populations from overweight and obese children to intensively training adolescents. Geraldine has been part of several multidisciplinary school-based interventions to reduce sedentary behaviour and improve physical and social health of children and adolescents.

Cathrine Neilsen-Hewett is Director of the Early Years at the University of Wollongong, Australia and has been a lecturer and researcher in early childhood for over 19 years. Cathrine has delivered workshops and invited addresses to parents, educators, corporations and government bodies both in Australia and overseas and has served on both state and federal government advisory committees. Her research expertise includes development in early childhood, the importance of positive peer relationships, bullying, early childhood pedagogy and practice, and childhood socialisation. Cathrine's current research projects focus on quality early childhood education and care environments, and enhancing access to early childhood education and health services as well as promoting social inclusion in Indigenous communities.

Jan Nicholson is Inaugural Roberta Holmes Professorial Chair at the Judith Lumley Centre at La Trobe University, Australia. She holds honorary research positions as Principal Research Fellow at Murdoch Children's Research Centre, and Adjunct Professor at Queensland University of Technology, Australia. Her research examines the influence of contemporary family, social, and organisational environments on children's healthy development, with a focus on vulnerable families.

Anita Nelson Niehues is Assistant Professor in Occupational Therapy at Lenior-Rhyne University, North Carolina, USA. Her research examines parental perception of risk and the influence on children's daily activities. She has interests in early intervention and public school settings.

Andrea Nolan is Professor of Early Childhood Education at Deakin University, Australia. Andrea has taught and researched in the early years for many years. Her research interests include early childhood workforce capabilities with a particular interest in professionalisation and practice, and the professional learning of teachers.

Natalie Parletta is Senior Research Fellow at the University of South Australia and a Nutritionist/Accredited Practising Dietitian at the Centre for Health and Wellbeing in Adelaide. She holds a PhD, Bachelor of Psychology (Honours) and Master of Dietetics, has published over 50 scientific papers and given over 200 talks/interviews. For over 10 years she has researched links between nutrition and mental health and parental influences on children's food choices. In clinical practice, Natalie is particularly interested in the role of nutrition and dietary food intolerance in children's behaviour, and helping parents to instil healthy eating behaviours in their children.

Sivanes Phillipson is Associate Professor of Family Studies at the Faculty of Education, Monash University Clayton Campus, Australia. Sivanes is also the Routledge Editor for the Evolving Families Series. She has diverse international experience and knowledge base in the broad field of measurements and systems approach to families and children's education, with expertise in large data set analysis and modelling. Her current projects include an Australian Research Council funded project on numeracy learning at home and a nationwide survey on family perspectives around educational resources.

Beth Saggers is Senior Lecturer in the School of Cultural and Professional Learning at Queensland University of Technology, Australia. She currently lectures in autism spectrum disorders (ASD), catering for diversity, inclusive practices, and behaviour support. She has over 20 years of experience working with students on the autism spectrum across a range of age groups and in a variety of educational settings.

Margaret Sims is Professor of Early Childhood at the University of New England, Australia. Her research interests centre around quality community-based services for young children and families. These arise from her experiences as a community worker in range of services, and include early intervention, inclusion, family support and child care.

Kerry Smith is Lecturer in the School of Human Services and Social Work, Griffith University, Australia. She has extensive experience in the field of children's services including managing and owning a school-age care service, experience in adult learning, teaching, and researching and is currently involved in the delivery of social, emotional learning to educators throughout Queensland. Her areas of expertise are childhood studies and professional development for children's services. She is completing a Masters of Philosophy using an evaluative approach to examine Talking Circles as a method of listening to the voices of children.

Karen Stagnitti is Professor, Personal Chair of the School of Health and Social Development at Deakin University, Australia. For over 30 years Karen has mainly worked in early childhood intervention programs in community-based settings as part of a specialist paediatric multidisciplinary team. Her area of research is children's play where she has published prolifically and presents her work on the play ability of children nationally and internationally.

Ann Taket is Chair in Health and Social Exclusion and Director of the Centre for Health through Action on Social Exclusion at Deakin University, Australia. She leads programs of research in social exclusion and health; prevention and intervention in violence and abuse; and human rights-based approaches in public health.

Maryanne Theobald is Senior Lecturer in the School of Early Childhood at Queensland University of Technology, Australia. Maryanne has methodological expertise in qualitative approaches including ethnomethodology and conversation analysis, and participatory research using video-stimulated accounts. She has research experience in communication and classroom talk, friendships and disputes in the school, playground, therapy and in multilingual contexts.

Catherine Thompson is now retired from active research with Queensland University of Technology, Australia, although still maintains a keen interest in research involving early childhood. In addition to research work, her career background includes devising and implementing intervention programs for children with physical impairments, learning difficulties and developmental delays both within Australia and in the UK. Cathy is currently working on the further development of her book and resources for fine motor skills to help children to become more independent and confident in their classroom setting.

Karen Thorpe is Professor at the Centre for Children's Health Research, Queensland University of Technology, Australia. Her research examines the effect of early experience, both within the family and child-care settings, on development and learning across the life-course. She has conducted a range of studies using large-scale longitudinal designs that include observational methods.

Kerryann Walsh is Associate Professor in the Faculty of Education at Queensland University of Technology, Australia. She has researched and published in the areas of school-based child sexual abuse prevention programs, parent-child communication about sexual abuse prevention, professionals' reporting of child abuse and neglect, and teacher training for child protection.

Manjula Waniganayake is Professor of Early Childhood at Macquarie University, Australia. Over three decades, Manjula has been involved in the early childhood sector as teacher, parent, advocate, policy analyst, teacher educator, and researcher. She was awarded an Honorary Doctorate from the University of Tampere, Finland for her contribution to early childhood leadership. Manjula's research and teaching interests focus on childhood socialisation, family diversity, educational leadership and professional learning. She believes in diversity and social justice, and values learning from others within Australia and beyond.

Susan Whatman is Senior Lecturer in Health and Physical Education and Sports Pedagogy in the School of Education and Professional Studies at Griffith University, Australia. Susan's expertise resides in teaching and learning in health and physical education and sports coaching contexts, and also in Indigenous education. She has a particular interest in power and control relations in curriculum decision-making in education systems and finding ways to empower educationally disadvantaged learners and communities.

Christine Woodrow is a Senior Researcher in the Centre for Educational Research at Western Sydney University, Australia. Through her research work in high poverty early childhood contexts in Chile and Australia, Christine has developed a framework for sustainable leadership that supports the development of innovative pedagogies for teaching and family engagement through a funds of knowledge approach. This work has had a significant impact on educators' re-conceptualisation of their work as leadership. This shift has been evident in the transnational research Christine has undertaken about early childhood professional identities.

Shirley Wyver is Senior Lecturer in Child Development at the Institute of Early Childhood, Macquarie University, Australia. Her research interests are in early play and cognitive/social development. She is a Chief Investigator on the Sydney

Playground Project which examines use of loose parts play and risk-reframing on school playgrounds. Shirley also conducts research in the area of blindness/low vision and development.

Hoi Yin Bonnie Yim is Associate Professor and Course Director of the Bachelor of Early Childhood Education Honours (BECE-Hons) and BECE (International) course at Deakin University, Australia. Bonnie's research interests include early childhood education and policy, child development, curriculum development and evaluation, cross-cultural studies, active learning engagement, and teacher education.

Preface

The age range birth to 12 years is recognised as crucial with significant consequences for ongoing educational success and future participation in society. Professionals in this critical phase need specialist preparation along with the skills and knowledge to understand and manage issues related to health and wellbeing.

This book will assist educators, academics, pre-service student teachers and teachers in their quest to successfully develop and implement effective practices for children's health and wellbeing. The book brings together the expertise of academics in the field of early years and the primary years of school. It is not exhaustive in its coverage – several books would be required to document and detail all of the relevant aspects of health and wellbeing, and each chapter could easily be expanded into a book in its own right.

The organisation of the book reflects the key priorities for health and wellbeing for children aged birth to 12 years of age. Each chapter concludes with questions that guide reflection of the concepts developed in the chapter. In addition to meeting editorial requirements, each chapter has been peer reviewed. The book is a collaborative effort, drawn from a range of scholars and practitioners who responded to the open call for contributions made by the editors in 2012 and then again in 2016 for a second edition. The book fills a gap in the resources available for health and wellbeing in Australia, bringing together sound scholarly debates and practical applications.

Professor Susanne Garvis and Professor Donna Pendergast

Acknowledgements

The editors wish to thank the wonderful authors of this second edition. We thank the reviewers for their insightful comments and the publishers for their confidence and assistance in this project.

PART 1

Context

CHAPTER 1

The importance of health and wellbeing

Donna Pendergast and Susanne Garvis

Introduction

According to the United Nations, the world population was 7.3 billion in mid-2015 and is projected to increase to over 8.5 billion in 2030 (United Nations, Department of Economic and Social Affairs, Population Division, 2015). In 2015, 26 per cent of the world population was aged between birth and 15 years (United Nations, 2015). It is predicted that by 2050 the relative percentage of young people aged 0–9 will decline – see Figure 1.1 (United Nations, 2015). More than half the global population growth up to 2050 is expected to occur in Africa. These demographic trends result from a combination of increased life expectancy, along with the effects of birth and population controls affecting fertility rates. What is evident is that the proportion of the world population in the birth-through-childhood group is large and, although it will decrease proportionately in the future, it will continue to be a dominant group in the world population (see Figure 1.1).

Children currently aged 0–15 years are all members of Generation Z. A **generation** is typically defined as the average interval of time between the birth of parents and the birth of their offspring with on average a birth generation 20–22 years, and a lifespan four times that generational length (Pendergast & Garvis, 2014). Every person is a member of a generation and this is based on their year of birth. Generational theory seeks to understand and characterise cohorts of people according to their birth generation. It is a dynamic socio-cultural theoretical framework that employs a broad brush-stroke approach, rather than an individual focus (Pendergast, 2008).

Generation: the average interval of time between the birth of parents and the birth of their offspring with on average a birth generation 20–22 years, and a lifespan four times that generational length (Pendergast & Garvis, 2014).

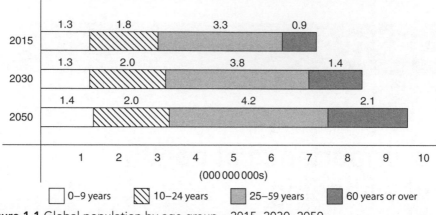

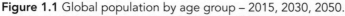

Figure 1.1 Global population by age group – 2015, 2030, 2050.

Generations are defined not by formal process, but rather by demographers, the press and media, popular culture, market researchers, and by members of the generation themselves (Pendergast, 2007). The basic notion is that as members of a generation, we typically share a birth year range, which is more likely to expose us to experiences that are typical of that time, and to a set of social and economic conditions that shape our generation in particular ways. The effect is the emergence of patterns and influences on collective thinking which leads to the acquisition of broad and common values and beliefs. The acquisition of values and belief systems principally occurs during the formative or childhood years of each generation (Pendergast, 2008).

The birth years for Generation Z commenced in 2002 and in 2017 incorporates our current young people up to the age of 15. The values and beliefs of the emerging generation are being shaped and defined, with contemporary world and local events impacting on this generation in ways never before experienced. According to McCrindle (2013), three words summarise Generation Z: global, visual, digital (see Figure 1.2). He explains that this group of young people are being shaped by the shifts in society resulting from acceleration and rapid change in complex times. Features of these times include the advancement of digital technology into almost every avenue of people's lives, along with a global perspective and visual pedagogies that come with the tools of technology. Peers remain a significant shaping force.

Along with the establishment of values and belief systems, the early years from birth to 12 years are increasingly recognised as the crucial time for laying the foundations for life with significant consequences for ongoing educational success, resilience and future participation in society. The formative years are the years where the capacity to make a difference can and does have profound effects. Carers and educators need specialist preparation as they are required to promote and teach health and wellbeing and to have the skills and knowledge to understand and manage the plethora of issues related to young children. Around the world, including in Australia, **early years** education is undergoing significant reform

Early years include preschool and the first two years of formal schooling.

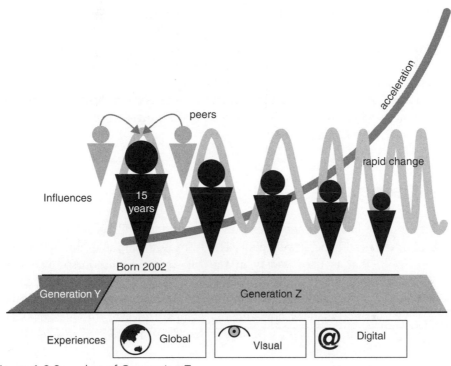

Figure 1.2 Snapshot of Generation Z.

as the potential to improve quality of life is better understood. These reforms place health and wellbeing as central constructs of this agenda. This chapter will explore the concepts of health and wellbeing and will share some of the initiatives that have put health and wellbeing on the agenda for early years learners in contemporary times.

Health

According to the World Health Organization (WHO), in a definition that has stood the test of time and remains unamended since 1948, '**health** is a state of complete physical, mental and social wellbeing and not merely the absence of disease or infirmity' (WHO, 1948). The first international conference for the promotion of health was held in 1986, and it was here that the *Ottawa Charter for Health Promotion* (*The Charter*) to encourage action to achieve health for all by the year 2000 and beyond was formalised, and the public health agendas around health promotion were shaped globally for the first time. According to *The Charter*, the fundamental conditions and resources for health are: peace; shelter; education; food; income; a stable ecosystem; sustainable resources; social justice; and equity. Improvement in health requires a secure foundation in these basic prerequisites (WHO, 1986).

> **Health** is a state of complete physical, mental and social wellbeing and not merely the absence of disease or infirmity (World Health Organization, 1948).

Consistent with this view, the Australian Institute of Health and Welfare (AIHW) (2012) notes that a person's health and wellbeing result from a complex interplay between biological, lifestyle, socio-economic, societal and environmental factors, many of which can be modified to some extent by health care and other interventions. Given the scope and complexity of these fundamental conditions and resources, the challenge of achieving health for all is patently obvious. For early years learners, who are reliant upon others for the provision of these conditions and resources, the challenges are even greater.

Wellbeing

The definition of health is dependent upon an understanding of the concept of 'physical, mental and social wellbeing'. The term **wellbeing** is a ubiquitous term that is used widely in the full range of discourses in society, including in policy and legal arenas, in education and the academy, in the workplace, in commercial settings and in media discourses such as television and magazines. However, there is no single definition of this commonly used term, which is in use around the world.

Wellbeing is a way of considering an overall state of being that might be measured using a range of indicators that are typically context specific.

SPOTLIGHT 1.1: DEVELOPING AN EVIDENCE BASE ABOUT HEALTH AND WELLBEING

In the last two decades the Organisation for Economic Co-operation and Development (OECD) has worked with a number of researchers to develop a sound evidence base that can inform policy makers and citizens to better understand the notion of wellbeing and to develop measures in order to improve wellbeing. For example, recent work on subjective wellbeing links the concept with happiness and quality of life (OECD, 2013). The OECD's Better Life Initiative, launched in 2011, aims to measure society's progress across 11 domains of wellbeing, ranging from income, jobs, health, skills and housing, through to civic engagement and the environment.

In a study conducted by Ereaut and Whiting (2008) titled *What do we mean by well being? And why might it matter?* the researchers concluded that 'we can see the complexity of definition and possible meaning for contemporary ideas of wellbeing … in fact, the research showed that the word "wellbeing" behaves somewhat strangely, and contains many anomalies and puzzles' (p. 6). The researchers settled on six key discourses that each hold a place in our understanding and use of the term wellbeing:

- *Wellbeing and the medical heritage.* This is where wellbeing is regarded as being closely aligned with the notion of health. This version of wellbeing is considered to be the dominant discourse for the term wellbeing.
- *Wellbeing as an operationalised discourse.* This is where wellbeing is formalised into measures which can be used as indicators of wellbeing, including desired outcomes and indicators of achievement.
- *Wellbeing as sustainability discourse.* This notion of wellbeing incorporates the idea of responsible society and the capacity to be replicable and more widely available for people; not just the individual.
- *Wellbeing within a discourse of holism.* The notion that not only the mind and body are the focus but also the social, environmental and other facets of life.
- *Wellbeing and philosophy.* In this understanding of wellbeing the notion of aiming for an ideal state, with a vision of what is best and desirable for a person, is the core meaning.
- *Wellbeing, consumer culture and self-responsibility.* This is a discourse where people are encouraged to strive for resilience, independence and achievement and to take personal responsibility for decision-making, their health and ultimately their sense of wellbeing.

For the purposes of this book, we are taking the multiple meanings of wellbeing, along with the dominant discourse connecting it to the health agenda, thereby incorporating the broad discourses of wellbeing and considering these in terms of early years learners. Bradshaw, Hoelscher and Richardson (2007) assist in honing the definition of wellbeing for the early years. They define child wellbeing as 'the realisation of children's rights and the fulfilment of the opportunity for every child to be all she or he can be in the light of a child's abilities, potential and skills' (p. 8). So, what are children's rights?

Global context: Health and wellbeing

The Convention on the Rights of the Child (CRC) is the most recognised international treaty setting out the basic rights of children, along with the obligations of governments to fulfil those rights. It has been accepted and ratified by almost every country in the world. The treaty was adopted by the United Nations General Assembly in 1989 and ratified by Australia in 1990 but is yet to be incorporated into Australian law. The Convention has 54 articles, with numbers 43–54 specifying how adults and governments should work together to make sure that all children realise their rights. The articles have four fundamental principles:

1. *Non-discrimination.* Children should neither benefit nor suffer because of their race, colour, gender, language, religion, national, social or ethnic origin, or because of any political or other opinion; because of their caste, property or birth status; or because they are disabled.
2. *The best interests of the child.* Laws and actions affecting children should put their best interests first and benefit them in the best possible way.

3. *Survival, development and protection.* The authorities in each country must protect children and help ensure their full development – physically, spiritually, morally and socially.
4. *Participation.* Children have a right to have their say in decisions that affect them and to have their opinions taken into account (UNICEF, 2013).

The United Nations Committee on the Rights of the Child monitors compliance with the CRC, with governments reporting every five years on what they are doing to ensure that children's rights are being met.

In their working paper developed for the United Nations Children's Fund (UNICEF) *Child Well-being in Advanced Economics in the Late 2000's,* Martorano et al. (2013) set out to develop a Child Well-Being Index in order to rank countries according to their performance in advancing child wellbeing, as underpinned by the framework of the Convention on the Rights of the Child. This is a challenging undertaking, as there is no consensus on how to operationalise and measure the concept of child wellbeing, although there have been many attempts to construct indexes over recent years. Most of these attempts are fraught with problems due to the lack of generalisability beyond country contexts or other factors such as a lack of measureable indicators. Utilising the Bradshaw et al. (2007) aforementioned definition of child wellbeing, Martorano et al. (2013) captured data for 13 components aggregated into five dimensions which they regard as representing child wellbeing, these being: material wellbeing; health; education; behaviour and risks; and housing and environment (see Table 1.1). Thirty-five countries received a score on the indicators and combinations of variables. Several did not have enough data for each indicator so were excluded from comprehensive analysis and commentary, including the countries of Australia, Japan and New Zealand.

Martorano et al. (2013, p. 41) concluded that:

> most countries have at least some or several dimensions or components that show a relatively disappointing performance. Some countries do relatively well on most dimensions (the Netherlands and the Scandinavian countries, except Denmark) and some countries perform relatively badly on most dimensions and components (Bulgaria, Romania, the United States). The Child Well-Being Index and the results on its dimensions, components and indicators reveal that serious differences across countries exist; suggesting that in many countries improvement could be made in the quality of children's lives.

An important initiative that set out to make substantial progress against the global problems of poverty, health, education and the environment was the establishment in the year 2000 of the United Nations Millennium Development Goals (MDGs) for 2015 (United Nations, 2000). All 189 member states of the United Nations including Australia committed to eight goals and targets, as outlined in Table 1.2.

Without exception the MDGs have the potential to impact on the health and wellbeing of early years learners around the world. In particular, Goal 2 – to achieve universal primary education – is particularly pertinent to health and wellbeing as

Table 1.1: Child Well-Being Index – dimensions, components and performance.

Dimension	Component	Examples of indicators used	Best performers	Worst performers
Material wellbeing	Monetary deprivation	Relative child poverty Child poverty gap	Netherlands and Nordic regions	Romania, Eastern European countries, United States
	Material deprivation	Deprivation index Family affluence scale		
Child health	Health at birth	Birth rate Infant mortality rate	Finland, Iceland, Luxembourg, the Netherlands and Sweden	United States, Romania, Latvia and Lithuania
	Child mortality	Child death rate		
	Preventive health services	Immunisation against DPT3, measles and polio		
Education	Educational achievement	OECD PISA reading, maths and science literacy	Nordic European countries, Belgium, Germany and the Netherlands	Romania, Greece and the United States
	Participation	Early childhood education Youth education Neither employment nor education		
Behaviour and risks	Experience of violence	Fighting in schools Bullying in schools	Nordic and Western European countries	Southern, Central and Eastern European countries
	Health behaviour	Eat breakfast daily Eat fruit daily 1 hour physical activity daily Overweight according to body mass index		
	Risk behaviour	Cigarettes, alcohol and cannabis consumption Teenage fertility rate		
Housing and environment	Overcrowding	Number of rooms / person / household with children	Switzerland, Ireland and Norway	Central and Eastern European countries, Greece, Italy and the United States
	Environment	Homicide rates Outdoor air pollution measure		
	Housing problems	Moisture Darkness No bath or shower No flush toilet		

Source: Developed from Martorano et al. (2013).

Table 1.2: The United Nations Millennium Development Goals (MDGs) for 2015.

Goals	Targets
Eradicate extreme poverty	• Halve, between 1990 and 2015, the proportion of people whose income is less than $1 a day • Achieve full and productive employment and decent work for all, including women and young people • Halve, between 1990 and 2015, the proportion of people who suffer from hunger
Achieve universal primary education	• Ensure that, by 2015, children everywhere, boys and girls alike, will be able to complete a full course of primary schooling
Promote gender equality	• Eliminate gender disparity in primary and secondary education, preferably by 2005, and in all levels of education no later than 2015
Reduce child mortality	• Reduce by two-thirds, between 1990 and 2015, the under-five mortality rate
Improve maternal health	• Reduce by three-quarters, between 1990 and 2015, the maternal mortality ratio • Achieve universal access to reproductive health
Combat HIV/AIDS, malaria, other diseases	• Have halted by 2015 and begun to reverse the spread of HIV/AIDS • Achieve, by 2010, universal access to treatment for HIV/AIDS for all those who need it • Have halted by 2015 and begun to reverse the incidence of malaria and other major diseases
Ensure environmental sustainability	• Integrate the principles of sustainable development into country policies and programs and reverse the loss of environmental resources • Reduce biodiversity loss, achieving, by 2010, a significant reduction in the rate of loss • Halve, by 2015, the proportion of people without sustainable access to safe drinking water and basic sanitation • Have achieved by 2020 a significant improvement in the lives of at least 100 million slum dwellers
Develop a global partnership for development	• Address the special needs of least developed countries, landlocked countries and small island developing states • Develop further an open, rule-based, predictable, non-discriminatory trading and financial system • Deal comprehensively with developing countries' debt • In cooperation with pharmaceutical companies, provide access to affordable essential drugs in developing countries • In cooperation with the private sector, make available benefits of new technologies, especially information and communications

Source: United Nations (2000).

the notion of a minimum global attainment for all children by 2015 would serve to lift the levels of literacy, numeracy and scientific literacy, thereby improving health and wellbeing status globally.

Australian context: Health and wellbeing

SPOTLIGHT 1.2: AUSTRALIA'S CHILDHOOD POPULATION

On 8 April 2016 the resident population of Australia was projected to be 24 039 377 (Australian Bureau of Statistics, 2016). Children aged 0–9 years make up 12.6 per cent of the population, and is a total of 18.8 per cent if the age group is extended to include all children up to 14 years of age (AIHW, 2012).

There are many agencies in Australia that provide updates of indicators related to children's health, development and wellbeing. A report compiled by the AIHW (2014) set out to map the indicators and reporting frameworks and their possible intersections, revealing that the Key Child National Indicators reported by the AIHW is the most comprehensive with 56 indicators. For that reason we will turn to these indicators to consider the current state of play for child health and wellbeing in Australia (see Table 1.3).

What these data indicate is a wide range of variability in the health, development and wellbeing of young Australians aged 0–14 years, and a lack of comprehensive knowledge in some core areas where we might expect to have a clear understanding of our practices, especially with regard to proportion of children attending early childhood education programs. The variability is geographic and between some population groups. New South Wales, Victoria, Western Australia, South Australia and the Australian Capital Territory had results better than, or similar to, the national average across either all or most of the indicators, with available data. Queensland, Tasmania and the Northern Territory had poorer results than the national average on several indicators, with Queensland's and the Northern Territory's results on all education-related indicators less favourable than the national average and with higher teenage birth rates. Aboriginal and Torres Strait Islander children, children living in remote areas and children living in socio-economically disadvantaged areas were all markedly extremely less favourable on many of the indicators, especially when the compounding effects were taken into effect.

Australia's child vulnerability in 2013 was reported to be 22 per cent (Australian Government, 2013), which refers to the percentage of young people who are developmentally vulnerable on one or more domains, as measured using the Australian Early Development Index (AEDI). The AEDI measures five areas of early childhood development from information collected through a teacher-completed checklist for children in their first year of formal full-time school.

Table 1.3: Trends for Australia's children aged 0–14 years: Health, development and wellbeing.

Priority area	Indicator	Explanation	Trend ✓ = favourable X = unfavourable = = no change or clear trend ? = no trend data available
Healthy	Mortality	Infant and child mortality is a key indicator of the hygiene and health conditions prevailing in a country, and the effectiveness of the health system in maternal and perinatal health.	✓
	Morbidity	Chronic conditions can affect normal growth and social, emotional and physical wellbeing.	✓
	Disability	Disability can have diverse effects that may restrict children's full involvement in society.	=
Promotion of healthy child development	Breastfeeding	Breastmilk provides the best nutritional start for infants and promotes their healthy growth and development.	?
	Dental health	The dental health of children affects their wellbeing and self-esteem. Untreated dental decay is a risk factor for infection and chronic disease in adult life. Most dental diseases are, however, preventable.	?
	Early learning	Children who attend early childhood educational programs 0–2 show better performance and progress in their early school years in both intellectual and social domains.	?
Learning and development	Transition to primary school	Children entering school with basic skills for life and learning have higher levels of social competence and academic achievement, increasing their likelihood of achieving their full potential.	?

Priority area	Indicator	Explanation	Trend √ = favourable X = unfavourable = = no change or clear trend ? = no trend data available
	Attendance at primary school	School attendance helps children develop the basic building blocks for lifelong learning and educational attainment, as well as social skills.	?
	Literacy and numeracy	Literacy and numeracy skills enable children to engage in learning and ultimately to fully participate in society and lead productive lives.	=
Adverse factors	Teenage births	Teenage motherhood poses significant long-term risks for both mother and child, including poorer health, educational and economic outcomes.	√
	Smoking in pregnancy	Smoking during pregnancy is an important modifiable risk factor for low birth weight, pre-term birth, placental complications, birth defects, respiratory problems and perinatal mortality.	?
	Alcohol use during pregnancy	Alcohol use during pregnancy is associated with adverse outcomes. These include fetal alcohol syndrome, alcohol-related birth defects and neuro-developmental disorders.	√
	Birth weight	Infants who are born with low birthweight are at greater risk of poor health, disability and death than other infants.	=
	Overweight and obesity	Overweight and obese children are at risk of serious health conditions, such as asthma, cardiovascular conditions and type 2 diabetes, in both the short and long term.	=
	Environmental tobacco smoke	Exposure to tobacco smoke puts children at risk of serious health problems including asthma and SIDS.	√

(continued)

Table 1.3: Trends for Australia's children aged 0–14 years: Health, development and wellbeing (*continued*).

Priority area	Indicator	Explanation	Trend ✓ = favourable X = unfavourable = = no change or clear trend ? = no trend data available
	Tobacco use	Tobacco smoking is the leading cause of preventable death in the world today. Tobacco use at a young age is a predictor of continued smoking in adulthood.	✓
	Alcohol misuse	Alcohol use at young ages is associated with more frequent use during late adolescence and an increased risk of later dependence.	✓
Family and community	Family economic situation	Low family income can adversely affect the health, education and self-esteem of children.	=
	Children in non-parental care	Some parents are unable to provide adequate care for their children.	X
	Parental health status	Raising children involves physical, emotional and financial demands that can pose significant challenges to a parent with physical or mental health problems or disability.	✓
	Neighbourhood safety	Children are shaped not only by their family environment but also by the neighbourhood in which they live.	=
	Social capital	Families with rich social networks have greater access to friends and neighbours to assist in managing their daily lives and problems.	=
Safety and security	Injuries	Injury is a leading cause of death among Australian children; however, the vast majority of injuries are preventable and occur as a result of hazards in the child's environment, which can be controlled.	✓

Priority area	Indicator	Explanation	Trend √ = favourable X = unfavourable = = no change or clear trend ? = no trend data available
	Child abuse and neglect	Abuse and neglect victims may experience lower social competence, poor school performance, impaired language ability, and are at increased risk of criminal offending and mental health problems.	X
	Children as victims of violence	Physical and sexual assault can have a range of short- and long-term negative effects on the physical and psychological health of children.	?
	Homelessness	Children who are homeless are more likely to continue to be homeless into adulthood.	=
	Children and crime	Children in the juvenile justice system are a particularly disadvantaged group and are vulnerable to continued and more serious offending later in life.	=
System	Childhood immunisation	Timely and complete immunisation is essential to protect children against communicable diseases that can have serious health consequences.	=
	Survival for leukaemia	Leukaemia survival among children continues to improve through advances in early detection, treatment, research and technology, and the development of specialised treatment centres and protocols for children.	√
	Child protection re-substantiations	Re-substantiation rates are one measure of how well child protection systems are performing in preventing the recurrence of child abuse or neglect.	?

Source: Developed from Australian Institute of Health and Welfare (2012a).

SPOTLIGHT 1.3: THE COST OF AUSTRALIA'S EARLY CHILDHOOD VULNERABILITY

In 2013 the Australian Research Alliance for Children and Youth (ARACY) released *The Nest action agenda: Improving the wellbeing of Australia's children and youth while growing our GDP by over 7 per cent* (ARACY, 2013). This plan provides a guiding framework for improving wellbeing and is based on the concept of aligning government and non-government actions to achieve collective traction and improve wellbeing. It is based on two imperatives – a possible decline in life expectancy for the first time in generations, and the impact of young people's wellbeing on Australia's economic productivity. ARACY estimates from international comparatives that 'the cost of early childhood vulnerability is between $1.75 and $2.7 trillion dollars' annually.

The areas measured by the AEDI are: physical health and wellbeing; social competence; emotional maturity; language and cognitive skills (school-based); and communication skills and general knowledge. In 2012, 96.5 per cent of children in their first year of formal full-time school were included in this study.

In 2015, the AEDI was renamed the Australian Early Development Census (AEDC) to clearly recognise the fact that the instrument is used as a population-based measure to child development. The timing and scope of the study remains the same and hence trends from three data sets taken in 2009, 2012 and 2015 can now be used to reveal trends. A total of 96 per cent of children were included in the 2015 data collection. The trends in the five domains are as follows:

- *Physical health and wellbeing.* The proportion of children developmentally vulnerable in the physical health and wellbeing domain was quite stable at 9.4 and 9.3 per cent in 2009 and 2012, but increased to 9.7 per cent in 2015.
- *Social competence.* Developmental vulnerability in the social competence domain decreased from 9.5 per cent in 2009 to 9.3 per cent in 2013, and has increased to 9.9 per cent in 2015.
- *Emotional maturity.* The number of children developmentally vulnerable in the emotional maturity domain has fluctuated over time. It decreased from 8.9 per cent in 2009 to 7.6 per cent in 2012, then increased to 8.4 per cent in 2015.
- *Language and cognitive skills.* Significant improvements were made in children's language and cognitive skills. The proportion of children who are developmentally vulnerable across the language and cognitive skills domain has decreased from 8.9 per cent in 2009 to 6.5 per cent in 2015.
- *Communication skills and general knowledge.* Developmental vulnerability across the communication and general knowledge domain has steadily decreased from 9.2 per cent in 2009 to 8.0 per cent in 2015 (Australian Government, 2015).

ARACY sets out five outcomes for their agenda: being loved and safe; having material basics; being healthy; learning; and participating (ARACY, 2013). These contribute to the enhancement of the wellbeing of young people in the Australian society. With this in mind, there are six directions recommended for action:

1. Improving early childhood learning and development
2. Improving the educational performance of young Australians
3. Improving the physical health of young Australians
4. Improving the social and emotional wellbeing of young Australians
5. Promoting the participation of young Australians
6. Addressing income disparity and its impacts.

In line with this action plan, there are many initiatives that work on the development of social and emotional learning, or resilience, such as an initiative of the Australian Government Department of Health and Ageing called Response Ability. It aims to promote the social and emotional wellbeing of children and young people by supporting the pre-service training of school teachers and early childhood educators, regarding mental health issues in children and young people (Commonwealth of Australia, 2013).

Furthermore, trends and development in early years education indicate major reform, such as the development of a national curriculum from Foundation to Year 12 by the Australian Curriculum, Assessment and Reporting Authority, which has been informed by the *Melbourne Declaration on Educational Goals for Young Australians* (Curriculum Corporation, 2008). The Declaration strongly positions schools for their importance in 'promoting the intellectual, physical, social, emotional, moral, spiritual and aesthetic development and wellbeing of young Australians, and in ensuring the nation's ongoing economic prosperity and social cohesion' (Curriculum Corporation, 2008, p. 4).

The *Victorian Early Years Learning and Development Framework For all Children from Birth to Eight Years* (State of Victoria, 2011) specifies five outcomes:

Outcome 1: Children have a strong sense of identity.
Outcome 2: Children are connected with and contribute to their world.
Outcome 3: Children have a strong sense of wellbeing.
Outcome 4: Children are confident and involved learners.
Outcome 5: Children are effective communicators.

In this context, Outcome 3 highlights the importance of wellbeing, with children expected to 'become strong' and 'take responsibility for their own health and physical wellbeing' (p. 23). This framework highlights the importance of fostering personal responsibility while acknowledging that enabling skills must be developed in educators to ensure this aspiration is achieved.

Conclusion

The proportion of the world population in the birth-through-childhood group is large and while it will decrease proportionately in the future, it will continue to be a dominant group in the world's population. The birth years for Generation Z commenced in 2002, and in 2017 incorporates our current young people up to the age of 15. The values and beliefs of the emerging generation are being shaped and defined, with contemporary world and local events impacting on this generation in ways never before experienced. Three words summarise Generation Z: global, visual and digital. These words have relevance when we consider the health and wellbeing of the young members of our society. There are many agencies globally and in Australia that provide updates of indicators related to children's health, development and wellbeing. What these data indicate is a wide range of variability in the health, development and wellbeing of young Australians aged 0–14 years – and a lack of comprehensive knowledge in some core areas where we might expect to have a clear understanding of our practices, especially with regard to the proportion of children attending early childhood education programs. The variability is geographic and between some population groups.

Summary

Key messages from this chapter include:

- The period from birth to 12 years is increasingly recognised as a crucial time for laying the foundations for life, with significant consequences for ongoing educational success and future participation in society.
- Carers and educators need specialist preparation as they are required to promote and teach health and wellbeing and to have the skills and knowledge to understand and manage the plethora of issues related to young children.
- Health is a state of complete physical, mental and social wellbeing and not merely the absence of disease or infirmity.
- The term 'wellbeing' is a ubiquitous one; however, there is no single definition of this commonly used term.
- Measuring wellbeing is a challenging undertaking because there is no consensus on how to operationalise and measure the concept. However, there have been many attempts to construct indexes over recent years.
- There is a global imperative to improve the health and wellbeing of children and there are many initiatives in place to support this goal.

Questions

1.1 How can educators assist young learners to take responsibility for their health and to foster wellbeing? Provide examples of curriculum and pedagogical strategies.

1.2 Select one of the United Nations Millennium Development Goals (MDGs) for 2015. Outline how achieving the target will assist in fostering health and wellbeing for early years learners.

1.3 Conduct an internet search for Australian policies related to children in the early years. Map the frequency of health- and wellbeing-related aspects incorporated in the policy.

1.4 What is the relationship between health, wellbeing and resilience?

References

Australian Bureau of Statistics (2016). *Population Clock.* Retrieved 8 April 2016 from http://www.abs.gov.au/ausstats/abs@.nsf/0/1647509ef7e25faaca2568a 900154b63?OpenDocument

Australian Government (2013). *A Snapshot of Early Childhood Development in Australia 2012 – AEDI National Report,* Canberra: Australian Government.

—— (2015). *Emerging trends from the AEDC.* Retrieved 8 April 2016 from https:// www.aedc.gov.au/resources/detail/fact-sheet--emerging-trends-from-the-aedc

Australian Institute of Health and Welfare (AIHW) (2012a). *A picture of Australia's children 2012. Cat. no. PHE 167.* Canberra: AIHW.

—— (2012b). *Australia's health 2012. Australia's health series* no. 13. Cat. no. AUS 156. Canberra: AIHW.

—— (2014). *Mapping of children and youth indicator reporting frameworks.* CWS 48. Canberra: AIHW.

Australian Research Alliance for Children and Youth (ARACY) (2013). *The Nest Action Agenda.* Retrieved 20 September 2013 from www.aracy.org.au/documents/item/162

Bradshaw, J., Hoelscher, P. & Richardson, D. (2007). *Comparing child wellbeing in OECD countries: Concepts and methods.* Innocenti Working Paper No. 2006-03. Florence: UNICEF Innocenti Research Centre.

Commonwealth of Australia (2013). *Response Ability.* Retrieved 20 September 2013 from www.responseability.org

Curriculum Corporation (2008). *Melbourne Declaration on Educational Goals for Young Australians.* Melbourne: Ministerial Council on Education, Employment, Training and Youth Affairs (MCEETYA).

Ereaut, G. & Whiting, R. (2008). *What do we mean by well being? And why might it matter?* Research Report DCSF-RW073. United Kingdom: Department for Children, Schools and Families.

Martorano, B., Natali, L., de Neubourg, C. & Bradshaw, J. (2013). *Child well-being in advanced economics in the late 2000's. Working paper 2013-01.* Florence: UNICEF Office of Research.

McCrindle, M. (2013). *Generation Z Defined: Global, visual, digital.* Retrieved 1 October 2013 from www.mccrindle.com.au/the-mccrindle-blog/generation_z_defined_global_visual_digital

Organisation for Economic Co-operation and Development (OECD) (2013). *OECD Guidelines on Measuring Subjective Well-being,* OECD Publishing. dx.doi.org/10.1787/9789264191655-en Retrieved 20 September 2013.

Pendergast, D. (2007). The MilGen and society. In N. Bahr & D. Pendergast (eds), *The Millennial Adolescent.* Camberwell: Australian Council for Educational Research.

—— (2008). Generational Dynamics – Y it matters 2 u & me. In: Pendergast, D. (ed.). *Home Economics: Reflecting the Past; Creating the Future.* Switzerland: International Federation of Home Economics, 99–114.

Pendergast, D. & Garvis, S. (2014). The importance of health and wellbeing. In S. Garvis & D. Pendergast (eds). *Health and Wellbeing in Childhood.* Port Melbourne, Australia: Cambridge University Press.

State of Victoria (2011). *Victorian Early Years Learning and Development Framework For all Children from Birth to Eight Years.* Melbourne: State Government, Department of Education and Early Childhood Development.

UNICEF (1989). Convention on the Rights of the Child. Retrieved 30 September 2013 from www.unicef.org.au/Discover/What-We-Do/Convention-on-the-Rights-of-the-Child.aspx

United Nations (2000). *United Nations Millennium Development Goals* (MDGs) for 2015 Retrieved 20 September 2013 from www.undp.org/content/undp/en/home/mdgoverview/

United Nations, Department of Economic and Social Affairs, Population Division (2015). *World Population Prospects: The 2015 Revision, Key Findings and Advance Tables. Working* Paper No. ESA/P/WP.241.

World Health Organization (WHO) (1948). *Preamble to the Constitution of the World Health Organization as adopted by the International Health Conference.* New York: World Health Organization. Retrieved 19 September 2013 from www.who.int/about/definition/en/print.html

—— (1986). *The Ottawa Charter for Health Promotion.* Retrieved 19 September 2013 from www.who.int/healthpromotion/conferences/previous/ottawa/en/

CHAPTER 2

Classifying health and wellbeing: Applying the *International Classification of Functioning, Disability and Health* to early years learners

Jane McCormack and Sharynne McLeod

Introduction

For many years, researchers, clinicians and educators have debated the relative influence of nature (biology) versus nurture (the social environment) in children's health and development. Those who emphasise the importance of biological factors are guided by a model of health known as the medical model. Within the medical model, disability is regarded as 'a problem of the person, directly caused by disease, trauma or other health condition, which requires medical care' (World Health Organization [WHO], 2007, p. 15). Those who emphasise the importance of the environment/context are guided by a social model. Within the **social model** of health, disability is regarded as 'a complex collection of conditions, many of which are created by the social environment' rather than an individual attribute (WHO, 2007, p. 18).

The **medical model** views disability as a problem of the person, directly caused by a health condition, which requires medical care provided by professionals in order to cure the individual (WHO, 2007).

The **social model** views disability as a socially created problem which requires action by society at large in order to make the environmental modifications necessary.

These two models of health and disability differ in their identification of where the health problem lies (the individual or the environment), differ in how it should be addressed (medical care/social action) and by whom (health professionals/society). However, very often both medical needs and social needs must be considered. Take for example, the case of childhood communication impairment. Many children with communication impairment benefit from direct intervention to address their speech or language difficulties. However, this is most beneficial when undertaken in conjunction with environmental interventions such as family education about the impairment – educating family members on how to stimulate language skills and support communication attempts. Thus, when we think about the health and wellbeing of children, we need a model of health that is holistic in its conceptualisation and comprehensive in its design in order to ensure we gain the best understanding of their health needs and can provide the most effective support. The *International Classification of Functioning, Disability and Health* (ICF) (WHO, 2001) was developed by the WHO to provide a comprehensive and holistic framework for conceptualising health. The WHO first defined health in a holistic way in 1946, regarding it as 'the state of complete physical, mental and social wellbeing and not merely the absence of disease or infirmity' (p. 100); however, more recently, they recognised a need for a framework to enable professionals, services and governments to enact that definition. The ICF is based on a **biopsychosocial** framework, and aims to integrate the medical and social models of health. Following the release of the ICF, a *Children and Youth* version was developed (ICF-CY, WHO, 2007) to specifically cover the ages from birth to 18 years in order to reflect the differences between children and adults in terms of their development and life activities (Lollar & Simeonsson, 2005). In this chapter, we provide an overview of the components of the ICF-CY and describe clinical and research applications of the framework to early years learners.

Biopsychosocial model views health (and disability) as an interaction of biological and contextual factors, and so integrates the medical and social models in a more holistic perspective (WHO, 2007).

International Classification of Functioning, Disability and Health – Children and Youth Version (ICF-CY)

The **ICF** and **ICF-CY** were designed to provide a global common language for describing the impact of health conditions and disabilities on human functioning. The WHO has proposed multiple ways in which the ICF may be used by health professionals, services and/or governments. These include clinical, administrative and research applications. For instance, in clinical practice, categories and codes within the ICF can be used as a basis for summarising assessment findings, clarifying diagnostic information, prioritising intervention targets and measuring outcomes; in administrative practice, ICF categories and codes may be used to examine referrals, set eligibility criteria for services and record service provision; and in research, ICF codes may be used to standardise the characteristics of participants, the selection of assessment tools and/or the design of tools to measure health conditions and intervention outcomes (WHO, 2007).

ICF: *International Classification of Functioning, Disability and Health.*

ICF-CY: *International Classification of Functioning, Disability and Health – Children and Youth Version.*

When we consider the health and wellbeing of children, the ICF-CY can assist us to think about the range of factors (biological, social and environmental) that may influence and impact on their perceptions and experiences of health, and to consider the range of ways in which we can improve their experiences. According to the ICF and ICF-CY, health and wellbeing result from the interaction between Body Structures and Functions, Activities and Participation, and Personal and Environmental Factors.[1] These components and their interactions are illustrated diagrammatically in Figure 2.1 and described in greater detail in the following sections.

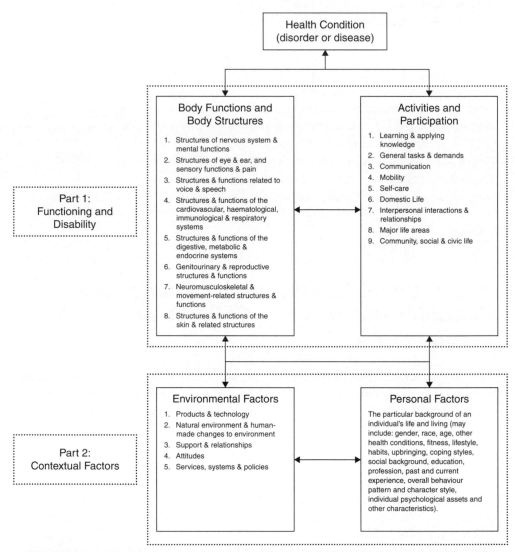

Figure 2.1 Parts, components and domains of the ICF and their interactions (adapted from the ICF and ICF-CY, WHO, 2001; 2007).

Source: Reprinted from McCormack et al. (2010).

---

1   Capitalisation has been used to be consistent with usage in the ICF-CY and to differentiate between everyday usage of these terms.

Body Functions and Structures

Within the ICF-CY, Body Structures refer to anatomical parts of the body (e.g. organs and limbs) and Body Functions refer to the functioning of body systems (e.g. speech and digestion). The ICF-CY lists eight main categories of each, which correspond to one another (see Table 2.1). These categories are then separated further according to common characteristics. For instance, in the category of Structures Related to Voice and Speech, listed structures include the hard and soft palate, tongue and teeth. If a problem with function or structure is identified, it is termed an 'impairment'. An impairment can involve anomaly, defect or loss and can range from mild to profound in severity. It may be temporary or permanent, progressive or static, and intermittent or continuous.

Table 2.1: Body Structures and Body Functions within the ICF-CY.

Body Structures	Body Functions
Structures of the nervous system	Mental functions
The eye, ear and related structures	Sensory functions and pain
Structures involved in voice and speech	Voice and speech functions
Structures of the cardiovascular, immunological and respiratory systems	Functions of the cardiovascular, haematological, immunological and respiratory systems
Structures related to digestive, metabolic and endocrine systems	Functions of the digestive, metabolic and endocrine systems
Structures related to the genitourinary and reproductive systems	Genitourinary and reproductive functions
Structures related to movement	Neuromusculoskeletal and movement-related functions
Skin and related structures	Functions of the skin and related structures

Source: Adapted from *International Classification of Functioning, Disability and Health: Children and Youth Version* (WHO, 2007).

Applying the Body Functions and Body Structures component to children's health

This list of structures and functions makes it possible to consider the biological aspect of health in a very comprehensive way. Thus, when thinking about the health and wellbeing of children in the early years, the ICF-CY guides us to consider: does the child have (or have they ever experienced) impairments that affect the integrity of structures or the capacity of structures to perform functions? These impairments may include congenital conditions such as Down syndrome or cerebral palsy, specific impairments such as blindness or asthma, acquired conditions such as hearing loss caused by recurrent otitis media (middle ear infections) or intellectual impairment subsequent to a neurological event. These impairments may also include conditions without a known cause, like speech and language disorders of unknown origin. Case study 2.1 guides you in how the Body Functions and Structures component can be used to understand the development of a child with communication difficulties.

CASE STUDY 2.1: MEET BEN

Ben (four years old) is a happy and active young boy who has been attending preschool for six months. He is the second of four children (the youngest is eight months old), lives on a farm 20 minutes from town and loves tractors! He also loves playing with his pet dogs. Ben has a history of ear infections and his preschool teachers have noticed that he is often difficult to understand. He is social but has become quite disruptive at preschool, and is obviously frustrated by his communication difficulties when talking to other children and staff.

Task: Look at the list of Body Structures and Body Functions in Table 2.1. What structures and functions might be impaired and contribute to Ben's communication difficulties? How could you find out more about the integrity of the structures and the level of the functioning?

Activities and Participation

A child may have a structural or functional impairment, but this may not affect their health and wellbeing if they are still able to perform daily activities and/or participate in chosen life experiences. Thus, in addition to considering a child's biological status, we need to consider their ability to participate in the activities of everyday life, in order to understand their level of health and wellbeing. In the ICF-CY, Activities refer to the tasks or actions that a child may perform, and Participation refers to their involvement in situations or events. Again, the ICF-CY provides a comprehensive list of what these factors may include. The list is divided into nine domains (see Table 2.2), which are further separated into a total of 132 items. For instance, Learning and Applying Knowledge includes activities such as Learning to Read and Learning to Write.

If a problem performing any of these activities is identified, it is termed an 'Activity Limitation' or 'Participation Restriction' (WHO, 2007, p. 12). A limitation or restriction is recognised when the performance of an individual with an impairment (such as speech and language) is significantly different to that of an individual without the impairment.

Table 2.2: Activities and Participation within the ICF-CY.

Activity and Participation	Description
Learning and applying knowledge	Actions necessary for acquiring new information and skills or the actions of putting those skills into practice, including attention, early literacy and calculation skills
General tasks and demands	Actions necessary for completing everyday tasks and for dealing with problems when task performance breaks down
Communication	Skills necessary for producing and comprehending verbal and non-verbal messages, and for using communication strategies or devices
Mobility	Skills required for moving oneself or objects, or using forms of transportation
Self-care	Skills required for looking after health
Domestic life	Tasks associated with acquisition of a house/food, completing household tasks and caring for objects/others
Interpersonal interactions and relationships	The actions of engaging with peers, teachers, family members, strangers or others
Major life areas	Activities required for education and/or employment
Community, social and civic life	Tasks required for engaging in social activities outside the family

Source: Adapted from *International Classification of Functioning, Disability and Health: Children and Youth Version* (WHO, 2007).

Applying the Activities and Participation component to children's health

In applying the Activities and Participation component of the ICF-CY to the health and wellbeing of children in the early years, we may consider: what activities does this child engage in or want to engage in? This may include specific tasks such as talking, painting and running, or activities that incorporate a range of skills, such as ballet, attending preschool or completing a spelling test. We also need to consider: where does this child participate in the activities? For instance, are activities undertaken in the lounge room, the backyard, McDonald's, the playground, the classroom or the supermarket? Furthermore, who does this child interact with? Possibilities may include parents, siblings, other relatives, friends, teachers, sporting teams and strangers.

When we understand the activities that the child undertakes and the settings in which they occur, we can begin to conceptualise what is needed from those environments and activities to ensure the child is able to participate fully and experience a sense of wellbeing as a result. The ICF-CY encourages consideration of what a child is capable of doing in an environment that has been adjusted for their needs (the child's *capacity*), as well as what they do in their everyday environment (the child's *performance*), in order to guide us in ways to modify environments to support children's performance. For instance, we might assess a child's capacity to execute an activity in their regular environment when assistance is provided; for example, dynamic assessments (Lidz, 1987). Thus, a child's experience of health and wellbeing is also dependent on contextual factors. The task below follows the earlier activity and shows you how the Activities and Participation component can be used to determine a child's strengths, challenges, needs and goals.

PAUSE AND REFLECT 2.1: THE IMPACT OF BEN'S COMMUNICATION DIFFICULTIES

You might like to look back over the information that was provided earlier about Ben. Now look at the list of Activities and Participation provided in Table 2.2. What do you know about Ben's Activity Limitations and Participation Restrictions? How might these have been influenced by his communication difficulties? What other activities might be difficult for him, due to his communication difficulties? What activities might he like to do? How will you find out more about his strengths and areas of difficulty?

Contextual (Environmental and Personal) factors

In the ICF-CY, contextual factors are divided into Environmental Factors and Personal Factors. Environmental Factors reflect external influences on functioning and disability and Personal Factors reflect internal influences. As such, Environmental Factors refer to a child's physical, social and attitudinal environment, while Personal Factors refer to a child's individual demographics or characteristics.

Environmental Factors

During childhood, the nature of children's environments, and the levels of competence and independence children demonstrate, undergo significant changes. In early childhood, the family environment exercises the most influence; however, in later childhood and adolescence, the school environment and larger community become more significant. According to the ICF-CY, 'negative environmental factors often have a stronger impact on children than on adults' (WHO, 2007, p. xvi), thus reinforcing the need to evaluate, modify and enhance children's environments as part of programs to promote/improve children's health and wellbeing. Addressing environmental factors may include altering legislation or national policies to ensure children have access to necessary health care and education.

Within the ICF-CY, Environmental Factors are further classified into two different levels: individual and societal. Individual Environmental Factors are those in the immediate environment of the individual (such as home and school) including the physical and material features of the environment as well as the people within that environment. Societal Environmental Factors are structures and systems in the community or society that govern and impact on individuals (e.g. organisations and services, government agencies, laws, regulations, formal and informal rules, as well as attitudes and ideologies) (see Table 2.3).

Table 2.3: Environmental Factors within the ICF-CY.

Environmental Factors	Description
Products and technology	Products (natural or man-made), equipment and technology in an individual's environment that are available, created or manufactured
Natural environment and human-made changes to environment	Elements of the natural or physical environment, and man-made changes, as well as characteristics of human populations within that environment
Support and relationships	Practical physical or emotional support, nurturing, protection, and assistance provided by individuals to other persons, in their everyday activities/environments
Attitudes	Customs, practices, ideologies, values, norms, factual beliefs and religious beliefs that influence behaviour
Services, systems and policies	Services that provide programs to meet the needs of individuals with society, systems that control and organise the services and policies that govern and regulate the systems/services

Source: Adapted from *International Classification of Functioning, Disability and Health: Children and Youth Version* (WHO, 2007).

Applying the Environmental Factors component to children's health

When thinking about the association between Environmental Factors and the health and wellbeing of children in the early years, we may consider: how is the child's physical environment contributing to their experiences of health and wellbeing? This includes features of the physical environment that may impact on health such as access to water/food, population density and pollution, as well as features of a particular context, such as the amount of light/noise in a classroom. It also means considering the social environment; for example, what is the family's background and how does this influence their attitudes towards health, wellbeing and accessing health services? For instance, a child's access to services may be impacted by their family's understanding of the roles of health/education professionals and how/when to access them for support, or by cultural beliefs about health and illness. Furthermore, we need to consider the health, education and disability services that are available for the child/family to access. This means also being aware of the limitations to service access, such as the lack of health services in some locations (e.g. rural and remote areas of Australia), and government policies impacting eligibility, prioritisation and duration of services in some settings. In the exercise below, you are encouraged to consider how the Environmental Factors component can be used to gain a greater understanding of Ben's life context and to plan appropriate support.

> ## PAUSE AND REFLECT 2.2: ENVIRONMENTAL FACTORS AND COMMUNICATION
>
> Remember the information that was provided about Ben earlier in the chapter? Now, consider the list of Environmental Factors in Table 2.3. What do you know about Ben's physical and social environment? How might this impact on his communication skills? How might it influence his ability to access and engage with health services? How could you find out more information? How could you support Ben?

Personal Factors

Unlike other components within the ICF-CY, a list of Personal Factors is not provided within the framework. However, suggestions are made as to the range of factors that could be considered to fall within this component. These include: 'gender, race, age, other health conditions, fitness, lifestyle, habits, upbringing, coping styles, social background, education, profession, past and current experience (past events and concurrent events), overall behaviour pattern and character style, individual psychological assets and other characteristics' (WHO, 2007, pp. 15–16). Threats (2007) has suggested that Personal Factors can be further divided into those that are unchanging; that is, those that provide the demographic details of an individual's life and background (e.g. gender, race, age and other health conditions), and those that have the potential to change or be changed (e.g. fitness, lifestyle, habits, social background, and education).

Applying the Personal Factors component to children's health

When thinking about the association between Personal Factors and the health and wellbeing of children in the early years, we may consider: how does this child like to learn? What does this child enjoy doing? How does this child respond in different situations? What has contributed to this child's life experiences so far? By understanding the child's background, lifestyle, temperament and so on, we can gain an understanding of what is important to the child and family and what has contributed to their experiences of health or illness. This, in turn, enables us to prepare environments and activities that maximise good health and minimise the impact of any impairments that exist.

Application of the ICF-CY

The ICF-CY has been designed to guide research and professional practice, as well as education, policy design and implementation. In the following sections the application of the ICF-CY in the field of childhood communication impairment is discussed in order to illustrate how such a framework might impact on the education and care of children.

Applying the ICF-CY in professional practice: A case study

It is often the case that children with speech and/or language difficulties are first identified with concerns when they commence their early childhood education. Earlier in this chapter, you were introduced to Ben, a four-year-old boy with speech and language difficulties living with his family in rural Australia. Throughout the chapter you have been asked to reflect on how the ICF-CY might help us to learn more about Ben's health experiences. In this section, we are going to review Ben's health experiences and consider how the ICF can ensure appropriate support is provided to him and his family.

The Body Functions and Structures component can be used to guide us to think about the potential causal factors contributing to Ben's communication difficulties, such as the recurrent period of hearing loss (an impairment of the function of hearing) associated with the ear infections. Consequently, we might suggest the family contact their local doctor or audiologist to investigate the child's current hearing status. We might also take note of the particular speech and language difficulties which Ben is demonstrating, such as sound errors, limited vocabulary or grammatical errors. Again, we might suggest a referral to another health professional, such as a speech pathologist who specialises in identifying and managing such difficulties.

The Activities and Participation component might guide us to examine the activities that Ben particularly enjoys (e.g. playing with friends and show-and-tell) and the communication needs associated with those activities (e.g. requesting help, answering questions, explaining activities and storytelling). We might think about the kinds of words that he needs to be able to say and the ways in which we can model those, and we might think of other cues we could use to support Ben's communication attempts. For instance, we might suggest to the family that they provide us with a photo diary for show-and-tell so we have contextual information to aid our understanding of Ben's recount.

The Environmental Factors component might guide us to think about ways we can modify the physical environment to improve the likelihood of successful interactions. For instance, we might ensure Ben is seated near the front of the room to better hear the modelling of sounds/words, and we might use rugs and soft furnishings to lessen reverberation and background noise. We might also modify the social environment through our attitudes, support and relationships. For instance, we might examine our response to communication breakdowns and identify ways in which to reduce them; for example, by encouraging Ben to use additional communication modalities to support speech (e.g. demonstrating or showing), through modelling a slower speech rate, and through repeating and clarifying his message. Finally, the Personal Factors component might guide us to remember Ben's interests and strengths so we utilise these in addressing any challenges he might experience.

Applying the ICF-CY in research

The ICF-CY also provides a useful framework to guide research. For instance, it may be used to guide prevalence studies through providing consistent definitions of the impairments being investigated, or it may enable a clearer understanding of the impact of health conditions, and intervention strategies, through providing comprehensive lists of activities that can be included as outcome measures.

To date, the ICF-CY has been used in the field of communication to examine both prevalence and impact of childhood speech and language impairment (McLeod & Threats, 2008). Research framed around the ICF-CY has indicated there is a high prevalence of speech and language impairment in children, and that Personal and Environmental Factors can act as factors that increase (risk) or decrease (protective) the likelihood of a child experiencing these difficulties (Harrison & McLeod, 2010). For example, the risk of having a speech and language impairment increases if you are male and have ongoing hearing problems. Additionally, childhood speech and language impairment can impact educational, social, behavioural and occupational outcomes throughout life (McCormack et al., 2009; McCormack et al., 2011). That is, children's Activities and Participation (e.g. academic achievement in literacy and mathematics, social relationships and behaviour) may be limited by their communication (Body Function) impairment. Furthermore, research has indicated many Australian children do not have sufficient access to targeted services (including speech pathology) to ameliorate the impact of their communication disability (McAllister et al., 2011). That is, Environmental factors are affecting their ability to access much-needed support. Consequently, formulation of national strategies to support children's communication is required (McLeod et al., 2014).

Conclusion

The ICF is a framework that enables us to consider health and health conditions in a holistic way. Within the ICF-CY, an impairment is considered the result of a problem with a Body Structure or Function. The impact of impairment can be seen by examining the way in which an individual's ability to perform Activities has been limited, or their Participation has been restricted. The degree of disability experienced by an individual is dependent on the Environmental and Personal Factors surrounding the individual and the degree to which they act as barriers or facilitators to health.

For all health conditions, it is the interrelationship that exists between biology and context that determines whether an impairment/disability exists. All health conditions may be considered disabilities when there is a lack of awareness and understanding of the impact of the condition and a lack of resources/support to facilitate children's health and development. That is, society's beliefs about health and wellbeing, and responses to identified health needs, can act as significant facilitators or barriers to children's perceptions and experiences of health. For management of impairments to be functional and effective, and for experiences of disability to be minimised and the best outcomes achieved and maintained, a holistic approach which addresses both biological and contextual factors is required (Howe, 2008).

Summary

Key documents discussed in this chapter are:

- The International Classification of Functioning, Disability and Health (ICF; WHO, 2001) and Children and Youth version (ICF-CY; WHO, 2007) were released by the World Health Organization as holistic frameworks for considering health and wellbeing.
- The ICF and ICF-CY comprise the following components: Body Functions and Structures, Activities and Participation, Environmental Factors and Personal Factors.
- The ICF and ICF-CY recognise that health and wellbeing are the result of the interaction between biological factors, everyday life activities and contextual factors that are intrinsic and extrinsic to the individual.

Questions

2.1 Consider a child you know who experiences an impairment of a Body Structure or Body Function (e.g. difficulty seeing, being diabetic). How does this impact their Activities and Participation?

2.2 Now think about the Environmental Factors that are in place to enhance the child's ability to participate in regular classroom and extra-curricular activities.

2.3 Attitudes are included in the Environmental Factors section of the ICF-CY. What are your attitudes towards children with hearing loss, children who are blind, children who have speech and language impairment, and children who have a physical disability? Are there strategies that you can employ to promote positive attitudes towards all children within the playground, classroom and community?

2.4 The WHO has identified other applications of the ICF which include education, policy design and implementation. How do you think the ICF could be used for these purposes?

References

Harrison, L.J. & McLeod, S. (2010). Risk and protective factors associated with speech and language impairment in a nationally representative sample of 4- to 5-year-old children. *Journal of Speech, Language, and Hearing Research, 53*(2), 508–29.

Howe, T.J. (2008). The ICF Contextual Factors related to speech-language pathology. *International Journal of Speech-Language Pathology, 10*(1-2), 27–37.

Lidz, C.S. (1987). *Dynamic assessment: An interactional approach to evaluating learning potential.* New York, NY: Guilford Press.

Lollar, D.J. & Simeonsson, R.J. (2005). Diagnosis to function: Classification for children and youths. *Journal of Developmental and Behavioral Pediatrics, 26*(4), 323–30.

McAllister, L., McCormack, J., McLeod, S. & Harrison, L.J. (2011). Expectations and experiences of accessing and engaging in services for speech impairment. *International Journal of Speech-Language Pathology, 13*(3), 251–67.

McCormack, J., Harrison, L.J., McLeod, S. & McAllister, L. (2011). A nationally representative study of the association between communication impairment at 4–5 years and children's life activities at 7–9 years. *Journal of Speech, Language, and Hearing Research, 54*(5), 1328–48.

McCormack, J., McLeod, S., Harrison, L.J. & McAllister, L. (2010). The impact of speech impairment in early childhood: Investigating parents' and speech-language pathologists' perspectives using the ICF-CY. *Journal of Communication Disorders, 43*(5), 378–96.

McCormack, J., McLeod, S., McAllister, L. & Harrison, L.J. (2009). A systematic review of the association between childhood speech impairment and participation across the lifespan. *International Journal of Speech-Language Pathology, 11*(2), 155–70.

McLeod, S., McAllister, L., McCormack, J. & Harrison, L.J. (2014). Applying the World Report on Disability to children's communication. *Disability and Rehabilitation, 36*(18), 1518–28.

McLeod, S. & Threats, T. T. (2008). The ICF-CY and children with communication disabilities. *International Journal of Speech-Language Pathology, 10*(1), 92–109.

Threats, T. (2007). Access for persons with neurogenic communication disorders: Influences of Personal and Environmental Factors of the ICF. *Aphasiology, 21*(1), 67–80.

World Health Organization (WHO) (2001). *International Classification of Functioning, Disability and Health (ICF).* Geneva, Switzerland: World Health Organization.

—— (2007). *International Classification of Functioning, Disability and Health – Child and Youth version (ICF-CY).* Geneva, Switzerland: World Health Organization.

PART 2

Dimensions of health and wellbeing

CHAPTER 3

Addressing developmental challenges to improve the wellbeing of children

Matthew Manning

Introduction

This chapter introduces the life-course approach, defining developmental prevention and early intervention. Principles of prevention are discussed, including risk and protective factors, functional capabilities, contexts and the importance of prevention. Following this is a brief review of the effectiveness of the developmental approach, and some solutions are proposed to address the complexity of human development in enhancing the wellbeing of vulnerable groups. This chapter focuses mostly on the benefits that arise from interventions implemented in the early years (e.g. preschool) on outcomes well after intervention in later life (e.g. adolescence). The outcomes discussed mainly relate to non-health outcomes such as cognitive development, educational success, social-emotional development, deviance, social participation and family wellbeing. There is also a small discussion regarding the evidence on the mental health of Australian Indigenous children compared to non-Indigenous children.

Policy questions

A number of important questions emerge when developing policy to improve the wellbeing of children. Two critical questions are:

- What is it about individuals, families, communities and institutions (e.g. schools) that can adversely affect an individual's life and their wellbeing?
- What measures can be implemented early in life to promote healthy development that enhances wellbeing?

To begin to answer the first question, it is necessary to examine the key theories that explain differences in human developmental trajectories. The theories propose that the risk of adverse wellbeing exists within the individual as well as within the environment in which they live. Further, how the individual interacts with their environment is implicitly affected by a number of systems, including the family system, school and community systems, and the broader economic and political environments.

Answering the second question involves a systematic review of the scientific evidence base. This exercise allows us to make objective assertions regarding efficacy of interventions in both the short and long term. Answering these questions goes some way towards developing strategies that allow for the adoption of a holistic approach aimed at promoting collective action in institutions of care and education, in order to enhance the wellbeing of vulnerable children. In Australia, the focus is often on those who present early manifestations of behavioural problems such as conduct disorder, or are exposed to child abuse, sexual assault (either by an adult or another child) and domestic violence. In addition, academics and practitioners attempt to coordinate their activities in order to develop strategies and programs that will assist those from diverse backgrounds (e.g. those from immigrant, refugee, low socio-economic or Aboriginal and Torres Strait Islander backgrounds) to negotiate a range of obstacles they face in everyday life.

SPOTLIGHT 3.1: OBJECTIVE AND SUBJECTIVE WELLBEING

'Objective wellbeing assumes that people have basic needs and rights, ranging from adequate food and water to physical health and education' (UK Government, 2011, p. 1). Objective wellbeing can be assessed through an analysis of observable indicators that measure the extent to which these needs/rights (e.g. household income and wealth, educational attainment, life expectancy, level of pollution, water quality and fish stocks) are met. Objective wellbeing measures are paternalistic, assuming that certain things are good or bad for wellbeing.

A subjective wellbeing approach avoids this paternalism by aiming to directly capture an individual's perceived wellbeing. Subjective wellbeing measures factors such as how satisfied people are with their lives, their health status, job satisfaction and perceived level of happiness (UK Government, 2011).

Life-course perspective

Evidence from empirical studies indicates that children who display early signs of disruptive behaviour, who are unprepared for school, perform poorly at school, are developmentally vulnerable or who live in a disadvantaged home environment are at a greater risk of developing social, health and psychological problems later in life (Homel, Elias & Hay, 2001). Examples of potential negative consequences include poor educational outcomes (e.g. school drop-out), reduced economic success (e.g. welfare dependency), increased deviance and contact with the criminal justice system, poor employment prospects and family dysfunction (Manning, 2004; 2008; Manning, Homel & Smith, 2010).

Glaring differences between cognitive and developmental vulnerability are observed between Indigenous and non-Indigenous children. Evidence reveals that the cognitive test score gap between groups at ages four to five is between 0.3 and 0.4 standard deviations. This suggests that the average five-year-old Indigenous child has the test scores of the average four-year-old non-Indigenous child in the sample (Leigh & Gong, 2009) (see Figure 3.1).

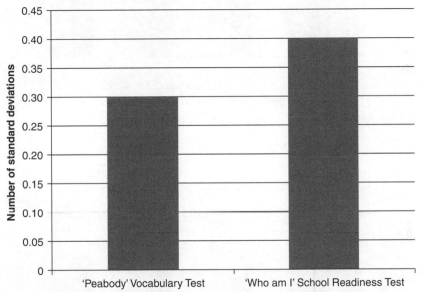

Figure 3.1 LSAC Indigenous to non-Indigenous gap in cognitive outcomes at 4–5 years of age.

Source: Adapted from Leigh & Gong (2009).

Similarly, scores in reading and maths (Figures 3.2 and 3.3) show that Indigenous children are less likely to meet the minimum standards than are non-Indigenous children, and the gap holds through time (i.e. at school years 3, 5, 7 and 9) (Australian Curriculum, Assessment and Reporting Authority, 2014).

Evidence also suggests that a lack of health screening for those most at risk (e.g. children in foster care) in the early years of life can heighten the risk of later potential emotional and mental health disorders, resulting in the provision of costly treatment and services for psychiatric disorders such as schizophrenia, depression, anxiety or substance abuse (Kortenkamp, 2002). Focusing again on Australian Indigenous children (from Western Australia) we can see that there is a stark difference with respect to the mental health of Indigenous children compared to non-Indigenous children (Figure 3.4).

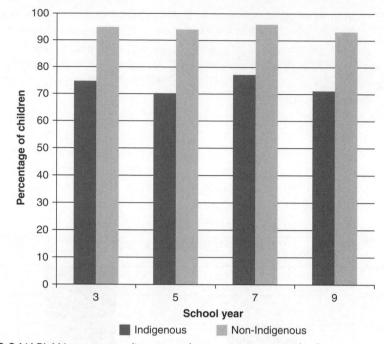

Figure 3.2 NAPLAN scores: reading at or above minimum standards.
Source: ACARA (2014).

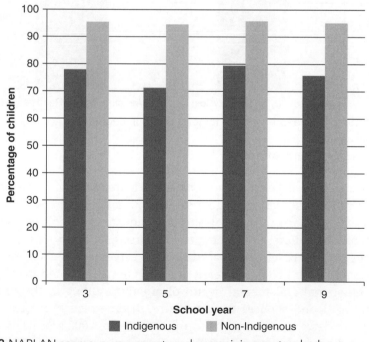

Figure 3.3 NAPLAN scores: numeracy at or above minimum standards.
Source: ACARA (2014).

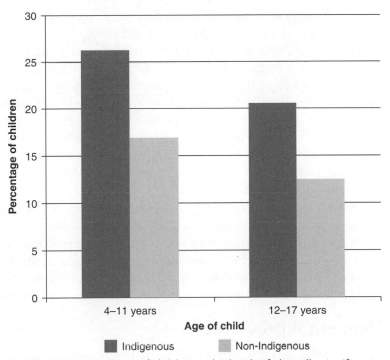

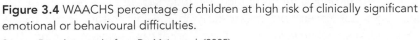

Figure 3.4 WAACHS percentage of children at high risk of clinically significant emotional or behavioural difficulties.

Source: Based on results from De Maio et al. (2005).

The Western Australia Aboriginal Child Health Survey (WAACHS) provides the best current data to compare the mental health of Indigenous children relative to that of non-Indigenous children, at various stages in life. In summary, the results show that Indigenous children have higher rates of clinically significant emotional or behavioural difficulties than non-Indigenous children. These results held for children aged 4 to 11 years (i.e. 26.3 per cent of Indigenous children were at risk of having clinically significant emotional or behavioural difficulties, compared to 16.9 per cent of non-Indigenous children), as well as for children aged 12 to 17 years (i.e. 20.5 per cent of Indigenous children were at risk of having clinically significant emotional or behavioural difficulties, compared to 12.5 per cent of non-Indigenous children) (De Maio et al., 2005).

The life-course perspective acknowledges the influence of factors – individual, cultural, social, environmental and economic – that potentially affect vulnerability. To fully understand vulnerability, and make changes to protect the individual, one must consider the multiple causal factors that act upon individuals at the various stages within their lives – such as birth, and transition from home to formal schooling – acknowledging that different factors may be more or less important at varying stages across the life-course.

Key transition points can either serve to initiate or reinforce vulnerability or, if protective steps are taken, can reduce vulnerability. Most transitions require an individual to identify with new social institutions, many of which require an individual to cope with a new set of developmental tasks and challenges (Laub & Sampson, 2005). For example, some children are particularly vulnerable when moving from home to a formal school environment, such as kindergarten, prep or primary school. The transition into a new institution can be frightening and overwhelming if strategies are not in place to both protect the child and equip them with the necessary skills and resources to cope with the transition. These strategies can occur before the transition (e.g. preparing to learn in the kindergarten years) or at the time of the transition (such as strategies aimed at reducing stress and uncertainty). They could be as simple as having an older 'buddy' assist the child in negotiating a new and unfamiliar environment.

Developmental prevention and early intervention, which are aligned with the life-course perspective, offer individuals, who are considered to be at risk or vulnerable, opportunities to overcome an array of problems associated with their development, health, learning, behaviour and overall wellbeing in the short and long term (Hayes, 2006). However, there are subtle differences between the terms 'developmental prevention' and 'early intervention'; these are now addressed.

Developmental prevention

Developmental prevention is underpinned by four key principles. First, 'early intervention' does not necessarily mean early in life, but rather 'early in the pathway'. Second, it is acknowledged that the context is always changing. This includes, but is not limited to, social policies, institutions and neighbourhoods in which people live. Third, risk and protective factors do matter. Finally, interventions are most effective when they focus on those most vulnerable at or around the time of an important transition in their life.

SPOTLIGHT 3.2: DEVELOPMENTAL PATHWAY

Loeber and Burke (2011) define developmental pathway as '... the orderly behavioural development between more than two problem behaviours with individuals differing in their propensity to progress along the successive problem behaviour represented by the pathway during development. Thus, pathways are a window into dynamic rather than static individual differences in youths' progression to serious problem behaviours' (p. 34).

Developmental prevention involves planning and organising efforts to reduce negative pathways, while preserving or increasing positive pathways for individuals (Little, 1999). Developmental prevention refers to interventions that target risk and protective factors in order to alter potential negative pathways that lead to reduced wellbeing (Homel, 2005). Interventions of this nature place significant emphasis on investing in institutions (e.g. schools or other learning environments such as play groups) as well as communities and social policies that manipulate multiple risk and protective factors at different levels of the social ecology, and at crucial transition points across the life-course – such as the commencement of school, or graduation from primary to high school (Freiberg, Homel & Branch, 2010). Therefore, developmental prevention is about providing resources to overcome adversity at critical points in the individual's life, not only in the early years.

Developmental pathways are distinguished from the causal pathways models proposed by Hertzman (1999). Causal pathways are written from a medical or epidemiological perspective, where there is an emphasis on 'linear causal chains of events' (Homel, 2005, p. 83). For example, one condition, such as poor school readiness, leads to another (e.g. disability and absenteeism in the fifth decade of life) via intermediate events – perhaps poor educational outcomes, and working in a highly stressed, low-control job (Homel et al., 2006).

The developmental pathways model and the causal pathways model are similar in many ways. However, they differ regarding one issue: the developmental pathways model acknowledges that human agency and the possibility of changing one's ways are achievable because of changes in social circumstances and opportunities that arise during an individual's life-course (Elder, 1998; Homel, 2005).

Early intervention

Early intervention begins by identifying individuals early in the life-course (e.g. preschoolers) who are seen as members of vulnerable groups, and providing resources to assist them to mediate vulnerability through risk-minimisation and protective factor-enhancement strategies. Enhancing protective factors, with the goal of enriching the available pathways for an individual, typically involves the provision of access to experiences and services that compensate for adverse life circumstances, disadvantage and vulnerability (Hayes, 2006). For example, parenting programs like the Triple P Positive Parenting Program (Sanders, Markie-Dadds & Turner, 2003) aim to reduce negative parenting behaviours such as harsh, coercive and inconsistent parenting, and enhance a parent's sense of self-confidence by enabling them to learn positive parenting skills (Hayes, 2006). Early intervention groups may be classified according to whether efforts are focused on the whole population (universal prevention), targeted population sub-groups identified as being at risk (selective prevention) or individuals identified with a given problem, or those at increased risk of a problem's future development (indicated prevention) (Gordon, 1983).

Risk and protective factors

Risk and protective factors underpin the life-course perspective (including developmental prevention and early intervention). **Risk factors** are measurable characteristics that precede an outcome, and are used to divide the population of interest into a range of risk groups (e.g. high and low risk). Risk factors can be classified as fixed (e.g. race and gender) or variable (e.g. parental child-rearing practices and levels of social and educational support).

Risk factors are a set of characteristics, variables or hazards that are correlated with the onset of future delinquency. They increase the probability of an individual developing a disorder when compared to a randomly selected individual from the general population (Hawkins, Catalano & Miller, 1992).

Protective factors mitigate the negative effects of risk factors and buffer the individual from negative life events, therefore reducing the chance of future delinquency (Kochenderfer-Ladd & Skinner, 2002).

Protective factors are variables – such as the presence of a stable emotional bond with a caregiver – that reduce the probability of negative outcomes.

This does not mean that the absence of a risk factor works in the same way as a protective factor. Rutter (2000) posits that little is achieved by calling the low-risk end of a risk dimension a protective factor. For example, if having parents who do not provide a nurturing and emotionally supportive environment is a risk factor, the absence of a poor emotional family environment will not necessarily protect you against other risk factors that might be encountered throughout life. Rather, a protective factor really means something that is more than just the absence of a risk factor. Further, what may be a risk factor in one situation may be a protective factor in another. Therefore, risk and protective factors may function simultaneously. For example, the divorce of a child's parents might have a negative impact on some children and may constitute a risk factor. On the other hand, a stressful family environment due to marital discord and perhaps even domestic violence is likely to have a negative impact on the child's social and emotional wellbeing, so divorce may actually act as a protective device from children being subjected to further stress. Das (2010) found this to be the case in minority ethnic families whose culture is highly resistant to divorce.

Functional capabilities

Sen and Nussbaum (1996) emphasise the role of functional capabilities (e.g. live to an old age, engage in economic transactions and participate in political activities) of individuals when evaluating social states in terms of wellbeing. In this context, poverty would be classified as a capability deprivation. Sen and Nussbaum suggest that emphasis should not be placed on how humans actually function, but rather their capability to function. Capability deprivation could come about as a result of ignorance, government oppression, lack of financial resources or false consciousness. As such, freedom of choice and the acknowledgement of individual heterogeneity (i.e. individual differences) when considering the wellbeing of individuals are important. This has important implications for educators, as modern pedagogy emphasises the significance of acknowledging the individual and their unique strengths, as well as their ability to have input into their learning across the life-course.

Understanding the context of prevention

In the later half of the twentieth century, we saw general improvements in quality of life for many in our society. However, Bronfenbrenner (2005) also argues that these changes have begun to threaten the social and ethical development of children – particularly those who grow up outside mainstream communities – and thus have been somewhat marginalised by changes in the social, economic and environmental fabric of modern society. The functional capabilities of these children are somewhat limited. Alongside the general improvements we have witnessed in mainstream communities lie growing rates of disruptive behaviours, delinquency, depression, suicide, substance use and abuse, lack of connection and poor school performance of the more marginalised communities (Stanley, Richardson & Prior, 2005).

Ecological theory (Bronfenbrenner, 1979) and developmental systems theory (e.g. Lerner & Overton, 2008) are both used to examine child development, and to explain the adverse trajectories in the developmental outcomes of vulnerable children (see further Chapter 8). According to these theories, social change partly explains a range of modern conditions (e.g. stress, family breakdown and dysfunction, poverty and inadequate parental engagement) that have begun to interfere with 'proximal processes' (Freiberg, Homel & Branch, 2010) that are important to positive development and also functional capabilities. These proximal processes include nurturing and responsive parenting, and strong supportive relationships within the family environment and between the family and institutions in which children live and operate – home, school, neighbourhood and community.

Bronfenbrenner (1979) identifies four systems that contain rules, norms and roles that help to shape human development.

1. The *microsystem* defines the immediate environment – the layer in which the child has the most direct contact (e.g. family, school, peer group). This layer is bi-directional in terms of impact away from and towards the child.
2. The *mesosystem* comprises connections between the child's immediate environments (e.g. if a child experiences difficulties at school, it is likely that the child's parents will need to interact with teachers and administrators at the school).
3. The *exosystem* contains other external and social systems that affect a child's development (e.g. the parents' workplaces, neighbourhood institutions, the local economy).
4. The *macrosystem* contains all of the various sub-systems and the various beliefs and values that are embedded within a culture via unwritten principles that regulate individual and collective behaviour.

Later, Bronfenbrenner and Morris (2006) added an additional system: the *chronosystem*. This system comprises all other systems and refers to the bi-directional influence of each system and the importance of history regarding a child's development.

Freiberg, Homel and Branch (2010, p. 30) argue that when schools become distracted or overwhelmed by the 'by-products of "toxic" developmental settings', they tend to expend resources and energy and are often 'locked in a continuing cycle of reaction to developmental difficulties'. As a consequence, teachers become too exhausted by stress 'to work proactively to create conditions that support children's learning and promote developmental competence' (p. 30). Distracted teachers increase the likelihood that vulnerable children will fall further behind and, in turn, jeopardise long-term prospects and future quality of life (Knudson et al., 2006).

This raises an important question: how do we provide children with the opportunity to succeed – particularly those who are considered vulnerable in our society? According to developmental systems theory, prevention should be holistic in nature and draw upon the strengths of individuals and their communities. In Lerner's words, 'the role of developmental science is to identify those relations between individual strengths and contextual assets in families, communities, cultures, and the natural environment, and to integrate strengths and assets to promote positive human development' (2006, p. 12). The next question concerns when we begin intervention efforts and the length of time for which we maintain them.

Why we begin interventions early

The consensus among developmental scientists is that we begin as early as we can. Some describe the temporal boundaries of prevention as 'womb to tomb'. In other words, we begin providing resources to expectant mothers and continue to provide resources and opportunities over the entire life-course. We should not, however, fall into the trap of believing that if we miss the early years then all is lost. Early childhood should be considered the first point in a series of important life phases, each of which contains aspects of vulnerability and opportunity (Laub & Sampson, 2005). Rather than suggesting that once past the age of three there is no possibility of brain development and restructuring, we should consider this point to be a critical time for learning, as suggested by Hockfield and Lombroso (1998). The point is that it is never too late to learn or change, but the process becomes increasingly complex and difficult.

Does developmental prevention work?

McCain et al. (1999) suggest that there is clear evidence that good developmental programs, which involve parents or other primary caregivers, can influence how caregivers relate to and care for the children, and can vastly improve a child's outcomes for behaviour, learning and health in later life. They also suggest that not only can the programs benefit the child and their family, they can also benefit all socio-economic groups in society. Unfortunately, intervention programs are often implemented at a point where the problem – for instance a behavioural issue – is considered to be serious (Golly, Stiller & Walker, 1998). Further, responses to these problems are unfortunately extremely complex and expensive to undertake successfully (Manning, 2004).

Early childhood intervention programs (from birth to five years) that employ a risk-focused approach can have positive impacts on outcomes of children who are considered at risk at an early age (Homel, 2005). Evidence is available to demonstrate the short- and long-term effects of early childhood intervention projects. Projects such as the Perry Preschool Project (Schweinhart, 2004), the Elmira Prenatal/Early Infancy Project (Eckenrode et al., 1998; Olds, 2002) and the Seattle Social Development Project (Hawkins et al., 1999) have gone some way to confirming this position.

Several studies show that a systematic delivery of basic services or resources to disadvantaged or vulnerable families improves outcomes for those targeted across multiple domains, including improved educational outcomes, decreases in child maltreatment, reductions in child and youth antisocial behaviour, lower levels of substance abuse, and increases in income and workforce participation (Brooks-Gunn, Fuligni & Berlin, 2003; Olds, 2002; Reynolds et al., 2001). Heckman, Stixrud and Urzua (2006) also stress the importance of the family in mediating the cognitive and social-emotional skills of children in their early years. Research conducted by Heckman, Stixrud, and Urzua (2006) highlight that families that *do* invest in developing their child's cognitive and social-emotional (non-cognitive) skills significantly improve their child's life trajectory – with reductions in subsequent involvement in crime, teenage pregnancy and improvements in educational outcomes. James Heckman's research has shown the importance of cognitive and non-cognitive skill development, and the role families play in nurturing this development, to overcome social disadvantage and vulnerability in a sustainable manner.

Finally, evidence shows that the early health screening (including mental health) of children mediates future problems and promotes healthy development and transitions along positive developmental pathways. For example, research suggests that children in foster care are at higher risk of developing, or in fact having, mental health problems than those who are not (Kortenkamp, 2002). Understandably, a compelling argument can be made for the early provision of mental health screening and services, particularly when evidence suggests that mental health problems can be identified in early childhood (Zeanah & Zeanah, 2009) and that the early provision of services helps reduce emotional disorders in later life (young adulthood) (Nelson et al., 2003).

A number of meta-analyses have recently been conducted that highlight the effectiveness of prevention models (e.g. family-based prevention, home visitation, parenting programs, enriched preschool programs) on a range of outcomes, such as cognitive development, educational attainment, social-emotional development, deviance, social participation, and health and familial wellbeing, ranging from directly after the intervention to early adulthood. Summaries of the findings of these important empirical studies can be found in MacLeod and Nelson (2000), Nelson et al. (2003), Farrington and Welsh (2003) and Manning, Homel and Smith (2010).

Evidence also exists showing the importance of providing supportive and nurturing early childhood education and care (ECEC) for Indigenous children with respect to their cognitive and developmental outcomes. Arcos Holzinger and Biddle (2015) used the Longitudinal Study of Indigenous Children (LSIC) to examine the effects of ECEC participation across a range of cognitive and developmental outcomes using linear regression models. The data in Figure 3.5 report outcomes at various ages of primary schooling. They compare the outcomes of Indigenous children who had attended preschool or preschool and child-care services, relative to those of children who did not attend. Model 1 controls only for ECEC attendance, while Model 2 controls for ECEC attendance as well as for a range of other demographic characteristics that could potentially impact the test score outcomes analysed. Shaded bars signify statistically significant effects of ECEC participation, and the vertical axis measures the difference in standard deviations. In terms of developmental outcomes, ECEC attendance in Model 2 led to a statistically significant decrease in the behavioural difficulties estimated by the SDQ total difficulties test, which points to fewer developmental difficulties (Figure 3.5).

important collaborative relationships with key institutions within communities; this is especially the case in socially and economically disadvantaged areas.

A challenge that faces policy-makers is that systems embedded in communities (e.g. education systems and the individual schools within those systems) are not 'system-ready' – or, for that matter 'evidence-ready' (Little & Maughan, 2010). Three fundamental goals exist: (1) to assist the community to build their own set of structured processes and resources that strengthen the developmental system in socially disadvantaged communities with the goal of making possible sustainable improvements in the wellbeing of children; (2) to ensure funds that are spent on services and programs are optimally allocated and efficiently used; and (3) to test the processes for both efficacy in fostering community coalitions empowered to achieve collective impact and transportability to new communities.

In terms of an integrated strategy, we need to ensure that the constituent elements (programs, policies, action plans, initiatives): (1) are explicitly linked via appropriate performance indicators to the intermediate goal in question; and (2) have clearly defined, mutually consistent responsibilities and appropriate arrangements for coordinating activities.

Critically, a central objective is to make such an advance possible in disadvantaged or vulnerable areas. This would require the development of a national infrastructure that would attempt to move away from the funding of individual services in isolation to a more coordinated approach. This scenario would require diverse organisations and communities to come together as clearly focused, well-resourced, skilled and fully collaborative partnerships to solve a small number of specific problems that they have identified as priorities on the basis of local data. These collaborative partnerships would empower the community, schools (and the teachers in those schools) and community agencies to transcend system silos, foster ethical practice and respectful relationships, and deliver goal-directed, quantitatively evaluated, evidence-based resources that promote child wellbeing.

Conclusion

A number of important questions emerge when developing policy to improve the wellbeing of children. Two questions in particular need to be answered when developing effective policy. First: what is it about individuals, families, communities and institutions that can adversely affect an individual's life and their wellbeing? Second: what measures can be implemented early in life to promote healthy development that enhances individual wellbeing? Successfully answering these questions allows for a holistic approach to be adopted that promotes collective action. A collective approach moves away from the funding of individual services in isolation to a more coordinated approach that potentially provides better outcomes for individuals living in socially and economically disadvantaged areas, thereby enhancing individual and societal wellbeing.

Summary

To improve the wellbeing of children and transcend system silos, policy-makers should aim to:

- increase the efficacy of individual child-serving organisations (e.g. schools)
- enhance the capacity of people at every level of an organisation (e.g. teachers)
- facilitate openness and commitment to change and organisational reform where needed
- motivate clear-headed reflection on the appropriateness of current practice, and reduce the use of ineffective and inefficient strategies, and
- translate knowledge about the causes of poor developmental outcomes into well-implemented evidence-based developmental prevention programs.

Questions

3.1   What is it about individuals, families, communities and institutions that can adversely affect an individual's life and their wellbeing?

3.2   What measures can be implemented early in life to promote healthy development that enhances individual wellbeing?

3.3   Describe the importance of risk and protective factors. Why do they need to be addressed?

3.4   Why is collective action important when addressing individual and societal wellbeing?

References

Arcos Holzinger, L. & Biddle, N. (2015). *The relationship between early childhood education and care (ECEC) and the outcomes of Indigenous children: evidence from the Longitudinal Study of Indigenous Children (LSIC)* (CAEPR Working Paper No. 103/2015). Canberra: Centre for Aboriginal Economic Policy Research (CAEPR).

Arthur, M., Hawkins, J., Brown, E., Briney, J. & Oesterle, S. (2010). Implementation of the Communities That Care prevention system by coalitions in the Community Youth Development Study. *Journal of Community Psychology, 28*(2), 245–58.

Australian Curriculum, Assessment and Reporting Authority (ACARA) (2014). *NAPLAN Achievement in reading, persuasive writing, language conventions and numeracy: National Report for 2014.* Sydney: ACARA.

Bronfenbrenner, U. (1979). *The ecology of human development: Experiments by nature and design.* Cambridge, MA: Harvard University Press.

—— (2005). Growing chaos in the lives of children, youth, and families: How can we turn it around. In U. Bronfenbrenner (ed), *Making human beings human: Bioecological perspectives on human development* (pp. 185–97). Thousand Oaks, CA: Sage.

Bronfenbrenner, U. & Morris, P. (2006). The ecology of developmental processes. In W. Damon & R. Lerner (eds), *Handbook of child psychology* (6th edn, pp. 992–1028). New York: Wiley.

Brooks-Gunn, J., Fuligni, A.S. & Berlin, L.J. (2003). *Early child development in the 21st century: Profiles of current research initiatives.* New York: Teachers College Press.

Das, C. (2010). Resilience, risk and protective factors for British-Indian children of divorce. *Journal of Social Sciences,* 25(1-2-3), 97–108.

De Maio, J.A., Zubrick, S.R., Silburn, S.R., Lawrence, D.M., Mitrou, F.G., Dalby, R.B. et al. (2005). *The Western Australian Aboriginal Child Health Survey: Measuring the social and emotional wellbeing of Aboriginal children and intergenerational effects of forced separation.* Perth: Curtin University of Technology and Telethon Institute for Child Health Research.

Eckenrode, J., Olds, D., Henderson, C.R., Kitzman, H., Luckey, D., Pettitt, L.M. et al. (1998). Long-term effects of nurse home visitation on children's criminal and anti-social behaviour. *Journal of the American Medical Association,* 280(15), 1302.

Elder, G.H. (1998). The life-course as developmental theory. *Child Development,* 69(1), 1–12.

Farrington, D. & Welsh, B.C. (2003). Family-based prevention of offending: A meta-analysis. *The Australian and New Zealand Journal of Criminology,* 36(2), 127–51.

Freiberg, K., Homel, R & Branch, S. (2010). Circles of care: The struggle to strengthen child developmental systems through the Pathways to Prevention Project. *Family Matters,* 84, 28–34.

Golly, A.M., Stiller, B. & Walker, H.M. (1998). First step to success: Replication and social validation of an early intervention program. *Journal of Emotional and Behavioural Disorders,* 6(4), 243–50.

Gordon, R.S.J. (1983). An operational classification of disease prevention. *Public Health Reports,* 98(2), 107–9.

Hawkins, D.J., Catalano, R., Kosterman, R., Abbot, R. & Hill, K. (1999). Preventing adolescent health-risk behaviours by strengthening protection during childhood. *Archives of Pediatrics and Adolescent Medicine,* 153, 226–34.

Hawkins, J.D., Catalano, R.F. & Miller, J.Y. (1992). Risk and protective factors in alcohol and other drug problems in adolescence and early adulthood: Implications for substance abuse prevention. *Psychological Bulletin,* 112(1), 64–105.

Hayes, A. (2006). Maintaining the gains: Sustainability in prevention and early intervention. *Family Matters,* 75, 66–9.

Heckman, J., Stixrud, J. & Urzua, S. (2006). The effects of cognitive and non-cognitive abilities on labour market outcomes and social behaviour. *Journal of Labour Economics,* 24(3), 411–82.

Hertzman, C. (1999). Population health and human development. In D.P. Keating & C. Hertzman (eds), *Developmental health and the wealth of nations:*

Social, biological, and educational dynamics (pp. 21–40). New York: Guilford Press.

Hockfield, S. & Lombroso, P. (1998). Development of the cerebral cortex: IX. Cortical development and experience: I. *Journal of American Academic Child Adolescence Psychiatry,* 37(9), 992–3.

Homel, R. (2005). Developmental crime prevention. In N. Tilley (ed), *Handbook of crime prevention and community safety* (pp. 71–106). Cullompton, UK: Willan.

Homel, R., Elias, G. & Hay, I. (2001). Developmental prevention in a disadvantaged community. In R. Eckersley, J. Dixon & B. Douglas (eds), *The social origins of health and well-being* (pp. 269–78). Cambridge: Cambridge University Press.

Homel, R., Freiberg, K., Lamb, C., Leech, M., Carr, A., Hampshire, A. et al. (2006). *The Pathways to Prevention project: The first five years 1999–2004.* Brisbane: Griffith University and Mission Australia.

Knudson, E., Heckman, J., Cameron, J. & Shonkoff, J. (2006). Economic, neurobiological, and behavioral perspectives on building America's future workforce. Paper presented at the National Academy of Sciences, 5 July.

Kochenderfer-Ladd, B. & Skinner, K. (2002). Children's coping strategies: Moderators of the effects of peer victimization? *Developmental Psychology* 38(2), 267–78.

Kortenkamp, K. (2002). *The well-being of children involved with the child welfare system: A national overview.* Washington, D.C: The Urban Institute.

Laub, J.H. & Sampson, R.J. (2005). A general age-graded theory of crime: Lessons learned and the future of life-course criminology. In D. Farrington (ed.), *Advances in criminological theory, Volume 13: Testing integrated developmental/ life-course theories of offending* (pp. 165–81). New Brunswick, NJ: Transaction.

Leigh, A. & Gong, X. (2009). Estimating cognitive gaps between Indigenous and non-Indigenous Australians. *Education Economics,* 17(2), 239–61.

Lerner, R. (2006). Developmental science, developmental systems, and contemporary theories of human development. In R. Lerner (ed.), *Handbook of child psychology (Vol. 1: Theoretical models of human development)* (pp. 1–17). Hoboken, NJ: John Wiley & Sons.

Lerner, R. & Overton, W. (2008). Exemplifying theory, research, and application to promote positive development and social justice. *Journal of Adolescent Research,* 23, 245–55.

Little, M. (1999). Prevention and early intervention with children in need: Definitions, principles and examples of good practice. *Children and Society,* 13, 304–16.

Little, M. & Maughan, B. (eds) (2010). *Effective interventions for children in need.* Aldershot: Ashgate.

Loeber, R. & Burke, J. (2011). Developmental pathways in juvenile externalizing and internalizing problems. *Journal of Research on Adolescence,* 21, 34–46.

MacLeod, J. & Nelson, G. (2000). Programs for the promotion of family wellness and the prevention of child maltreatment: A meta-analytic review. *Child Abuse and Neglect,* 24(9), 1127–49.

Manning, M. (2004). *Measuring the costs of community-based developmental prevention programs in Australia*. Masters (Hons), School of Criminology and Criminal Justice, Griffith University.

—— (2008). *Economic evaluation of the effects of early childhood intervention programs on adolescent outcomes*. PhD, Key Centre for Ethics, Law, Justice and Governance, Griffith University.

Manning, M., Homel, R. & Smith, C. (2010). A meta-analysis of the effects of early developmental prevention programs in at-risk populations on non-health outcomes in adolescence. *Children and Youth Services Review*, 32(4), 506–19.

McCain, M.N., Mustard, F.J., Coffey, C., Gordon, M., Comis, J., Offord, D. et al. (1999). *Early Years Study: Reversing the real brain – final report*. Ontario: Ontario Children's Secretariat.

Nelson, G., Westhues, A., Laurier, W. & MacLeod, J. (2003). A meta-analysis of longitudinal research on preschool prevention programs for children. *Prevention and Treatment*, 6, 1–35.

Olds, D. (2002). Prenatal and infancy home visiting by nurses: From randomized trials to community replication. *Prevention Science*, 3(3), 153–72.

Reynolds, A.J., Temple, J.A., Robertson, D.L. & Mann, E.A. (2001). Long-term effects of an early childhood intervention on educational achievement and juvenile arrest: A 15-year follow-up of low income children in public school. *Journal of the American Medical Association*, 285(18), pp. 2330–46.

Rutter, M. (2000). Resilience considered: Conceptual considerations, empirical findings, and policy implications. In J. Shonkoff & S. Meisels (eds), *Handbook of early childhood intervention* (2nd edn, pp. 651–82). New York: Cambridge University Press.

Sanders, M., Markie-Dadds, C. & Turner, K. (2003). *Theoretical, scientific and clinical foundations of the Triple P Positive Parenting Program: A population approach to the promotion of parenting competence*. Parenting Research and Practice Monograph No. 1, Brisbane: University of Queensland.

Schweinhart, L.J. (2004). *The High/Scope Perry Preschool Study through age 40: Summary, conclusions, and frequently asked questions*. Ypsilanti, MI: High/Scope Educational Research Foundation.

Sen, A. & Nussbaum, M. (1996). Functioning and capability: The foundation of Sen's and Nussbaum's development of ethic. *Political Theory*, 24(4), 584–612.

Stanley, F., Richardson, S. & Prior, M. (2005). *Children of the lucky country? How Australia has turned its back on children and why children matter*. Sydney: Pan Macmillan.

UK Government (2011). *Objective vs. subjective well-being*. Retrieved 18 July 2013 from http://webarchive.nationalarchives.gov.uk/20110422103457/well-being. dxwconsult.com/2011/02/24/objective-vs-subjective-well-being

Zeanah, C., & Zeanah, P. (2009). The scope of infant mental health. *Handbook of Infant Mental Health*, 3(1), 5–21.

CHAPTER 4

Communication development

Jane McCormack, Sharynne McLeod and Linda Harrison

Introduction

Humans are social beings. They play, chat, sing, tell jokes, share stories, discuss issues, ask questions, follow directions, write emails, send text messages, follow Twitter, post on Facebook and do countless other activities every day that enable connections with others. Communication skills are core to these activities. Communication skills allow us to participate in our everyday lives and interact with the world around us.

In this chapter, we identify key stages in the development of communication skills in the early years, explore the milestones associated with each stage, and identify features that may indicate concerns at each stage. We discuss the links between oral and written communication skills and we suggest strategies for stimulating and supporting communication development across the early years.

> **Communication** is the production and comprehension of verbal (language-based) and/or non-verbal messages between two or more individuals within a particular context.
>
> **Language** is communication that occurs through the use of symbols which represent meaning (e.g. sounds, letters, gestures) and which are governed by rules specific to the context in which the language is used (e.g. country, age-group, status).

What is communication?

Communication is the sharing of ideas and information through verbal and non-verbal messages. Verbal messages are those that have a word (or **language**) base and include speaking, writing and signing. Non-verbal messages are not word-based and might include tactile or visual communication (e.g. a hug or a facial expression) (Crystal, 2006). Verbal communication (i.e. language) may be described as expressive (producing a message) or receptive (understanding a message).

Verbal communication is often considered in terms of three key areas: form, content and use (Bloom & Lahey, 1978). Form refers to the symbols used within the language (e.g. sounds, letters, words, gestures) and rules for combining those symbols (e.g. the sound combinations [phonology] or word combinations [syntax] allowed in a language). Content refers to the meaning communicated by specific symbols/words/sentences and/or the combinations of these (often called semantics). Use refers to the way in which rules are applied and content is chosen to reflect the context in which the communication is occurring (also known as pragmatics). Form, content and use are interdependent, as illustrated in Figure 4.1.

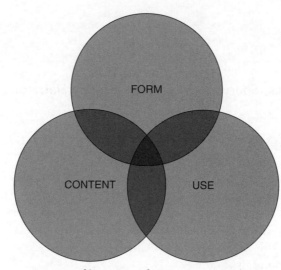

Figure 4.1 Three components of language: form, content and use.

Source: Adapted from Bloom & Lahey (1978).

Your ability to communicate in different contexts is a skill that has been developing since you were born. Initially, your communication with others would have been non-verbal (through eye gaze, pointing, smiling etc.), while they would have communicated in non-verbal and verbal (language-based) ways with you. As you were exposed to verbal communication, you began to imitate this and produce this yourselves. For most of us, the first form of verbal communication that we develop is **speech**, and later we develop reading/writing (literacy) as well. Speech involves the planning and executing of precise and coordinated oral motor movements in order to produce a message orally. While it is a common way in which language is expressed, it is not essential for verbal communication. For children who cannot speak, communication through gesture, sign and/or pictorial symbols

Speech is the process by which we produce verbal (language-based) communication in oral form (compared to writing, the process for production in written form, and sign language, the process for production in gestural form).

can be learned from an early age. For other children, their speech may be unclear or their language delayed, and they may need support to acquire speech and language skills. Without support, difficulties with speech can lead to problems with written communication and learning, as well as difficulties developing and maintaining social relationships at school (Harrison et al., 2009; McCormack et al., 2011).

The following sections outline the communication skills that appear at different stages in a child's development. In the appendix to this chapter, you will find Table 4.1 which is a summary of this information and strategies to support children's communication development within each stage.

PAUSE AND REFLECT 4.1: THE ROLE OF THE SPEAKER AND THE ROLE OF THE LISTENER

'We need to draw ears on so people can hear what we're saying' (Child).

What does this quote suggest about children's perceptions of roles and responsibilities in communication exchanges? Do you agree? What do you think influences this perception?

Figure 4.2 Tim's (4.3) drawing of himself talking to his sister.

Source: Illustration copyright 2012 by S. McLeod, L. McAllister, L. J. Harrison & J. McCormack. Reprinted with permission.

Laying the foundations: 0–12 months (babies)

Before babies develop words, they develop *prelinguistic* (non-verbal) behaviours, many of which are required for successful communication later (e.g. eye contact, shared attention and turn-taking) (Wetherby & Prizant, 1993). From 8 to 12 months, babies demonstrate a dramatic increase in their use of social communication skills, particularly in their use of gesture to express a message (Reilly et al., 2006). Babies learn these behaviours from hearing and watching others communicate, but also from receiving feedback on their own communication attempts (Miller & Lossia, 2013). Thus, a language-rich environment in which non-verbal and verbal communication skills are frequently modelled for babies, and speech is directed specifically towards babies, is essential for assisting them to attend to language, to enhance their communication systems and to foster social interactions (Golinkoff et al., 2015; Miller & Lossia, 2013).

During the first 12 months of life, anatomical and neurological changes take place that lay the foundations for children to learn verbal (language) communication skills. These changes primarily affect the oromotor structures (e.g. lips, tongue, jaw and palate), laryngeal and respiratory systems. Initially, the vocalisations produced by children are vegetative or reflexive (e.g. hiccups, crying), then infants begin to experiment with producing sounds, particularly vowels and bilabial (lip) sounds (b, p, m). This babbling, or vocal play, is a feature of communication development in the first year. Initially, the babbling is reduplicated, so that the same consonant and vowel patterns are repeated (e.g. *mamamama*); however, soon afterwards infants develop variegated babbling – the ability to change consonants and vowels (e.g. *bamenama*) (Oller et al., 1999). The sound sequences in variegated babbling increasingly imitate the sound sequences of adult speech. This occurs as infants are exposed to variations in phonological patterns and intonation in the care-givers' responses to the infants' own babbling (Goldstein & Schwade, 2008). This change in babbling reflects an improvement in the accuracy and consistency of oromotor movements and, with further practice and improvement, infants develop the ability to produce adult-like forms – their first words.

Along with the growth and development of anatomical structures, the production of first words also requires the development of an infant's *lexicon*, or internal representation of words and word meanings. In the very first days of life, infants learn to perceive auditory information and can distinguish between voices (and there is some evidence to suggest they have some perceptual ability while in the womb) (Ruben, 1997). As this first year progresses, they continue to rely on auditory input to make sense of their world. Infants learn to associate a word (i.e. a combination of sounds) with an object, person or place through continuous exposure to, and repetition of, that vocabulary item.

In this early stage of language development, impairments of oral structures (such as cleft lip and/or palate) and impairments of sensory functions (such as temporary or permanent hearing loss) can impact on the acquisition of speech and language, through affecting an infant's ability to perceive and/or imitate spoken language. Typically, children at risk of communication difficulties due to structural or sensory impairments will be under the management and care of a team of professionals, which may include audiologists, speech pathologists and ear, nose and throat surgeons.

Other infants with communication difficulties may present as unresponsive to the communication of others, and/or may demonstrate minimal attempts at vocalisations without an identifiable cause. While children vary in their degree of babbling, attempts to communicate messages in some form (i.e. pointing, vocalising) are expected in the first year. The following section describes ways in which early communication skills can be supported.

Supporting communication development: Let's play

To assist babies to develop prelinguistic behaviours, parents and educators can engage in activities that focus on interaction. Repetitive games, such as peek-a-boo, teach babies turn-taking skills and the process of interacting with others through initiating an action and then expecting and awaiting a response.

Babies learn words by imitating others. Parents and educators need to talk to babies but also be responsive to their baby's attempts to initiate communication. For example, by noticing what has captured the infants' attention (e.g. through following their eye-gaze or pointing), adults can provide the words for objects that have taken the infant's interest. It will be the words for these items that babies are most motivated to learn. Thus, it is important to follow the infant's lead when deciding what to talk about. Talking *for* the baby, by explaining their actions, or *with* the baby about what is happening around them, provide the language-rich environments that encourage language development. Reading and looking at books with young children can also support their language and cognitive development through exposing them to new vocabulary (Murray & Egan, 2014).

First words: 1–2 years (toddlers)

When infants/toddlers first hear a particular combination of sounds (a new word), they develop a series of representations (or entries) that are stored within their lexicon (word memory). The *semantic* representation is knowledge of what the word means, the *phonological* representation is knowledge of what the word sounds like, and the *motor plan* is knowledge of how the word is produced (e.g. the sound combinations required and movements needed to make those sounds) (Stackhouse & Wells, 1997). When infants use a vocabulary item to refer to a person/object consistently for the purpose of communication, a word may be considered learnt.

During this time of word learning, children sometimes over generalise the meanings of words. For example, a child may overuse the word *juice* to refer to any drink, such as a glass of water or milk. Over time, children's representations become more refined and connections are made between the stored word and other words that are related in some way – semantically (e.g. part/whole objects, categories, synonyms, antonyms) or phonologically (e.g. rhymes, same initial sound). This occurs as they are exposed to the word more often, learn more about variations of the word (e.g. instead of saying *dog*, begin to identify a Labrador, a Border Collie, or a Cocker Spaniel) and/or as they use the word and receive feedback on the effectiveness of their use.

First words typically consist of high-frequency ones (those that the child has heard often) which include common nouns (names of foods, animals, body parts, games) and people's names (and kinship terms). These first word groups are common across different languages, although some differences in the rate of use have been found. For instance, children learning Mandarin and Cantonese tend to produce more words describing family relationships (e.g. grandma, grandpa, sister, brother, aunt, uncle) than English-speaking children, while English-speaking children tend to produce more animal and object names (Tardif et al., 2008). During this stage, toddlers' lexicons grow exponentially. The words produced still tend to be simple in structure (e.g. consonant-vowel-consonant combinations such as *cat*); however, as toddlers learn a greater range of words (adjectives, verbs and prepositions, in addition to nouns), they begin combining words to form short phrases (e.g. *more milk, doggie run*). As toddlers begin to combine words to form phrases and sentences, difficulties with fluency might become apparent, such as when children repeat sounds or words while trying to plan and produce their message.

During these first two years of life, toddlers communicate for a number of purposes: demonstrating interest; questioning; negating and agreeing; requesting; playing; and participating in daily rituals (greetings and goodbyes). The purpose of the communication impacts on the words children are motivated to learn and vice versa, which reflects the overlap between *content* and *use* (see Figure 4.1). During this stage, children will typically understand many more words than they can produce, and start to understand these words outside routines, although some contextual support may still be required (e.g. the toddler can point to body parts outside of bathtime). They also begin to understand different questions, including *What? Who?* and *Where?* although may respond by pointing if they do not have the vocabulary items to communicate verbally.

Toddlers learn to pronounce many speech sounds (e.g. p, b, m, t, d, n, h, w) between one and two years of age and as a result, their speech becomes easier to understand. However, it is common for toddlers to make some errors with their speech sound production from time to time and to simplify words (e.g. 'biscuit' becomes *bibi*). The speech of toddlers can be more difficult to understand when they are using longer sentences. However, a good guide to keep in mind is that at two years, half of toddlers' speech should be understood.

Supporting communication development: Let's model

To assist communication development, parents and educators can use modelling to provide toddlers with opportunities to repeat what is said, particularly when children make speech sound errors. A speech pathologist should be contacted for advice if a toddler's speech is very difficult for familiar people to understand; if gestures (and grunts) are used in place of words, if stuttering is present; if the toddler's communication difficulties are associated with an emotional response (e.g. frustration, withdrawal, distress); or if there is a family history of these difficulties.

When parents or educators are concerned about the child's speech and language development, it is also advisable to have the child's hearing checked by an audiologist, as hearing is important for children to learn how to reproduce sounds correctly and has been identified as a risk factor in the development of speech and language difficulties (Harrison & McLeod, 2010).

Putting it into practice: 2–5 years (preschoolers)

During the preschool years, children communicate for a wider range of purposes and with a wider range of people than in their infant and toddler years. This reflects changes to the activities in which children engage during the preschool years and the larger environmental context in which these activities are undertaken. Instead of communicating primarily with family and other familiar adults about items in the here and now, preschool children begin communicating about more abstract and complex ideas. They are also more likely to be exposed to a larger number of peers and adults (including educators, parents of peers, coaches and instructors). Preschoolers use speech and language in their social interactions and play to request inclusion, suggest ideas, explain rules and tell stories; in short, to develop and maintain relationships with others. Furthermore, they use speech and language in more formal settings, such as preschool or kindergarten, to request help, show comprehension and make inferences; in short, to learn new skills/ knowledge or demonstrate learning.

As children communicate with more people in more environments, they are exposed to new vocabulary and begin to learn more specific terms. For instance, preschool children know the names of shapes, sizes, letters and numbers. They understand and use a growing range of sentence forms, including complex sentences, where two ideas are joined by a conjunction (e.g. I'm wearing a jacket *because* it's cold outside), and questions, such as *why? when?* and *how?*

In an Australian study examining the experiences of children with communication (speech) difficulties, preschoolers were asked to draw a picture of themselves talking to someone and then to describe the picture to the interviewer (the illustrations in this chapter are from this study). The range of communication partners portrayed in the pictures, which included parents, siblings, friends, teachers and pets, as well as the range of activities, reflects the diversity of what and with whom children communicate in the early childhood years (McCormack et al., 2010).

Preschool children use much longer sentences than toddlers and their speech is typically more intelligible to familiar and unfamiliar listeners. By four years, children can say most speech sounds correctly, although some are easier to pronounce than others. Shriberg (1993) divided the 24 English consonants according to the ease of pronunciation within spontaneous conversational speech:

- Early-8 (averaging more than 75 per cent correct in preschoolers' speech): m, b, y, n, w, d, p, h
- Middle-8 (averaging 25 to 75 per cent correct): t, ng, k, g, f, v, ch, j
- Late-8 (averaging less than 25 per cent correct): sh, s, z, th (<u>th</u>umb), th (<u>th</u>is), l, r, zh (televi<u>si</u>on).

Shriberg's categories show the sounds that develop later and which may be more difficult for children to produce. For instance, preschool children commonly have difficulty with 'r' (e.g. saying *wed* for 'red'), 'v' (e.g. saying *berry* for 'very'), and 'th' (e.g. saying *fankyou* for 'thank you'). Sometimes, preschool children will produce sounds correctly in short words (e.g. 's' in *sun*) but may have difficulty when saying those in longer words (e.g. 'spaghetti' might become *begetti*).

Preschoolers can use many *consonant clusters*, which are combinations of two or more sounds (e.g. tw, sp, gl, scr) that can be produced at the start (e.g. <u>bl</u>ue) or end of words (e.g. ha<u>nd</u>). Some preschool children are still developing the ability to say more complex combinations of sounds together (e.g. <u>scr</u>ibble and <u>str</u>awberry). By four to five years of age children should be almost always intelligible to everyone, including strangers (McLeod, Harrison & McCormack, 2012).

Another important communication milestone that is achieved during the preschool years is children's early development of skills that will be important for learning to read and write. *Phonological awareness* refers to knowledge about the sound structure of words and skills to manipulate sound structures; specifically syllable-level awareness, onset-rime (rhyme) awareness and phonemic awareness (Rvachew & Grawburg, 2006). In the preschool years, children learn that words can be segmented into parts (syllables) and that words are made up of sounds. They learn to identify syllables (e.g. *am-bu-lance*), units of rhyme (e.g. *cat – bat*) and individual sounds in spoken words (e.g. *d-o-g*). Later, they learn to blend the onset + rime (e.g. 'd' + 'og' = *dog*), blend individual phonemes (e.g. 'd' + 'o' + 'g' = *dog*), segment words into phonemes (e.g. 'dog' = 'd' + 'o' + 'g') and delete phonemes (e.g. 'dog' – 'g' = *do*) (Anthony et al., 2003). Once children become proficient at tasks involving spoken words, they can transfer their knowledge and skills to written words. That is, they learn to read/spell through their ability to map sounds to letters, and to recognise sound and letter patterns in words.

Supporting communication development: Let's expand

Building a child's communication skills in the early preschool years requires the introduction of new vocabulary and modelling ways to expand on their utterances. For instance, when a child identifies a *blue car*, parents and educators can

CASE STUDY 4.1: THE IMPACT OF COMMUNICATION DIFFICULTIES

'As the years progressed he's started to use gestures more' (Teacher).

Owen has very unintelligible speech compared to his peers. He drew a picture of himself talking with his mother. First he drew the faces, bodies and legs in red and yellow, then scribbled over their faces with black.

Reflect on how communication success or failure influences children's subsequent communication attempts.

How do you support communication in children? How could you encourage communication when children have speech and/or language difficulties?

Figure 4.3 Owen's (4.6) drawing shows him (left) 'talking' to his mother.

Source: Illustration copyright 2012 by S. McLeod, L. McAllister, L. J. Harrison & J. McCormack. Reprinted with permission.

acknowledge and respond by commenting (expansion) that *the blue car is driving on the road* or *the blue car is travelling slowly* or asking for more information: *I wonder where the blue car is going?*

In later preschool years, parents and educators may engage in a range of activities to help children develop early literacy skills. For instance, parents can read to children, sing songs and play rhyming games, or games such as 'I spy' that encourage children to think about sounds and letters. Due to the strong link between sound production and the development of early literacy skills, it is important that preschool children produce sounds accurately. A visit to the speech pathologist is recommended if children cannot be understood, if they are frustrated with attempts to communicate, if they are using very few words, or if they are not using sounds in particular word positions (e.g. saying *ish* for 'fish' or *bu* for 'bus').

Language for learning: 5–12 years (school-aged children)

When children commence school, their communication development shifts from a focus on learning language to using language for learning. At school, children's oral language skills continue to develop, and their written language skills are consolidated. In the school years, children experience growth in their vocabulary and develop *metalinguistic skills* (Gombert, 1992). These skills relate to the ability to think about and talk about words. School-aged children have a more complex and mature understanding of words, and can recognise connections or relationships between words. For instance, they learn that words can have multiple meanings (e.g. noses that *run* and feet that *smell*), that words can sound the same, but be spelt differently (*bare* vs. *bear*), or be spelt the same but pronounced differently (e.g. *live* in a house vs. a *live* performance). They also learn that words can have literal meaning and figurative meanings (e.g. *pull up your socks*). As children's language knowledge increases, they can use language for a greater range of purposes, including telling or understanding jokes and riddles based on lexical ambiguity.

During the early school years, children produce narratives (Liles, 1993). These often form a bridge between oral and written language tasks. Early narratives typically comprise a basic plot structure, which includes an introduction to the setting and the characters (*once upon a time …*), followed by a period of conflict or a problem to be resolved, and finally a solution to the problem (*… and everyone lived happily ever after*). These narratives become more complex, the characters become more developed and the descriptions become more detailed as children progress through the school-age years. As children's literacy skills improve, these narratives take on written language form, often as a task to be completed in story-writing time. However, first, children need to be able to match sounds to letters consistently, and learn spelling rules.

During the school-age years, children's speech should be intelligible to everyone, both familiar and unfamiliar to the child, but there are some common difficulties. Children might have trouble producing 'th' sounds correctly (e.g. _thumb, this_) until age eight to nine years, and may have difficulty saying 's' and 'z' when they lose their front teeth. Children may produce some clusters of sounds together, but may still have trouble with other sound combinations (e.g. _scwatch_ for '_scratch_'). They may also have difficulty producing polysyllabic words (e.g. _hippopotamus_) (McLeod, 2013).

Signs of more serious or lasting communication difficulties in the school-age years might present as behavioural problems, as children may struggle to remember or follow instructions or class rules, due to difficulty recalling information or inability to understand particular vocabulary. Children may have difficulty initiating and maintaining friendships with peers, which may be caused by problems with understanding particular social rules of language (or _pragmatics_). This can lead children to say the wrong thing at the wrong time, misunderstand jokes/sarcasm, or fail to pick up on non-verbal cues (facial expression and gesture). Other signs of communication difficulties may present as poor performance in classroom activities or academic tasks. For instance, children may take a long time to process information and respond to questions, use non-specific vocabulary (such as _thing_ and _stuff_) and produce narratives (stories) that lack detail or coherence.

Supporting communication development: Let's read

Reading together, as a group in the classroom, and encouraging children to participate in individual reading activities at school or at home will introduce them to new narrative forms, and provide a guide for them to develop their own stories. The more practice children have at decoding words, the better they will become at word recognition, which will enable them to concentrate more on comprehending the message in what they read (rather than just the individual words).

Reading to children is a valuable way of introducing new vocabulary. Educators might encourage the class to work together to come up with broad definitions for new words, to think about related words, to identify categories that the words fit into, and to find synonyms and antonyms for these words. This will help all students to increase their vocabulary as well as their ability to describe and explain.

Students with receptive language difficulties often have trouble following instructions, particularly if the instructions involve multiple steps or include complex concepts and grammatical structures (e.g. 'Before you put your books away, glue the worksheets in and then write your name on the front cover'). Segmenting instructions into individual steps, and repeating instructions in the order in which they are to be completed, may help students to process the information and recall small chunks at a time. Providing a visual support by writing the instructions on the board will also assist many students.

PAUSE AND REFLECT 4.2: THE SUPPORTIVENESS
OF THE ENVIRONMENT

'Can others understand your child?'
'Depends on if they're listening well enough' (Parent).

Discuss the way in which a communication difficulty might impact on a child's participation in life activities. Next, discuss the challenges faced by communication partners. Consider how environmental (physical and social/attitudinal) factors can facilitate or limit a child's communication success. What are some strategies for supporting communication for all children?

Figure 4.4 Kaitlin (4.8) talking to her friend (left) about 'playing and picking and smelling flowers'.

Source: Illustration copyright 2012 by S. McLeod, L. McAllister, L. J. Harrison & J. McCormack. Reprinted with permission.

Conclusion

Communication is an essential part of children's daily lives and enables them to interact with the world around them. Being able to communicate is considered a human right, recognised by the United Nations Conventions on the Rights of the Child (UNICEF, 1989). Consequently, it is essential that all children are supported to develop effective communication skills.

This chapter has outlined the development of communication skills from birth through the primary school years. We have seen how children first communicate through non-verbal means (e.g. eye contact and pointing), and later through verbal communication (e.g. speech and writing), and how this is strongly linked to anatomical, cognitive and motor development. We have discussed key milestones in children's communication development, relating to both receptive (understanding) and expressive (production) language skills. Furthermore, we have seen how oral language skills (speech) form the basis for written language skills. Finally, we have seen how children learn, extend and refine their communication through interacting with their environment, and so have examined a range of strategies that we can use to support children learn these essential skills.

Summary

The key messages highlighted in this chapter are:

- Communication is the sharing of ideas and information through verbal and non-verbal messages; language is a rules-based system, common to a particular group of people, which enables the production and comprehension of messages; speech is one way in which messages may be expressed.
- Prior to the development of words, babies engage in non-verbal communicative behaviours such as eye contact, gestures and turn-taking to initiate interactions and respond to others.
- Children learn language through exposure to language, modelling of language and feedback on their use of language. Verbal communication (language) can be encouraged through providing a language-rich environment in which children's communication is acknowledged, child-directed speech is demonstrated and opportunities to practise are provided.
- Strong speech and oral language skills lay the foundation for the development of written language skills. Supporting children's development of phonological awareness skills will assist their development of literacy skills.
- Communication difficulties at school may present as social or behavioural difficulties.

Questions

4.1   Infants begin communicating long before they begin using words. List some specific examples of what and how they communicate. How can parents and educators respond in ways that support communication development?

4.2   If a parent/friend/educator is concerned about a toddler's production of some sounds, what information would be useful to give them about typical speech development?

4.3   Many preschool children enjoy reading Dr Seuss books and other rhyming stories. What skills do such books assist children to develop? Generate a list of books that may stimulate and support communication development, and describe the ways in which they do so.

4.4   How might receptive language difficulties present in the school years and what are some practical strategies that parents and educators could implement to support children's understanding at school?

References

Anthony, J.L., Lonigan, C.J., Driscoll, K., Phillips, B.M. & Burgess, S.R. (2003). Phonological sensitivity: A quasi-parallel progression of word structure units and cognitive operations. *Reading Research Quarterly*, 38, 470–87.

Bloom, L. & Lahey, M. (1978). *Language development and language disorders*. New York, NY: Wiley.

Crystal, D. (2006). *How language works*. Melbourne, Australia: Penguin.

Goldstein, M.H. & Schwade, J.A. (2008). Social feedback to infants' babbling facilitates rapid phonological learning. *Psychological Science*, 19(5), 515–23.

Golinkoff, R.M., Can, D.D., Soderstrom, M. & Hirsh-Pasek, K. (2015). (Baby) talk to me: The social context of infant-directed speech and its effects on early language acquisition. *Current Directions in Psychological Science*, 24(5), 339–44.

Gombert, J.E. (1992). *Metalinguistic development* Chicago, IL: University of Chicago Press.

Harrison, L.J. & McLeod, S. (2010). Risk and protective factors associated with speech and language impairment in a nationally representative sample of 4- to 5-year-old children. *Journal of Speech, Language, and Hearing Research*, 53, 508–29.

Harrison, L.J., McLeod, S., Berthelsen, D. & Walker, S. (2009). Literacy, numeracy and learning in school-aged children identified as having speech and language impairment in early childhood. *International Journal of Speech-Language Pathology*, 11(5), 392–403.

Liles, B.Z. (1993). Narrative discourse in children with language disorders and children with normal language: A critical review of the literature. *Journal of Speech, Language, and Hearing Research*, 36(5), 868–82.

McCormack, J., Harrison, L.J., McLeod, S. & McAllister, L. (2011). A nationally representative study of the association between communication impairment at 4–5 years and children's life activities at 7–9 years. *Journal of Speech, Language, and Hearing Research*, 54(5), 1328–48.

McCormack, J., McLeod, S., Harrison, L.J., McAllister, L. & Holliday, E.L. (2010). A different view of talking: How children with speech impairment picture their speech. *ACQuiring Knowledge in Speech, Language and Hearing*, 12(1), 10–15.

McLeod, S. (2013). Speech sound acquisition. In J.E. Bernthal, N.W. Bankson & P. Flipsen Jnr (eds), *Articulation and phonological disorders: Speech sound disorders in children* (7th edn, pp. 58–113). Boston, MA: Pearson Education.

McLeod, S., Harrison, L.J. & McCormack, J. (2012). Intelligibility in Context Scale: Validity and reliability of a subjective rating measure. *Journal of Speech, Language, and Hearing Research*, 55, 648–56.

Miller, J.L. & Lossia, A.K. (2013). Prelinguistic infants' communicative system: Roles of caregiver social feedback. *First Language*, 33(5), 524–44.

Murray, A. & Egan, S.M. (2014). Does reading to infants benefit their cognitive development at 9-months-old? An investigation using a large birth cohort survey. *Child Language Teaching and Therapy*, 30(3), 303–15.

Oller, D.K., Eilers, R.E., Neal, A.R. & Schwartz, H.K. (1999). Precursors to speech in infancy: The prediction of speech and language disorders. *Journal of Communication Disorders*, 32, 223–45.

Reilly, S., Eadie, P., Bavin, E.L., Wake, M., Prior, M., Williams, J. et al., (2006). Growth in infant communication between 8 and 12 months: A population study. *Journal of Paediatrics and Child Health*, 42, 764–70.

Ruben, R.J. (1997). A time frame of critical/sensitive periods of language development. *Acta Otolaryngology*, 117, 202–5.

Rvachew, S. & Grawburg, M. (2006). Correlates of phonological awareness in preschoolers with speech sound disorders. *Journal of Speech, Language, and Hearing Research*, 49(1), 74–87.

Shriberg, L D. (1993). Four new speech and prosody-voice measures for genetics research and other studies in developmental phonological disorders. *Journal of Speech and Hearing Research*, 36, 105–40.

Stackhouse, J. & Wells, B. (1997). *Children's speech and literacy difficulties: A psycholinguistic framework.* London, UK: Whurr.

Tardif, T., Fletcher, P., Liang, W., Zhiang, Z., Kaciroti, N. & Marchman, V.A. (2008). Baby's first 10 words. *Developmental Psychology*, 44(4), 929–38.

UNICEF (1989). *The United Nations Convention on the Rights of the Child (UNCRC).* Retrieved from: http://www2.ohchr.org/english/law/crc.htm

Wetherby, A. & Prizant, B. (1993). *Communication and symbolic behavior scales.* Baltimore, MD: Paul H. Brookes.

Appendix

Table 4.1: Communication development and strategies to support children.

	Ages and stages			
	0–1 year	1–2 years	2–5 years	5–12 years
Speech	Infants produce sounds made with the lips (e.g. b and m). Later, they start to produce other sounds (e.g. d, m, n, h, w, t) in their babble.	Sounds and speech become easier to understand. At 2 years, half of a toddler's speech should be understood. Toddlers can say a range of speech sounds when talking (e.g. p, b, m, t, d, n, h, w). However, many toddlers have difficulty saying sounds correctly all the time. It's common for children to make some sound errors (e.g. 'tat' for 'cat' and 'pan' for 'pram') and for speech to be less clear when they are using longer sentences.	Preschool children can say most sounds correctly, but may have difficulty with 'r' (e.g. saying 'wed' for 'red'), 'v' (e.g. saying 'berry' for 'very'), and 'th' (e.g. saying 'fankyou' for 'thank you'). Some children may still produce 's' as 'th' (e.g. lisp) They can use many consonant clusters, which are combinations of two or more sounds (e.g. tw, sp, gl, dr). Children may use clusters at the start (e.g. <u>bl</u>ue) or end of words (e.g. ha<u>nd</u>). Some children are still developing the ability to say some combinations of sounds together (e.g. <u>str</u>awberry), or saying all the sounds correctly in longer words (e.g. caterpillar, and spaghetti).	When children commence school, their speech should be easily understood by everyone. Children might still have trouble with 'th' sounds (e.g. <u>th</u>umb, <u>th</u>is) until 9 years, and might have difficulty saying sounds such as 's' and 'z' when baby teeth fall out. Children can produce clusters of sounds together, but may still have trouble with individual sounds (e.g. such as 'r' and 'l') in combinations (e.g. '<u>scr</u>atch' for 'scratch') or longer words (e.g. hippopotamus, pumpkin)

(continued)

Table 4.1: Communication development and strategies to support children (continued).

	Ages and stages			
	0–1 year	1–2 years	2–5 years	5–12 years
Language (expressive)	Initially, infants communicate by crying, smiling, eye contact, laughing, pointing and reaching. They experiment with sounds by babbling (e.g. 'babamada'), and around 12 months may start to use words (typically names of familiar people and objects, words relating to routines ['bye'], communicative games and songs, and recurrence (e.g. 'more'). Words are used to request objects/actions, refuse ('no'), agree ('yeah'), play games (e.g. peek-a-boo). It's common for them to simplify words (e.g. 'biscuit' becomes 'bi').	Toddlers triple the number of words they can say between one and two years of age. By 18 months, toddlers can say about 50 words (e.g. labels for people, objects, actions, locations, possession) and start to put two words together (e.g. 'Daddy car'). They use language primarily to request information/objects, comment on their experiences and answer questions.	Preschool children start to use longer sentences, and use conjunctions (and, when, so, because, if) to join sentences. They use terms for colours, basic shapes (circles, squares), sizes (big, small) and spatial relationships (in, on, under). They ask what, who, where (2–3 years), why (3–4 years), when and how questions (4–5 years). They create narratives, with increasing structure as they get older. They use language to recall events, reason, predict and maintain interaction.	Sentence length and complexity increases (greater in written than spoken language). Children demonstrate mastery of grammatical rules (and exceptions). Story narratives are complex and include goals/motivations of characters, and multiple episodes. Vocabulary includes more abstract and specific terms.
Language (receptive)	Infants hear/recognise the sounds of their parents' language and understand simple words (approx. 3–50) and sentences.	Words and sentences start to be understood outside routines but some contextual support may be required. Toddlers understand 2-word combinations similar to those they express, as well as more complex requests, explanations, and instructions from adults.	Preschool children understand colours, family relationship terms, basic shapes (circles, squares), sizes (big, small) and spatial terms (in, on, under) Understand what, who, where (2–3 years), why (3–4 years), when and how questions (4–5 years).	Children understand passive sentences and words with multiple meanings. Develop critical reading/thinking skills; are able to analyse, synthesise and reflect on language meaning in oral and written communication.

	Ages and stages			
	0–1 year	**1–2 years**	**2–5 years**	**5–12 years**
Play/ socialising	Infants enjoy communicative games and songs focused on turn-taking and imitation.	Early forms of symbolic play such as feeding the dolly commence in the toddler years.	Use of language in play increases, and imaginary play develops in the preschool years.	Language is increasingly used by school-age children to maintain social connections. The ability to use and understand jokes/riddles based on language develops.
Literacy	Babies enjoy being read picture books and simple stories, and will open the flaps to look for a hidden object or turn pages with support.	Toddlers enjoy joint book-reading; learn to hold books the correct way and to turn pages; distinguish between print and pictures; and learn to hold a crayon and scribble or make dots.	Preschool children start to develop skills that will be important for learning to read and write (called 'pre-literacy skills'). They can recognise and produce rhymes (e.g. 'cat – bat'), segment words into syllables/beats (e.g. 'am-bu-lance'); and isolate initial sounds and recognise/produce words with the same initial sound (e.g. 'big brown bear'). Preschool children recognise that letters are associated with particular sounds, can name letters, and may recognise own name and familiar words in print (e.g. 'McDonalds'). They may be able to write their own name and/or some letters and attempt other words.	In the early years of formal schooling, children learn to read independently and the complexity of the texts they read increases as they progress through their schooling. Children can blend sounds to form words of increasing length, segment words into phonemes and manipulate sounds in words. Children know letter names and sounds for consonants/vowels, and can match these. Children can decode individual sounds in words and start to recognise words by sight. As more words are recognised by sight, reading becomes more fluent and attention shifts to comprehension of texts. Children start to spell using phonetic correspondence, then learn spelling patterns. Complexity of written work develops and types of writing styles increase.

(continued)

Table 4.1: Communication development and strategies to support children (*continued*).

	Ages and stages			
	0–1 year	**1–2 years**	**2–5 years**	**5–12 years**
Support	Infants who do not progress through this stage of 'playing with sounds' are at risk of speech difficulties later. Talk to infants, respond to and repeat their babbling, and respond to any attempts at communication that infants make.	Show you understand what the child is saying and model the correct way of saying words, particularly when children make occasional sound errors. If a toddler's speech is very difficult for parents to understand, or if children are using gestures (and grunts) in place of words, suggest referral to a speech pathologist for further advice.	In the preschool years, parents might want to have their child's hearing checked as hearing is important in order to learn how to say sounds correctly. Also, parents can visit a speech pathologist if concerned about their child's speech/language development, particularly if they are using very few words, cannot be understood or if they are frustrated with attempts to communicate, if their speech appears very effortful, or if they are not using initial sounds. Read to children, sing songs and play rhyming games, or games such as 'I spy' which encourage children to think about sounds and letters.	In the early years of school, provide many examples of print. Include phonological awareness and metalinguistic activities in daily activities. Pre-teach new or difficult vocabulary to enable students to focus on understanding concepts rather than remembering words and word meanings. Encourage children to use contextual information to aid decoding and comprehension of written texts.

CHAPTER 5

Physically educated: Developing children's health and wellbeing through movement and motor skills

Timothy Lynch

Introduction

This chapter complements the chapter 'Human movement and motor skills' (Williams, 2014) published in the first edition of this text. As the title suggests, the purpose is to extend Williams' work by investigating examples of practical human movement development embedded within the field of physical education. Thus, the chapter answers the questions: What does human movement theory look like in practice? How can it be optimised for all children? Why is it vital for the advancement of 'health and wellbeing in childhood'?

The physical dimension is significant within children's learning because it offers powerful and meaningful connections across all learning and development areas. The socio-cultural perspective suggests that the curriculum be connected to the child's world and everyday interests (Arthur et al., 2015). As children have a natural play structure, learning through movement heightens interest. 'Play' sits within the physical dimension – 'where children are learning through their interactions, as well as adopting and working through the rules and values of their own cultural group' (Arthur et al., pp. 99–100). The socio-cultural benefits of play enable 'the development of imagination and intelligence, language, social skills, and perceptual-motor abilities in infants and young children' (Frost, 1992, p. 48).

Hence, this chapter adopts the same goal as Williams' chapter: 'to highlight the importance of early childhood educators integrating bio-physical and socio-cultural understandings' (2014, p. 62). This is an important goal affirmed by Callcott, Miller & Wilson-Gahan: 'It is now evident that practice and encouragement as well as correct and quality instruction are necessary for children to become proficient in fundamental movement skills' (2015, p. 32).

To enable a deeper understanding of the advancement of 'health and wellbeing in childhood' through 'belonging, being and becoming' physically educated, two major underpinning themes are investigated: approaching quality physical education, and human movement and motor skills in childhood.

Approaching quality physical education

Health and wellbeing

Implementing quality physical education increases the likelihood of children experiencing positive health and wellbeing outcomes. One popular and simple definition of wellbeing is 'a state of feeling good about ourselves and the way our lives are going' (Commonwealth of Australia, 2014a, p. 1). Research provides evidence that regular physical activity promotes mental and social wellbeing (Commonwealth of Australia, 2014a; Lynch, 2015a; Parkinson, 2015; Public Health England, 2015; Richards, 2016; Salmon et al., 2011). For social, emotional, intellectual and health benefits, it is recommended that toddlers and preschoolers have at least three hours of physical activity per day, and children aged 5 to 12 years 60 minutes a day of moderate-to-vigorous intensity physical activity (Commonwealth of Australia, 2014b).

Socio-cultural approach: an inclusive approach to learning which considers all social and cultural environments and influences affecting children. Social and cultural backgrounds are also considered in providing socially just learning experiences.

The marriage of human movement and the **socio-cultural approach** promotes quality physical education which has driven the last two Australian Curriculum reforms (1994 and 2013) for the learning area of 'Health and Physical Education' (HPE) (Lynch, 2016b; 2014). Thus, the HPE Australian Curriculum offers a national policy balanced in theory and pedagogy, one that is inclusive, promotes social justice and where students are assisted to make well-judged decisions in relation to good health and wellbeing (Queensland School Curriculum Council [QSCC], 1999).

The connections between the physical dimension and wellbeing are evident in the Early Years Foundation Stage (EYFS) in the National Curriculum of England and Wales. The EYFS consists of six areas of learning and development which are equally important and connected. Social and Emotional Learning (SEL) has a strong presence relating to the first of the six areas listed:

- Personal, Social and Emotional Development
- Communication, Language and Literacy
- Problem Solving, Reasoning and Numeracy
- Knowledge and Understanding of the World
- Physical Development
- Creative Development (Department for Children, Schools and Families, 2008, p. 11).

It is stated that 'none of these areas can be delivered in isolation from the others. They are equally important and depend on each other to support a rounded approach to child development' (2008, p. 11). Furthermore, 'all the areas must be delivered through planned, purposeful play, with a balance of adult-led and child-initiated activities' (2008, p. 11).

As the title suggests, the Early Years Learning Framework for Australia (EYLFA) (Department of Education, Employment and Workplace Relations for the Council of Australian Governments [DEEWR], 2009) was influenced by the EYFS National Curriculum of England and Wales, along with socio-cultural theory in the United Kingdom, Australia and New Zealand (Cliff, Wright & Clarke, 2009). The *Victorian Early Years and Development Framework: For all Children from Birth to Eight Years* (VEYDF), devised from the EYLFA, clarifies an important aspect of the HPE and wellbeing relationship that no other Australian document has achieved to date, elucidating the relationship and responsibilities between the learning area of HPE and wellbeing. For Outcome 3, 'children have a strong sense of wellbeing', it categorises wellbeing into two aspects:

Figure 5.1 A child's personal, social and emotional development is interconnected with their physical development.

- children become strong in the social, emotional and spiritual wellbeing;
- children take increasing responsibility for their own health and physical wellbeing (DEECD, 2009, p. 23).

It is important to note that while HPE is the only learning area explicitly associated with wellbeing in curricula, it is not and cannot be responsible for all wellbeing development. This statement acknowledges that all areas of wellbeing need to be explicitly taught and that wellbeing does not necessarily occur as a direct result of being physically educated. Similar to what the EYFS proposes, learning needs to be purposefully planned. This is supported by Bailey et al. (2009) who summarised (from a review of educational research papers) that many educational benefits claimed by physical education are highly dependent on contextual and pedagogic variables.

Robbins, Powers & Burgess (2011) establish seven strongly connected dimensions of wellness: physical, intellectual, emotional, social, spiritual, environmental, and occupational. A study that explored the dimension of spirituality in the HPE learning area across three Queensland case study schools (Lynch, 2015b) found that regular quality inclusive HPE lessons increased children's potential for spiritual experiences. Hence, curriculum frameworks and research studies illustrate the power of an inclusive socio-cultural approach.

While the HPE learning area recognises and advocates the development of all health dimensions, the core of 'Health and Physical Education' – as the nomenclature states – is the 'physical' dimension. For this reason, health and wellbeing associated with being physically educated is the key wellbeing development responsibility of HPE. An example of where this occurs is Hellison's Teaching Personal and Social Responsibility (TPSR) model (2011) which 'offers a primary emphasis on the often under-represented affective domain without devaluing or limiting the physical activity taught in physical education' (Walsh, 2016, p. 8). The model consists of five levels: (1) respecting the rights and feelings of others; (2) self-motivation; (3) self-direction; (4) leadership; and (5) transfer outside of physical education.

Socio-cultural approach: Addressing hidden messages

The introduction of the socio-cultural perspective recognises that children are influenced by the different physical, social, cultural, political, economic and environmental forces affecting their wellbeing (Queensland School Curriculum Council, 1999). Therefore, this approach offers a 'holistic' learning approach for physical education. Throughout history, physical education has often focused on the body as an object, in contrast to the 'whole' child. This occurs 'in a society when man [and woman] has gained the capacity of looking at his [or her] own body as if it were a thing' (Broekhoff, 1972, p. 88). Critically examining literature and taken-for-granted assumptions within the physical education field from a cultural and historical perspective illustrates the pertinence of the socio-cultural approach.

Discourses: socially constructed and reasoned messages.

Hidden curriculum: when children acquire both unintentionally and intentionally delivered messages as a consequence of being in the school environment. Often educators are unaware of the existence of some messages because they become culturally accepted and are not recorded in curriculum materials.

Discourses that have influenced the 'body as an object' philosophy include military, scientific, health and sport. They portray ideologies that include sexism, elitism, healthism, individualism and mesomorphism (Colquhoun, 1991; 1992; Hickey, 1995; Kirk, 1992; Kirk & Twigg 1993; Scraton, 1990; Tinning, 1990; Tinning & Fitzclarence, 1992; Tinning, Kirk & Evans, 1993). Such ideologies often pass on false messages to the child and on many occasions these are unintentional and/or the teacher is unaware of their existence. Ideologies are not recorded in curriculum documents; rather, they are traits taught and learnt through various mediums within society, in what is termed the '**hidden curriculum**'.

Military discourse involved physical education through drilling and exercising. This military-style training existed in Australian schools from 1911 to 1929 and was the first and only national system of physical training. Kirk and Spiller described this period as a time of *schooling* rather than education, as 'physical education was deeply implicated in the project of schooling the docile body, in knowing it and shaping it to meet particular circumstances and fulfil particular social and political projects' (1991, p. 108).

Science has had a major influence on physical education through technology and medicalisation, the scientific discourse having particular relevance to the bio-physical foundations of human movement. The influence of science on education began after the launch of the first Sputnik on 4 October 1957. It was thought at the time that schools were not producing enough scientists, so financial support was directed towards this goal. This continues to be a concern but in the 1950s, physical education curricula became 'technocratically rationalised' (Kirk, 1988) and the 'new look' physical education curriculum focused on biomechanics, exercise physiology, sports medicine, psychology of sport and history of sport (Kirk, McKay & George, 1986).

Health as an **ideology** has influenced both society and physical education. Healthism is described by Crawford as 'a belief that health can be unproblematically achieved through individual effort and discipline directed mainly at regulating the size and shape of the body' (1980, p. 366). The television program *The Biggest Loser* is a prime example of healthism, where the body is associated with morally disciplined behaviour and people experience guilt if they are seen as undisciplined.

Ideology: generally accepted beliefs, values and commitments within society.

The sporting discourse has developed beliefs about physical education and sport that are not always necessarily true. The National Curriculum in England's 'Physical Education Programme' states as the 'purpose of study' for the subject in Key stage 1 (5–7 years) and 2 (8–11 years):

> A high-quality physical education curriculum inspires all pupils to succeed and excel in competitive sport and other physically demanding activities. It should provide opportunities for pupils to become physically confident in a way which supports their health and fitness. Opportunities to compete in sport and other activities build character and help to embed values such as fairness and respect (Department for Education (DfE), 2016, p. 1).

PAUSE AND REFLECT 5.1: YOUR EXPERIENCES OF PHYSICAL EDUCATION AND SPORT

Reflecting on your experiences of physical education and sport, do you take for granted assumptions raised for educators? Can all children excel in competitive sport? Will playing sport build character for all children? Is fairness and respect an outcome of all sporting experiences?

It is argued by some that this is not possible, suggesting that 'competing drags us down, devastates us psychologically, poisons our relationships and interferes with our performance' (Kohn, 1992, p. 114). Hickey shares other assumptions and contradictions about sport:

- By being involved in sport, people naturally develop positive attitudes about healthy lifestyle.
- Friendship, teamwork, sharing and cooperation are incontestable manifestations of involvements in physical education and sport.
- If you are prepared to work hard and make the necessary sacrifices, you can achieve what you want to in sport and physical education.
- Boys and girls receive equal opportunity and recognition in their involvement in sport and physical education.
- Children get most of their understandings and interpretations about physical education and sport through the school curriculum (Hickey, 1995, p. 5).

As evidenced by the literature, over the years 'belonging, being and becoming' physically educated has not always been achieved. In the past it has been argued that 'where physical education is poorly or insensitively taught it is more likely to have a negative influence on learners than a positive one' (Tinning et al., 2001, p. 181).

> ## PAUSE AND REFLECT 5.2: OPTIMISING POSITIVE EXPERIENCES
>
> Reflecting on your experience of physical education and sport, have there been times where you have had a negative experience? What can educators do to optimise positive experiences?

The Australian HPE curriculum adopts the socio-cultural approach. It identifies that being physically educated has health and wellbeing developmental outcomes and benefits for children. It also suggests that wellbeing benefits are optimised when existing cultural messages, associated with the hidden curriculum, are addressed:

> The Health and Physical Education curriculum will draw on its multi-disciplinary base with students learning to question the social, cultural and political factors that influence health and wellbeing. In doing so students will explore matters such as inclusiveness, power inequalities, taken-for-granted assumptions, diversity and social justice, and develop strategies to improve their own and others' health and wellbeing (Australian Curriculum, Assessment and Reporting Authority (ACARA), 2012, p. 5).

As the literature implies, it is essential for educators to adopt a holistic approach towards physical education. Adopting the socio-cultural approach has important implications, 'because its attention to social and cultural influences on health put it in opposition to notions which locate responsibility for health almost solely in the individual and their decisions' (Cliff, Wright & Clarke, 2009, p. 165). It is proposed that the marriage of human movement and the socio-cultural approach enables quality physical education.

Quality physical education

Quality Physical Education (QPE) needs to be provided for all children. Therefore, all educators must understand how to provide inclusive practice where correct movements can be mastered. QPE is defined by the United Nations Educational, Scientific Cultural Organisation (UNESCO) as:

> the planned, progressive, inclusive learning experience that forms part of the curriculum in early years, primary and secondary education. In this respect, QPE acts as the foundation for a lifelong engagement in physical activity and sport. The learning experience offered to children and young people through physical education lessons should be developmentally appropriate to help them acquire the psychomotor skills, cognitive understanding, and social and emotional skills they need to lead a physically active life (2015, p. 9).

Human movement and motor skills in childhood

Motor control

Williams focuses on the bio-physical foundations of human movement in his chapter 'Human movement and motor skills', giving explicit importance to the sub-discipline of motor control: 'Motor control is a field of natural scientific research that attempts to understand the processes whereby movement is controlled, coordinated and learned through the integrated operation of the nervous, skeletal and muscular systems' (2014, p. 66). These movements can be divided into two categories: reflexes and skills (motor skills).

Motor skills 'can be defined as goal-directed, improvable actions that require movement of all or part of the body in order to be performed successfully' (Williams, 2014, p. 63). While a diverse range of movements fit this definition, Williams gives the early years' examples of writing one's name, tying shoelaces and catching a ball. Of these three movements, catching a ball is synonymous with physical education, in particular Fundamental Movement Skills (FMS).

Fundamental Movement Skills (FMS) are also referred to as Fundamental Motor Skills and are the building blocks to more complex human movements. The Australian Curriculum for HPE shares that FMS 'provide the foundation for competent and confident participation in a range of physical activities' (ACARA, 2016). FMS can be categorised as locomotor skills, non-locomotor skills and manipulative skills (object control). Locomotor and non-locomotor skills include running, jumping, hopping, skipping, leaping, landing, galloping, rolling, sliding, stopping, twisting, turning, swinging, dodging, walking, balancing, jogging, floating and moving the body through water (ACARA, 2016; Australian Sports Commission, 1997). Manipulative skills include: ball control (bouncing and catching), throwing, tracking/trapping, kicking and striking (ACARA, 2016; Australian Sports Commission, 1997).

FMS build a foundation for movements, often relating to games and sports, but they are also, more importantly, the foundation to movements that assist with life skills. Closely related to the child's life-skill movements, and sitting alongside FMS, are gymnastics movements referred to as Dominant Movement Patterns (DMP). The building blocks of gymnastics are synonymous with movements used on adventure playground equipment such as monkey bars, swings and slides; they include landings, locomotions, swings, statics, springs and rotations (Australian Council for Health, Physical Education and Recreation (ACHPER), 1998). It is argued that gymnastics sits at the core of being physically educated (Lynch, 2016a). Because many parents value gymnastics, before- and after-school clubs for children are popular but this is an area of the curriculum that is often limited in schools.

Ideally, FMS (and DMPs) should be mastered as early as possible. This is supported by the Australian Curriculum for HPE where 'FMS' is listed as a focus area to be taught from Foundation to Year 6. One of the five aims listed for the HPE national curriculum is to develop the knowledge, understanding and skills to enable students to 'acquire, apply and evaluate movement skills, concepts

PAUSE AND REFLECT 5.3: DOMINANT MOVEMENT PATTERNS IN THE PLAYGROUND

Reflecting on children's activities in an adventure playground, which rides, climbing frames or activities involve landing, locomotions, swings, statics (non-movement such as balance), springs (leaps and jumps) and rotations?

and strategies to respond confidently, competently and creatively in a variety of physical activity contexts and settings' (ACARA, 2016). Similarly, the National Curriculum in England for Physical Education states in Key stage 1 that 'pupils should develop fundamental movement skills' and specifically 'master basic movements including running, jumping, throwing and catching, as well as developing balance, agility and co-ordination, and begin to apply these in a range of activities' (DfE, 2016, p. 2).

Research suggests that the best time for children to learn and refine their motor skills is in the pre-foundation year and early primary school years (Branta, Haubenstricker & Seefeldt, 1984; Commonwealth of Australia, 1992; Espenschade & Eckert, 1980; Lynch, 2011; 2014). During this early developmental phase, children have a natural play structure and more time to focus on developing their motor skills. Another advantage relating directly to the socio-cultural approach is the early detection of motor difficulties where subsequent intervention programs can reduce many physical and related emotional problems (Arnheim & Sinclair, 1979; Commonwealth of Australia, 1992; Johnson & Rubinson, 1983; Lynch, 2013a; Seefeldt, 1975; Smoll, 1974).

Acquisition of motor skills model

Williams refers to 'motor control' as 'the processes by which motor skills are performed' and identifies the use of models, metaphors and analogies to assist with this process. One model described by Fitts & Posner (1967) is the 'acquisition of motor skills'. The first stage of this model is the 'Cognitive Phase' where the learner receives and uses information on how the skill is to be performed; for example, when a driving instructor explains to a novice the various apparatus used for driving a car. The learner cautiously proceeds to drive the car, often with large errors such as 'kangaroo jumps' or 'bunny hops'. The second stage is the 'Associative Phase' where the learner refines the mechanics of the skill through practice, using feedback offered by the driving instructor, their own intrinsic feedback and their sense of proprioception. Errors are still common at this stage.

The third stage described by Fitts & Posner is the 'Autonomous Phase' where the learner can perform the skill automatically; that is, without having to think about the movement and just doing it when they choose to. In the example of learning to drive a car, this happens when the driver finds that they no longer have to think about the process of each action they are making. The driver in this phase may even be tempted to combine motor skills while driving the car, such as adjusting

> ## PAUSE AND REFLECT 5.4: CHILDREN'S MOVEMENT AND DEVELOPMENT
>
> Reflecting on children learning particular movements, can you identify times where a child has been in each of the three phases of acquiring motor skills? What was the movement and why would you identify the child as being in the particular phase?

the radio. This analogy of learning to drive a car can be transferred to represent the various movement progressions throughout life – from the baby rolling to sitting up, crawling to bear walking, standing with support to standing without support, and taking first steps. Likewise, children learning the various FMS in the early years of school can often be identified as moving through one of the three stages.

When associating the acquisition of motor skills model to children's learning, the ideal is to have children performing motor skills automatically before placing them in more physically demanding situations, such as high-pressure games during physical education. If children are able to perform the necessary skills during a game situation, without having to apply the thinking involved in the first two stages of Fitts & Posner's model, they are then able to focus on other aspects of the game, such as strategies.

Motor development (Figure 5.2 later in this chapter) and national curricula indicate that many children will be ready to be placed in high-pressure games from the age of seven. While some children will be ready before seven, in diverse classes with children from various physical experiences and socio-cultural backgrounds, the reality is that often children in upper primary schools may still be in the first or second stage of the acquisition of skills model for FMS used in particular games or modified sports. Research indicates that many children unfortunately have limited FMS at the beginning of secondary school (Barnett et al., 2013). This is another socio-cultural aspect of physical education of which educators need to be mindful because it is not inclusive practice to play a game or modified sport when not all children have had opportunities to develop the skills required. Such practices in schools needs to be critically examined since the children who have had prior experiences are often favoured over those who have not.

> ## PAUSE AND REFLECT 5.5: TEACHING A PHYSICAL EDUCATION CLASS
>
> In a Year 5 class of 27 children, 18 children play basketball regularly for a club and have mastered all the necessary motor skills and strategies for this sport. How would you inclusively implement the skills of dribbling and passing with this class? Can the basketball players be extended while the other nine children are offered opportunities to develop these skills?

Educators are therefore challenged to be creative when implementing physical education adopting a socio-cultural approach. At all times the aim should be to maintain inclusivity, by catering for the diverse needs of the class. This is easier said than done and is the greatest modern-day challenge for physical educators. The ability to implement strategies that cater for all needs, while enabling enjoyment, engagement and challenges, is evidence of a teacher's expertise as a quality physical educator.

As the National Curriculum of England for Physical Education 'Purpose of study' accentuates, sport sits within the physical education curriculum. There is a misconception at times that physical education is only sport. This becomes confusing for educators in the early years when children's motor control is not developmentally ready to combine a number of motor skills with game rules and strategies (Figure 5.2). Using the analogy of learning to read, throwing a child into a complex game is like introducing early years' children to phonics using a novel. It is not developmentally appropriate.

The National Curriculum of England identifies this issue but also recognises that there are simple games that do play a vital role in children's progression in becoming physically competent and confident in the early years. The curriculum policy states that in Key stage 1, children 'should be taught to: participate in team games, developing simple tactics for attacking and defending' (DfE, 2016, p. 2). The Australian curriculum for HPE also espouses this essential motor development understanding for quality physical education. From Foundation stage through to Year 6, the focus area 'Active play and minor games' is addressed within the curriculum. On the other hand, the focus area 'Games and sports' is only recommended for Year 3 upwards (ACARA, 2016), after which time children have ideally mastered FMS.

Hence, embedded in QPE are quality games that include simple, developmentally appropriate games in the early years, requiring limited FMS and rules (Arthur et al., 2015). Simple games include hopscotch, tiggy, 'What's the time Mr. Wolf?' and 'stuck in the mud', as well as others that the children may create themselves. These simple games play an important developmental role because they lead to more complex games where variables such as space, objects, number of participants, number of games, time and speed are introduced through supplementary rules. Such rules increase the challenge for participants and the FMS required. Four guidelines are identified for implementing quality games, including both simple and more complex games:

1. Safe for all players.
2. Inclusive – all players can participate. This involves having the skill level to participate safely and at an enjoyable level.
3. Engaging – the players' participation is optimised. Waiting time is eliminated or minimal.
4. Enjoyment is prioritised (Lynch, 2013b, p. 19).

Motor development

If educators are to use models, metaphors and analogies to enhance their understanding and the understanding of the children, then motor development is

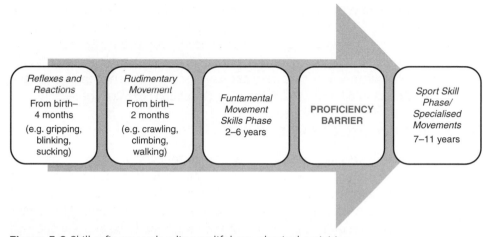

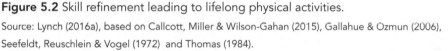

Figure 5.2 Skill refinement leading to lifelong physical activities.

Source: Lynch (2016a), based on Callcott, Miller & Wilson-Gahan (2015), Gallahue & Ozmun (2006), Seefeldt, Reuschlein & Vogel (1972) and Thomas (1984).

important. This is 'the specialised area of study within the sub-discipline of motor control that deals with the description and explanation of these changes from the beginning to the end of life' (Williams, 2014, p. 68). The progression through stages of motor development illustrates the difficulties that children confront when opportunities to master FMS are not provided. Figure 5.2 is adapted from Callcott, Miller & Wilson-Gahan (2015), Gallahue & Ozmun (2006), Seefeldt, Reuschlein & Vogel (1972) and Thomas (1984).

The proficiency barrier generally occurs around Year 3 at school (seven years of age, turning eight) and culminates with myelination, the production of the myelin sheath. Myelination enables smooth coordinated and subsequently increased complexity in children's movement skills and it 'permits the transmission of nerve impulses and is not complete at birth' (Gallahue & Donnelly, 2003, p. 31). Hence, children's motor development is capitalised if FMS are mastered before Year 3 and myelination.

It is important that children experience a wide range of physical activities and that they have opportunities for physical creativity. Using the analogy of learning to read, it is only after having learnt to read that one can explore the many stories in the library. Likewise, mastering FMS enhances creativity, and specifically child-directed play through movement learning experiences relating to games, dance, gymnastics and swimming. From a socio-cultural approach, it is a priority that children are equipped with the FMS to enhance their ability to share and cooperate through movement with friends. This often leads to connections within the greater community. Therefore, educators need to be experts in early movement if opportunities are to be provided for children to master a wide variety of motor skills, develop motor control and optimise their motor development.

This point is extremely pertinent when teaching physical education in the early years of primary school and one that is often overlooked (Lynch, 2016b). For the same reasons that early years teachers are required to have developmentally appropriate phonics and numeracy expertise, schools need to provide expertise for learning in the physical area. Consistent with the socio-cultural approach and comparable to play-based pedagogy, learning motor skills requires scaffolding and guidance from an expert to assist the child to become competent. Scaffolding sits within Vygotsky's zone of proximal development and expertise may involve family and community partnerships. While tasks may be initially challenging for the child, practising should be enjoyed regularly if the child is to master the skill.

Information processing model

Another model Williams discusses in relation to motor control is the information-processing model which 'stresses the importance of the internal cognitive processing of the learner' (Rink, 2010, p. 24). This model 'posits three distinct and sequential stages of movement control: perceiving, deciding, and acting' (Williams, 2014, p. 66). Children require a clear idea of the task, need to be actively engaged in the learning process, have plentiful opportunities to practice, and be offered external feedback as well as opportunities to self-assess through internal feedback. Furthermore, 'knowledge of how learners process information [information processing theory] helps educators to select appropriate cues and to design appropriate feedback for learners' (Rink, 2010, p. 24). During practice, formative feedback such as 'Assessment for Learning' is vital.

Popular metaphors are adopted by many educators and coaches. For example, in swimming the instructor may remind the children to glide through the water like an arrow, long and straight with arms outstretched, or to have 'long legs' and 'kick their socks off' during the flutter kick. An analogy for landing safely in gymnastics is 'land on your motorbike', with arms reaching forwards (holding the handlebars), legs bent and shoulder-width apart (sitting on a motorbike).

It is commonly recommended that no more than three cues be used so that children can retain the information (Anshell, 1990). For example, three cues for the underarm throw might be: swing back, step forwards (on opposite leg to hand holding the ball) and release. Further detail and a demonstration can accentuate that the arm swings forwards and releases when the hand is directed towards the target. Also, that the opposite arm comes out to the side of the body to assist with balance. Further, pedagogy may involve questioning and exploring to enable children to discover what they think are the most effective steps in this FMS.

PAUSE AND REFLECT 5.6: EXPERIENCES OF MOVEMENT

Reflecting on your experiences of movement, what are some other effective analogies you are familiar with?

For a number of motor skills to be performed simultaneously – for example, skipping (locomotor) while dribbling a basketball – it is essential that at least one of the motor skills (either dribbling or skipping) is automatic (Figure 5.3).

The information processing model suggests 'the ability to perform two motor tasks simultaneously means that at least one set of actions can be conducted automatically (without cognition)' (Anshell, 1990, p. 19). Emphasis should be placed on correct practice because 'ingrained, highly learnt errors in movement execution (or technique) may be extremely difficult, if not impossible, to correct' (Abernethy, 1991, p. 93).

Consistent with the socio-cultural approach, pedagogy will relate to the cultural contexts of the child and school. Groupings, motor development, location, time, resources, facilities and expertise within the community will influence how opportunities are provided. Research indicates that the Perceptual Motor Program (PMP) (Figure 5.3) implemented with parental assistance is a successful structured program for the early years of primary schools (Lynch, 2005).

Figure 5.3 A PMP can be implemented using parental assistance.

Source: Getty Images/DGLimages.

Conclusion

This chapter investigated quality physical education in practice, complimenting 'Human movement and motor skills' (Williams, 2014) published in the first edition of this text. It was established that implementing QPE as espoused by the United Nations requires educator knowledge, and ideally expertise, in the bio-physical foundations of human movement and the inclusive socio-cultural approach. Exploring this blend involved examination of literature, curriculum policies and research, determining that children's health and wellbeing is enhanced through QPE.

Summary

Educators are encouraged to be creative in their provision of inclusive movement activities and to offer progressive and developmentally appropriate learning experiences. The key messages highlighted in this chapter are:

- Quality physical education enhances children's health and wellbeing.
- Quality physical education is a planned, progressive and inclusive learning experience.
- It is strongly recommended that all children have opportunities to master FMS before seven years of age.
- Educators require expertise in the fundamentals of movement and the inclusive socio-cultural approach.
- The physical dimension is significant within children's learning as it offers powerful and meaningful connections across all learning and development areas.

Questions

5.1   What does human movement theory look like in schools?

5.2   How can 'belonging, being and becoming' physically educated be successfully implemented in early years settings?

5.3   Why is 'belonging, being and becoming' physically educated vital in childhood?

5.4   What hidden curriculum messages about movement have been brought to your attention after reading this chapter?

References

Abernethy, B. (1991). Acquisition of motor skills. In F.S. Pyke (ed.), *Better Coaching – Advanced Coach's Manual*, (pp. 69–98). Canberra, Australia: Australian Coaching Council.

Anshell, M. (1990). An information processing approach to teaching sport skills to inexperienced athletes. *Sports Coach*, 13, 16–22.

Arnheim, D.D. & Sinclair, W.A. (1979). *The clumsy child* (2nd edn). London: C. V. Mosby.

Arthur, L., Beecher, B., Death, E., Dockett, S. & Farmer, S. (2015). *Programming and planning in early childhood settings* (6th edn). South Melbourne, Australia: Cengage Learning.

Australian Council for Health, Physical Education and Recreation (ACHPER) (1998). *Gymnastics lower primary*. Richmond, South Australia: ACHPER.

Australian Curriculum, Assessment and Reporting Authority (2012). *Draft shape of the Australian curriculum: health and physical education*. Retrieved from http://www.acara.edu.au/hpe.html

—— (2016). *The Australian curriculum health and physical education.* Retrieved from http://www.australiancurriculum.edu.au/download/f10

Australian Sports Commission (1997). *Sport it! Towards 2000 teacher resource model: developmental sports skills program.* Canberra: Pirie Printers.

Bailey, R., Armour, K., Kirk, D., Jess, M., Pickup, I. & Sandford, R. (2009). The educational benefits claimed for physical education and school sport: An academic review. *Research Papers in Education, 24,* 1–27.

Barnett, L.M., Hardy, L.L., Lubans, D.R., Cliff, D.P., Okely, A.D., Hills, A.P. et al. (2013). Australian children lack the basic movement skills to be active and healthy. *Health Promotion Journal of Australia.* Retrieved from http://www.qorf.org.au/wpcontent/uploads/2014/03/Children_lack_Basic_Movement_Skills.pdf

Branta, C., Haubenstricker, J. & Seefeldt, V. (1984). Age changes in motor skills during childhood and adolescence. *Exercise & Sport Sciences Reviews, 12,* 467–520.

Broekhoff, J. (1972). Physical education and the reification of the body. *Gymnasion, 4,* 4–11.

Callcott, D., Miller, J. & Wilson-Gahan, S. (2015). *Health and physical education: preparing educators for the future* (2nd edn). Port Melbourne, Australia: Cambridge University Press.

Cliff, K., Wright, J. & Clarke, D. (2009). What does a 'sociocultural perspective' mean in health and physical education? In M. Dinan-Thompson (ed.) *Health and physical education: issues for curriculum in Australia and New Zealand* (pp. 165–182). South Melbourne: Oxford University Press Australia and New Zealand.

Colquhoun, D. (1991). Health based physical, the ideology of healthism and victim blaming. *Physical Education Review, 14(1),* 5–13.

—— (1992). Technocratic rationality and the medicalisation of the physical education curriculum. *Physical Education Review, 15(1),* 5–11.

Commonwealth of Australia (1992). *Physical and sport education – A report by the senate standing committee on environment, recreation and the arts.* Canberra: Senate Printing Unit.

—— (2014a). *Wellbeing and self-care fact sheet.* Retrieved from http://www.responseability.org/__data/assets/pdf_file/0011/10541/Wellbeing-and-self-care-Final.pdf

—— (2014b). *Does your child get 60 minutes of physical activity everyday? Make your move-sit less be active for life! Australia's physical activity and sedentary behaviour guidelines: 5-12 years.* Retrieved from http://www.health.gov.au/internet/main/publishing.nsf/content/F01F92328EDADA5BCA257BF0001E720D/$File/brochure%20PA%20Guidelines_A5_5-12yrs.PDF

Crawford, R. (1980). Healthism and the medicalisation of everyday life. *International Journal of Health Services, 10,* 365–89.

Department for Children, Schools and Families (2008). *Statutory framework for the Early Years Foundation Stage – setting the standards for learning, development and care for children from birth to five.* Nottingham, UK: Department for Children, Schools and Families.

Department for Education (DfE) (2016). *National curriculum in England: physical education programmes of study.* Retrieved from https://www.gov.uk/government/uploads/system/uploads/attachment_data/file/239040/PRIMARY_national_curriculum_-_Physical_education.pdf

Department of Education and Early Childhood Development (DEECD) (2009). *Victorian early years learning and development framework for all children from birth to eight years.* Melbourne: DEECD.

Department of Education, Employment and Workplace Relations for the Council of Australian Governments (DEEWR) (2009). *Belonging, being and becoming: The Early Years Learning Framework for Australia.* Canberra, Australia: DEEWR.

Espenschade, A.S. & Eckert, H.M. (1980) *Motor development* (2nd edn). Sydney: Merrill.

Fitts, P.M. & Posner, M.I. (1967). *Human performance.* Belmont, CA: Brooks/Cole Publishing.

Frost, J.L. (1992). *Play and playscapes.* Albany, New York: Delmar Publishers.

Gallahue, D.L. & Donnelly, F.C. (2003). *Developmental physical education for all children* (4th edn). Champaign, IL: Human Kinetics.

Gallahue, D.L. & Ozmun, J.C. (2006). *Understanding motor development: Infants, children, adolescents, adults* (6th edn). Boston, MA: McGraw-Hill.

Hickey, C. (1995). Can physical education be physical education? *ACHPER Healthy Lifestyles Journal,* 42(3), 4–7.

Hellison, D. (2011). *Teaching responsibility through physical activity* (3rd edn). Champaign, IL: Human Kinetics.

Johnson, R. & Rubinson, R. (1983). Physical functioning levels of learning disabled and normal children. *American Corrective Therapy Journal,* 37, 56–59.

Kirk, D. (1988). *Physical education and curriculum study: a critical introduction.* London: Croom Helm.

—— (1992). Physical education, discourse and ideology: Bringing the hidden curriculum into view. *Quest,* 44, 35–36.

Kirk, D., McKay, J. & George, L.F. (1986). All work and no play? Hegemony in the physical education curriculum. *Proceedings of Trends and Developments in Physical Education: the VIII Commonwealth and International Conference on Sport, Physical Education, Dance, Recreation and Health* (pp. 170–177). London: E. & F. N. Spon.

Kirk, D. & Spiller, B. (1991). Schooling the docile body: the social origins of physical education in Victorian elementary schools. In P. Jeffrey (ed.). *Proceedings of the Australian Association for Research in Education (AARE) Conference.* Gold Coast, Australia: AARE.

Kirk, D. & Twigg, K. (1993). The militarization of school physical training in Australia: The rise and demise of the junior cadet training scheme, 1911–1931. *History of Education,* 22(4), 319–414.

Kohn, A. (1992). *No contest: the case against competition.* Boston, USA: Houghton Mifflin Company.

Lynch, T. (2005). *An evaluation of school responses to the introduction of the Queensland 1999 health and physical education (HPE) syllabus and policy developments in three Brisbane Catholic primary schools (Unpublished doctoral thesis).* Australian Catholic University, Australia.

—— (2011, December 17–23). What does a role model Australian primary school Health and Physical Education (HPE) programme look like? Paper presented at the 53rd International Council Health, Physical Education, Recreation, Sport and Dance (ICHPER-SD) Anniversary World Congress & Exposition, Cairo (Egypt). Retrieved from http://www.ichpersd.org/i/publications/Proceedings_for_Cairo.pdf doi:10.13140/2.1.2783.1682

—— (2013a). Health and physical education (HPE) teachers in primary schools: supplementing the debate. *Australian Council for Health, Physical Education and Recreation (ACHPER) Active and Healthy Magazine, 20*(3/4), 10–12. doi:10.13140/2.1.2889.6644

—— (2013b). 'Poison ball' or a magic potion? Secrets within an infamous game. Australian Council for Health, Physical Education and Recreation (ACHPER) *Active and Healthy Magazine,* 20(2), 19–21 doi:10.13140/2.1.3282.8806

—— (2014). Australian curriculum reform II: Health and Physical Education (HPE). *European Physical Education Review, 20*(4), 508–524. doi:10.1177/1356336X14535166

—— (2015a). Health and physical education (HPE): Implementation in primary schools.*International Journal of Educational Research, 70*(c), 88–100. doi:10.1016/j.ijer.2015.02.003

—— (2015b). Investigating children's spiritual experiences through the health and physical education learning area in Australian schools. *Journal of Religion and Health 54*(1), 202–20.

—— (2016a). Australian football: leading children's fundamental movement and sporting skill development. In M. Drummund & S. Pill (eds), *Advances in Australian Football: a sociological and applied science exploration of the game* (pp. 110–19). Hindmarsh, South Australia: Australian Council for Health, Physical Education and Recreation (ACHPER).

—— (2016b). *The future of health, wellbeing and physical education: optimising children's health and wellbeing through local and global community partnerships.* London, UK: Palgrave Macmillan. doi:10.1007/978-3-319-31667-3

Parkinson, E. (2015, August 16). Dick Telford's study finds sport can improve NAPLAN scores. *Financial Review.* Retrieved from http://www.afr.com/news/special-reports/afr16srsportyourchildseducation---20150814-giyyh4

Public Health England (2015). *Promoting children and young people's emotional health and wellbeing: a whole school and college approach.* Retrieved from https://www.gov.uk/government/uploads/system/uploads/attachment_data/file/414908/Final_EHWB_draft_20_03_15.pdf

Queensland School Curriculum Council (1999). *Health and physical education initial in-service materials.* Brisbane: Publishing Services, Educational Queensland.

Richards, R. (2016). *School sport.* Retrieved from https://www.clearinghouseforsport.gov.au/knowledge_base/organised_sport/value_of_sport/school_sport

Rink, J.E. (2010). *Teaching physical education for learning* (6th edn). Boston: McGraw-Hill.

Robbins, G., Powers, D. & Burgess, S. (2011). *A wellness way of life* (9th edn). New York, USA: McGraw-Hill.

Salmon, J., Arundel, L., Hume, C., Brown, H., Hesketh, K., Dunstan, D. et al. (2011). A cluster-randomized controlled trial to reduce sedentary behaviour and promote physical activity and health of 8-9 year olds: the transform-us! Study. *BMC Public Health,* 11, 759.

Scraton, S. (1990). *Gender and physical education.* Geelong, Australia: Deakin University Press.

Seefeldt, V. (1975, March). *Critical learning periods and programs of early intervention.* Paper presented at the AAPHER Convention, Atlantic City, NJ.

Seefeldt, V.B., Reuschlein, S. & Vogel, P. (1972). *Sequencing motor skills within the physical education curriculum.* Paper presented at the meeting of American Association of Health, Physical Education and Recreation, Houston.

Smoll, F.L. (1974). Motor impairment and social development. *American Corrective Therapy Journal,* 28, 4–7.

Tinning, R. (1990). *Ideology and physical education: Opening Pandora's box.* Geelong, Australia: Deakin University Press.

Tinning, R. & Fitzclarence, L. (1992). Postmodern youth culture and the crisis in Australian secondary school physical education. *Quest,* 44(3), 287–303.

Tinning, R., Kirk, D. & Evans, J. (1993). Healthism and daily physical education. In Deakin University, *Critical curriculum perspectives in physical education – Reader* (pp. 77–94). Geelong, Australia: Deakin Print Services.

Tinning, R., McDonald, D., Wright, J. & Hickey, C. (2001). *Becoming a physical education teacher: Contemporary and enduring issues.* Frenchs Forest, Australia: Pearson Education.

Thomas, J.R. (1984). Developmental motor skill acquisition. In J.R. Thomas (ed.). *Motor Development During Childhood and Adolescence* (p. 125). Minneapolis, MN: Burgess.

United Nations Educational, Scientific and Cultural Organization (UNESCO) (2015). *Quality physical education: guidelines for policy makers.* Paris, France: UNESCO Publishing.

Walsh, D. (2016). Teaching the teaching personal and social responsibility model through developmental stages. *Active & Healthy: Promoting Active & Healthy Living,* 23(2/3), 8–11.

Williams, B.J. (2014). Human movement and motor skills. In S. Garvis & D. Pendergast, (eds), *Health & wellbeing in childhood* (pp. 61–72). Port Melbourne, Australia: Cambridge University Press.

CHAPTER 6

Sexual abuse prevention education

Kerryann Walsh, Donna Berthelsen and Jan Nicholson

Introduction

Child sexual abuse is a serious problem that has received increased attention in recent years. From an ecological perspective, in which social problems are viewed in the context of characteristics of individuals, families and broader societal systems (Prilleltensky, Nelson & Peirson, 2001), preventing child sexual abuse involves strengthening capacity to intervene at individual, family/relationship, school and community levels.

School-based education programs have been developed in efforts to prevent child sexual abuse before it happens, and to provide children who may already be experiencing it with information about the importance of and strategies for seeking help. Design of these programs must be based on evidence rather than ideology. Evaluations have demonstrated that sexual abuse prevention education can provide children with improved knowledge and skills for responding to, and reporting, potential sexual abuse. School-based programs typically present information to children via a series of core concepts and messages, which are delivered using engaging pedagogical strategies such as multimedia technologies, animations, theatre and songs, puppets, picture books and games. This chapter outlines the key characteristics of effective child sexual abuse prevention programs and identifies directions for future research and practice.

Definition of sexual abuse, prevalence and effects

The World Health Organization (WHO) defines child sexual abuse as 'the involvement of a child in sexual activity that he or she does not fully comprehend; is unable to give informed consent to; or for which the child is not developmentally prepared and cannot give consent; or that violates the laws or social taboos of society' (1999, p. 15). The WHO further defines child sexual abuse as involving sexual activity 'between a child and an adult or another child who by age or development is in a relationship of responsibility, trust or power' (WHO, 1999, p. 16). Some examples include, but are not limited to, sexual watching of a child while dressing or bathing; sexual touching of a child's genitals or nipples; taking photographs of a child's genitals, involving a child in making pornography; masturbation of an adult by a child; vaginal or anal penetration; or involving a child in prostitution.

In these cases, the sexual activity is illegal and exploitative, and is being used to gratify or satisfy the needs of the abuser. It typically involves coercion or inducement of the child to participate, and the abuser will try to manipulate the child and hide what is happening. The abuser will often be known to the child, and will lure the child by engaging in a relationship with them, gaining their trust and gradually sexualising the relationship over time. This is known as '**grooming**' behaviour. Sexual abuse may occur over weeks, months or years. The age of greatest vulnerability is 7 to 12 years (Finkelhor & Baron, 1986).

Grooming is when an adult builds a relationship with a child and/or their family to gain trust for the purposes of abuse. Grooming can happen online or face-to-face. It can involve lures, secrecy, isolating the child and gradually sexualising the relationship.

Research with large samples of individuals in countries worldwide have shown that sexual abuse is experienced by 10 to 20 per cent of girls and 5 to 10 per cent of boys before the age of 18 years (Stoltenborgh et al., 2011). Although child sexual abuse occurs in all societies, not all children are at equal risk. Children who are more vulnerable include girls, unaccompanied children, children with disabilities, children living in foster care, children living with only one biological parent or with parents who have a mental illness or alcohol or drug dependencies, and children living in situations of war or armed conflict. Despite its prevalence, child sexual abuse is often not disclosed by the child and is under-reported to authorities. Many cases are not revealed until adulthood and still more remain completely concealed for life. When children do disclose, it is often to their mother and, as they get older, to a friend or teacher.

Child sexual abuse causes serious short- and long-term consequences for the health and wellbeing of those victimised. Beyond the immediate confusion and pain, child sexual abuse is associated with other serious psychological and behavioural problems such as depression, anxiety, post-traumatic stress disorder, inappropriate sexual behaviours, anti-social and suicidal behaviours, eating disorders, alcohol and substance abuse, and sexual revictimisation (Putnam, 2003). Health problems recently identified include cardiac and gastro-intestinal diseases, obesity and, in females, gynaecologic and reproductive issues (Irish,

Kobayashi & Delahanty, 2010). Of particular note for educators is that being sexually abused can affect a child's ability to pay attention, participate and learn in the context of normal school activities. Children who have experienced sexual abuse are at much greater risk of dropping out of school and not completing their education.

A brief history of child sexual abuse prevention education

More than 40 years ago, in response to growing public concern about the problem of child abuse, the USA enacted the world's first child abuse prevention law: the Child Abuse Prevention and Treatment Act 1974. This Act established the National Center on Child Abuse and Neglect (NCCAN) and, through this agency, funding was made available for prevention initiatives. This enabled women's rape crisis centres and violence prevention organisations in the USA to develop the first child sexual abuse prevention programs. They were delivered in preschools and schools, and were soon widely adopted across the country (Berrick & Gilbert, 1991; Plummer, 1986). In 1984, California enacted legislation making school-based child sexual abuse prevention 'training' compulsory for all children. Children were to receive this training five times during their schooling from preschool through to high school (Kohl, 1993). By the mid-1990s, a large number of programs (400–500) were reportedly in use (Plummer, 1986). Research at that time revealed that approximately 67 per cent of 10–16-year-olds in the USA had been exposed to a diverse array of programs (Finkelhor & Dziuba-Leatherman, 1995). This research also showed that children exposed to programs that provided opportunities for practice, prompted discussions with parents and taught ways of dealing with bullies were more likely to actually use protective strategies when threatened (Finkelhor, Asidigian & Dziuba-Leatherman, 1995a). Twelve months later, a follow-up study with the same individuals showed program exposure was not linked with reduced incidence of victimisation, but rather was associated with increased likelihood of disclosure, higher levels of self-protective efficacy and decreased levels of self-blame – all of which are clinically significant and positive indicators in child sexual abuse recovery (Finkelhor, Asidigian & Dziuba-Leatherman, 1995b).

Two studies with mixed findings conducted in the USA in the early 2000s attempted to determine, retrospectively, whether participation in sexual abuse prevention programs reduced the incidence of victimisation. First, a study with over 900 female undergraduate university students found that 28 per cent of students had been exposed to a prevention program in preschool and 92 per cent had experienced a program in primary (elementary) school. Age at program exposure was around six to seven years. Those students who had not participated in school-based prevention program were twice as likely to have experienced child sexual abuse (Gibson & Leitenberg, 2000). Second, a study with 126 high school students found 53 per cent of students had attended a school-based child sexual abuse prevention program. Students exposed to programs had higher levels of sexual abuse knowledge about four important concepts: knowing children are not to blame; knowing abusers can be familiar people; knowing both boys and girls can be victimised; and understanding the need for reporting. Forty per cent of program participants believed the program helped them avoid threatening circumstances; however, data from the a small group of children who were abused by family members suggested the strategies learnt were less effective with known perpetrators (Ko & Cosden, 2001).

Prevention

Prevention of child sexual abuse is a difficult outcome to measure. Assessing whether preschool or school-based prevention education actually prevents sexual abuse entails long-term follow-up with cohorts of learners who have been exposed to programs, and comparing them with learners who have not. This is an expensive and logistically difficult exercise due to the resources required to undertake such studies and the practical issues of data collection, as well as attrition owing to children's absences from school among other factors. Not surprisingly, there is no research that has yet been able to assess adequately whether prevention education is effective in the long term. For this reason, the field urgently requires research that collects longitudinal follow-up data which is able to rigorously investigate the link between prevention education and actual prevention. These studies need to be prospective (i.e. following individuals forwards over time), rather than retrospective (i.e. having individuals reflect back on their experience). Despite the unavailability of such data, researchers and advocates tend to conclude that prevention education has:

> additional, important objectives beside those of preventing victimization, including promoting the reporting of victimization, reducing the stigma and self-blame that victimized children feel, and educating parents, teachers, and other community members about the problem ... The programs could be justified solely on the basis of these goals even if actual prevention was relatively uncommon (Finkelhor, 2007, p. 642).

A **systematic review** is a literature review that identifies and critically assesses *all* the research undertaken on a particular intervention.

Several **systematic reviews** which collate research evidence into a combined report have shown that school-based programs are effective in increasing children's conceptual knowledge of child sexual abuse (measured via interviews or questionnaires) and their self-protective skills (measured in simulated scenarios). However, as mentioned, few studies have done long-term follow-up. The high-quality studies that have measured retention of knowledge, up to six months after program delivery, find that such knowledge is retained over time (see, for example, Walsh et al., 2015).

Where does child sexual abuse prevention education fit into the early years and school curricula?

Child sexual abuse prevention education aims to provide children with knowledge and skills to protect themselves, to avoid unsafe situations and to disclose abusive events to a trusted adult. These interventions also raise teacher, parent and community awareness of sexual abuse, and provide adults with the knowledge and skills to protect children.

Internationally, the long-standing **Health Promoting Schools Framework** developed by the WHO (1986, 1998) encourages a whole-school approach to addressing health issues, including relationships and sexual health education, which acts as an umbrella curriculum area for child sexual abuse prevention education. Within the Health Promoting Schools Framework, primary prevention strategies aim to prevent problems before they occur. Such strategies or initiatives can be delivered to whole populations (known as universal interventions) or to particular groups at higher risk (known as targeted or selective interventions). Child sexual abuse prevention education was originally designed as a primary or universal prevention intervention to be delivered to all children, but research shows that this seldom occurs. Its coverage in the preschool and school curricula relies to a large extent on system-level directives as well as individual teacher discretion. This is the case with most curriculum content.

The most robust international instruments to assist schools and early childhood centres in locating child sexual abuse prevention education in the curriculum can be found in the form of guidelines for sexuality education developed by the United Nations Educational, Scientific and Cultural Organization (UNESCO) and the Sexuality Information and Education Council of the United States (SIECUS).

UNESCO (2009) has developed the two-volume *International Technical Guidance on Sexuality Education*. Based on a systematic review of studies of the effectiveness of sexuality education curricula worldwide and an extensive review of existing standards, the UNESCO guidance sets out key concepts, topics, learning objectives and key ideas grouped according to four age levels: level 1 (ages 5–8), level 2 (ages 9–12), level 3 (ages 12–15) and level 4 (ages 15–18). Sexual abuse prevention content is embedded within three of the six key concepts (Key Concepts 2, 3 and 4) as detailed with a few examples in Table 6.1.

For children aged birth to five years in child-care and preschool settings, SIECUS (1998) has developed the *Right from the Start: Guidelines for Sexuality Issues: Birth to Five Years*, in response to the need for age-appropriate guidance for sexuality education

Child sexual abuse prevention education typically occurs in schools or early learning centres and involves the use of programs, curricula, books and other resources designed to raise awareness and reduce risk of child sexual abuse. Other terms used include: body safety (Wurtele, 2007), child safety training, child assault prevention, child protection education (New South Wales Department of School Education, 1997), personal body safety (Miller-Perrin, Wurtele & Kondrick, 1990), personal safety education (National Center for Missing and Exploited Children [NCMEC], 1999), and protective behaviours (Flandreau-West, 1984).

The **Health Promoting Schools Framework** was developed by the World Health Organization to encourage a whole-of-school approach to addressing key health issues, including sexuality education.

PAUSE AND REFLECT 6.1: CURRICULUM-TO-PRACTICE EXAMPLES FOR CHILDREN OF DIFFERENT AGES

Table 6.1: Curriculum-to-practice examples by age level.

Key Concept 2: Values, Attitudes and Skills	Key Concept 3: Culture, Society and Human Rights	Key Concept 4: Human Development
↓	↓	↓
Topic 2.5: Finding help and support	Topic 3.4: Gender-based violence, sexual abuse and harmful traditional practices	Topic 4.5: Privacy and body integrity
↓	↓	↓
Key ideas (Level 1: Ages 5–8)	Key ideas (Level 2: Ages 9–12)	Key ideas (Level 1: Ages 5–8)
• All people have the right to be protected and supported • Trusted adults can be sources of help and support in the school and community	• There are ways to seek help in the case of sexual abuse and rape	• Everyone has the right to decide who can touch their body, where, and in what way
↓	↓	↓
Exercise Consider reading children's picture books with these themes. Examples include *Jasmine's Butterflies* by Justine O'Malley & Carey Lawrence or *Hattie and the Fox* by Mem Fox & Patricia Mullins.	**Exercise** Take a look at the lesson plans available in The *Body Safety Training Curriculum for Teachers* by Sandy K Wurtele or *Preventing Sexual Abuse* by Carol Plummer.	**Exercise** Consider reading children's picture books with these themes, such as *Some Secrets Should Never Be Kept* by Jayneen Sanders & Craig Smith and *Everyone's Got A Bottom* by Tess Rowley & Jodi Edwards.

Source: Adapted from UNESCO (2009, Vol II, pp. 16, 20, 25).

for younger children. These guidelines were designed by a taskforce of professionals for use by educators in centre-based care to lay the foundation for children's sexual health. The guidelines are built around six key concepts and related topics, with key messages for children at three developmental levels: infancy (birth to age one year); toddlers and preschool-aged children (ages one to four years); and older preschoolers (ages four to five years). Child sexual abuse prevention content is embedded in one of the six key concepts (Key Concept 5). Spotlight 6.1 provides some examples of content relating to sexual abuse prevention for children aged four to five years.

SPOTLIGHT 6.1: A CURRICULUM PLANNING SEQUENCE FOR YOUNG CHILDREN

Table 6.2: Examples of content for sexual abuse prevention

Key Concept 5: Health
↓

Topic 17: Sexual Abuse Prevention
↓

Some examples of key messages for older preschoolers (ages 4–5):
- Children have the right to tell others not to touch their bodies when they don't want to be touched.
- It's wrong for an older, stronger or bigger person to look at or touch a child's penis, vulva or bottom without good cause.

Source: SIECUS (1998, pp. 11, 55–7).

Within specific countries, child sexual abuse prevention education for early years learners is generally located in the curriculum domain of health education, where it is typically taught in two strands: (1) safety education/injury prevention; and/or (2) wellbeing/healthy relationships. In some school curricula, content will be explicitly stated, while in others it will be implicit and must be inferred from learning statements.

SPOTLIGHT 6.2: EXPLICIT AND IMPLICIT CURRICULUM STATEMENTS

An example of an explicit approach would include clear statements about providing children with opportunities to learn about and understand *appropriate and inappropriate touching, safe and unsafe situations, and identifying people who can help*. An implicit approach would be less specific and more subject to interpretation, such as: *children should be able to demonstrate behaviours and identify people to keep them safe and healthy*.

In an ideal world, education systems would have the following:

- a child-protection policy with several key elements relating specifically to child sexual abuse prevention education: a clear statement explaining the compulsory or voluntary nature of provision; expectations for directors and principals for reporting on compliance; procedures for dealing with student disclosures of past or current child sexual abuse, including staff reporting obligations; explicit statements about the location of sexual abuse prevention content in the curriculum

- assessment and reporting of student learning
- support for educators in the form of materials, teaching resources and lesson plans in easily accessible formats
- specialist training opportunities for educators and support staff
- opportunities for integration of content across the curriculum (e.g. in language and literacy via children's literature)
- parent packages and communication strategies for working with parents, particularly about the timing and content
- well-established links with relevant community support agencies and services, including statutory child protection services (Walsh et al., 2013).

Children spend a large part of their lives in early learning environments, including care and education settings. Educators working in these environments are in an ideal position to intervene in cases of known or suspected child sexual abuse. In contexts in which school systems lack these features, there is much that educators can do. Australian teacher educator, Vivienne Watts (1997) encapsulates this idea well in her conceptualisation of educators' roles in child protection as multidimensional, involving:

- developing their own knowledge and understanding of child sexual abuse via attending training and undertaking professional development
- knowing the warning signs and indicators of child sexual abuse, legal reporting obligations in cases of known or suspected child sexual abuse, and procedures for reporting
- making reports to child-protection authorities or police in appropriate circumstances
- responding to the needs of abused children in their learning communities
- teaching children self-protection and help-seeking strategies
- supporting children by cooperating with child-protection and other support agencies.

Types of prevention programs, program contents, methods and resources

An anchor for teaching child sexual abuse prevention education can typically be found in school curricula, as noted above. But specific programs have also been developed by non-government agencies and community organisations worldwide, such as Bravehearts (Australia – Ditto's Keep Safe Adventure), Child Help (USA – Speak up, Be Safe), the Council of Europe (European Union – The Underwear Rule), Plan International (India – Break the Silence) and the Canadian Red Cross (Canada – Be Safe!).

Since 1987, there have been more than 25 meta-analyses, systematic reviews and narrative reviews of research that focuses on child sexual abuse prevention programs. These reviews have revealed considerable variability in the overall methodological quality of the research in program evaluation studies. None of these reviews has identified program typologies, and few have been able to isolate the characteristics of effective prevention programs. However, some reviews have identified characteristics that are 'common' to programs. For example, researchers have detailed eight concepts typically taught in prevention programs:

1. *Body ownership.* This is also known as body integrity, where children are taught about ownership of their bodies, including private parts, their right to control access to their bodies, and the limited range of situations in which adults or other children would need to touch/see their private parts or take photos of them.
2. *Touch.* Children are taught to distinguish types of touching, including sexually abusive touch.
3. *Assertiveness.* Children are taught strategies to use in relation to grooming scenarios, inappropriate touching and other sexual threats.
4. *The 'No–Go–Tell' sequence.* Children are taught to say 'No' loudly when someone tries to or does touch them inappropriately, to 'Go' or get away from a situation and to 'Tell' an adult who can help.
5. *Secrecy.* Children are taught to distinguish types of secrets, the difference between secrets and surprises, and the concept that secrets should never be kept.
6. *Intuition.* This is a controversial component, especially for young children, in which children are taught to trust their feelings when they feel something is not right.
7. *Support systems.* Children are taught to identify adults in their social system and agencies (e.g. Helplines) who can help, which is especially important in the event of disclosure of current or past sexual abuse.
8. *Blame.* Children are taught that they are never to blame if they have been or have almost been abused or victimised; the fault always lies with the adult perpetrator (Bogat & Martinez-Torteya, 2010; Duane & Carr, 2002).

The topics most frequently recalled by the 2000 children in Finkelhor's studies, cited above, included telling an adult (recalled by 95 per cent); kidnapping (81 per cent); good touch/bad touch (81 per cent); yell/scream (80 per cent); sexual abuse definitions (80 per cent); incest (74 per cent); abuse is not the child's fault (74 per cent); confusing touch (70 per cent); and dealing with bullies (63 per cent).

In programs, this content is typically taught using a range of pedagogies. Specific pedagogies associated with more effective programs include a combination of instruction, modelling, role-play, rehearsal/practice, social reinforcement, feedback, discussion, group mastery and review. Delivery formats are varied, and include film/video/DVD, theatrical plays and performances, and multimedia presentations, with additional resources including songs, puppets, mascots, comics, colouring books, storybooks and games.

Some researchers have categorised programs dichotomously as either active (i.e. involving modelling-rehearsal-practice in delivery) or passive (i.e. involving lecture-type delivery). However, this approach is limited because most effective programs employ multimodal delivery approaches and use several integrated pedagogies, as noted above. Additionally, many effective programs are multi-systemic in that they target multiple members of children's social systems – for example, teachers and parents (Duane & Carr, 2002). This multi-systemic focus is crucial because sexual abuse prevention education should *never* be seen as a replacement for adult responsibility to protect children.

What is best practice?

Program facilitators of sexual abuse prevention education have been waiting for the identification of a set of 'best practice' guidelines. Although there is no definitive source, there are tools that, when combined, can assist with answering the question 'What is best practice?' Such guidelines can provide a mechanism for making informed judgements about the most promising or potentially effective education programs for specific settings.

In Australia, a report on respectful relationships education in Victorian schools identified five criteria for good practice:

1. a whole-school approach
2. a program framework and logic
3. effective curriculum delivery
4. relevant, inclusive and culturally sensitive practice
5. impact evaluation (Flood, Fergus & Heenan, 2009, p. 5).

Similarly, six national standards for sexual assault prevention education were developed in Australia after a rigorous process of program mapping and consultation:

1. coherent conceptual approaches to program design
2. use of a theory of change
3. comprehensive program development and delivery
4. inclusive, relevant and culturally sensitive practice
5. effective evaluation strategies
6. training and professional development of educators (Carmody et al., 2009, p. 23).

In the USA, guidelines for programs to reduce child victimisation are broader still because these can aim to prevent all forms of violence, with a focus on child sexual abuse. An education taskforce proposed that these programs should:

- be based on accepted educational theories
- be appropriate for the age and educational and developmental levels of the child
- offer concepts that will help children build self-confidence in order to better handle and protect themselves in all types of situations
- have multiple program components that are repeated several years in a row
- utilise qualified presenters who use role-playing, behavioural rehearsal, feedback and active participation (National Center for Missing and Exploited Children, 1999, pp. 6–8).

Researchers internationally generally agree on what should be considered best practice, and this is best captured by the six practices identified by Daro (1994, p. 215):

1. Instruction must encompass repeated opportunities for children to practise safety strategies.
2. Programs must be tailored to the unique cognitive and learning capacities of different age groups.
3. Content must be presented in a stimulating and integrated way sufficient to capture children's interest and promote their learning.
4. General concepts should be part of programs, on account of their value in strengthening children's responses to everyday situations generally, as well as sexual abuse prevention specifically.
5. Children must be encouraged to tell adults if they are touched in a way that does not seem right without creating negative perceptions of healthy human affection.
6. Longer, staged and more detailed programs are best integrated into the school curriculum for maximum benefit.

Parental roles in child sexual abuse prevention education

In recent years, parents have become more aware of child sexual abuse through media reporting of cases and coverage of the topic in popular movies and television series. Parents can be the most readily available sources of information for their children about child sexual abuse prevention. Although parents admit to hesitancy in discussing these issues, they generally have positive attitudes towards the teaching of this content at school (Walsh & Brandon, 2012). Different studies have shown that 78 to 100 per cent of parents surveyed in Australia, Canada, China and the USA favour coverage of prevention education in school curricula, and slightly fewer parents prefer coverage in before-school settings (Briggs, 1988; Chen & Chen, 2005; Chen, Dunne & Han, 2007; Elrod & Rubin, 1993; Wurtele et al., 1992).

Over time, parents have become more willing to discuss child sexual abuse prevention with their children at home. In the USA, for example, research shows that the proportion of mothers who talked with their children about sexual abuse had increased from 59 per cent in 1992 to 79 per cent in 2010 (Deblinger et al., 2010; Wurtele et al., 1992). Parents' readiness to enter into dialogue with their children is influenced by many factors, including gender, personal experience of child sexual abuse, access to resources or models, beliefs about age-appropriateness and perceptions of negative consequences. Parents who were exposed to child sexual abuse prevention education at school and/or who reported having family discussions about sexual abuse when they were children reported a higher likelihood of talking with their own children about this topic (Walsh & Brandon, 2012). This appears to be part of an inter-generational cycle of prevention with potential to gain momentum. The challenge for early years educators and providers of prevention education is to find ways to partner with parents to harness their strengths as children's first teachers.

Conclusion

Child sexual abuse has serious short- and long-term effects for individuals and societies. Teaching of prevention education in the early years is one component of a comprehensive prevention approach. Official curriculum documents are always the starting point for considering what can be taught within different school systems and contexts. Curricula can be both complemented and supplemented by judicious use of other evidence-based materials and resources covered in this chapter.

Summary

Key messages from this chapter include:

- Child sexual abuse is experienced by 10 to 20 per cent of girls and 5 to 10 per cent of boys worldwide.
- Child sexual abuse prevention education is taught in early years and school curricula under the broad domain of health education.
- Research shows that sexual abuse prevention education can provide children with improved knowledge and skills for responding to and reporting potential sexual abuse.
- Child sexual abuse prevention education can be taught using a range of innovative and age-appropriate pedagogies.
- Parents have an important role to play in child sexual abuse prevention, and their information needs in terms of program content and methods must be carefully addressed.

Questions

6.1   What are some common concepts taught in child sexual abuse prevention education?

6.2   What are key considerations for early years educators when planning to teach child sexual abuse prevention education?

6.3   A parent asks what will be taught as part of child sexual abuse prevention education, and specifically asks whether anatomically correct terms for body parts will be used. What do you say and do?

6.4   How might child sexual abuse prevention concepts be integrated into the teaching of other key learning areas such as English/literacy?

Acknowledgement

The research informing this chapter was funded by the Australian Research Council's Discovery Project Scheme (DP 1093717). The authors acknowledge the research assistance provided by Leisa Brandon.

References

Berrick, J.D. & Gilbert, N. (1991). *With the best of intentions: The child sexual abuse prevention movement*. New York: Guilford Press.

Bogat, G.A. & Martinez-Torteya, C.M. (2010). Child sexual abuse education: Developmental and practical issues. In M.A. Paludi & F.L. Denmark (eds),

Victims of sexual assault and abuse: Resources and research (pp. 121–65). Santa Barbara, CA: ABC-CLIO.

Briggs, F. (1988). South Australian parents want child protection programs to be offered in schools and preschools. *Early Childhood Development and Care,* 34(1), 167–78.

Carmody, M., Evans, S., Krogh, C., Flood, M., Heenan, M. & Overden, G. (2009). *Framing best practice: National standards for the primary prevention of sexual assault through education.* Retrieved from http://www.nasasv.org.au/PDFs/Standards_Full_Report.pdf

Chen, J.Q. & Chen, D.G. (2005). Awareness of child sexual abuse prevention education among parents of grade 3 elementary school pupils in Fuxin City, China. *Health Education Research,* 20(5), 540–7.

Chen, J.Q., Dunne, M.P. & Han, P. (2007). Prevention of child sexual abuse in China: Knowledge, attitudes, and communication practices of parents of elementary school children. *Child Abuse & Neglect,* 31(7), 747–55.

Daro, D.A. (1994). Prevention of child sexual abuse. *The Future of Children,* 4(2), 198–223.

Deblinger, E., Thakkar-Kolar, R.R., Berry, E.J. & Schroeder, C.M. (2010). Caregivers' efforts to educate their children about child sexual abuse. *Child Maltreatment,* 15(1), 91–100.

Duane, Y. & Carr, A. (2002). Prevention of child sexual abuse. In A. Carr (ed.), *Prevention: What works with children and adolescents? A critical review of psychological prevention programmes for children, adolescents and their families* (pp. 181–204). New York: Brunner-Routledge.

Elrod, J.M. & Rubin, R.H. (1993). Parental involvement in sexual abuse prevention education. *Child Abuse & Neglect,* 17(4), 527–38.

Finkelhor, D (2007). Prevention of sexual abuse through educational programmes. *Pediatrics,* 120, 640–5.

Finkelhor, D., Asidigian, N. & Dziuba-Leatherman, J. (1995a). Victimization prevention programs for children: A follow-up. *American Journal of Public Health,* 85(12), 1684–9.

—— (1995b). The effectiveness of victimization prevention instruction: An evaluation of children's responses to actual threats and assaults. *Child Abuse & Neglect,* 19(2), 141–53.

Finkelhor, D. & Baron, L. (1986). Risk factors for child sexual abuse. *Journal of Interpersonal Violence,* 1(1), 43–71.

Finkelhor, D. & Dziuba-Leatherman, J. (1995). Victimization prevention programs: A national survey of children's exposure and reactions. *Child Abuse & Neglect,* 19(2), 29–39.

Flandreau-West, P. (1984). *Protective behaviors: Anti-victim training for children, adolescents and adults.* Madison, WI: Protective Behaviors Inc.

Flood, M., Fergus, L. & Heenan, M. (2009). *Respectful relationships education: Violence prevention and respectful relationships education in*

Victorian secondary schools. Retrieved from http://www.education.vic.gov.au/Documents/school/teachers/health/respectful

Fox, M. & Mullins, P. (1987). *Hattie and the fox.* New York: Simon & Schuster Books for Young Readers.

Gibson, L.E. & Leitenberg, H. (2000). Child sexual abuse prevention programs: Do they decrease the occurrence of child sexual abuse? *Child Abuse & Neglect,* 24(9), 1115–25.

Irish, L., Kobayashi, I. & Delahanty, D.L. (2010). Long-term physical health consequences of childhood sexual abuse: A meta-analytic review. *Journal of Pediatric Psychology, 35*(5), 450–461.

Ko, S.F & Cosden, M.A. (2001). Do elementary school-based child abuse prevention programs work? A high school follow-up. *Psychology in the Schools,* 38(1), 57–66.

Kohl, J. (1993). School-based child sexual abuse prevention programs. *Journal of Family Violence,* 8(2), 137–50.

Miller-Perrin, C.L., Wurtele, S.K. & Kondrick, P.A. (1990). Sexually abused and nonabused children's conceptions of personal body safety. *Child Abuse & Neglect,* 14(1), 99–112.

National Center for Missing and Exploited Children (NCMEC) (1999). *Guidelines for programs to reduce child victimization: A resource for communities when choosing a program to teach personal safety to children.* Retrieved from https://mbfchildsafetymatters.org/wp-content/uploads/2015/07/Guidelines-for-Chid-Safety-Programs.pdf

New South Wales Department of School Education (1997). *Child protection education: Curriculum materials to support teaching and learning in Personal Development, Health and Physical Education.* Sydney: New South Wales Department of School Education, Student Welfare Directorate. Retrieved from http://www.curriculumsupport.education.nsw.gov.au/primary/pdhpe/safe/cpe.htm

O'Malley, J. & Lawrence, C. (2002). *Jasmine's butterflies.* Perth, Australia: Protective Behaviours Western Australia.

Plummer, C.A. (1984). *Preventing sexual abuse: Activities and strategies for those working with children and adolescents.* Washington, DC: National Criminal Justice Reference Service.

—— (1986). Prevention education in perspective. In M. Nelson & K. Clark (eds), *The educator's guide to preventing child sexual abuse.* Santa Cruz, CA: Network.

Prilleltensky, I., Nelson, G. & Peirson, L. (2001). *Promoting family wellness and preventing child maltreatment: Fundamentals for thinking and action.* Toronto: University of Toronto Press.

Putnam, F.W. (2003). Ten-year research update review: Child sexual abuse.*Journal of the American Academy of Child and Adolescent Psychiatry, 42*(3), 269–278.

Rowley, T. & Edwards, J. (2007). *Everyone's got a bottom.* Fortitude Valley, Qld: Family Planning Queensland.

opportunities for children to explore, experiment, predict and take managed risks. The balance can be achieved when the indoor and outdoor environment is arranged in a way that manages risk but still allows children to make decisions and do things for themselves. The balanced environment allows children to experience success in what they are doing through their own independence. The role of the educator is therefore to monitor the environment but also to demonstrate trust and respect for children's abilities to make decisions and to help keep challenges within current capacities for children.

To help us start thinking about safe environments, it is important to critically discuss attitudes towards 'risk'. Take five minutes to write down what your own understanding of 'risk' is, and what you would consider to be a danger to children. Why do you think this way? Does it align with other educators' understanding of 'risk'? When would a 'risky activity' be considered more beneficial to children's learning and outweigh any possible negative outcomes?

Figure 7.1 Managing risks during meal times.

Source: Getty Images/Ruth Jenkinson.

Potential risk: capable of becoming a possible risk to young children.

Managed risks are those that have controls in place. The educator has considered the child's ability, past experience, family/home environment and personal dispositions to identify and reduce the **potential risk**.

SPOTLIGHT 7.1: FOCUS ON MANAGING THE USE OF GLASS AND CROCKERY WITH YOUNG CHILDREN

Some Victorian early childhood services use real glass and crockery at children's mealtimes. This has been an embedded practice for over 70 years at some services. Children are trusted and supported to take managed risks to help build important life skills. If glass or plates are broken, children are encouraged to help clean up. To minimise potential risks, educators engage with small groups of children and are mindful of the age and level of skill of children.

Promoting children's health and safety, and ensuring their total wellbeing – including their physical and psychological welfare – requires that educators think critically about the routines, environment and relationships in their early-childhood setting. Educators need to know about the life circumstances of each child so they are able to use this understanding in their daily work and to provide each child with a sense of belonging within each setting. Identifying potential areas for reflection in indoor and outdoor safety to promote children's safety is discussed below.

Indoor safety

Sleeping

Sleeping areas for young children is an important area for consideration. Educators need to reflect on the location, material for sleeping and sanitisation of sleep material.

Educators should avoid placing infants on beanbags, sheepskins or synthetic pillows, and toys should be removed from the crib or sleeping area. Overheating is another important factor for children when sleeping (Kemp et al., 2000). Too much bedding, clothing that is too heavy and an environment that is too warm can contribute to an unsafe sleeping environment. In some instances, sudden infant death syndrome (SIDS) has been attributed to sleeping environments that are too warm (American Academy of Paediatrics, 2005).

Appropriate sanitisation of sleeping areas for young children is also necessary. In early childhood services, it is important that preventive measures are taken to regularly wash sleeping materials and to sanitise floors if children are sleeping on mattresses on the floor.

Environmental hazards

Inadequate ventilation is a safety risk that is often considered to be an environmental hazard. It is important that air moves sufficiently so there is no gathering of fumes, germs or other safety risks. Ventilation and natural light are also stipulated as a requirement under the Education and Care Services National Regulations. Regulation 110 is listed in Spotlight 7.2 (NHMRC, 2013).

Other irritants to a child's air quality environment also need to be considered. These could include the use of air fresheners, perfumes worn by staff and other artificial fragrances. These need to be considered, and either removed or modified as they are an environmental hazard.

SPOTLIGHT 7.2: VENTILATION AND NATURAL LIGHT

REGULATION 110 VENTILATION AND NATURAL LIGHT

The approved provider of an education and care service must ensure that the indoor spaces used by children at the education and care service premises:

(a) are well ventilated; and

(b) have adequate natural light; and

(c) are maintained at a temperature that ensures the safety and wellbeing of children.

Penalty: $2000.

Note: A compliance direction may be issued for failure to comply with this regulation.

General materials in the inside environment also pose a potential risk to children and need to be monitored. Examples of materials are as follows:

- Cleaning supplies are a risk to children, and should be stored in a locked cupboard.
- Paints and some craft supplies may present a risk if a child ingests them.
- Children may be allergic to certain materials in the inside environment, such as latex products.

It is important that educators have a working understanding of allergies in children and know how to reduce opportunities for exposure.

Space and shared space

In classrooms, there should be adequate space for children to move around so they do not have to compete for space with other children. As part of the Education and Care Services National Regulations (NHMRC, 2013), education and care services are required to have at least 3.25 square metres of unencumbered indoor space. This space does not include passageways, toilets and hygiene facilities, nappy-changing areas, areas used for storage of cots, general storage areas, rooms for staff and administration, or the kitchen (unless the kitchen is used by children as part of an education program provided by the service).

The educator needs to also ensure that the set-up of the environment allows children sufficient space to be able to move around without any barriers that impair visibility of all children to staff at all times. The space may also be used for multiple functions, meaning it has to be continually assessed. For example, where children sit on the floor might also be the location for group work, art projects and science experiments. The area's safety and cleanliness standards need to be maintained.

SPOTLIGHT 7.3: FOCUS ON LATEX

Children attending education and care services may be at significant risk of exposure to latex and acquiring a latex allergy for the following reasons:

- Education and care services are more likely to use cheaper, powdered supermarket brands of latex gloves rather than the more expensive, low-protein, powder-free, medical-grade examination gloves used in health care.
- Children may be regularly exposed to latex, including via their mucous membranes (e.g. when educators and other staff wear powdered latex gloves to prepare and handle food, and to change a child's nappy; from inhaling latex powder when educators and other staff remove powdered gloves near children; and from touching surfaces that are contaminated with latex powder, such as nappy change mats).
- Some authorities suggest that latex gloves should not be used in education and care services because of latex allergy risks to children, educators and other staff (NHMRC, 2013, p. 25).

Design is also important for children's sense of safety. In a recent study, Agbenyega (2011) explored how children made sense of safe and unsafe learning spaces, and how this understanding affected the ways in which they engaged with their learning spaces in an Australian early childhood centre. Findings suggested that the children felt safe in spaces that offered them the best opportunities for play. These were the spaces where they behaved well, laughed freely, reacted positively and played without too much restriction.

PAUSE AND REFLECT 7.1: EDUCATION SPACES

Think of an indoor space in a classroom. Were there any spaces that were used for multiple functions? Were there any safety procedures that needed to be followed? Would the same risks be there if the space hadn't been shared?

Interpersonal safety

In early childhood education settings, injuries caused by children to other children include biting, kicking, scratching and fighting. The role of the educator is to intervene when behaviours threaten other children. However, it is important that educators understand the cause of the behaviour and utilise suitable conflict-resolution strategies. For example, children under three years of age might use taste through biting as a way to explore the world, with limited language to express their ideas and feelings. The biting might also occurr because of teething, insecurity, over-stimulation or the child asserting their independence. It is important for the educator to act immediately by taking the following action:

- Intervene in the situation. Never bite the child back. Give immediate first aid if needed.
- Talk to the child who bit and tell them that biting is not okay. Encourage the child to apologise and help the child they just bit.
- Talk to the child who was bitten and give reassurance. Encourage the child who was bitten to tell the biter they were hurt.
- Alert other staff and complete an injury report. The families of both children will need to be informed.
- Examine the early-childhood setting to see whether any areas needed to be modified to lessen the risk.

Immunisation: when a vaccine is given to a person to allow them to become immune or resistant to a disease.

The **National Health and Medical Research Council (NHMRC)** is a leading body for developing health advice for the Australian community, health professionals and governments.

Immunisation is a reliable way to prevent some infections. According to the **NHMRC** 'Immunisation works by giving a child a vaccine – often a dead or modified version of the germ – against a particular disease. This makes the child's immune system respond similarly to the way it would respond if the child had actually contracted the disease, but with far less severe symptoms' (2013, p. 19). Table 7.1 provides details of funded vaccinations in Australia through the National Immunisation Program in Australia.

If a child is ill with an infectious disease, exclusion from the classroom should be considered in discussion with the family. Sometimes excluding children is the only way to limit the spread of the infection. It is difficult for some families to have children excluded, 'leading to stress and conflict between families and educators' (NHMRC, 2013, p. 13). The NHMRC (2013) suggests a good approach is to have a written policy about exclusion periods when ill. An example of an exclusion period outlined by the NHMRC is provided in Table 7.2.

Developmental-level risks

Developmental-level risks are risk factors that are dependent on the child's age.

It is important that educators begin the process of defining the boundaries for indoor safety and screening the environment for hazards based on the child's developmental level. Safety hazards can be broken down to developmental age and vulnerabilities associated with a particular stage.

Infants

Young infants must be carefully watched to protect and prevent risks. Young infants should never be left alone on a bed or table in case they fall. Toys should also be large in diameter, have smooth round edges and be soft to reduce the risk of choking and suffocation. All toys should also be removed from the crib.

As infants become more mobile and develop new motor skills at a rapid rate, an increased number of hazardous situations present themselves. The early

Table 7.1: Vaccines funded through the National Immunisation Program.

Child programs	
Age	**Vaccine**
Birth	Hepatitis B
2 months	Hepatitis B, diphtheria, tetanus, acellular pertussis (whooping cough), *Haemophilus influenzae* type b, inactivated poliomyelitis (polio) (hepB-DTPa-Hib-IPV)
	Pneumococcal conjugate (13vPCV)
	Rotavirus
4 months	Hepatitis B, diphtheria, tetanus, acellular pertussis (whooping cough), *Haemophilus influenzae* type b, inactivated poliomyelitis (polio) (hepB-DTPa-Hib-IPV)
	Pneumococcal conjugate (13vPCV)
	Rotavirus
6 months	Hepatitis B, diphtheria, tetanus, acellular pertussis (whooping cough), *Haemophilus influenzae* type b, inactivated poliomyelitis (polio) (hepB-DTPa-Hib-IPV)
	Pneumococcal conjugate (13vPCV)
	Rotavirus
12 months	*Haemophilus influenzae* type b and Meningococcal C (Hib-MenC)
	Measles, mumps and rubella (MMR)
18 months	Measles, mumps, rubella and varicella (chickenpox) (MMRV)
4 years	Diphtheria, tetanus, acellular pertussis (whooping cough) and inactivated poliomyelitis (polio) (DTPa-IPV)
	Measles, mumps and rubella (MMR) (to be given only if MMRV vaccine was not given at 18 months)
At-risk groups	**Vaccine**
6 months and over	Influenza (flu) (people with medical conditions placing them at risk of serious complications of influenza)
12 months	Pneumococcal conjugate (13vPCV) (medically at risk)
12–18 months	Pneumococcal conjugate (13vPCV) (Aboriginal and Torres Strait Islander children in high-risk areas)
12–24 months	Hepatitis A (Aboriginal and Torres Strait Islander children in high-risk areas)
4 years	Pneumococcal polysaccharide (23vPPV) (medically at risk)

Source: Australian Government Department of Health (2013).

childhood environment should be constantly monitored for potential objects that could be put in mouths and become a choking hazard (see Spotlight 7.4). It should also be monitored to check for any recalls of toys or infant equipment that might pose a risk.

During increased mobility, infants will also be exposed to different terrains that might lead to a fall. The environment needs to be monitored to ensure that

Table 7.2: Exclusion period.

Condition	Exclusion of case	Exclusion of contacts
Conjunctivitis	Exclude until discharge from the eyes has stopped, unless a doctor has diagnosed non-infectious conjunctivitis.	Not excluded
Herpes simplex (cold sores, fever blisters)	Not excluded if the person can maintain hygiene practices to minimise the risk of transmission. If the person cannot comply with these practices (e.g. because they are too young), they should be excluded until the sores are dry. Sores should be covered with a dressing where possible.	Not excluded
Influenza and influenza-like illnesses	Exclude until the person is well.	Not excluded
Measles	Exclude for four days after the onset of the rash.	Immunised and immune contacts are not excluded. For non-immunised contacts, contact a public health unit for specialist advice. All immuno-compromised children should be excluded until 14 days after the appearance of the rash in the last case.
Mumps	Exclude for nine days or until swelling goes down (whichever is sooner).	Not excluded
Pertussis (whooping cough)	Exclude until five days after starting appropriate antibiotic treatment, or for 21 days from the onset of coughing.	Contact a public health unit for specialist advice about excluding non-vaccinated contacts, or antibiotics.
Rubella (German measles)	Exclude until the person has fully recovered or for at least four days after the onset of the rash.	Not excluded
Varicella (chickenpox)	Exclude until all blisters have dried – this is usually at least five days after the rash first appeared in non-immunised children, and less in immunised children.	Any child with an immune deficiency (for example, leukaemia) or who is receiving chemotherapy should be excluded for their own protection as they are at high risk of developing severe disease; otherwise, not excluded.

Source: NHMRC (2013).

SPOTLIGHT 7.4: EXAMPLES OF CHOKING AND SUFFOCATION HAZARDS FOR YOUNG CHILDREN

- marbles
- balloons
- plastic bags
- popcorn
- toys with strings or cords long enough to encircle a child's neck
- coins
- pins
- pencils
- dress-up jewellery
- games
- hard lollies
- staples
- buttons

if a child does fall, it is not from a height and there is no sharp-edged furniture. Falling is important for infant development; however, it must be in a managed environment. Adolph (2008) argues that when infants fall, they do not merely learn by cue-association to prevent future tumbles. Instead, they learn to problem solve in what Adolph (2008) refers to as 'learning to learn'.

Toddlers

Toddlers are at a cognitive level that allows them to think and solve problems, with continual testing of their limits to understand and make meaning of their environment. Toddlers will draw upon their senses to make meaning of the world around them. For example, educators at a painting stand would need to monitor the child to make sure the child did not ingest art supplies. Thus it is important for educators to teach about food and non-food groups.

SPOTLIGHT 7.5: FOCUS ON HAND HYGIENE

Equipment that uses water, such as toilets and sinks, should be monitored and cleaned frequently. Children and staff should be encouraged to wash their hands often, as hand **hygiene** is one very effective way to control the spread of infection. Hand hygiene is a general term that refers to washing hands with soap and water, or using an alcohol-based hand sanitiser.

Hygiene refers to cleanliness habits to maintain optimal health and prevent the spread of disease.

Preschoolers

Preschool-aged children are able to understand aspects of cause and effect. Preschoolers can be engaged to help to monitor and observe the indoor environment for hazards. Children can help to develop strategies and safety approaches within the inside environment. These include interpersonal strategies as well as monitoring the environment.

School age

School-aged children are much less prone to indoor safety hazards compared with young children. However, it is important that the classroom is still monitored to ensure safety. The placement of furniture should also be considered carefully to allow adequate space. Any electronic technology used in the classroom also requires monitoring to reduce risks associated with electricity. Children in this age range can learn preventive measures and can help the educator monitor the environment.

SPOTLIGHT 7.6: FOCUS ON CELEBRATION CAKES AND BLOWING OUT CANDLES

According to the NHMRC (2013, p. 60):

Many children like to bring a cake to share with their friends on their birthday. Children love to blow out their candles while their friends are singing 'happy birthday'. Cakes and candles may also be brought into the education and care service for other special occasions. To prevent the spread of germs when the child blows out the candles, parents should either:

- provide a separate cupcake (with a candle if they wish) for the birthday child and enough cupcakes for all the other children
- provide a separate cupcake (with a candle if they wish) for the birthday child and a large cake that can be cut and shared.

Outdoor safety

Equipment

Some materials in the outside environment of early-childhood settings and schools require maintenance to ensure child safety.

Let's look at the example of sandpits, an item common in some educational settings. While sandpits can be fun for children, they also pose a number of risks. Good practices include the following:

- Cover the sandpit when not in use to prevent contamination from animal faeces, and to protect children from sharp or dangerous objects that have been discarded.
- Sandpits should be of a depth that can easily be raked over before each use to screen for foreign objects.
- Children and adults should wash their hands with soap and water or use an alcohol-based sanitiser before and after playing in the sandpit (NHMRC, 2013, p. 60).

Equipment may also require regular washing to deter germs. Toys should be washed regularly with all dirt removed.

All outside playground equipment should also have energy-absorbing material underneath to cushion falls and prevent serious injuries. Materials such as soft, loose sand and rubber are shock absorbers and require a minimum depth. The surface should be checked and maintained regularly.

Sun protection

Two in three Australians will develop some form of skin cancer before the age of 70 (SunSmart, 2011). Sun exposure during childhood has a significant impact on a person's risk of skin cancer. It is important that children in early childhood services and schools implement effective sun-protection measures. These include:

- slipping on sun-protective clothing
- slopping on SPF30+ sunscreen
- slapping on a hat
- seeking shade
- sliding on sunglasses (SunSmart, 2011).

In Australia, it is critically important to provide shade for children when they spend time outdoors, particularly from September to April. Permanent shade or temporary canopies can help create inviting spaces that encourage children to stay out of direct sunlight.

One of the most powerful and effective ways to convey messages about the need to balance getting enough sun with sun protection is to enact it in daily practice with children, and to talk about it with them.

Travel

Young children should learn about being safe as a pedestrian, cyclist or passenger in a car and on public transport. They should also learn the importance of where to play safely, away from traffic and roads. There are many programs available to assist educators from child safety and road safety organisations.

SPOTLIGHT 7.7: FOCUS ON THINKING ABOUT SAFETY

Primary-aged children require adult supervision around roads and car parks to keep them safe from moving vehicles. While children understand road safety rules, they may not follow these all of the time. Adult supervision is necessary.

Fire

A visit from a local fire department is a tradition for many early childhood education and care centres and schools in Australia. While funding cuts have seen this practice become less regular (Barr, Saltmarsh & Klopper, 2010), Saltmarsh believes that 'many centres continue to include a fire safety visit in their annual activities where possible' (2010, p. 291). During visits, children will be introduced to fire-prevention concepts and presented with information about what to do if they encounter a fire. Children may be introduced to fire safety equipment and be made aware of the appearance of fire fighters in the community. This approach is important in the Australian context, given that one in four set fires typically involves children aged six years or younger (Cole, Crandall & Kourofsky, 2004).

Developmental-level risks

The child's developmental level allows for identification of potential risks in the outdoor environment. Since the majority of accidents happen outdoors, it is important that educators have a working understanding of potential hazards. Potential risks include travelling in motor vehicles, drowning and falls from inappropriate equipment.

Infants and toddlers

In a motor vehicle, infants and toddlers should always be in a safety seat secured in the back seat of the vehicle. The outdoor play area for infants should also consist of flexible materials that offer no hazards if they are placed in the child's mouth. The emphasis for this age group is sensory motor activity, so any outdoor equipment needs to reflect this need.

Children should also be supervised around water features and pools at all times. Pools should be fenced and have locked gates.

Preschoolers

Educators of preschoolers needs to ensure that the outdoor play area is suitable and safe for children to engage in play events. This includes ensuring that equipment is of an appropriate height, playground equipment has suitable cushioning material underneath and the structures are free from sharp edges. Children should always be observed in the outdoor environment. Children in this age range will be able to engage in understanding about their own personal safety and procedures when using equipment.

School age

Children of this age have developed coordination and are physically capable of most outside activities. The role of the educator is to offer equipment that will allow children the ability to use their skills. The educator needs to ensure there is enough appropriate equipment for all children, and should consider how to balance challenging children's skills without the activity being a threat to their physical safety. Children in this age range also need to learn to manage and monitor their own risks.

Conclusion

In this chapter you have learned about child safety standards and procedures in Australia for both inside and outside spaces. Differences exist in procedures for infants/toddlers, preschool-aged children and school-aged children. It is important for professionals and families to know the current guidelines in regards to health, safety and hygiene. By having a working knowledge, we can ensure the safety of all children under the supervision of professionals.

Summary

This chapter has reinforced the need for providing safe learning spaces for children. The key messages highlighted in this chapter are:

- There are a number of threats to indoor safety, including indoor equipment, interpersonal behaviour, poisons, fires and shared space.
- Risks in the outdoor environment can occur on playgrounds and in the backyard. Potential risks include roads, water and the weather.
- An understanding of developmental levels of the child is important for knowing how to monitor and modify the environment.
- Through the use of observation, supervision and working with families, educators can promote safe behaviours in early childhood environments.
- Educators need to understand and be aware of the potential risks in indoor and outdoor environments, and know how to protect children.

Questions

7.1 Visit an early childhood service or school and audit it for indoor safety. What risks do you observe? How does the service manage the potential risks?

7.2 List the developmental-level risks for an 18-month-old, 5-year-old and a 12-year-old in an indoor environment and an outdoor environment. Compare the different age ranges and contexts. What do you notice?

7.3 If you were organising an excursion to the local art gallery for the children, what hazards would you need to consider?

7.4 Is it possible and desirable to completely remove risk from a classroom environment for child safety? Why/why not?

References

Adolph, K.E. (2008). Learning to move. *Current Directions in Psychological Science*, 17(3), 213–18.

Agbenyega, J. (2011). Researching children's understanding of safety: An auto-driven visual approach. *Contemporary Issues in Early Childhood*, 12(2), 163–74.

American Academy of Paediatrics (2005). The changing concept of sudden infant death syndrome: Diagnostic coding shifts, controversies regarding the sleeping environment, and new variables to consider in reducing risk. *Pediatrics*, 116, 1245–55.

Australian Children's Education and Care Quality Authority (2012). *National Quality Standard*. Retrieved 3 April 2017 from http://www.acecqa.gov.au/childrens-health-and-safety

Australian Government Department of Health (2013). *National Immunisation Program Schedule.* Retrieved 20 February 2014 from http://www.immunise.health.gov.au/internet/immunise/publishing.nsf/Content/4CB920F0D49C61F1CA257B2600828523/$File/nips-oct2013.pdf

Barr, J., Saltmarsh, S. & Klopper, C. (2010). Early childhood safety education: An overview of safety curriculum and pedagogy in outer metropolitan, regional and rural NSW. *Australasian Journal of Early Childhood,* 34(4), 31–6.

Boreham, C. & Riddoch, C. (2001). The physical activity, fitness and health of children. *Journal of Sports Sciences,* 19(12), 915–29.

Cole, R.E., Crandall, R. & Kourofsky, C.E. (2004). We CAN teach young children fire safety. *Young Children,* 59(2), 14–18.

Kemp, J.S., Unger, B., Wilkins, D., Psara, R.M., Ledbetter, T.L., Graham, M.A. et al, (2000). Unsafe sleep practices and an analysis of bedsharing among infants dying suddenly and unexpectedly: Results of a four-year, population-based, death-scene investigation study of Sudden Infant Death Syndrome and related deaths. *Pediatrics,* 106, E41.

National Health and Medical Research Council (NHMRC) (2013). *Staying healthy: Preventing infectious diseases in early childhood education and care services* (5th edn). Canberra: NHMRC.

Saltmarsh, S. (2010). Lessons in safety: Cultural politics and safety education in a multiracial, multiethnic early childhood education setting. *Contemporary Issues in Early Childhood,* 11(3), 288–98.

SunSmart (2011). *Be SunSmart, play SunSmart.* Retrieved 22 May 2013 from http://www.sunsmart.com.au/downloads/resources/booklets/be_sunsmart_play_sunsmart.pdf

Towner, E. & Towner, J. (2001) The prevention of childhood unintentional injury. *Current Paediatrics,* 11(6), 403–8.

CHAPTER 8

Social determinants of health and wellbeing

Margaret Sims

Introduction

> *… the most significant influences on child development and parenting capacity stem from the structural inequities which currently run throughout … society* (Jack, 2005, p. 301).

Despite universal access to health care and education, Australia is currently ranked in the bottom third of all OECD countries on a range of health and wellbeing indicators for children (Australian Research Alliance for Children and Youth, 2013). Such differences in health and wellbeing outcomes are now recognised as a 'wicked problem' (Moore, 2011) because they are extremely complex and very difficult to address (https://www.wickedproblems.com/1_wicked_problems.php). The United Nations has recognised this and created a special unit whose role it is to take the lead in addressing the factors contributing to this wicked problem (http://www.who.int/social_determinants/en/). This chapter examines this 'wicked problem', with the aim of supporting early childhood educators to reflect on the role they can play in addressing these issues.

The chapter begins by looking at social inequality, particularly in relation to health and wellbeing. Despite huge improvements in the resources we have available to us – think for a moment about the early childhood experiences of your grandparents/parents, who were growing up before antibiotics were available – internationally we see significant declines in population health and wellbeing, and increasingly large gaps between the rich and the poor in countries all around the world.

The chapter goes on to explore how governments are attempting to address issues of social inequality. While early childhood educators are rarely involved at the level of policy – although it is very important that we advocate at this level – it is necessary to understand the context, as this influences how we work with young children. The chapter concludes with practical suggestions for some actions early childhood educators can take to contribute to managing this problem.

PAUSE AND REFLECT 8.1: WICKED PROBLEMS

What are wicked problems? Study Figure 8.1 and explore these at: https://www.wickedproblems.com/1_wicked_problems.php
Read through the material and watch the video.

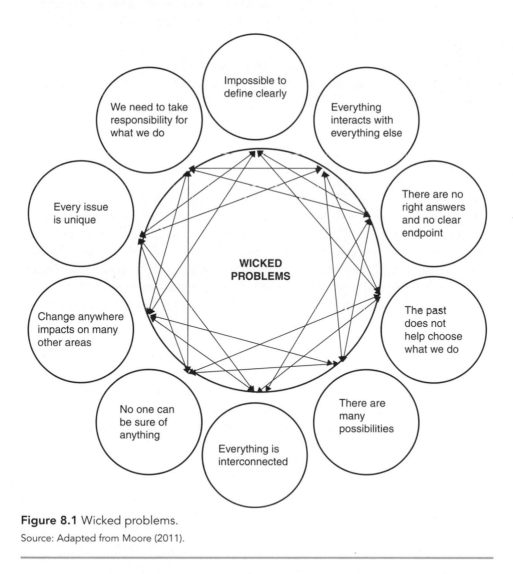

Figure 8.1 Wicked problems.

Source: Adapted from Moore (2011).

PAUSE AND REFLECT 8.2: THINKING ABOUT SOCIAL DETERMINANTS

Before we begin, think about the community in which you live.

- Are there some families who appear to be financially better off than other families? What characteristics did you use to make this judgement?
- Are there services that these families access which other families cannot afford?
- Do their children attend different schools?
- What differences do you see in the houses – size, outdoor play space, heating and cooling, safety?
- What kinds of differences do you see in the different neighbourhoods? What local shops are there? What infrastructure is there? What parks are there and what is in these parks?

Write a case study about an imaginary *advantaged* family living in your community. Write a case study about an imaginary *disadvantaged* family living in your community.

Social inequality

Living conditions have improved across the Western world and these better living conditions are associated with better outcomes. We have an increased life expectancy compared with a century ago, better health and improved wellbeing. Yet, despite these overall better outcomes, within each society we still see some people living in poorer conditions than others. These poorer conditions (usually associated with lower socio-economic status or **social disadvantage**) include poorly resourced neighbourhoods; low family income leading to poorly resourced homes; poor parental education levels; increased risks for unemployment or low-paid, stressful employment; and insecure housing. These conditions are associated with lower levels of social support, more risky behaviours (including substance abuse and criminal behaviours) and higher levels of unhappiness. This leads to greater exposure to stress and negative life events that require the use of additional physical and emotional resources as coping strategies. Because people have fewer physical and emotional resources available to them, they quickly exhaust their resources, and are therefore less likely to manage subsequent stressors effectively, resulting in a downward spiral of increasing inability to cope.

Social disadvantage: there is no absolute definition of disadvantage; rather it is judged in comparison with advantage. Social disadvantage normally includes some or all of the following: poor health, limited education, unemployment, financial hardship, experiencing violence, being the victim of crime and/or having limited or no social support.

Income inequity (one of the key measures of the gap between those who 'have' and those who 'have not' and thus an indicator of family stress) is recognised by the World Economic Forum as a top international economic risk. In Australia this gap has been growing steadily over the past years resulting in Australian income inequity being larger than the OECD average (Australian Council of Social Services, 2015). Rising income inequality across the OECD is linked to a 5 per cent decline in economic growth and is thought to have contributed to the global financial crisis (Australian Council of Social Services, 2015). The richest 100 people in the world added enough money to their portfolios in 2012 to have ended world poverty four times over (Oxfam, 2013). The 10 richest Australians in 2015 – according to Fairfax Media – had between them over $21 billion (Pash, 2015) and the richest 10 per cent of Australians hold 45 per cent of the wealth. In contrast, the bottom 40 per cent of Australian income families hold only 5 per cent of Australian wealth (Australian Council of Social Services, 2015) and around 10 per cent of Australians do not have enough money to buy adequate food each week (Salvation Army, 2015). The 1.73 million families making up the bottom 20 per cent of Australian wealth have together less than the money held by the seven richest individuals in Australia (Richardson & Denniss, 2014).

Humanitarian migrants are much more likely to be living on a low income, with an average family income of $22 920 in 2010 to 2011 (Australian Bureau of Statistics, 2015). Asylum seekers have no rights to employment or study and have limited access to welfare, making them some of the most disadvantaged groups seeking assistance from support agencies (Salvation Army, 2015). Wages increased by 72 per cent for the 10 per cent of top Australian income earners in the 25 years up to 2010, but only increased by 14 per cent for the lowest 10 per cent of income earners (Australian Council of Social Services, 2015) while the unemployment benefit in 2011 remained 20 per cent below the poverty line (Douglas et al., 2014).

As nations become richer, inequities in health and wellbeing grow larger. This 'gap' between those who 'have' and those who 'have not' is called a social gradient. **Social gradients** result in inequities that are reflected as disparities in a range of life outcomes. For example, on average Indigenous males have a life expectancy of 69.1 years whereas non-Indigenous males are expected to live to an average of 79.7 years. Indigenous males living in outer regional, remote and very remote areas are estimated to live 0.7 years less than Indigenous males living in major cities and inner regional areas (Australian Government, 2014). Social inequality has an impact on self-image and self-esteem and, through these, lifelong wellbeing. Being lower in the social hierarchy implies one is less worthy of value and esteem. Considerable research demonstrates that feelings of inferiority, lack of control over one's destiny and powerlessness (both in the workplace and in life generally) have a significant negative impact on both health and wellbeing. For example, Wilkinson (2011) refers to a World Bank study indicating that children from high and low castes in India asked to complete puzzles did equally well until they were made aware of their caste differences. Once this had occurred, the children from the lower castes performed more poorly.

Social gradients are differences in outcomes observed across different levels of social and economic advantage/disadvantage. Better outcomes are universally observed in those who are more advantaged. Inequity in outcomes such as health (at the individual and group/population levels) are related to the social position of individuals/families/groups.

There is strong evidence that citizens in countries where there is little difference between those who are rich and those who are poor (a small social gradient) have better community lives, higher levels of trust, lower levels of violence, longer life expectancies, better rates of educational attainment, and better health and happiness (Wilkinson, 2011). It is not simply that countries with a high social gradient have more poor people who directly contribute to poorer national outcomes. Rather, in these countries, even people in the middle classes living on good incomes have poorer outcomes: they have poorer health and wellbeing than middle-class people in more egalitarian societies. Social gradients are therefore not about absolute levels of wealth or poverty, but rather about relative levels.

Causes of social inequality

Social determinants are the overall social, physical and economic environments into which people are born, grow and live out their lives. Bronfenbrenner's bio-ecological theory (2005) identifies these as all the factors in each level of the ecosystem that impact on children, their families, communities and societies.

In order to address the **social determinants** of health, it is necessary to understand the contributing factors. One line of thought argues that differences in people's behaviour are the root cause. People in disadvantaged groups are more likely to engage in behaviours that compromise their health – for example, smoking, drug/alcohol use and criminal behaviours tend to be higher in families with members who are stressed and/or living in poverty. Violence is also more common in such families and communities, so children learn that it is a normal way to manage challenges. In addition, adults are less likely to engage in healthy exercise, so members tend to become overweight – with all the attendant health risks.

Other explanations centre around the ability to acquire resources. People living in poverty generally have a much poorer diet than those with adequate income. Healthy foods – such as fruit and vegetables – are more expensive, and those on a low income are less able to afford them. Foods with a high fat content are more filling at a lower cost than healthy foods. Two-thirds of the children in families supported by the Salvation Army in 2014 went without basic necessities (Salvation Army, 2015). Epigenetic research now suggests that when food supply is irregular, the body adapts by ensuring that maximum advantage is taken of the food that is ingested, increasing the risk of obesity at times when the food supply is more plentiful.

People on lower incomes are less able to afford comfortable housing and safe, well-resourced neighbourhoods. Therefore, homes may be more overcrowded, with little space for school children to complete homework. Clothing and bedding are more likely to be inadequate, causing the body to use excess energy to keep warm, thus having fewer resources available to fight illness.

Neighbourhoods are likely to be more risky, so children are either kept inside where it is safe, or they play in areas where they are exposed to bullying, violence and crime. Families who perceive their neighbourhood as dangerous are less likely to participate in neighbourhood events, thus further limiting their social contacts and opportunities for social support. Neighbourhood playgrounds either do not exist, or are dangerous – for example, with syringes buried in sandpits, and play equipment defaced with graffiti or vandalised. Education is often of a poorer quality and fewer children access early childhood programs, impacting on educational outcomes. For example, the Australian Early Development Census identifies that Indigenous children are more than twice as likely to be developmentally vulnerable compared to non-Indigenous children and children who speak a language other than English at home and who are not yet proficient in English have a 93.7 per cent risk of being identified as developmentally vulnerable (Australian Government, 2013).

Alternatively, a life-course perspective suggests that disadvantage accumulates: lack of access to resources in early childhood results in poor health and wellbeing, which in turn can impact on ability to manage schooling, which ultimately impacts on educational attainment, employment prospects and income generation potential in adulthood. Lower education levels are linked to less secure employment, lower wages and poorer working conditions, which impact on the physical and emotional resources available to support family members.

This perspective positions disadvantage in the parental generation as transferring to the children's generation, and research suggests that it is also likely to transfer to the next generation – the children's children. We know that children born into families with less access to life resources (such as income and education) are less likely to be able to overcome this disadvantage and thus are strongly influenced by their parents' socio-economic position (Dabla-Norris et al., 2015). Families whose lack of resources require them to live in poorer housing demonstrate poorer health and wellbeing. The lives of these at-risk families are often complicated by additional problems associated with high stress: family violence, unsafe neighbourhoods, a lack of housing stability – all associated with poorer health and wellbeing. In addition, for those who are part of an ethnic minority group, constant exposure to racism is stressful, and has a significant and negative impact on mental health, physical health and wellbeing (Priest et al., 2013).

PAUSE AND REFLECT 8.3: SOCIAL INEQUALITY

Think about the imaginary disadvantaged family for whom you developed a case study in Pause and Reflect 8.2.

- What parental behaviours can you add to your case study that contribute to the family's disadvantage?
- What resources are either totally lacking or in short supply in this family?
- What do you think could be the combined impact of all of these factors on the health and wellbeing of the children in this family?

Addressing social inequality

Addressing social determinants is important for a range of reasons. Economic arguments abound. For example, in the UK The Equality Trust (2014) estimated that inequality lost the UK economy annually £12.5 billion because of reduced healthy life expectancy, £25 billion because of poorer mental health, £1 billion because of increased imprisonment rates and £678 million because of increased numbers of murders. In Australia, a recent review argued that we could save $2.3 billion annually on hospital costs alone if social determinants were addressed. In addition, 170 000 additional people would be healthy enough to work, generating an additional $8 billion in earnings coupled with a $4 billion annual saving in welfare payments (Brown, Thurecht & Nepal, 2012). The alternative argument suggests that the driving force for change should not be economics, but rather a vision of a more just society – one in which every individual has a fair opportunity to participate. Arguments based on morality (what is right rather than what is expedient) have little purchase in modern politics, so the interventions that are available tend to focus around the more pragmatic, economic rationalisations.

There is considerable debate regarding how best to address the social determinants of health. A focus on working towards equality of outcomes has led to policies that aim to redistribute resources – for example, creating minimum income levels through welfare payments and providing universal access to health care and education. Welfare payments are targeted specifically at those people who are more disadvantaged, with an expectation that those with resources will support themselves. The assumption is that if all people have equal *access* to resources (either through their own efforts or through targeted state intervention), inequity in *outcomes* will no longer exist. However, universal access to services does not ensure universal participation or equal outcomes. We know, for example, that Australia continues to have significant health and wellbeing inequities despite its claim to be a country where all people have access to basic welfare and health services. We also know that equal access to education does not ensure equal academic outcomes.

There is growing recognition that targeting resources to those who are most disadvantaged will not address social gradients (Marmot, 2010). This is partly because inequality is a wicked problem: simply addressing income disadvantage, for example, does not mitigate the impact of the lack of intellectual stimulation provided in a home where parents have a low education level nor the lack of community facilities in a low-income neighbourhood. In addition, something rather like a catch 22 operates: if the health of those who are most disadvantaged is targeted and therefore improved, then those who were just above them in status will become the new disadvantaged, and, because their health issues were not targeted, they will become less healthy. Marmot argues that it may be impossible to eliminate social gradients, so we should target reducing the gap. This can only be achieved, he argues, through 'proportionate universalism' (2010, p. 16); that is, services available to all, delivered with greater intensity to those who are more disadvantaged, with sufficient flexibility to address local priorities.

There is an assumption that social inequity will be addressed if there is a focus on developing a socially inclusive society. Social inclusion occurs when people are *not* marginalised and when there is *no* inequity (EFA Global Monitoring Team, 2010). The complexities of defining social inclusion are illustrated in Figure 8.2. Two major initiatives have been put in place to attempt to address social inclusion. The first

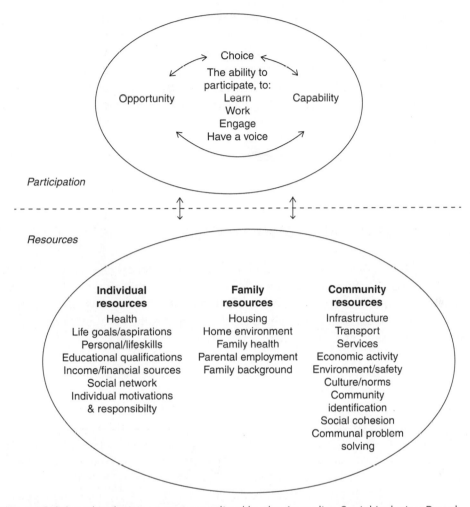

Figure 8.2 Social inclusion as conceptualised by the Australian Social Inclusion Board.
Source: Australian Social Inclusion Board (2012, p. 13).

is the Australian *Closing the Gap* agenda that focuses specifically on Indigenous disadvantage across a range of outcomes, including health and wellbeing. In the most recent evaluation, the aim of ensuring all Indigenous four-year-old children in remote communities have access to a quality early childhood program by 2013 was not met – 85 per cent rather than the targeted 95 per cent of Indigenous children were enrolled. The aim to halve the gap in mortality rates for Indigenous children under five by 2018 is identified as on track. However, the aim to halve the gap in reading, writing and numeracy by 2018 is not on track with no improvements identified since 2008 (Abbott, 2015).

The second initiative operates out of the federal Department of Social Services. *Communities for Children*, a program in some ways similar to *Closing the Gap*, focuses on families who are disadvantaged or live in disadvantaged areas, and aims to improve family functioning, and child safety, wellbeing and development (http://www.dss.gov.au/our-responsibilities/families-and-children/programs-services/family-support-program/family-and-children-s-services). The Communities for Children model uses a facilitating partner whose role involves working with other local agencies so they can deliver services in partnership. The aim is to create child-friendly communities which will, in turn, deliver positive outcomes for children and families. Services offered as part of the program need to be responsive to community needs and are therefore quite different across different communities. Overall, the program has seen smaller numbers of children living in households where there was no employment, fewer parental reports of hostile or harsh parenting behaviours and improved parental self efficacy (Muir et al., 2009).

Social inequality and stress

Children growing up in 'risky' households are likely to experience a range of chronic stressors. Their families have limited physical and emotional resources to use in parenting so they are likely to lack opportunities to develop resilience. Parents under stress are more likely to develop punitive, inconsistent and irritable parenting styles. Parents themselves are more likely to experience high levels of relationship conflict, and there is increased risk for child abuse/neglect. These all have a major negative impact on children's health and wellbeing.

The early years of life are therefore critical when it comes to setting the foundations for lifelong health and wellbeing outcomes. Epigenetic research is now providing us with some understanding of how the social world in which children participate impacts on their biology and neurology, and thus shapes these lifelong outcomes (Maggi et al., 2010). Some of these are *latent* processes – that is, exposure to certain environmental factors in the early years only becomes evident many years later. For example, birth weight, the size of the placenta and the amount of weight gain over the first year of life impact on risk of cardiovascular disease between 50 and 60 years of age, no matter what other factors operate in the intervening years. Other processes are *cumulative* – for example, the impact of low parental socio-economic status is greater if children experience this throughout their childhood than if they experience it for a short time only. Other impacts follow a *pathway* effect, where one factor influences another, which then influences another. For example, children from disadvantaged backgrounds are less prepared for school, which impacts on their ability to succeed at school, which then impacts on their employment options in adulthood, which ultimately impacts on their adult health and wellbeing, and the health and wellbeing of their children (and potentially their children's children).

The pathway model in particular is useful in conceptualising chronic disease in later life (Gustafsson et al., 2004). Exposure to stresses throughout childhood and early adulthood (such as growing up in a disadvantaged family and community) result in 'wear and tear' on many of the body's physiological systems. In particular, when the body's stress mechanisms (the hypothalamic–pituitary–adrenal [HPA] axis) are triggered many times, and for long periods of time, compensatory changes occur in secondary metabolic systems in order to maintain homeostasis. Over time, these changes develop into a multi-systemic disease state called *allostatic load*. Think of it as an elastic band that is stretched to capacity for so long that it is no longer able to snap back – the accumulated load has fundamentally changed the elastic. In a similar manner, if a person's physiology is 'stretched' almost to breaking point for long enough, it can be fundamentally changed so that it cannot go back to the way it was supposed to be. This state of high allostatic load means the body is at significant risk of developing a range of illnesses of the metabolic and cardiovascular systems.

In children, we see this in a range of outwardly observable behaviours. Children can become hyperactive, impulsive and irritable. They may display significant levels of externalising behaviour problems, become depressed and struggle with memory problems. Conversely, we may see children adapt in the opposite manner: displaying high levels of internalising behaviours, and high levels of underactivity and passivity. They are likely to be at risk of developing a range of health problems, including diabetes, malnutrition, immune disorders, fibromyalgia, allergies, asthma and cardiovascular disease.

Social determinants and the role of early childhood educators

Children begin to accumulate allostatic load while still in utero. Maternal nutrition and stress impact on the developing foetus. For example, the typical Western diet eaten by pregnant women increases the risk of their children being obese throughout their lives (Muhlhausler & Ailhaud, 2013). Poverty and malnutrition during pregnancy result in a greater risk of low birth weight and infant mortality. A lack of fatty acids in utero in particular is related to visual and behavioural problems in the infant (Maggi et al., 2010). Early childhood educators play an important role in supporting parents through pregnancy. They are an important source of health and wellbeing information, but they also need to consider the support they can offer (either themselves or through brokering relationships between families and other community members and/or agencies), aimed at both reducing parental stress levels throughout the pregnancy and supporting parental health and wellbeing.

Allostatic load accumulates through childhood. Families who are living in poor neighbourhoods, with minimal access to resources, poor housing, low income and poor health care, create a child-rearing environment that chronically stresses children's developing HPA systems. Such families are usually characterised by limited availability of support for parents, low parental education, high parental stress levels, poor parental mental health and wellbeing, poor nutrition and limited opportunities for children to engage in rich learning opportunities. Parenting is often more punitive and less responsive to children's needs.

In these contexts, children develop physiological coping mechanisms that enable them to function as best they can. For example, infants whose parents respond inconsistently to their attempts to communicate learn to cry more loudly and for longer, in their attempts to elicit parental responses. These infants often display extreme signs of arousal; it is as if the infant believes that normal distress is not going to succeed in gaining comfort, so displays of affect have to become more and more extreme in order to elicit attention. In an early childhood environment, such behaviours are often perceived as problematic, whereas in the home environment they are actually adaptive. Early childhood educators need to be aware they not only reflect on children's behaviour in the early learning context, but across the totality of children's lives. Strategies that focus on punishing the child for prolonged crying, or reducing the crying by using techniques such as ignoring, serve to reduce the child's ability to cope with the home environment and, in the long term, reduce resilience and increase the risk of poor long-term health and wellbeing.

Families (and early-childhood settings) exist in the context of communities, and communities themselves can function to increase or decrease allostatic load. Parenting is more likely to be effective in neighbourhoods where parents feel they know their neighbours and they feel safe. Perceptions of neighbourhood safety influence residents' ability to be physically active, and parents' willingness to permit children to play in outdoor areas. Where there are more easily accessible shops selling healthy food, residents' diets are likely to be healthier; poor access to supermarkets is associated with higher levels of obesity. High levels of transport noise and feelings of neighbourhood chaos are associated with

Protective factors are those factors ameliorating the impact of the risks children and families face in their daily lives. Protective factors help children and families cope with the stresses in their lives.

higher levels of depression and mental health problems. Early childhood educators need to consider the wider community in which families live. There are a range of **protective factors** that support family functioning, and early childhood educators can be involved in supporting, mentoring, coaching and engaging with families and communities to create better child-rearing environments through a focus on:

- supporting parents to build effective friendships and social supports
- facilitating an increase in parental knowledge and skills around parenting and daily living (remembering that different families will have different dreams for their children and different approaches in working towards those dreams)
- brokering parental access to relevant services and community groups
- liaising with other services in the area to create a more integrated approach to service delivery to make access easier for families
- advocating for community resources with families – for example, a local library, play spaces, family-friendly shops and so forth
- increasing the understanding of community members, business owners and community organisations about the importance of early childhood.

Bronfenbrenner's (2005) model of bio-ecological development emphasises the importance of considering early years learners in the context of their biology and microsystems as well as in the context of broader systems (exo-, meso- and macrosystems). Early childhood educators addressing social determinants of health also need to consider these various levels of the system. Social determinants are 'wicked problems' (Moore, 2011), and tackling them requires sophisticated, complex approaches fed by a commitment to social justice and equity.

PAUSE AND REFLECT 8.4: ADDRESSING DISADVANTAGE

Think of the imaginary disadvantaged case study family from Pause and Reflect 8.2. What kinds of support would be useful in supporting this family? Remember that disadvantage is caused through a multiplicity of factors so that addressing disadvantage (a wicked problem) is going to need a range of opportunities (wicked solutions).

   Might any of the following be useful? Explain your answer.

- facilitated playgroup
- parent education
- linking parents with other parents in the neighbourhood
- organising car pools for shopping, outings etc.
- organising a babysitting club
- advocating with the council to improve facilities and safety at the local park
- cooking club
- homework club

Conclusion

Inequities in children's health and wellbeing represent a 'wicked problem' that is the focus of much international attention. These inequities are a 'wicked problem' because of the complexity of underlying causes and contributing factors identified in this chapter as the social determinants of health. Social determinants arise not only out of individual neurobiology/physiology differences, but from the world around children impacting not only directly on them, but on their parents (and even their grandparents). Attempts to address these issues to create a more socially just society need to be complex and sophisticated. Early childhood educators play a significant role in contributing to these initiatives.

Summary

The key messages highlighted in this chapter are:

- Despite improved conditions, social inequality is getting worse.
- The gap between the 'haves' and the 'have-nots' is called a social gradient. The steeper the social gradient, the worse the health and wellbeing outcomes of a nation.
- Social inequalities in health and wellbeing may be caused by people who are disadvantaged engaging in more problematic behaviour, by unequal access to resources and/or by an accumulation of disadvantage over a lifetime.
- Governments attempt to address social inequality through: (1) redistribution of resources; or (2) targeting of resources only to those who are disadvantaged. Neither works well. Proportionate universalism has recently been suggested as another option.
- The impact of the social environment on long-term health and wellbeing outcomes operates through latent, cumulative and/or pathway impacts on neurobiology/physiology.
- The concept of allostatic load is used to conceptualise the impact of the social environment on the biology of an individual. The higher the allostatic load, the greater the risk for poor health and wellbeing.
- Early childhood educators need to take a bio-ecological approach to deal with the complexity of this 'wicked problem'. Supports can be offered to the child, family and community to address a range of social determinants.

Questions

8.1 Think about a family with which you work. Identify the factors in the child that contribute to health and wellbeing. Identify family factors. What could early childhood educators do to facilitate better health and wellbeing outcomes for this child and family?

8.2 Think about the community in which this family lives. Is this a family-friendly community – one in which it is relatively easy to be a parent? What are the factors that contribute towards its family-friendly (or family-unfriendly) nature? What could early childhood educators do to make this community a place where children would have better health and wellbeing outcomes?

8.3 Identify your local members of parliament (state and federal). To what parties do they belong? What are their policies in relation to early childhood health and wellbeing? Do they support the idea that individuals are responsible for their own health and wellbeing, or do they see the state as having a role in addressing systemic disadvantage? Do they support universal or targeted services to address health and wellbeing inequities? Write a two-paragraph statement explaining why you think these politicians should consider the social determinants of health in their thinking and their policies.

8.4   Explore the Australian Early Development Census website (http://www.aedc.gov. au/). See if you can find the AEDC results for your communities (the community in which you live and the community in which you work.)

References

Abbott, T. (2015). *Closing the Gap. Prime Minister's Report 2015.* Canberra: Commonwealth of Australia.

Australian Bureau of Statistics (2015). *3418.0 – Personal Income of Migrants, Australia, Experimental, 2010–11* (p. 45). Canberra, ACT: Australian Government.

Australian Council of Social Services (2015). *Inequality in Australia. A nation divided.* Strawberry Hills, NSW: Australian Council of Social Services.

Australian Government (2013). *A Snapshot of Early Childhood Development in Australia 2012 – AEDI National Report.* Canberra, ACT: Australian Government.

—— (2014). *Aboriginal and Torres Strait Islander Health Performance Framework 2014 Report..* Canberra, ACT: Australian Government.

Australian Research Alliance for Children and Youth (2013). *Report Card. The wellbeing of young Australians.* Braddon, ACT: Australian Research Alliance for Children and Youth.

Australian Social Inclusion Board (2012). *Social Inclusion in Australia. How Australia is faring* (2nd edn.). Canberra, ACT: Department of the Prime Minister and Cabinet, Commonwealth of Australia.

Bronfenbrenner, U. (ed.) (2005). *Making human beings Human. Bioecological perspectives on human development.* Thousand Oaks, CA: Sage Publications.

Brown , L., Thurecht, L. & Nepal, B. (2012). *The Cost of Inaction on the Social Determinants of Health.* The National Centre for Social and Economic Modelling (NATSEM), University of Canberra.

Dabla-Norris, E., Kochhar, K., Suphaphiphat, N., Ricka, F. & Tsounta, E. (2015). *Causes and Consequences of Income Inequality: A Global Perspective.* Washington DC: International Monetary Fund.

Douglas, B., Friel, S., Denniss, R. & Morawetz, D. (2014). *Advance Australia Fair? What to do about growing inequality in Australia.* Weston, ACT: Australia 21 and The Australia Institute.

EFA Global Monitoring Team (2010). *Reaching the marginalised.* Oxford: Oxford University Press and UNESCO.

The Equality Trust (2014). *The cost of inequality*. London: The Equality Trust, p. 7.

Gustafsson, P.E., Allansson, E., Gustafsson, P.A. & Nelson, N. (2004). Cortisol levels in children and relation to psychosocial factors. *Journal of Psychosomatic Research*, 56, 640.

Jack, G. (2005). Assessing the impact of community programmes working with children and families in disadvantaged areas. *Child and Family Social Work*, 10, 293–304.

Maggi, S., Irwin, L., Siddiqi, A. & Hertzman, C. (2010). The social determinants of early child development: An overview. *Journal of Paediatrics and Child Health*, 46(11), 627–35.

Marmot, M. (2010). *Fair Society, Healthy Lives. The Marmot Review*. London: Department of Health.

Moore, T. (2011). *Wicked problems, rotten outcomes and clumsy solutions. Children and families in a changing world.* Paper presented at the NIFTeY/CCCH Conference 2011. Children's place on the agenda … past, present and future, Sydney. http://www.netsvic.org.au/emplibrary/ccch/NIFTeY_CCCH_ Conference_11_-_paper.pdf

Muhlhausler, B. & Ailhaud, G. (2013). Omega-6 polyunsaturated fatty acids and the early origins of obesity. *Current Opinion in Endocrinology, Diabetes & Obesity*, 20(1), 56–61. doi:10.1097/MED.0b013e32835c1ba7

Muir, K., Katz, I., Purcal, C., Patulny, R., Flaxman, S., Abelló, D. et al. (2009). *National evaluation (2004–2008) of the Stronger Families and Communities Strategy 2004–2009.* (Vol. 24). Canberra, ACT: Commonwealth of Australia.

Oxfam (2013). *The cost of inequality: how wealth and income extremes hurt us all.* Oxfam Media Briefing (p. 5). London: Oxfam.

Pash, C. (7 October 2015) *The 10 richest families in Australia. Business Insider Australia*. Retrieved from http://www.businessinsider.com.au/ the-10-richest-families-in-australia-2015-10

Priest, N., Paradies, Y., Trenerry, B., Truong, M., Karlsen, S. & Kelly, Y. (2013). A systematic review of studies examining the relationship between reported racism and health and wellbeing for children and young people. *Social Science & Medicine*, 95, 115–117. doi:/10.1016/j.socscimed.2012.11.031

Richardson, D. & Denniss, R. (2014). *Income and wealth inequality in Australia*. Canberra, ACT: The Australia Institute.

Salvation Army (2015). *National Economic & Social Impact Survey 2015* (p. 40). Blackburn, Vic & Sydney, NSW: The Salvation Army Australia Southern Territory and the Australia Eastern Territory.

Wilkinson, R. (2011). *What difference does inequality make?* Public Lecture (p. 11). Loughborough University: Human Rights and Equalities Charnwood. Retrieved 27 January 2017 from http://humanrightsandequalitiescharnwood. aj-services.com/uploads/Annual%20Lecture%202011.pdf

CHAPTER 9

Friendships

Maryanne Theobald, Susan Danby, Catherine Thompson and Karen Thorpe

Introduction

This chapter investigates friendships and children's wellbeing in the early years of schooling. Having a friend, and being a friend, is closely connected to children's health and wellbeing in the early years. Friendship safeguards children from social isolation and is associated with academic attainment and social success. In early childhood, children often make friends through play and other shared activities.

Through young children's direct accounts and visual representations about friendships, we explore characteristics of friendship and the strategies that children use to make friends and manage disputes as they negotiate their social and emotional relationships through play and shared spaces. Three aspects of friendships are evident in the children's accounts: friendship is enduring, friendship is a mutual relationship, and friendship involves an emotional investment. This chapter provides educators with an understanding of the important role of friendships in young children's everyday lives, and to their happiness and wellbeing in the early years.

Importance of friendships in the early years

Children's **friendships** are accomplished in the social and educational spaces outside of family contexts, and include child care, preschool and school settings. These settings provide children with opportunities to interact with other children and make friends.

> **Friendship** involves interactions between two or more participants where the relationship is one of emotional and social connectedness. Being a friend means being available emotionally for each other, and trusting and supporting each other.

Having a friend is associated with a child's success at school. Children with friends enjoy school more, and are happier to attend preschool and school (Buhs & Ladd, 2001). Friendships are particularly important when children attend their first year of school because children with friends tend to adjust more quickly and have more positive attitudes towards schooling (Dunn, Cutting & Fisher, 2002). When at preschool or school, children with friends join in with activities more often than those without friends (Tomada et al., 2005), and participation in class activities is associated with positive effects on children's achievement at school.

Friendships provide children with social and emotional support that is important for resilience in times of change, and feelings of happiness and wellbeing (Danby, 2008; Dunn, 2004). Friends offer strong supports that can reduce feelings of anxiety, confusion, angst and social isolation for children. In the early years, friendships facilitate positive outcomes for children and can reduce stress in times of change, such as transition to school (Dunn, 2004; Hartup, 1992).

Being left out of social activities and not having friends may be a threat to children's physical and mental health and their social and emotional wellbeing (Dunn, 2004; Laursen et al., 2007). Statistics show that up to 9 per cent of Australian children and adolescents are diagnosed with mental illness, such as anxiety or depression, that lasts longer than six months (Australian Institute of Health and Welfare [AIHW], 2012). These problems affect children's healthy development trajectories and may result in youth substance abuse, violence and suicide. A key preventative measure for mental health is having strong relationships with others.

Children's friendships share many of the same elements as adult friendships, including having positive feelings, happiness and intimacy. It is a misconception to think that children's friendships are in some way lesser than adults' friendships. Studies emphasise the mutuality of friendships and show strongly that children appreciate having friends, as being 'together' means being able to spend time together doing things, and sharing ideas and activities. In their study of friendships of Swedish children, aged 10 to 11 years, Kostenius and Ohrling (2008) found that friends play an important role of being helpful to each other and supporting each other – particularly in difficult times. As one child in their study reported, 'friendship is like having an extra parachute to unfold when your own is not opening up' (pp. 29–30). Both being a friend and having a friend 'plays a critical part in their acquisition of social identity and selfhood' (James, 1993, p. 2001) which occurs in **peer culture** and across the lifespan.

Peer culture is 'a stable set of activities or routines, artefacts, values and concerns that children produce and share in interaction with peers' (Corsaro, 2009, p. 301; Corsaro & Molinari, 1990, p. 214).

To be a friend requires particular skills and affective states. Having a friend offers social opportunities to become skilled at understanding the standpoints of others – an important consideration for helping children to participate in peer groups and activities in early years settings. The capacity to be able to recognise another's point of view and get along with others is an important communication skill and a key predictor of successful relationships in later life (Hartup, 1992). Sometimes, young children need help to build these skills and affective stances, and it is here that the role of the educator is critical – not least in modelling how to communicate with empathy and care for others, regardless of their age and status.

Friendships do not always go to plan, however, and may result in the relationship being fractured through **disputes**. When the bond between children is strong, young children are capable of engaging in repair during such challenges. Sometimes, children need additional support and targeted intervention to develop skills for building and maintaining friendships. Some children, for example, may have more difficulty in understanding the perspective of another child (Rendle-Short, 2003). Educators can provide encouragement and specific strategies to build and manage relationship disputes. These are important points for social learning in which educators can provide guidance in presenting the perspective of others. Indeed preschool rooms with greater social diversity have been found to be those where there is opportunity for deeper quality of friendships among children (Thorpe et al., 2010).

> A **dispute** is a social practice where participants may disagree or argue about a matter. A dispute, often built around disagreement, is actually a collaborative activity as it involves two or more to participate.

Researching children's friendships

To investigate friendships in the early years, this chapter draws upon young children's accounts of friendships from two studies. The first study aimed to understand friendship from the children's own perspectives, about how they made friends when starting school. The second study explored how children made friends when they did not share a common language. There were two cohorts of children. In Study 1, there were 70 preschool-aged children aged three to four years and in Study 2, there were 162 children in the first year of formal schooling aged five to six years. In both studies, researchers engaged in informal interviews with small groups of three to four children.

The children were invited to draw pictures of their experiences of friendship as they talked with the researcher, and some of these images are included in this chapter. The drawings were designed to help children feel comfortable about expressing their views. The researchers encouraged the participants to use their own images and words to communicate their perspectives on friendship (Danby, Ewing & Thorpe, 2011; Kostenius & Ohrling, 2008) and our approach recognised the child's agency as a research participant (Danby & Farrell, 2004; Thorpe et al., 2007).

The audio-recorded interviews were transcribed using pseudonyms to protect the participants' anonymity. The children's accounts discuss who their friends are and what they like to do as friends. As well as identifying the qualities of friendship that they share, they identify the strategies that they use to build friendships.

Characteristics of friendships

Friendships are not the same as other peer relationships in children's lives. While shared experiences may be evident in peer interactions, there are additional aspects of being a friend, including 'doing things together' (Corsaro & Molinari, 1990, p. 221) and having common interests and shared moments. Reciprocity and commitment are elements of friendships that make friendship mutual among children (Hartup, 1992).

The next section presents case study extracts of research conversations with young children about making friends. In Case Study 9.1, Angela and a researcher explore dimensions of friendship, with a particular focus on playing together and sharing intimate moments.

Angela begins with an account of what friends do – that is, friends 'play together'. She then elaborates on 'what sorts of things' friends do and provides examples, suggesting friends 'play with each other', 'hug each other' and 'sit together'. The researcher adds 'chat together', to which Angela agrees. In this way, Angela and the researcher build a collaborative account of the activities that friends do together that highlights reciprocity and sharing some form of intimacy. An aspect of friendship identified by Dunn (2004) Figure 9.1 is Angela's representation of her and her friend sitting together.

CASE STUDY 9.1: WHAT DO FRIENDS DO TOGETHER?

Researcher: When you think about friends, what do you think of?

Angela: They play together.

Researcher: Playing together. That's a good idea. What sorts of things do friends do together?

Angela: They play with each other. They hug each other.

Researcher: They do, don't they? Could you make a drawing about what you think friends do together?

Angela: Mmmm . . . and sit together.

Researcher: They do sit together.

Angela: I'll just draw the sitting one.

Researcher: And I expect they even chat together?

Angela: Yep.

Researcher: Do you do that?

Angela: Yep.

Researcher: And what sorts of things do friends chat about?

Angela: Lots of things.

Researcher: Just any old thing?

Angela: Yep.

Figure 9.1 Friends 'sit together' (Angela, Case Study 9.1).
Source: Thorpe et al. (2006–2008).

In Case Study 9.2, the researcher asks Ophea about the expected behaviours of friends.

Evident in Ophea's account is an emphasis that friends are 'nice' and 'would look after you'. This attention to the caring role of friendships shows the emotional elements that children expect and invest in friends. When asked about her drawing

CASE STUDY 9.2: HOW DO FRIENDS BEHAVE?

Researcher: What sorts of behaviour do friends have with each other?

Ophea: Nice.

Researcher: That's true. Can you think of other things that friends are together?

Ophea: Nice.

Researcher: Yeah, they certainly are nice. What about if you fell over when you were playing puppies?

Ophea: They would look after you.

Researcher: They would, wouldn't they?

Ophea: They would tell the teacher.

Researcher: They would. And if you're a good friend to somebody, you would do the same thing, wouldn't you? Can you think of anything else that friends do?

Ophea: Play together.

(Figure 9.2), Ophea replies that it is about 'puppy games', her favourite game to play with her friends.

In Case Study 9.3, Angela is asked to talk more about how friends 'respect' each other. She identifies a number of characteristics of friendship that provide a more detailed description of friendship.

As Angela explains, friends 'share things' and have similar passions that continue over time. She provides the example of her interests shared with her friend; they 'play, like, a lot of times' and 'both love horses'. When asked further about 'respect', Angela suggests that a friend 'sits next to me when I'm sad', which the researcher names as being 'kind'. These times demonstrate shared activities that they both enjoy, and also the characteristic of friendship that friends have empathic responses and care when they see that their friend needs additional

Figure 9.2 'We always do puppy games' (Ophea, Case Study 9.2).
Source: Thorpe et al. (2006–2008).

CASE STUDY 9.3: HOW DO YOU RESPECT A FRIEND?

Researcher: I was just asking you how you respected your friend, Amy.

Angela: Well I share things with her. We do play, like, a lot of times, more than you could ever imagine and we both love horses.

Researcher: That's great. What do you think Amy does that shows you she respects you?

Angela: Well, she sits next to me when I'm sad.

Researcher: So she's kind as well?

support. Angela's response highlights that being a friend involves seeing each other as equals with an expectation of emotional support. She emphasises key elements of friendship: that friendships are enduring, with shared interests that occur a number times, and are mutual – with friends liking the same things.

In Case Study 9.4, a new aspect of friendship is introduced when Maya suggests that friends 'could help you learn'.

Case Study 9.4 begins as the researcher introduces 'play' as an activity done with friends. When asked about what other activities friends might do, Maya suggests that an attribute of friendship is 'they help you learn'. Maya elaborates that 'they help you do books at school'. Her suggestion that friends help each other in learning tasks is one that is matched by studies that suggest the associated influence of friends on success at school (Ladd, 1990). The researcher summarises Maya's account that friends support each other: 'friends can help you learn, and they can also play with you'. Maya's drawing of the monkey bars and oval where she plays with her friends (Figure 9.3) highlights the importance of sharing place

CASE STUDY 9.4: DO FRIENDS DO OTHER THINGS?

Researcher: They do play. Do they do other things as well, if they're your friends?

Maya: They could help you . . . Sometimes, if they know something, they could help you learn. Sometimes they do some . . . Sometimes they help you do books at school.

Researcher: So, friends can help you learn; and they can also play with you.

Figure 9.3 'The monkey bars that me and Tom use' (Maya, Case Study 9.4).
Source: Thorpe et al. (2006–2008).

Figure 9.4 Friends are 'kind' (Petra, Case Study 9.5).

Source: Thorpe et al. (2006–2008).

(such as playgrounds) and also having time together to participate in these shared activities.

Across many interviews, children provided similar accounts of friendship, and identified similar characteristics of friends. For the children, having friends was associated also with protecting access to play spaces (Cromdal, 2001). Case Study 9.5 shows that friends offer support to participate in peer activities.

As in previous case studies, the children first identify the attribute of being 'kind' and the activity of 'play' as aspects of being a friend. In this Case Study 9.5, Paul provides information about gaining access to peer groups and activities: 'Some kids are very, very nice that they play with me. When they let me play'. His comment about being a member of a peer group suggests the importance of being included and gaining membership in social interaction. Calling upon a friend is one strategy used by young children to access peer groups (Corsaro, 1985; Danby & Baker, 2000; Theobald, et al., in press). David asks Paul a clarifying question, 'Like so

CASE STUDY 9.5: WHAT IS A FRIEND LIKE?

Researcher: How do you know if someone is a friend to you? What is a friend like to you?

Petra: Kind.

Researcher: They're kind, Petra. How else? How do you know if someone is being your friend, David? How do you know if someone is your friend?

David: They play with you.

Researcher: They play with you. What about you, Paul, how do you know if someone is being a friend to you?

Paul: Some kids are very, very nice that they play with me. When they let me play.

David: Like so they don't leave you out?

Paul: Yeah.

Researcher: Friends definitely don't leave you out.

they don't leave you out?' Paul agrees, and the researcher says, 'Friends definitely don't leave you out'. The sense of being included is very strong here – the idea of not being isolated and alone, but of belonging and having membership in a friendship pair or group. The sense of inclusion comes across in the children's drawings as well: Petra skipping with her friends (Figure 9.4) and David playing crocodiles (Figure 9.5).

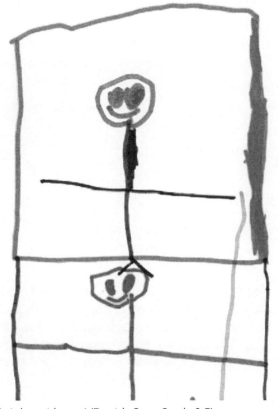

Figure 9.5 Friends 'play with you' (David, Case Study 9.5).
Source: Thorpe et al. (2006–2008).

Making friends in the early years

Children's friendships are built as they play and interact with others. Influencing factors include the location of the activity, the timing of interactions, the involvement of participants and the activity itself. These influences show that friendships are continuously being built and maintained.

Children use a variety of strategies to make friends in the early years. As Danby et al. (2012) show, children use three main strategies: requesting to join in an already occurring game; forming a team or a club with other children who have common interests; and helping others. These strategies require children to understand the intricacies of relationships, and skills such as picking up on other children's displays of emotion and understanding what they mean (Dunn, Cutting & Fisher, 2002). Children may spend time 'surveying the scene', or they may have experiences in a particular setting – such as the playground – before they employ one strategy over another (see Case Study 9.6).

CASE STUDY 9.6: HOW DID YOU MAKE YOUR FRIENDS?

Researcher: What was the best thing about starting school, or what was the worst thing about starting school?

Sally: I went to school and I didn't know it was so fun. And then I knew it was fun and I made lots of new friends.

Researcher: How did you make your friends?

Ben: By asking them.

Sally: When they needed to do something or when they . . .

Researcher: So you helped them when they needed to do something.

Having friends helps children transition into new school contexts more easily (Dunn, Cutting & Fisher, 2002). When the researcher asks Sally and Ben about what was 'the best' or 'the worst' thing about starting school, Sally suggests that she did not think that school could be so much fun and that it was a bit unknown. Sally then explains that her feelings about school changed once she made 'lots of new friends', making her experience of the transition to school enjoyable and positive. When asked how the children make friends, Ben answers that he used the strategy of asking others to be friends. Sally says that she looked out for others needing assistance. The researcher formulates that helping others was a strategy that Sally used to make friends. Sally's drawing (Figure 9.6) illustrates her sad face, representing her initial feelings of sadness before she made a friend at school.

In Case Study 9.7, Tim describes his strategies for making new friends. His drawing shows a number of friends lined up, as he 'asked people if they wanted to play' (Figure 9.7).

Tim outlines a successful strategy for making friends: 'asking others to play'. He explains that he used a technique of asking everyone their names. When Tim was asked about how long it took to become friends, he replies that it took a little while to get to know each other. His insight provides a glimpse into understanding the complexities of children's friendships. For most, friendship does not happen instantaneously, and friendships need time and attention in order to flourish, as shown in Case Study 9.8.

Figure 9.6 Making friends at school (Sally, Case Study 9.6).

Source: Thorpe et al. (2006–2008).

CASE STUDY 9.7: HOW DID YOU MAKE A NEW FRIEND?

Researcher: How did you decide how to make a new friend?

Tim: I asked people if they wanted to play with me and they would.

Researcher: How did you find Cam to be your friend?

Tim: Because I asked everyone their names and they told me.

Researcher: Yeah, and what made you pick Cam to be a special friend? Were you his friend right from the very first day you started here or did it take you a little while to get to know each other?

Tim: It took a little while to get to know each other.

Ryan elaborates on his suggestion that friends do things together. Not only do friends engage in shared activities, they spend 'a lot of the time' together. Ryan provides a historical account of the length of time that he and John played together 'when we were in prep'. He explains that he and John played together even more

Figure 9.7 'I asked people if they wanted to play' (Tim, Case Study 9.7).
Source: Thorpe et al. (2006–2008).

now than when they were in the prep class: 'in prep he did it 15 and now he does it with me 100'. In Ryan's description, friendship clearly requires a quantifiable, sustained and shared interaction. In Case Study 9.3, Angela similarly emphasised the sustained time spent in interaction, saying: 'We do play, like, a lot of times, more than you could ever imagine'. These accounts highlight the time needed to foster friendships, and that 'doing things together' offers opportunities to build a social relationship that endures. When considered within a school context, it means that educators should offer both opportunity and time for children to make friends.

CASE STUDY 9.8: WHAT IS A FRIEND TO YOU?

Researcher: So Ryan, what is a friend to you?

Ryan: John.

Researcher: John is a friend. Why is he a friend?

Ryan: Because he plays with me. A lot of time. I think it's 20.

Researcher: He plays with you a lot of the time. So a friend is someone that spends a lot of time with you?

Ryan: Yeah and he does it when we were in prep he did it 15 and now he does it with me 100.

Researcher: 100? Wow!

Ryan: He still plays with me.

Disputes among friends and within peer groups

Friendship relationships do not always run smoothly. In Case Study 9.9, Angela talks about a rupture in a friendship.

On hearing about the rupture in friendship, the researcher provides alternative ways to view what happened by talking through ideas about friendship and calling into account Angela's identity as a certain sort of friend. By asking, 'So do you think you would still be somebody's friend if it was just an accident?', the researcher suggests that the action was an accident and that the lack of intention would not jeopardise the friendship. In other words, if an accident, such an action might be allowable.

The researcher does not accept Angela's original formulation of what happened, nor provide a lecture on what to think. Rather, questions were asked that sought to explore aspects of Angela's identity-formation to consider the matter from both her perspective and those of others. These kinds of conversations are relevant for

CASE STUDY 9.9: FRIENDSHIP 'BUMPS'

Angela: Yeah. Well my cousin, well she . . . well one of her best friends bumped her and then didn't become her best friend at all.

Researcher: Oh, really?

Angela: Because she bumped her when she was supposed to do some neat colouring in.

Researcher: Oh, I see and so then they stopped being best friends, did they?

Angela: Yeah and then she came friends with other people.

Researcher: Do you think that's fair enough to not be a friend just because somebody bumped you?

Angela: No.

Researcher: No.

Angela: Because you got out of the lines.

Researcher: But do you think that she bumped her purposely or was it an accident, do you reckon?

Angela: It was an accident, I think.

Researcher: So do you think you would still be somebody's friend if it was just an accident?

Angela: Yeah.

classroom interactions, as they provide reflections on what happened and other potential ways to understand the event.

> ## PAUSE AND REFLECT 9.1: CONSIDER YOUR ACTIONS AS EDUCATOR IN THIS SITUATION
>
> Marnee and Rebecca often play together at preschool. One day, Marnee becomes upset when Rebecca plays with Johanna instead of her, and tells you Rebecca is not being her friend. As an educator in this situation, what would you do?

Making friends in multilingual settings

Making and maintaining friends when there are language differences among children may present challenges. Case Study 9.10 shows the perspectives of two children when asked about making friends if they did not share a common language.

Gestures and play objects enabled the children to invite peers (Theobald et.al, in press). Claire suggested making contact by waving at them, drawing on a universal meaning of a greeting able to be translated in any language. Sam's response was to identify playing a game of snakes and ladders, avoiding any confusion that may possibly occur when there is no common language. The game incorporates turn taking and focuses on participation, and might successfully avoid possible misunderstandings to do with talking. At the same time, though, such a game requires shared cultural understandings of games in general, and snakes and ladders in particular.

Multilingual: being able to understand and use two or more languages in oral, manual or written forms at a basic level (International Expert Panel on Multilingual Children's Speech, 2012).

Case Study 9.11 highlights that children choose to talk as a key way of making friends, even in **multilingual** settings.

CASE STUDY 9.10: WHAT IF YOU DIDN'T UNDERSTAND EACH OTHER?

Researcher: What if somebody came to preschool and they didn't understand what you said and you didn't understand what they said. How would you make friends then?

Claire: Wave so they can know what I'm doing.

Researcher: Yes. What would you do instead of talking? [to Sam]

Sam: Play snakes and ladders.

Researcher: You play snakes and ladders? Do a game.

CASE STUDY 9.11: LANGUAGE EXCHANGE

Researcher: What might you do if you couldn't understand what you were saying to each other? How would you make friends?

Owen: You'd say something what they say and they say something what you say.

Researcher: So talk in their language and they might talk in your language. Okay.

When Owen is asked how he would make friends if there were misunderstandings with language between he and another child, he suggests a language exchange. He explains: this is when he would talk in another child's language and they would reciprocate. This example illustrates children's attention to the co-production of a conversation in order to make friends.

Considering the quality of interactions among children and supporting their relationships with others while in school settings provides children with a healthy start to life. This is complex interactional work in which they engage. Play offers children occasions to construct real-life relationships through the pretend frame (Bjork-Willen, 2012). Such occasions give children a chance to work out and re-order the typical power relations of a peer group in ways that might otherwise not be afforded.

PAUSE AND REFLECT 9.2: CONSIDER YOUR ACTIONS AS EDUCATOR IN THIS SITUATION

It is Raj's first day at preschool, a few weeks into the school year. Raj has recently moved to Australia from India. He speaks Tamil and Gujarati (Indian dialects) and is learning to speak English. As an educator, what might you do to help Raj build friendships in the class?

Educators' role in supporting children's friendships

Educators are significant in supporting children's relationships. For example, Theobald and Danby (2012) show how an educator's intervention and enforcement of playground rules initiated a dispute between two children. Similarly, Svahn and Evaldsson's (2012) Swedish study shows that telling the teacher amplified the influence of bullying, with further exclusion of one child by the peer group after she had told the teacher about the bullying. Educators are not neutral participants in children's friendship attempts, as their interventions involve power relations and can have unintended consequences.

Educators are well placed to provide support for children as they attempt to build friendships. Children are often underestimated when making friends or sustaining relationships, as this view does not take into account their thoughtful accounts of what it means to be a friend. The specific role of educators is to understand the value of children's friendships and to support them to make friends through specific modelling and strategies. Encouraging children to 'have a go' and join in games, follow the rules of play and start conversations help them to build relationships in classrooms (Kidsmatter, 2016).

Early years settings are described frequently as 'places for meeting, bonding and bridging', with a focus on 'social connectedness and shared values' (Thorpe et al., 2010, p. 1). Children who are successful in making friends have well developed social skills. Educators can support children to take turns, share feelings and be good listeners (Kidsmatter, 2016).

All children require occasions where they are able to build relationships and make friends. Sometimes, there are occasions when children have trouble making a friend. For example, some children may find it difficult to maintain an extended conversation and to maintain eye contact (Rendle-Short, 2003). In these circumstances, children can make friends with sensitive and careful intervention by adults, helping them to develop skills such as maintaining eye gaze.

Conclusion

Having a friend is important for good health and wellbeing in the early years. Drawing on children's accounts of the characteristics and qualities of friendships, their descriptions implicated moral framings of friendship with associated rights and responsibilities. Three central features of friendship were highlighted in the accounts:

1. Friendships are enduring and involve doing things together, for sustained periods or a repeated number of times.
2. Friendships are mutual – there is affiliation based on shared interactions, similar interests and equal status.
3. Friendships involve feelings and displays of intimacy (such as hugging).

The children's accounts constructed the identity of a friend as someone who offered concern for a friend's wellbeing, help and support, such as easing a friend's entry into a peer group.

Summary

Children in the early years have strong friendships and understand the value of friendship. They display the same qualities of friendships that older children and adults value in terms of making friends and sustaining relationships. The key messages highlighted in this chapter are:

- Even one friend protects children from external influences, and helps them to feel comfortable and that they belong. In addition, having a friend means that children are more likely to experience transition into new school contexts more easily, as well as to do better at school.
- Friendships require time and opportunities for social interaction, shared conversation and finding a common interest.
- Playgrounds are important places for making friends in the school setting. Children need time away from regulated activities in school playgrounds to explore social relationships with others.
- Educators who support children to participate in games and spaces of the peer culture can help build social relationships in classrooms even when language difference occurs.
- Children who are successful in making friends have well developed social skills in turn taking, initiating a conversation, sharing feelings, being a good listener, being fair and playing by the rules of a game.

Questions

9.1 What are the qualities of friendships?

9.2 How can you, as an educator, support children in making friends in your classroom, especially if there are language differences?

9.3 How do you provide for children to spend sustained periods of time in activities that will assist them to make friends?

9.4 What do parents need to know to support their children's friendships?

Acknowledgements

This chapter draws on research from two projects. The first was supported under the Australian Research Council's Discovery Projects funding scheme (grant no. DP0666254). The Office of Education Research at Queensland University of Technology supported the second project. We thank the Australian Twin Registry and Australian Multiple Birth Association, Catholic Education (Queensland), Education Queensland, participating members of Independent Schools (Queensland), the Lady Gowrie Queensland Association and the Crèche and Kindergarten Association of Queensland for assistance in recruiting children to the study. We also thank the participating children, families, schools and teachers who gave their time. Thanks to Cathy Thompson, Maryanne Theobald, Toby Thompson and Sandy Houen, who conducted the child interviews.

References

Australian Institute of Health and Welfare (AIHW) (2012). *A picture of Australia's children*. Retrieved 25 February 2014 from http://www.aihw.gov.au/WorkArea/DownloadAsset.aspx?id=10737423340

Bjork-Willen, P. (2012). *Disputes in everyday life: Social and moral orders of children and young people*. Bingley: Emerald Group.

Buhs, E.S. & Ladd, G.W. (2001). Peer rejection as antecedent of young children's school adjustment: An examination of mediating processes. *Developmental Psychology,* 37(4), 555–60.

Corsaro, W.A. (1985) *Friendship and peer culture in the early years*. Norwood, NJ: Ablex.

—— (2009). Peer culture. In J. Qvortrup, W. A. Corsaro & M-S. Honig (eds), *The Palgrave handbook of childhood studies* (pp. 301–15). Hampshire, UK: Palgrave Macmillan.

Corsaro, W.A. & Molinari, L. (1990). From *seggiolini* to *discussione*: The generation and extension of peer culture among Italian preschool children. *International Journal of Qualitative Studies in Education,* 3(3), 213–30.

Cromdal, J. (2001). Can I be with? Negotiating play entry in a bilingual school. *Journal of Pragmatics,* 33(4), 515–43.

Danby, S. (2008). The importance of friends, the value of friends, friendships within peer cultures. In L. Brooker & M. Woodhead (eds), *Developing positive identities: Diversity and young children* (pp. 36–41). Milton Keynes: Open University Press.

Danby, S. & Baker, C.D. (2000). Unravelling the fabric of social order in block area. In S. Hester & D. Francis (eds), *Local educational order: Ethnomethodological studies of knowledge in action* (pp. 91–140). Amsterdam: John Benjamins.

Danby, S., Ewing, L. & Thorpe, K. (2011) The novice researcher: Interviewing young children. *Qualitative Inquiry,* 17(1), 74–84.

Danby, S. & Farrell, A. (2004) Accounting for young children's competence in educational research: New perspectives on research ethics, *Australian Educational Researcher,* 31(3), 35–50.

Danby, S., Thompson, C., Theobald, M. & Thorpe, K. (2012). Children's strategies for making friends when starting school. *Australasian Journal of Early Childhood,* 37(2), 63–71.

Dunn, J. (2004). *Children's friendships: The beginnings of intimacy.* Malden, MA: Blackwell.

Dunn, J., Cutting, A. & Fisher, N. (2002). Old friends, new friends: Predictors of children's perspective on their friends at school. *Child Development, 73*(4), 621–35.

Hartup, W.W. (1992). Having friends, making friends, and keeping friends: Relationships as educational contexts. *ERIC Digest.* Retrieved 14 April 2014 from http://ericeece.org/pubs/digests/1992/hartup92.html

International Expert Panel on Multilingual Children's Speech (2012). *Multilingual children with speech sound disorders: Position paper.* Bathurst, NSW, Australia: Research Institute for Professional Practice, Learning and Education (RIPPLE), Charles Sturt University.

James, A. (1993). *Childhood identities: Self and social relationships in the experience of the child.* Edinburgh: Edinburgh University Press.

KidsMatter (2016). *Helping children learn positive friendship skills.* Retrieved 24 June 2016 from https://www.kidsmatter.edu.au/families/about-friendship/ making-friends/helping-children-learning-positive-friendship-skills

Kostenius, D. & Ohrling, K. (2008). 'Friendship is like an extra parachute': Reflections on the way schoolchildren share their lived experience of well-being through drawings. *Reflective Practice, 9*(1), 23–35.

Ladd, G.W. (1990). Having friends, keeping friends, making friends, and being liked by peers in the classroom: Predictors of children's early school adjustment? *Child Development, 61*(4), 1081–100.

Laursen, B., Bukowski, W.M., Aunola, K. & Nurmi, J. (2007). Friendship moderates prospective associations between social isolation and adjustment problems in young children. *Child Development, 78*(4), 1395–404.

Rendle-Short, J. (2003). Managing interaction: A conversation analytic approach to the management of interaction by an 8-year-old girl with Asperger's syndrome. *Issues in Applied Linguistics, 13*(2), 161–86.

Svahn, J. & Evaldsson, A-C. (2012). 'You could just ignore me': Situating peer exclusion within the contingencies of girls' everyday interactional practices', *Childhood, 18*(4), 491–508.

Theobald, M., Bateman, A., Busch, G., Laraghy, M. & Danby, S. (in press). 'I'm your best friend': Peer interaction and friendship in a multilingual preschool. In M. Theobald (ed.). *Friendship and peer culture in multilingual settings.* London: Emerald.

Theobald, M. & Danby, S. (2012). A problem of versions: Laying down the law in the school playground. In S. Danby & M. Theobald (eds), *Disputes in everyday life: Social and moral orders of children and young people.* New York: Emerald.

Thorpe, K., Danby, S., Hay, D. & Stewart E. (2006–2008). 'Compromised or competent: A longitudinal study of twin children's social competencies, friendships and behavioural adjustment'. CSIRO. Project ID: DP0666254.

Thorpe, K., Tayler, C.P., Bridgstock, R.S., Grieshaber, S.J., Skoien, P.V., Danby, S.J. et al. (2007). *Preparing for school: Report of the Queensland Preparing for School Trial 2003/04*. Brisbane: School of Early Childhood, Queensland University of Technology.

Thorpe, K., Staton, S., Morgan, R., Danby, S. & Tayler, C. (2010). Testing the vision: Preschool settings as places for meeting, bonding and bridging. *Children and Society*, 26(4), 328–40.

Tomada, G., Scheider, B.H., de Domini, P., Greenman, P.S. & Fonzi, A. (2005). Friendship as a predictor of adjustment following a transition to formal academic instruction and evaluation. *International Journal of Behavioral Development*, 29(4), 413–22.

CHAPTER 10

Food for thought: The role of teachers and parents in children's food choices

Natalie Parletta

Introduction

Since the end of the twentieth century, children have been faced with a rapidly changing world that is having a significant influence on their health and wellbeing, including alterations to our food supply, marketing and other lifestyle factors that influence children's food consumption. The early years are a pivotal period for the establishment of food and nutrition literacy – that is, dietary education, behaviours and preferences – when children are forming their tastes and food preferences, and are most receptive to health messages. Schools and caregivers are ideally placed to assist early years learners to develop positive attitudes towards, and knowledge of, healthy food. This is also of relevance to schools because healthy children are better learners, and evidence suggests that a holistic approach to education that includes health and nutrition has wide-reaching benefits for children and staff.

Furthermore, lifestyle factors – including diet – are critical issues in developed countries that are facing alarming rates of childhood obesity, earlier onset of chronic diseases, and learning and behaviour problems. A good supply of essential nutrients from fresh, minimally processed whole foods, is a major contributor to optimal development of children's growing bodies and brains. Importantly, food preferences and dietary patterns established at this time can track into adolescence and adulthood, having a significant influence on children's physical and psychological health and wellbeing throughout life. The seriousness of the problem of child obesity was recently addressed by a citizens' jury run by researchers at the University of Adelaide (2016), who made 10 major recommendations. Although they acknowledge that the problem is complex and call for multi-level government intervention, their recommendations include school-based nutrition education and health promotion plus nutrition education programs targeted at new parents.

Early childhood educators and carers, teachers and parents can play a key role in influencing children's knowledge about healthy foods and food choices by creating a positive food environment with healthy food options, involving children in gardening and food preparation, role-modelling healthy food choices and contextualising the adoption of healthy eating habits within a warm, encouraging approach to education and child-rearing with clear healthy boundaries – thereby contributing to a healthy start to life for children.

Physical health and wellbeing

The 2007 Australian National Children's Nutrition and Physical Activity Survey (Commonwealth of Australia, 2008) identified that most children are not meeting dietary guidelines for healthy eating, with excessive consumption of non-core foods (high in unhealthy fats, sugar and salt with low nutritional value) and low intakes of essential whole foods such as fruit, vegetables and foods containing **omega-3 fatty acids**. A recent study of 435 Australian children aged 9 to 10 years, from low to high socio-economic backgrounds, suggests that this situation is not improving. For instance, 55 per cent of daily energy intake came from non-core foods and 91 per cent of children were not eating the recommended daily servings of vegetables. Median diet quality scores were only 26 for boys and 25 for girls, out of a maximum of 73 points (Whitrow et al., 2016).

Omega-3 fatty acids are healthy fats for the brain and body that we need to get from our diet: grean leafy vegetables, nuts (e.g. walnuts), seeds (e.g. linseeds), algae and oily fish (e.g. salmon, mackerel, sardines, tuna).

These poor eating patterns, combined with excess sedentary activities and insufficient physical activity, can contribute to greater risk of obesity and associated chronic diseases such as diabetes and heart disease. Previously seen only in adults, these are now starting to appear in children (Lobstein et al., 2004). On average, one in four Australian children is overweight or obese, carrying an increased risk of becoming an overweight or obese adult. Overweight and obesity is also associated with a myriad of psychological consequences, such as low self-esteem, stigma, reduced employment opportunities and poor mental health.

Conversely, eating nutritious whole foods, including fruits, vegetables, nuts, seeds, legumes and fish, is associated with better physical and mental health, and can significantly reduce the risk of developing chronic diseases. Healthy lifestyle is the most ideal and effective approach to preventing chronic disease onset. Established habits are difficult to break and chronic disease is more difficult to address than maintaining good health. Therefore, early childhood is the ideal time to develop healthy lifestyle habits when children are receptive to learning and are developing their attitudes and preferences – and those habits and views developed during the early years are most likely to track through to adolescence and adulthood. Biologically, children's taste buds continue to develop throughout childhood. Although taste buds are wired for sweet, salty foods if these are provided, exposure to healthy, whole foods will influence the development of a child's tastes while reinforcing learned and environmental influences on food preferences, so that the foods to which children are exposed early in life can have a lasting impact on future food choices and eating behaviours.

Healthy children are better learners
Nutrients for brain development and function

Not only do poor eating patterns affect physical health, they also have an impact on children's cognitive and emotional development. The adage that 'you are what you eat' reflects the fact that our brain, as well as our body, comprises essential nutrients that are required for its development and ongoing performance. Studies in malnourished children have established that nutrition and stimulation interact to produce optimal education outcomes. For instance, a sample of children who had been malnourished showed a gap of 10 to 12.5 fewer IQ points at several ages and a 60 per cent rate of attention deficit hyperactivity disorder (ADHD) compared with a 15 per cent rate in healthy matched controls from the same schools (Galler & Barrett, 2001).

A large longitudinal study on the island of Mauritius (Raine et al., 2003), controlling for psycho-social adversity, found that children who had been malnourished at the age of three had a loss of 15.3 IQ points and more anti-social and aggressive behaviour that was mediated by low IQ. These children also had greater incidence of aggression and motor excess at age 17. Notably, this study recruited a sub-sample of three-year-olds to take part in a two-year enrichment program (nutrition, physical activity and education), and compared their development with carefully matched controls. Results indicated improved maturation of the frontal cortex of the brain in the enrichment group, and significantly reduced schizotypal personality and anti-social behaviour 14 to 20 years later. These benefits were greatest for children who had been malnourished, with 23 to 53 per cent lower scores on a range of these adverse psychological outcomes, suggesting that the nutrition component played an important role.

Importantly, sub-clinical deficiencies of micro-nutrients may disrupt cognition and mental health when overt signs of malnourishment are not present, and sub-optimal levels of essential nutrients such as iron, zinc and omega-3s are widespread in children from developed countries like Australia. The brain has particularly high requirements for nutrients from food to develop and function. It accounts for over 50 per cent of the body's glucose requirements for its ongoing function, which in turn relies on nutrients to enable a steady supply of glucose to the brain. In addition, essential nutrients such as zinc, iron, magnesium and omega-3s have a range of interrelated roles in brain function, so inadequate intake of these nutrients can contribute to learning and behaviour problems associated with developmental disorders such as ADHD (Sinn, 2008) and learning difficulties. While it is well known that severe iodine deficiency can result in mental retardation, mild to moderate iodine deficiency is prevalent in developed countries, and has been associated with 6.9 to 10.2 lower IQ points in children under five years of age compared with iodine-replete children (Bougma et al., 2013). A **meta-analysis** across 15 schools reported a significant average increase of 3.2 IQ points following supplementation with vitamins and minerals versus placebo (Schoenthaler & Bier, 1999). The strongest effects were in under-nourished and under-performing children from lower socio-economic backgrounds, who showed an average increase of eight IQ points, and in one study that took blood samples intelligence scores

Meta-analysis: combining a range of different research studies together and running a statistical analysis to test the results of the combined data, which gives more powerful results than one study alone.

increased by 11 IQ points in children whose blood nutrient levels rose (Schoenthaler et al., 1991). Overall, diet quality has been associated with academic achievement. For instance, in a longitudinal population cohort study in the UK, children with a 'junk food' dietary pattern at age three had increased hyperactivity and lower school performance at age eight (Northstone et al., 2012). These children's dietary patterns at age three also predicted their later IQ scores: those with a diet characterised by processed foods high in fat and sugar at age three had a small reduction in IQ scores at eight years of age, while those with a healthy diet characterised by fruit, salad, pasta, rice and fish had a small increase in IQ scores at the age of eight.

Food additives and behaviour

It is now established by well-designed research studies that food additives can have a detrimental effect on children's learning and behaviour, and in some cases be associated with developmental problems like ADHD (Pelsser et al., 2011; McCann et al., 2007; Schab & Trinh, 2014). Even in children without a clinically diagnosed problem, food additives can contribute to mood swings, inattentiveness, hyperactivity, headaches and digestive problems. Although clearly there are multiple contributors to learning and behaviour problems, in some children the effect of food intolerances can be clearly noticeable, and the effect size in randomised controlled trials is clinically meaningful for children with ADHD (Pelsser et al., 2011). Even in children from a general population, food colourings and preservatives in amounts that children consume on average each day in the UK were shown to increase hyperactivity compared to placebo, which impacts on learning ability (McCann et al., 2007).

Former teacher and food additive expert Sue Dengate (2014) provides a useful website on food intolerance for parents and teachers, which presents information about food additives and their effects, links to scientific research, case studies and dietary guidance for parents and caregivers. The website is http://www. fedup.com.au.

CASE STUDY 10.1: FOOD INTOLERANCE AND BEHAVIOUR

Here is one example of a common case study reported on Sue Dengate's 'Fed Up' website (reprinted verbatim, with permission):

'I would like to say a very big thank you for helping change not only my son's life dramatically but in turn the whole family.

Last year I put my eight-year-old boy onto your elimination diet. Before the diet my son was in trouble at school every day, he was argumentative, angry, hyperactive, and overall his behaviour was negative and every day was a huge struggle. After discovering that he reacts severely to preservatives, colours, salicylates and amines, his overall wellbeing has completely changed.

Not only is the household a much . . . calmer place now, also so is his class room. He would [have] been considered to be one of the naughtiest children in the class but now he is achieving amazing results at school. He competed in the National Maths Competition and got a distinction (finished in the top 11 per cent in all of Australia), he also achieved very highly in the NAPLAN and has amazed his music teacher by performing songs that are way above his year level.

Not only is he a much happier boy, so are his siblings and both my husband and I. Not only has this diet given him a much better chance for a successful future, he is living testimony that this diet is truly life changing.' (Paula)

Cognition and behaviour: Breakfast and learning

As well as an ongoing need for essential nutrients for healthy brain function, the nature and timing of meals – particularly breakfast – can have a short-term effect on cognitive performance. Children and adults perform cognitively better if they eat breakfast. Children's brains have higher **metabolic activity** than adults. Combined with lower muscle mass, this results in both greater requirements for energy and a greater need for an ongoing energy supply. This increases children's need for an adequate breakfast to assist their cognitive performance during the day. A meta-analysis of studies that investigated the influence of breakfast on cognitive performance found that having breakfast resulted in better outcomes compared with not having breakfast, although this effect was more apparent in children whose nutritional status was below par (Hoyland, Dye & Lawton, 2009).

A subsequent UK study reported that a nutrient-rich breakfast with a low-**glycemic index (GI)** – muesli, milk and fruit – was superior to a nutrient-poor, high-GI breakfast (cornflakes, milk and white bread) or no breakfast (Cooper et al., 2012). It makes sense that, in addition to benefits provided by the variety of nutrients in the low-GI breakfast used in the latter study, the fibre provided by a low-GI breakfast will enable the slow release of glucose into the bloodstream and thereby support sustained cognitive performance levels throughout the day.

> **Metabolic activity:** all of the chemical reactions that take part in the body and brain that enable their functions and keep us alive.

> **Glycemic index (GI):** a ranking of carbohydrates in foods according to how they affect our blood glucose levels – lower GI (e.g. high fibre) foods raise blood sugar levels more slowly than high GI foods (e.g. refined carbohydrates like sugar and white bread).

> ### SPOTLIGHT 10.1: NUTRITION/DIET AND CHILDREN'S HEALTH AND WELLBEING – OVERVIEW OF MAIN POINTS
>
> - The early years are an optimal time to develop children's nutrition literacy and food preferences.
> - Obesity and other diet-related chronic diseases are a significant problem for children in developed countries like Australia.
> - Essential nutrients from a whole-food diet are important contributors to children's brain development, learning and behaviour.
> - A healthy breakfast will assist children's cognitive performance and learning throughout the day.
> - Additives in processed foods can contribute to learning and behaviour problems even in healthy children, and should be avoided.

Why should education settings be involved in children's nutrition literacy?

Next to the family, school has the biggest influence on children's lives. Therefore, in an environment of increased accessibility and aggressive marketing of highly processed, non-nutritious foods, schools can help to arm children with the knowledge and ability to make healthy food choices. Furthermore, schools can have a particularly important and consistent influence on children whose families who have limited time, knowledge and/or resources for providing and promoting healthy food in the family home. Schools can also benefit directly from healthy children in a number of ways, including improved attendance due to less absenteeism, more alert learners and better behaved students.

Accordingly, the World Health Organization (WHO) has played a key role in the global Health-Promoting Schools initiative (see WHO 2014), including nutrition as an essential element with the argument that 'health, education and nutrition support and enhance each other' (WHO 1998, Foreword). The alignment of health and education in the school setting is highlighted as a continuing issue by Valois, Slade and Ashford (2011), quoting the following landmark statement from *Health is Academic*:

> *Today's education climate in education is in a state of flux. Public debate centres on how schools can do what they do even better – despite shrinking budgets and new challenges. But as the authors of this volume assert, educational reforms will be effective only if students' health and well-being are identified as contributors to academic success and are at the heart of decision and policy making. Schools, in concert with students, their families, and communities, must consider how well schools are accomplishing their missions and how they can best help students realise their full potential* (Marx, Wooley & Northrop, 1998, p. 293).

Although the Healthy School Communities initiative that produced the report (Valois et al., 2011) is American, the same issues apply in Australian schools that face similar challenges, such as low budgets, competing demands on curriculum content and arguments that the main function of schools is to educate children academically (Setter, Kouris-Blazos & Wahlqvist, 2000).

The report includes a summary of research on schools that have included a focus on children's health and wellbeing as an integral part of the school's curriculum – they report higher levels of academic achievement; higher staff satisfaction and lower staff turnover; greater efficiency; a positive school climate; and a school-community culture that enhances student growth (Valois et al., 2011). Therefore, not only are schools and early caregivers ideally placed to have a significant influence on the development of children's nutrition knowledge, food preferences and attitudes; they also benefit from a school-wide approach to healthy food and nutrition.

Healthy food projects in Australian schools

Setter et al. (2000) conducted a review of Australian health-promoting school programs and made some recommendations such as: one-off talks by health professionals are ineffective; a central statewide database would be useful for teachers to access key information that can be used to develop a program; nutrition programs need to be implemented at every year level, starting from kindergarten (prep); programs that include health and nutrition in both the curriculum and the school canteen are most effective; integrating concepts about health and nutrition in a wide range of classes (e.g. using nutrition concepts as a basis for teaching interactive computer skills, English assignments), may be just as effective as delivering it in specialised nutrition classes; regular in-house nutrition training and education for teachers is needed; and home economics should be brought back to help children learn basic cooking skills.

Further to this, Drummond (Drummond & Sheppard, 2011) ran focus groups with teachers, parents, principals, canteen managers and students in South Australia to investigate the role of school canteens within the school system. She identified common obstacles to healthy school canteens that included a lack of volunteers to help prepare food, a lack of nutrition awareness, a perception of needing to profit from canteen sales, and a lack of school support. This research highlighted the importance of engaging the wider community in nutrition messages, volunteer support in school activities and the school canteen, encouraging older students to be positive role models or 'champions', and support at all levels for including healthy canteen food within a school-wide priority placed on health and nutrition.

An international workshop to examine the evidence base regarding school food and nutrition inspired a number of papers that were put together for a special issue of the journal *Public Health Nutrition* (Mikkelsen & Ohri-Vachaspati, 2013). One of these papers (Moore et al. 2013) used case studies from schools in the UK and Australia to highlight the importance of adopting a multi-level socio-ecological framework for implementation of effective school food policies and interventions.

All indications support the notion that nutrition messages need to be consistent to be effective as part of a whole school approach – for example, the food available in school canteens needs to reflect messages on health and nutrition that are taught in the school curriculum. Drummond (2010) notes that children's eagerness to consume healthy food following a two-week education program needs to be supported with food availability at home to be sustained. Indeed, there is evidence that children can be agents of change – for example, by requesting healthy food at home that they had grown, cooked, eaten and/or learned about at school.

A whole-of-school approach to nutrition literacy will include teaching of food and nutrition skills alongside examples of healthy eating via food availability in the school canteen as well as events – such as sports days and funding activities – that complement a school-wide focus on healthy lifestyles. A comprehensive approach to assisting children to choose a healthy diet, both at home and at child care or school, will include healthy food and snacks, teacher role-modelling and development of skills in food growing, handling, preparation, cooking and consumer literacy – that is, how to shop for healthy food, and how to understand food marketing and nutrition labels. Some schools have successfully implemented regular activities such as 'fruit' days, which encourage children to bring fruit from home to cut up and share. School-based nutrition programs also need to be consistent with environmentally sustainable and financially viable food systems. These are complementary – for instance, a school can promote home-prepared food in brown paper bags or reusable containers as part of a focus on environmental awareness, which will also be consistent with encouraging whole food rather than packaged, processed food.

The Australian government has published a resource kit for 'Healthy and active school communities' that includes examples of schools which have implemented healthy eating and/or physical activity, what they did and what

Figure 10.1 Girls gardening.

Source: Getty Images/Hero Images.

SPOTLIGHT 10.2: WAYS IN WHICH SCHOOLS CAN PROMOTE FOOD AND NUTRITION LITERACY TO EARLY YEARS LEARNERS

- Recognise schools as important leaders in the promotion of food and nutrition literacy and in developing healthy learners.
- Integrate healthy food and nutrition literacy throughout the school curriculum and at all year levels.
- Provide regular in-house nutrition training and education for teachers and canteen staff.
- Be congruent in food and nutrition literacy promotion throughout the school.
- Provide healthy food in the school canteen – recruit volunteers; involve children in food choice and promotion.
- Provide healthy food on school sports days, and at fundraising activities and other events.
- Grow a school vegetable garden and involve children in growing the vegetables.
- Involve children in food preparation, handling, cooking and eating healthy food.
- Integrate healthy food messages with environmental awareness.
- Incorporate healthy food messages into newsletters for parents.
- Promote partnerships with parents and the local community to support food and nutrition literacy, healthy food and vegetable gardens at the school.

Figure 10.2 Students cooking.

Source: Getty Images/Niedring/Drentwett.

worked (see Department of Health and Ageing, 2004). An excellent model has been developed in Berkeley, California, where they provide five days of onsite training for educators around the world each year (http://edibleschoolyard.org/).

How parents and caregivers can encourage healthy diets

Food environment: factors in the home, school and society that influence food consumption (e.g. food availability, child feeding strategies, mealtime structure, television viewing, cost of food, school canteens, food advertising).

The **food environment** provided by families and carers – particularly in the first five years – can have a lasting influence on young children's taste preferences, food knowledge and choices. The division of responsibility (Satter, 2007) model, or 'parents provide, child decides', states that parents are responsible for what food they provide, where and when, while children are responsible for whether and what they choose to eat. Role modelling of healthy food choices and attitudes can have a powerful influence, as can involving children in gardening, shopping, cooking healthy food and preparing healthy snacks – and making it fun. Having dinner as a family, with one meal for all, and ensuring it is a positive experience can create positive associations with healthy foods. Food aversion can easily develop after even one unpleasant experience.

It is advisable to avoid power struggles around food, and never force children to eat anything or bribe them with dessert – these tactics do not work in the long term. Pressuring children to eat has been shown to be counterproductive, resulting in lower food intake and greater negative associations with food (Galloway et al., 2006). Children will eat when they are hungry and if they are bribed with dessert they will perceive that to be the desired food rather than the vegetable that we are trying to get them to eat. Similarly, if children are exposed to highly processed foods and given 'anything' just to make sure they eat, or to entertain or soothe them, they will develop preferences for the unhealthy options and become 'fussy eaters'. Furthermore, if they are forced to eat or finish the food on their plate when they do not want to eat or have had enough, they will lose their innate ability to respond to internal satiety cues. Young children naturally tend to develop neophobia – that is, fear of unknown food– at around the age of two. Continued positive exposure to healthy foods, rather than pandering to fussiness, will help to mitigate this, and their willingness to try novel foods will naturally increase over time. These and other family environment/parental influences are reviewed by Scaglioni, Salvioni and Galimberti (2008). It is important for well-meaning parents to be aware of keeping it fun and positive. Drawing from many years of working with families, author and nutrition expert Jill Castle warns against too much nutrition talk at the table. She advises to let this be guided by children, and avoid nutrition messages that can be interpreted in a way that influences children's self-esteem (e.g. I am bad if I eat unhealthy food).

Other effective strategies include limiting exposure to commercial television and food advertising targeted at children. When badgered for unhealthy food in the supermarket, say 'no' and mean 'no'; a consistent, loving and encouraging but firm **authoritative parenting style** will effectively get the message across, and children will give up if you stand your ground. Offer healthy alternatives. A body of research has identified that restrictive feeding practices are not associated with healthy food choices. Conversely, permissive parenting practices (translated to allowing children to eat whatever they want) is also not effective. What is most effective is to give children *choices between healthy options* – that is, have healthy food and drinks available and simply keep the non-nutritious snack foods/cereals/desserts out of the environment. These are alright as 'sometimes' foods. Children can be encouraged to bake cookies, cakes, and muffins as well as helping out with other meals. The important point is to not make a big deal out of these by demonising them or alternatively making them into 'treats'. As indicated above, the foods to which young children are exposed, and which are familiar to them, can have a powerful influence on what they will accept and willingly eat. Researchers have shown that exposing children to a previously disliked vegetable for 14 consecutive days resulted in greater liking and likelihood of eating that vegetable compared with children in control groups. They investigated this further, and showed that toddlers who were visually exposed to vegetables via storybooks and then exposed to vegetable tastings were even more likely to like and eat them (Heath, Houston-Price & Kennedy, 2011).

The Commonwealth Scientific and Industrial Research Organisation (CSIRO) has put out an excellent resource for parents that includes practical ideas and recipes, *The CSIRO Wellbeing Plan for Kids* (see CSIRO, 2009).

Authoritative parenting style: a parenting style with high demandingness and high responsiveness which involves setting firm, clear boundaries with love and warmth. This parenting style is associated with healthier psychological outcomes and healthier behaviours.

Figure 10.3 Mother and son cooking together.

Source: Getty Images/Tetra Images.

SPOTLIGHT 10.3: WAYS IN WHICH PARENTS AND CAREGIVERS CAN PROMOTE HEALTHY FOOD PREFERENCES TO EARLY YEARS LEARNERS

- Provide healthy options: parents provide, child decides.
- Act as role models in healthy food choices and attitudes towards food.
- Provide children with consistently healthy food options in their environment.
- Eat family meals together (with no short-order cooking) and create a positive food environment.
- Limit exposure to commercial television.
- Maximise exposure to positive messages about, and associations with, healthy food.
- Never force children to eat, or to finish the food on their plate.
- Never bribe children to eat vegetables or other healthy foods.
- Do not use processed sweet, salty or high-fat foods as treats or rewards.
- Provide regular access to water and keep sugary drinks out of the house/environment.
- Do not cater for fussiness.
- Provide repeated positive exposure to healthy, whole foods.
- Involve children in growing vegetables, shopping and cooking.
- Talk to children about healthy food and help them to develop a critical awareness of non-nutritious food advertising and promotion.

Figure 10.4 Family eating together.

Source: Getty Images/Ariel Skelley.

Conclusion

It can be seen from other chapters in this book that there are multiple influences on the health and wellbeing of early years learners. As part of a holistic approach to health and wellbeing, food and nutrition literacy is a fundamental requirement for growing children. Consumption of and preference for healthy, whole foods helps to form a foundation for physical and mental health and wellbeing in childhood and throughout life and, along with healthy levels of physical activity, can assist children to develop resilience in dealing with challenges and benefit from opportunities provided to them.

In light of the availability and marketing of highly processed foods aimed at children, it is vital for parents, caregivers and schools to play a key role in helping children form healthy attitudes towards, knowledge of and preferences for, healthy food.

Summary

The key messages highlighted in this chapter are:

- Currently the majority of Australian children are consuming excess processed foods that are high in unhealthy fats, sugar and salt, and not enough whole foods such as fruit, vegetables, nuts, seeds, legumes, wholegrains and fish that provide essential nutrients for optimal growth and development.
- Provision of healthy food and development of healthy food preferences are significant contributors to children's physical and mental health, learning and behaviour.
- Schools can both provide and benefit from integration of nutrition and food literacy throughout the school curriculum, supported by healthy food availability in school canteens and special events in a whole-of-school approach.
- Parents and caregivers are important role models, and can help children to develop healthy food preferences and attitudes by creating a positive, healthy food environment, noting the division of responsibility in child feeding, involving children in gardening, shopping and cooking, eating meals as a family and providing healthy options.

Questions

10.1   What does food and nutrition literacy for children involve?

10.2   Why is food and nutrition literacy important? Provide at least four reasons.

10.3   What can parents and caregivers do to promote the development of healthy food preferences in children?

10.4   What can schools do to promote food and nutrition literacy for children?

References

Bougma, K, Aboud, F.E., Harding, K.B. & Marquis, G.S. (2013). Iodine and mental development of children 5 years old and under: A systematic review and meta-analysis. *Nutrients,* 5(4), 1384–1416.

Commonwealth of Australia (2008). *2007 Australian National Children's Nutritional and Physical Activity Survey.* Barton, ACT.

Commonwealth Scientific and Industrial Research Organisation (CSIRO) (2009). *The CSIRO wellbeing plan for kids.* Ringwood: Penguin. Retrieved 14 April 2014 from http://www.publish.csiro.au/pid/6175.htm

Cooper, S.B., Bandelow, S., Nute., M.L., Morris, J.G. & Nevill, M.E. (2012). Breakfast glycemic index and cognitive function in adolescent school children. *British Journal of Nutrition,* 107, 1823–32.

Dengate, S. (2014). Food Intolerance Network website. Retrieved 16 April 2016 from http://www.fedup.com.au

Department of Health and Ageing (2004). *Healthy and active school communities: A resource kit for schools.* Retrieved 16 April 2014 from http://www.healthyactive.gov.au/internet/healthyactive/publishing.nsf/Content/schoolcommu_resourcekit.pdf/$File/schoolcommu_resourcekit.pdf

Drummond, C.E. (2010). Using nutrition education and cooking classes in primary schools to encourage healthy eating. *Journal of Student Wellbeing*, 4(2), 43–54.

Drummond, C. & Sheppard, L. (2011). Examining primary and secondary school canteens and their place within the school system: A South Australian study. *Health Education Research*, 26(4), 739–49.

Galler, J.R. & Barrett, R.L. (2001). Children and famine: Long-term impact on development. *Ambulatory Child Health*, 7, 85–95.

Galloway, A.T., Fiorito, L.M., Francis, L.A. & Birch, L.L. (2006). 'Finish your soup': Counterproductive effects of pressuring children to eat on intake and affect. *Appetitie*, 46, 318–323.

Heath, P., Houston-Price, C. & Kennedy, O.B. (2011). Increasing food familiarity without the tears. A role for visual exposure? *Appetite*, 57, 832–8.

Hoyland, A., Dye, L. & Lawton, C.L. (2009). A systematic review of the effect of breakfast on the cognitive performance of children and adolescents. *Nutrition Research Reviews*, 22, 220–43.

Lobstein, T., Baur, L., Uauy, R. & IASO International Obesity TaskForce (2004). Obesity in children and young people: A crisis in public health. *Obesity Reviews*, 5 (Sup. 1), 4–104.

Marx, E. & Wooley, S.F. with Northrop, D. (1998) *Health is academic: A guide to coordinated school health programs.* New York: Teachers College Press.

McCann, D. et al. (2007). Food additives and hyperactive behaviour in 3-year-old and 8/9-year-old children in the community: A randomised, double-blinded, placebo-controlled trial. *Lancet*, 370, 1560–67.

Mikkelsen, B.E. & Ohri-Vachaspati, P. (2013). Editorials: Hunger, overconsumption and youth: future directions for research in school-based public health nutrition strategies. *Public Health Nutrition*, 16(6), 953–7.

Moore, G., Murphy, S., Chaplina, K., Lyons, R.A., Atkinson, M. & Moore, L. (2013). Impacts of the primary school free breakfast initiative on socio-economic inequalities in breakfast consumption among 9–11-year-old schoolchildren in Wales, *Public Health Nutrition*, 16(6), np.

Northstone, K., Joinson, C., Emmett, P., Ness, A. & Paus, T. (2012). Are dietary patterns in childhood associated with IQ at 8 years of age? A population-based cohort study. *Journal of Epidemiology and Community Health*, 66(7), 624–8.

Pelsser, L.M., Frankena, K.,Toorman, J.,Savelkoul, H.F., Dubois, A.E.,Pereira, R.R. et al. (2011). Effects of a restricted elimination diet on the behaviour of children with attention-deficit hyperactivity disorder (INCA study): A randomised controlled trial. *Lancet*, 377, 494–503.

Raine, A., Mellingen, K., Liu, J., Venables, P.H. & Mednick, S.A. (2003). Effects of environmental enrichment at ages 3–5 years on schizotypal personality and antisocial behavior at ages 17 and 23 years. *American Journal of Psychiatry,* 160, 1627–35.

Satter, E. (2007). The Satter Feeding Dynamics Model of child overweight definition, prevention and intervention. In W. O'Donahue, B.A. Moore & B. Scott (eds), *Pediatric and Adolescent Obesity Treatment: A Comprehensive Handbook* (pp. 287–314). New York: Taylor and Frances.

Scaglioni, S., Salvioni, M. & Galimberti, C. (2008). Influence of parental attitudes in the development of children's eating behaviour. *British Journal of Nutrition,* 99 (Sup. 1), S22–25.

Schab, D.W. & Trinh, N.T. (2014) Do artificial food colors promote hyperactivity in children with hyperactive syndrome: A meta-analysis of double-blind placebo-controlled trials. *Developmental and Behavioral Pediatrics,* 25, 423–34.

Schoenthaler, S.J., Amos, S.P., Eysenck, H.J., Peritz, E. & Yudkin, J. (1991). Controlled trial of vitamin-mineral supplementation: Effects on intelligence and performance. *Personality and Individual Differences,* 12(4), 351–62.

Schoenthaler, S.J. & Bier, I.D. (1999). Vitamin-mineral intake and intelligence: A macrolevel analysis of randomised controlled trials. *Journal of Alternative and Complementary Medicine,* 5(2), 125–34.

Setter, T., Kouris-Blazos, A. & Wahlqvist, M. (2000). *School-based healthy eating initiatives: Recommendations for success.* Melbourne: Monash Asia Institute.

Sinn, N. (2008). Nutritional and dietary influences on Attention Deficit Hyperactivity Disorder. *Nutrition Reviews,* 66(10), 558–68.

University of Adelaide (2016, May 23). 'Citizens' jury wants government action on child obesity' media release, https://www.adelaide.edu.au/news/news85042. html#.V1TTYr37LFo.twitter

Valois, R.F., Slade, S. & Ashford, E. (2011). *The healthy school communities model: Aligning health and education in the school setting – healthy school communities.* Alexandria, VA: ASCD. http://www.ascd.org/ASCD/pdf/siteASCD/publications/Aligning-Health-Education.pdf

Whitrow, M.J., Moran, L., Davies, M.J., Collins, C.E., Burrows, T.L., Edwards, S., et al. (2016). Core food intakes of Australian children aged 9–10 years: daily servings and diet quality in a community cross-sectional sample. *Journal of Human Nutrition & Dietetics,* doi:10.1111/jhn.12358

World Health Organization (WHO) (1998). *Healthy nutrition: An essential element of a health-promoting school,* WHO Information Series on School Health, Geneva: WHO. Retrieved 14 April 2014 from http://www.who.int/school_youth_health/media/en/428.pdf

—— (2014). What is a health-promoting school? Retrieved 15 April 2016 from http://www.who.int/school_youth_health/gshi/hps/en

CHAPTER 11

Body image of pre-adolescents

Galina Daraganova

Introduction

There is a growing amount of evidence that body image dissatisfaction is an issue of increasing concern and is associated with a number of damaging consequences for health and wellbeing (Cook, MacPherson & Langille, 2007; Croll, 2005; Liechty, 2010). This issue can affect anyone regardless of age, gender, ethnicity, body size and shape (UK Parliamentary Report, 2012). Historically, the onset of body image concerns was attributed to adolescence as this is the period when puberty begins and the most dramatic body changes are experienced (Cash, 2002b). However, a 'thin' ideal is already present among children in primary school years, and children as young as seven years old report dissatisfaction with their bodies (Dohnt & Tiggemann, 2006; Levine & Piran, 2004; Liechty, 2010).

This chapter uses a nationally representative sample of Australian children to demonstrate the importance of understanding the desired and perceived body images of 8- to 11-year-olds and the discrepancy between these images, as well as to highlight the extent to which physical health and socio-emotional wellbeing of children is already associated with body image dissatisfaction at ages 10–11 years.

Rationale: Impact of body image on health

Body image can be understood as the way children think and feel about their body. Negative self-evaluation of body shape may affect children's feelings and thoughts, and lead them to modify their behaviour and develop physical and psychological problems (Cash, 2002b). Studies have shown that children who are dissatisfied with their body size are more likely to follow unhealthy diets (Cash, 2002a; Stice et al., 1998), use anabolic steroids (mainly among boys) (Cohane & Pope, 2001), and have excessive levels of physical activity (Neumark-Sztainer et al., 2006). Dieting and excessive exercise in turn can lead to other health problems, such as fatigue and gastrointestinal problems, as well as joint or bone injuries (Neumark-Sztainer et al., 2006). Body dissatisfaction has also been found to be associated with a variety of risky behaviours, including early sexual activity, self-harm, and suicide planning (Cook, MacPherson & Langille, 2007). Dissatisfaction with one's own body not only affects physical health and behaviours but also may cause psychological distress. Children who report concerns with their body size are likely to report lower levels of global self-worth and poorer self-esteem (Tiggemann, 2005). Low self-esteem in turn might lead to limited engagement in everyday life and the development of social anxiety and depression (Stice et al., 2000; Stice & Shaw, 2002; Tiggemann, 2005). While the relationship between body image dissatisfaction and negative physical and psychological effects are evident in adolescents, the question of interest is whether the onset of this relationship emerges much earlier than adolescence. If children in middle primary years do experience socio-emotional problems (such as low self-esteem or negative mood) that are associated with dissatisfaction with their body, then prevention programs should take place earlier rather than later (Irving, 2000; McCabe, Ricciardelli & Salmon, 2006; Stice & Shaw, 2004).

Children in focus: Longitudinal Study of Australian Children

This chapter uses data from K cohort children from the Longitudinal Study of Australian Children (LSAC)[1] when they were aged 8–9 and 10–11 years. There were 2212 boys and 2119 girls of age 8–9 years and 2075 boys and 1975 girls of age 10–11 years. All analyses presented below were conducted separately for boys and girls. Some measures were collected only for 10- to 11-year-old children; that is, the analyses of the relationship between physical and psychological wellbeing and body image dissatisfaction exclude children at 8–9 years old.

Research in focus: Body image

Body image can be measured using different tools: pictorial scales (e.g. Collins, 1991; Truby & Paxton, 2002) and/or attitudinal scales (e.g. Multidimensional Body-Self Relations Questionnaire [Brown, Cash & Mikulka, 1990]). The choice of instrument usually depends on population (e.g. cross-cultural, race/ethnic related), age group, and dimension of body image (e.g. body size/shape, global body image, specific body parts, appearance, fitness, health, disordered eating, figure ratings).

---

1   LSAC is a nationally representative study of Australian children born in 2004 (B cohort) and in 2000 (K cohort).

Perceived and desired

In this study body image was measured using the Pictorial Body Image Instrument (Collins, 1991). This is a well-established method for assessing body image dissatisfaction. Boys and girls were presented with a set of seven drawings of children (matched to the respondent's gender), ranging in size from very thin to obese, and numbered from one (very thin) to seven (obese). Collins (1991) did not assign the pictures either to a body mass index range or classify them according to body mass status. For the purpose of this analysis, Picture 4 was chosen as the reference and other pictures were classified relative to Picture 4: Picture 1 or 2 = very thin; Picture 3 = thin; Picture 4 = average; Picture 5 = large; and Picture 6 or 7 = very large (see Figure 11.1).

SPOTLIGHT 11.1: THE CHILDREN'S PICTORIAL BODY IMAGE SCALE, BY GENDER

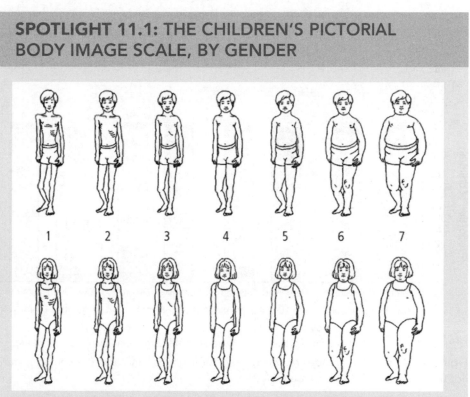

Figure 11.1 The children's pictorial body image scale, by gender.

Source: Collins (1991).

Proposed categorisation:

- Picture 1, 2 or 3 = very thin
- Picture 3 = thin
- Picture 4 = average
- Picture 5 = large
- Picture 6 or 7 = very large

Perceived body image is a child's perception of his/her own body size.

Desired body image is a child's perception of the ideal body size.

During the LSAC interview, every child was asked two questions about their body size. First, the child was asked to choose the picture that looked most like him/her. This picture was identified as the **perceived body image**. The perceived body image was derived for 2171 boys and 2075 girls aged 8–9 years and 2032 boys and 1937 girls aged 10–11 years. Then, the child was asked to choose the picture that showed the way he/she wanted to be. This picture was identified as the **desired body image**. The desired body image was derived for 2169 boys and 2073 girls aged 8–9 years and 2035 boys and 1938 girls aged 10–11 years.

At eight to nine years of age, almost half of the boys (46 per cent) reported being average, around 40 per cent reported being thinner than average (28 per cent, thin and 10 per cent, very thin), and the rest perceived themselves as being larger (14 per cent large and 2 per cent very large) (see Figure 11.2). As boys grew up, a similar proportion of them perceived themselves as average size, whereas a smaller number of boys reported being thinner than average (29 per cent thin and 5 per cent very thin) and a greater proportion reported being larger than average (24 per cent). A similar pattern was observed for girls, though the proportions varied slightly.

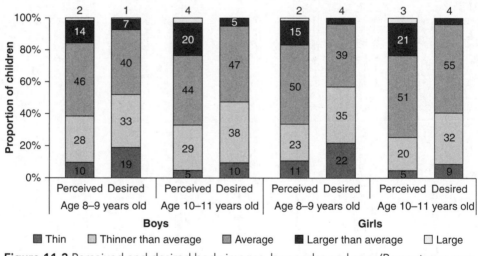

Figure 11.2 Perceived and desired body images, by gender and age. (Percentages may not total exactly 100% due to rounding.)

Source: LSAC, Kinder Cohort, boys and girls, age 8–11 years old, Commonwealth of Australia, CC BY 4.0.

At age eight to nine years, less than half of the children wanted to be average size, whereas the majority wanted to be thinner than average with 19 per cent of boys and 22 per cent of girls wanting to be very thin. A very small proportion wanted to be larger than average: 7 per cent of boys and 4 per cent of girls. Note, that no one wanted to be very large. As the children were growing up, a large proportion of them still wanted to be thinner than average (48 per cent of boys and 41 per cent of girls), though a healthy tendency was evident. The proportion of children who wanted to be very thin decreased substantially: one in ten children wanted to be very thin at age 10–11 years compared to two in ten children at 8–9 years of age. Also, the proportion of children who wanted to be average increased with age, from 40 per cent to 47 per cent in boys and from 39 per cent to 55 per cent in girls.

Body image dissatisfaction

The discrepancy between the perceived and the desired body images was used to measure the degree of **body image dissatisfaction**. A positive score suggested that the child wanted to be thinner, a negative score suggested that the child wanted to be larger and a score of zero suggested that the child was satisfied with their size (their current self-perception matched their desired body shape). For the body

> **Body image dissatisfaction** is the discrepancy between perceived and desired body image.

image dissatisfaction measure, the absolute discrepancy was also calculated to remove the direction of dissatisfaction. Some studies suggest that pictorial images are insufficient on their own for measuring body image dissatisfaction, as a discrepancy between perceived and desired body image may not actually indicate dissatisfaction with body (Vander Wal & Thelen, 2000). While it is important to collect attitudinal information on body image dissatisfaction rather than only relying on any discrepancy between perceived and desired body images, here we only focus on one aspect of body dissatisfaction – dissatisfaction with body size. Dissatisfaction with facial features, skin colour and physical attractiveness are not addressed.

At age eight to nine years, a majority of the children were dissatisfied with their body image (see Figure 11.3). Four in ten eight- to nine-year-old boys (40 per cent) wanted to be thinner and around two in ten boys (17 per cent) wanted to be larger than they perceived themselves. Slightly different proportions were observed for girls: 45 per cent of eight- to nine-year-old girls wanted to be thinner and only

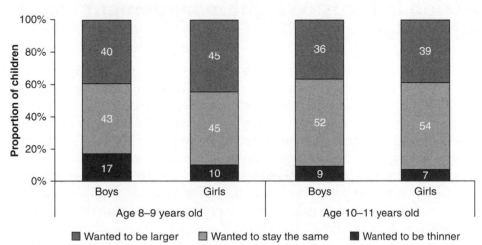

Wanted to be larger   Wanted to stay the same   Wanted to be thinner

Figure 11.3 Body image dissatisfaction, by gender and age. (Percentages may not total exactly 100% due to rounding.)

Source: LSAC, Kinder Cohort, boys and girls, age 8–11 years old, Commonwealth of Australia, CC BY 4.0.

10 per cent wanted to be larger than they thought they were. As the children were growing up, the proportion who were satisfied with their body increased in both boys and girls, though the proportion of those who were dissatisfied was still high. Overall, at 10–11 years of age, just over 50 per cent of children were satisfied with their body, around 40 per cent wanted to be thinner, and around 10 per cent wanted to be larger, regardless of gender.

PAUSE AND REFLECT 11.1: WHAT CAN EDUCATORS LEARN FROM PERCEIVED AND DESIRED BODY IMAGES OF 8- TO 11-YEAR-OLDS?

- A 'thin' ideal is evident from an early age.
- A positive trend is evident as children grow older: fewer want to be very thin and more want to be average size.
- About 50 per cent of children are dissatisfied with their body size, with proportions being slightly smaller among 10 to 11 year olds than 8–9 year olds.
- No gender differences are found.

Reflection questions:

- When should educators introduce discussions about body image with children?
- How can a positive body image be promoted and boosted in classrooms?
- How important is it to identify children at risk of body image dissatisfaction?

Action in focus: Weight management strategies

Weight management strategies are actions taken to control one's own weight.

It is of great importance to understand whether children of pre-adolescent age already engage in **weight management strategies** and whether there is a relationship between body image dissatisfaction and these behaviours (McCabe & Ricciardelli, 2005). To examine whether those who were dissatisfied with their body were more likely to engage in weight management behaviours, the children were asked whether they were trying to lose, gain or keep their weight; however, they were not asked exactly how they were doing it (e.g. limiting food intake to lose weight, eating 'junk' food or larger quantities to gain weight, or exercising). The analysis is presented separately for boys and girls of 10–11 years of age only, as these questions were not asked when children were younger. All the differences reported are statistically different at a 5 per cent level of significance.

At age 10–11 years, boys and girls were asked about their weight management strategies during the 12 months preceding the interview and at the time of the interview. First, they were asked whether they had done anything to control their weight (tried to lose weight or keep from gaining weight) during the last 12 months. Note that children were not asked whether they tried to *lose or gain* weight, but rather whether they *controlled* their weight. The majority of children had tried to manage their weight. This was true for both boys (61 per cent) and girls (56 per cent). The proportions were greater among boys and girls who were dissatisfied with their bodies than those who were satisfied, 50 per cent vs 72 per cent for boys and 42 per cent vs 73 per cent for girls.

The children then reported on their current weight management behaviours. In particular, they were asked to pick one option that best described what they were trying to do about their weight at the time of the interview: 'lose weight', 'gain weight', 'stay the same', or 'do nothing'. Among 10–11 year olds, 38 per cent of boys and girls were trying to lose weight, 8 per cent of boys and 5 per cent of girls were trying to gain weight, 33 per cent of boys and 31 per cent of girls were trying to stay the same weight, and only 20 per cent of boys and 26 per cent of girls did nothing. There were no gender differences among boys and girls who were trying to lose weight, but more boys tried to gain weight and fewer did nothing to control their weight compared to girls of the same age. The differences were observed by body image dissatisfaction (see Figure 11.4). Out of those who were satisfied with their body, a majority (75 per cent of boys and 79 per cent of girls) reported either doing nothing or trying to stay the same, 25 per cent reported trying to lose weight and around 5 per cent tried to gain weight. In contrast, out of those who were dissatisfied with their body image, a majority tried to lose weight (59 per cent of boys and 61 per cent of girls), almost one in ten tried to gain weight and only 30 per cent tried to stay the same or did nothing.

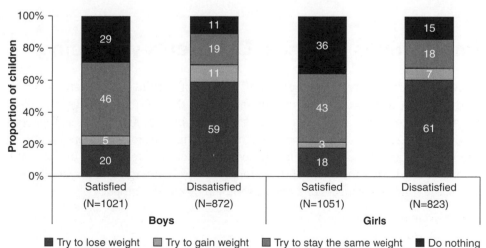

Figure 11.4 Weight management strategies of 10- to 11-year-olds, by age and body image dissatisfaction. (Percentages may not total exactly 100% due to rounding.)

Source: LSAC, Kinder Cohort, boys and girls, age 8–11 years old, Commonwealth of Australia, CC BY 4.0.

It is quite possible that among those boys and girls who were trying to lose or gain weight, some were engaged in positive strategies (such as limiting their energy-dense food intake, eating more fruit and vegetables, exercising), whereas others could be engaged in unhealthy or dangerous strategies such as severely restricting food intake or vomiting after a meal.[2] In the absence of detailed information about the methods children were using to lose, gain or keep the same weight, it is not possible to comment on the positive or negative effects of weight control strategies and their prevalence among children aged 10–11 years.

PAUSE AND REFLECT 11.2: WHAT CAN EDUCATORS LEARN ABOUT WEIGHT MANAGEMENT STRATEGIES OF 10- TO 11-YEAR-OLDS?

- A majority of children tried to control their weight.
- *Trying to stay the same* was the most common strategy among those who were satisfied with their body image.
- *Trying to lose weight* was the most common weight management strategy among those who were dissatisfied with their body image.

Reflection questions:

- Does dissatisfaction with one's own body image always lead to negative consequences?
- When should children be introduced to healthy weight management strategies?
- How can healthy eating and physical activities be promoted to boost positive body image?

Implications in focus: Children's wellbeing

Body dissatisfaction can affect different aspects of a child's life. There is strong evidence that adolescents who are dissatisfied with their body image are likely to experience social problems, depression symptoms and poor self-esteem (Tiggemann, 2005). Disentangling these relationships improves understanding of the role of positive body image in the socio-emotional development of the child. To examine whether the onset of these relationships is emerging in pre-adolescent years, the following aspects of a child's wellbeing were examined:

- physical health
- self-worth
- peer relationships
- emotional and behavioural problems.

---

2   At these ages, LSAC did not include detailed measures of the particular strategies that might be employed.

Physical health

As the focus of this chapter is on how children's dissatisfaction with their body interacts with their perceptions and feelings about themselves, children's perspectives rather than the objective measures of their physical health were of main interest. Three questions were asked to gain the children's perspective[3]:

- Have you felt fit and well [in the last week]?
- Have you felt full of energy [in the last week]?
- How much do you enjoy being physically active (doing things like sports, active games, walking or running, swimming)?

Response options were categorised as 'very/extremely' vs 'not at all/slightly/moderately' for the first two questions and 'a lot' vs 'quite a lot/not very much/not at all' for the third question.[4] Perception of physical health was measured as percentages of positive responses.

Figure 11.5 shows that the proportion of girls and boys who felt fit and well, full of energy and enjoyed physical activity was greater among boys and girls who were satisfied with their body image compared to those who were dissatisfied. While, overall, a majority of boys and girls, regardless of body image dissatisfaction, reported feeling fit and well, full of energy and enjoying physical activity, the corresponding proportions were smaller among children who were dissatisfied with their bodies. The difference was more evident in the proportion of feeling fit and well. In particular, out of those satisfied with their bodies, around 80 per cent of children felt fit and well compared to around 55 per cent of those who were dissatisfied with their body. There were no gender differences.

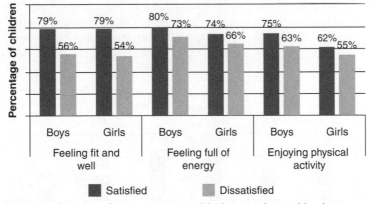

Figure 11.5 Physical health of 10- to 11-year-olds, by gender and body image dissatisfaction.

Source: LSAC, Kinder Cohort, boys and girls, age 8–11 years old, Commonwealth of Australia, CC BY 4.0.

---

3 The first two questions were from the KIDSCREEN-52 instruments (The KIDSCREEN Group, Europe, 2006).

4 Only around 6 per cent of boys and girls reported enjoy physical activity 'not very much/not at all'.

Self-concept and self-worth

Previous research has consistently found that, on average, adolescents who are dissatisfied with their body are more likely to have negative thoughts than those who are satisfied (Stice et al., 2000). Here, it has been investigated whether boys and girls in their pre-adolescent years who were dissatisfied with their body size were also likely to have a low level of self-worth or negative thoughts about themselves.

The level of self-worth was derived from the child's report on the General Self-Concept scale from the Self-Description Questionnaire-I (Marsh, 1990). The Self-Description Questionnaire is a well validated and widely used Australian measure of multidimensional self-concept in pre-adolescent children. The scale comprises eight items, with response options ranging from 1 (false) to 5 (true). The self-worth score is the mean of the responses to the questionnaire items, with a higher score indicating better outcomes. In this analysis, children in the bottom quintile (20 per cent) of the distribution of mean scores were distinguished from the remainder of the children. This bottom quintile represented a group of children with *relatively* low self-worth.

Two items from the Short Moods & Feelings Questionnaire (Angold et al., 1995) were adapted to measure signs of negative thoughts:

- I feel I am not good.
- I do not enjoy anything at all.

The reference period for these questions was the last two weeks, and response options were categorised as 'sometimes true/true' vs 'not true'. Overall, around 35 per cent of boys and girls felt they were not good, and around 17 per cent of boys and 11 per cent of girls did not enjoy anything at all.

The proportions of boys and girls who had low self-worth and negative thoughts were significantly greater among those who were dissatisfied with their body image compared to those who were satisfied (Figure 11.6). For example, 40 per cent of

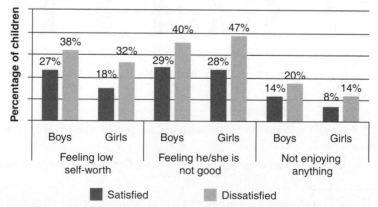

Figure 11.6 Self-worth and negative thoughts of 10- to 11-year-olds, by gender and body image dissatisfaction.

Source: LSAC, Kinder Cohort, boys and girls, age 8–11 years old, Commonwealth of Australia, CC BY 4.0.

boys and 47 per cent of girls who were dissatisfied with their body reported feeling that they were not good compared to 29 per cent of boys and 28 per cent of girls who were happy with the way they looked.

Relationships with peers

Adolescents who are dissatisfied with their body image are less likely to feel confident and more likely to lack social skills than those who are satisfied (Tiggemann, 2005). This sub-section examines whether pre-adolescent children who were dissatisfied with their body image were also likely to report poor relationships with peers and likely to report problems with peers.

The measure of the child's relationships with peers was derived from the child's report on the Peer Relations scale from the Self-Description Questionnaire-I (Marsh, 1990). This scale comprises eight items, with response options ranging from 1 (false) to 5 (true). The peer relations score is the mean of the responses to the questionnaire items, with higher scores indicating better outcomes. The peer relations scale items included statements such as 'I have many friends', 'I get along with kids easily' and 'I am popular with kids my own age'. Children at the bottom quintile (20 per cent) of the distribution of mean scores were distinguished from the remainder of the children and represent a group of children with *relatively* poor peer relationships.

The measure of whether the child had relationship problems with their peers was derived from the Strengths and Difficulties Questionnaire (Goodman, 2001).[5] This scale measures the degree of reported peer problems a child may be experiencing, and comprises five items with response options ranging from 0 to 10. Higher scores indicate higher levels of problems. The scale includes items such as 'picked on or bullied by other children', 'gets on better with adults than with other children' and 'rather solitary, tends to play alone'. To identify children with relatively high peer relationship problems, children at the top quintile (20 per cent) of the distribution of mean scores were distinguished from the remainder of children.

As for other outcomes, boys and girls who were dissatisfied with their body image were more likely to report poor quality peer relationships and peer relationship problems compared to boys and girls satisfied with their body image (Figure 11.7). Among boys who were dissatisfied with their body image, 34 per cent had poor quality relationships and 21 per cent had problems with their peers compared to 22 per cent and 15 per cent respectively among boys satisfied with their body image. Similar proportions were observed in girls. Among girls who were satisfied with body image, 30 per cent reported poor relationships and 18 per cent reported problems with their peers, compared to 22 per cent and 10 per cent respectively among girls satisfied with their body image.

---

5   This instrument is a brief screening questionnaire that includes scales assessing conduct problems, emotional symptoms, hyperactivity or inattention, pro-social behaviour and peer relationship problems.

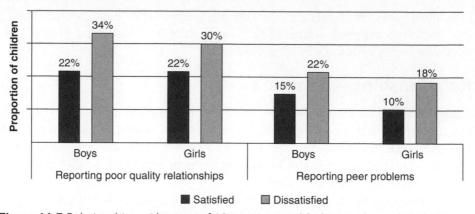

Figure 11.7 Relationships with peers of 10- to 11-year-olds, by gender and body image dissatisfaction.

Source: LSAC, Kinder Cohort, boys and girls, age 8–11 years old, Commonwealth of Australia, CC BY 4.0.

Emotional and behavioural problems

The emotional and behavioural problems of 10- to 11-year-old boys and girls were examined using childrens' reports on the emotional symptoms and conduct problems sub-scales from the Strengths and Difficulties Questionnaire (Goodman, 2001).[6] Each sub-scale has a possible range of 0 to 10, with higher scores indicating higher levels of socio-emotional problems. To identify children with relatively high emotional and behavioural problems, children in the top quintile (20 per cent) of the distribution of mean scores on both sub-scales were distinguished from the remainder of the children.

Consistent with previous results, the proportions of boys and girls who had high emotional and conduct problems were greater among those who were dissatisfied with their body image, compared to those who were satisfied (Figure 11.8), especially among girls with emotional problems. Out of girls who were dissatisfied with their body, one-third reported having relatively high level of emotional problems compared to one-fifth of girls who were satisfied with their body.

---

6   The SDQ emotional problems sub-scale comprises items like: 'often unhappy, downhearted or tearful', 'nervous or clingy in new situations, easily loses confidence' and 'many worries, often seems worried'. The SDQ conduct problems sub-scale comprises items like: 'often has temper tantrums or hot tempers', 'often fights with other children or bullies them' and 'often lies or cheats'.

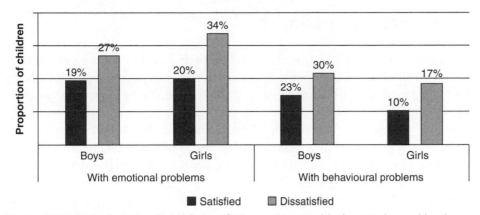

Figure 11.8 Socio-emotional problems of 10- to 11- year-olds, by gender and body image dissatisfaction.

Source: LSAC, Kinder Cohort, boys and girls, age 8–11 years old, Commonwealth of Australia, CC BY 4.0.

PAUSE AND REFLECT 11.3: WHAT CAN EDUCATORS LEARN FROM BODY IMAGE DISSATISFACTION AND SOCIO-EMOTIONAL WELLBEING OF 10- TO 11-YEAR-OLDS?

- Association between body image dissatisfaction and poor physical and socio-emotional wellbeing is already evident in pre-adolescents.
- Among children who are dissatisfied with their body image:
  - *boys* are at the same risk of showing signs of poor physical, social and emotional wellbeing as girls with only one exception
  - *girls* are at greater risk of feeling bad about themselves than boys.

Reflection questions:

- If the onset of such relationships already takes place in the pre-adolescent years, when should prevention and intervention take place to be successful?
- How important is it to create a school environment that supports and promotes positive body image?

Summary of research

The research presented in this chapter demonstrates that already at eight to nine years of age, around 60 per cent of children were dissatisfied with their body size and around 50 per cent of children wanted to be thinner than average body size, with almost one in five children choosing a very thin body as an ideal body. A positive change was apparent as children grew older. While still around 50 per cent of boys and 40 per cent of girls wanted to be thinner than average, a very small proportion of children wanted to be very thin, and a greater proportion of children were satisfied with their bodies.

But what does it mean for a child's physical and psychological health to be dissatisfied with the way he/she looks? The study showed that already at 10–11 years of age children engage in weight management strategies. The majority of children dissatisfied with their body size were trying to lose weight, whereas the majority of children satisfied with their body tried to stay the same or did nothing. Importantly, the strong relationships between body image dissatisfaction and children's wellbeing could also be observed already in pre-adolescents. Children who were dissatisfied with their body were more likely to report poor physical health and socio-emotional wellbeing compared to children satisfied with their body size. Surprisingly, no gender differences are found – neither in the desired body image nor in the relationship between body dissatisfaction and overall wellbeing of the child.

The pre-adolescent period appears to provide a great opportunity for parents and educators to intervene and promote healthy body image and help children to develop positive self-esteem in relation to their bodies. As children spend most of their daytime at school, schools are in an excellent position to help children to develop positive self-esteem in relation to their bodies and increase their resilience to any negative messages they may encounter later in their lives. Therefore, by tailoring the school curriculum and creating a school environment to promote positive body image, educators can have a positive impact on students' outcomes across different domains: education, physical and mental health and social engagement.

Body image education is increasingly becoming part of the Health and Physical Education Curriculum in Years 5/6 across Australia (Australian Curriculum, Assessment and Reporting Authority [ACARA], 2013). The Australian Curriculum for general capabilities – in particular, the framework for personal and social capability – provides clear, well-structured and scaffolded learning activities to assist early years educators in this regard. A number of national and international key standards in teaching body image have also been developed over the years (Australian Government Office for Youth, 2009; Knightsmith, 2016) and include: having a statement in the school mission about providing a body image-friendly environment and celebrating diversity; making available body image-friendly school and sports uniforms; discouraging fat-shaming and equation of human worth with body shape; using inclusive images wherever possible; providing an opportunity for all students to engage in regular physical activity in a non-competitive, non-weight loss-focused, safe and secure environment; providing a balance of food options from all food groups in the canteen; providing all teachers with training and information about the impact of body image issues; and focusing on the wellbeing of students.

In developing interventions, though, it is important to remember that being dissatisfied with one's own body size does not necessarily have only negative effects, especially among severely underweight or overweight children. For example, while children of normal weight who are dissatisfied with their own body are at risk of developing an unhealthy body weight, a desire among overweight children to lose weight or for underweight children to gain weight might motivate them to manage their weight.

Conclusion

The main challenge for policies and practice is to encourage children to manage their weight within a healthy range, while maintaining healthy self-worth and socio-emotional wellbeing. Thus, developing targeted intervention programs that concurrently address healthy body image and equip children with healthy weight management strategies, like healthy eating habits and regular exercising, as well as boost their self-confidence, might help not only to improve children's physical health but also to reduce the negative effects of body image dissatisfaction on the socio-emotional wellbeing of children.

Summary

The main take-home messages from the current research are:

- 'Thin ideal' is already apparent when children are eight to nine years old. Body image education in primary school might show great benefit for a child's long-term wellbeing as prevention (body image education in primary school) is more effective than intervention (poor socio-emotional outcomes in adolescence).
- Children as young as 10–11 years of age engage in weight management strategies. Educating children on healthy lifestyle choices and promoting healthy eating and physical activity is, therefore, crucial for positive physical health outcomes.
- Pre-adolescents who are dissatisfied with their own body are likely to report poor socio-emotional outcomes, including poor relationships with peers, poor self-worth, emotional and conduct problems as well as having negative thoughts about themselves. Education should be holistic and cover different populations: children, educators and parents.
- Even though no gender differences are found, consideration should be given as to whether to separate students by gender when sensitive topics are discussed.

Questions

11.1 How can educators promote positive body image in young children?

11.2 Why is it important to explore the body image perceptions of young children?

11.3 How do educators balance the need to address health concerns such as obesity without compromising children's self-esteem and body image?

11.4 How can schools and families work together to promote healthy body image?

Acknowledgements

This chapter adapts the work 'Body image of primary school children' published in the Longitudinal Study of Australian Children SAC Annual Statistical Report 2013 (© Commonwealth Government of Australia, Creative Commons Attribution 3.0 Australia licence [CC BY 3.0] https://creativecommons.org/licenses/by/3.0/au/deed.en). The report is produced by the Australian Institute of Family Studies and aims to provide valuable insights into family functioning and child development for researchers, policy-makers, and those who provide services and support, as well as the community at large.

References

All Party Parliamentary Group on Body Image and Central YMCA (2012). *Reflection on Body Image.* London: UK Parliamentary Report.

Angold, A., Costello, E.J., Messer, S.C., Pickles, A., Winder, F. & Silver, D. (1995). Development of a short questionnaire for use in epidemiological studies of depression in children and adolescence. *International Journal of Methods in Psychiatric Research,* 5, 237–49.

Australian Curriculum, Assessment and Reporting Authority (2013). *General capabilities in the Australian Curriculum: Personal and social capability.* Sydney: ACARA.

Australian Institute of Family Studies (AIFS) (2014). *The Longitudinal Study of Australian Children Annual Statistical. Report 2013.* Melbourne: AIFS.

Australian Government Office for Youth (2009). Body image: Information paper. Canberra: Australian Government.

Brown, T., Cash, T. & Mikulka, P. (1990). Attitudinal body-image assessment: Factor analysis of the Body-Self Relations Questionnaire. *Journal of Personality Assessment,* 55(1–2), 135–44.

Cash, T. (2002a). Cognitive-behavioral perspectives on body image. In T. Cash & T. Pruzinsky (eds), *Body image: A handbook of theory, research, and clinical practice* (pp. 38–46). New York: Guilford.

—— (2002b). A negative body image: Evaluating epidemiological evidence. In T. Cash & T. Pruzinsky (eds), *Body image: A handbook of theory, research, and clinical practice* (pp. 269–276). New York: Guilford.

Cohane, G.H. & Pope, H G. (2001). Body image in boys: A review of the literature. *International Journal of Eating Disorders,* 29(4), 373–79.

Collins M.E. (1991). Body figure perceptions and preferences among preadolescent children. *International Journal of Eating Disorders,* 10(2), 199–208.

Cook, S., MacPherson, K. & Langille, D. (2007). Far from ideal: Weight perception, weight control, and associated risk behaviours among adolescent females in Nova Scotia. *Canadian Family Physician,* 53, 678–84.

Croll, J. (2005). Body image and adolescents. In J. Stang & M. Story (eds), *Guidelines for adolescent nutrition services.* Minneapolis, MN: Center for Leadership, Education and Training in Maternal and Child Nutrition, Division of Epidemiology and Community Health, School of Public Health, University of Minnesota.

Dohnt, H.K. & Tiggemann, M. (2006). Body image concerns in young girls: The role of peers and media prior to adolescence. *Journal of Youth and Adolescence,* 35(2), 141–51.

Goodman, R. (2001). Psychometric properties of the Strengths and Difficulties Questionnaire (SDQ). *Journal of the American Academy of Child and Adolescent Psychiatry,* 40, 1337–45.

Irving, L.M. (2000). Promoting size acceptance in elementary school children: The EDAP puppet program. *Eating Disorders*, 8, 3–16.

The KIDSCREEN Group Europe (2006). *The KIDSCREEN Questionnaires - Quality of life questionnaires for children and adolescents. Handbook.* Lengerich: Pabst Science Publishers.

Knightsmith, P. (2016). *Teacher guidance: Key standards in teaching about body image.* UK: PSHE Association, Government Equalities Office.

Levine, M.P. & Piran, N. (2004). The role of body image in the prevention of eating disorders. *Body Image*, 1(1), 57–70.

Liechty, J.M. (2010). Body image distortion and three types of weight loss behaviors among nonoverweight girls in the United States. *Journal of Adolescent Health*, 47, 176–82.

Marsh, H.W. (1990). *Self Description Questionnaire-I (SDQ-I) manual.* Sydney: University of Western Sydney.

McCabe , M.P. & Ricciardelli, L.A. (2005). A longitudinal study of body image and strategies to lose weight and increase muscles among children. *Applied Developmental Psychology*, 26, 559–77.

McCabe, M.P., Ricciardelli, L.A & Salmon, J. (2006). Evaluation of a prevention program to address body focus and negative effect among children. *Journal of Health Psychology*, 11, 589–98.

Neumark-Sztainer, D., Paxton, S.J., Hannan, P.J., Haines, J. & Story, M. (2006). Does body satisfaction matter? Five-year longitudinal associations between body satisfaction and health behaviors in adolescent females and males. *Journal of Adolescent Health*, 39, 244–51.

Stice, E., Hayward, C., Cameron, R.P., Killen, J.D. & Taylor, C.B. (2000). Body image and eating disturbances predict onset of depression in female adolescents: A longitudinal study. *Journal of Abnormal Psychology*, 109, 438–44.

Stice, E., Mazotti, L., Krebs, M. & Martin, S. (1998). Predictors of adolescent dieting behaviors: A longitudinal study. *Psychology of Addictive Behaviors*, 12, 195–205.

Stice, E. & Shaw, H. (2004). Eating disorder prevention programs: A meta-analytic review. *Psychological Bulletin*, 130(2): 206–7.

Tiggemann, M. (2005). Body dissatisfaction and adolescent self-esteem: Prospective findings. *Body Image*, 2, 129–35.

Truby H. & Paxton, S. (2002). Development of the Children's Body Image Scale. *British Journal of Clinical Psychology.* 41(2), 185–203.

Vander Wal, J.S.& Thelen, M.H. (2000). Eating and body image concerns amont obese and average-weight children. *Addict Behavior*, 25(5), 775–8.

PART 3

Applications

CHAPTER 12

Teaching for social and emotional learning

Wendi Beamish and Fiona Bryer

Introduction

Teaching in the twenty-first century values social and emotional learning (SEL) as an integral part of student learning and success across the school years and into adult life. Community recognition of the substantial difficulties in coping faced by young people in our rapidly changing society is magnifying this value. Policy recognition from the Australian Curriculum, Assessment and Reporting Authority (ACARA, 2013) has converted these values into expectations for educational activity. By specifically embedding SEL content into the core curriculum, ACARA is acknowledging that students need to achieve social outcomes alongside academic success. However, the current status of Australian school efforts to deliver SEL instruction to all students is unknown because the action research is quite scattered and limited to social skills training (see, for example, Davies et al., 2015). At this time, therefore, there is little local evidence to inform and guide Australian teachers in understanding SEL content and integrating it into the teaching-learning process for their class of diverse learners.

In order to meet these community values and curriculum expectations, teachers are being pressed to ensure that their students experience social connectedness and emotional wellbeing as part of participating in learning, acquiring a sense of personal competence and using self-management strategies during classroom activities. Attending to tasks, regulating self and engaging with others are pivotal skills threading throughout daily classroom activities and routines. Many teachers need the knowledge and confidence to adopt a more strategic process for responding to the social and emotional challenges that some students face in mastering core learning tasks related to this attend-regulate-engage skill set. Assessing classroom difficulties in social and emotional learning provides a necessary starting point to identify adjustments across the classroom curriculum and embed these adjustments into the plan-implement-evaluate teaching cycle.

The focus of this chapter is threefold. First, we tap into the rich research on SEL from the USA. The translation of this knowledge into Australia has had some influence on ACARA but needs to be better disseminated to end users such as teachers. This research has clear application to teacher activity, especially with respect to knowing students and how they think, feel and learn (i.e. Standard 1 of the Australian Professional Standards for Teachers [Australian Institute for Teaching and Social Leadership Ltd., 2010]) and also with respect to making classroom environments more supportive for all students (Standard 4). Second, we identify the benefits of a school-wide approach to social-behavioural learning for academic success. These benefits can accrue for teachers and students when sufficient infrastructural school supports are in place to enable teachers to integrate SEL into classroom curriculum and instruction. Third, we highlight evidence-informed SEL strategies that teachers can use as part of their assess-plan-implement-evaluate cycle. On their own, however, many teachers struggle to translate this curriculum expectation into everyday practice.

What is SEL?

Social and emotional learning involves student acquisition of skills needed to recognise and manage emotions, develop empathy for others, form positive relationships and make responsible decisions.

Social and emotional learning (SEL) is a broad domain of learning that develops throughout life. As a domain, SEL draws on complex cognitive, emotional and behavioural processes that, with experience over time, strengthen students' capacity to attend to, self-manage and engage with others in their expanding personal and social worlds of learning, living and leisure. Therefore, explicit classroom instruction in SEL progressively supports a positive state of wellbeing, mental health and resourcefulness related to resilience in dealing with life challenges. Because of these multifaceted processes, the SEL domain can be viewed from a number of perspectives (Bear, Whitcomb & Elias, 2015). For example, this domain has been represented in the literature as a clustering of competencies, elements, skills and dispositions.

Framing SEL

The approach to SEL in the Australian Curriculum is consistent with that adopted internationally. Table 12.1 presents the SEL framework and competencies for school-age students put forward by the Collaborative for Academic, Social, and Emotional Learning (CASEL), which have gained widespread international consensus. The table also shows the linkage between the CASEL framing of SEL around five core groups of competencies (Zins et al., 2004) and international goal setting by UNESCO (2013).

Table 12.1: Relation between CASEL Competencies and other SEL Descriptors.

CASEL (2004) Competencies	UNESCO (2013) Sub-domains	ACARA (2013) Elements
Self-awareness Identifying and recognising emotions; accurate self-perception, recognising strengths, needs and values; self-efficacy	Emotional awareness Self-confidence and self-efficacy	Self-awareness
Self-management Impulse control and stress-management; self-motivation and discipline; goal-setting and organisational skills	Self-regulation	Self-management
Social awareness Perspective-taking; empathy; difference recognition; respect for others	Empathy	Social awareness
Relationship management Communication, social engagement and relationship-building; working cooperatively; negotiation, refusal and conflict management; help-seeking	Social relationships Conflict resolution	Social management
Responsible decision-making Problem-identification and situation analysis; problem solving; evaluation and reflection; personal, social and ethical responsibility	Moral, civic and ethical values	

Source: Zins et al., (2004); UNESCO (2013); ACARA (2013).

Moreover, the table makes it clear how ACARA (2013) drew on CASEL competencies to formulate four sets of personal and social capability (PSC) elements within the Australian curriculum. They adopted self-awareness, self-management and social awareness competencies; they also adapted relationship management into a social management element; and they excluded competencies around responsible decision-making.

This ACARA mapping for building student competence in SEL elements is consistent with the latest learning standards for SEL across the USA (Dusenbury et al., 2015). Standards guiding student SEL skill development in both countries aim to integrate these competencies across the curriculum for each age. Dusenbury and colleagues recommend additional guidelines to promote SEL implementation of standards (e.g. how to create school learning environments that are positive and culturally sensitive, and how to build teacher capacity in SEL instructional practice). These same recommendations are applicable in Australia and provide direction for progressing formal SEL implementation at the whole-school level in this country. The Australian Temperament Project provides an evidence-based case for age-by-skill capability building across all classrooms in a school, showing that 'at any one time-point approximately 25 per cent of all students exhibit significant adjustment difficulties of some sort' (Sanson, 2016, p. 24).

It can also be noted that ACARA mapping for SEL is becoming more closely aligned with the Australian teaching of social and emotional competencies in the early years. For example, the KidsMatter Australian Early Childhood Initiative (2014) notes the need to develop children's social and emotional skills and observes the connections to SEL in the Early Years Learning Framework and the National Quality Standard. Early years teachers routinely use everyday social and emotional situations to informally teach SEL. They use naturalistic strategies such as adult modelling and verbal coaching in teachable moments to build skills in SEL competencies for infants, toddlers and young children.

PAUSE AND REFLECT 12.1: RESPONSIBLE DECISION-MAKING

- Responsible decision-making is not included as an element in ACARA's Personal and Social Capability framework. However, teaching independence and responsibility begins in the early years with toddlers being asked to do simple things like tidying up toys after play. Consider the case for and against the formal teaching of personal, social and ethical responsibility to school-age students.

- Think about practical ways in which teachers can address this content in their daily teaching.

Situating SEL within the whole-school context

A reform agenda in Australian schools is intended to better meet student learning needs (Hattie, 2015). Current reform efforts in many schools use a National School Improvement Tool (Australian Council for Educational Research, 2012) to facilitate better student outcomes. With this tool, a school can benchmark its practice improvement across nine dimensions (e.g. expert teaching team, differentiated teaching and learning, effective pedagogical practices). These complementary trends are encouraging the emergence of differentiated instruction within a **multi-tiered framework** (McIntosh & Goodman, 2016; Stormont et al., 2012). Universal (Tier 1), targeted (Tier 2) and intensive (Tier 3) levels of student support across academic, social and emotional, and behavioural domains are being driven by data-gathering and assessment combined with evidence-informed teacher practice.

Multi-tiered framework of supports: a comprehensive system in a school for meeting the needs of all students (from *struggling* to *advanced*). The framework comprises three levels of student support and intervention (*universal* needed by most students, *targeted* needed by some students and *intensive* needed by a few students).

Multi-tiering acknowledges that the needs of most students can be met through explicit and purposeful classroom teaching (universal). However, it recognises that some students require more focused small group instruction (targeted) and that a few students need personalised teaching to become successful learners (intensive). For example, anxiety among most learners can be addressed through instructional support (e.g. explicit teaching, immediate feedback). Some students may not respond to this Tier 1 support and may require targeted group coaching in emotional skills development. A few students may require intensive intervention with personalised plans developed through education-health-family partnerships.

The school-wide approach within this reform agenda harnesses the advantages of teacher learning communities and scales up the opportunities for learning success (Hattie, 2015). Adoption means that a school can respond meaningfully to the contextual needs of their community; better catering to learning needs within a school boosts student academic and socio-behavioural outcomes. Successful adoption relies on school-wide infrastructure, which includes committed leadership and sufficient resources, documented decision-making procedures and data-gathering tools, as well as staff training and collaboration (Anderson & Borgmeier, 2010). This school-wide approach with effective infrastructure means that teachers are better supported to implement SEL instruction within class (Tier 1), SEL groupings across the school (Tier 2) and individualised SEL teaching (Tier 3).

Working through the SEL teaching cycle

Teaching routinely involves working through an assess-plan-implement-evaluate cycle, and this **teaching cycle** also applies to emerging practice in SEL instruction at school and classroom levels. The content descriptions and elaborations detailed in the PSC elements of general capabilities in the Australian Curriculum provide starting points for Australian schools and teachers in order to undertake SEL assessment and planning. Specific skills in each element are described in a PSC learning continuum from Prep to Year 10, with each skill also linked directly to skills in other PSC elements and in relevant learning areas.

The **teaching cycle** is based on the explicit and systematic teaching and learning of targeted SEL skills. The cycle is viewed as a dynamic assess-plan-instruct monitor process accompanied by ongoing evaluation and reflection.

At this point in time, those schools that have adopted a school-wide approach can also take advantage of several commercial programming packages or curricula (see Spotlight 12.1) to guide and formalise SEL instruction within and across classrooms. Some formal SEL measures are commercially available in association with mixed media curriculum packages (e.g. Social Skills Improvement System by Elliott and Gresham (2008); Strong Kids series Pre-K to Grade 12 by Merrell et al., [2007]). In these circumstances, inbuilt tools are routinely provided to ensure quality of instruction and consistency of approach across the teaching cycle.

SPOTLIGHT 12.1: THREE RECOMMENDED SEL RESOURCE PACKAGES WITH AGE-RELATED CURRICULUM ACROSS SCHOOLING YEARS

Skillstreaming	Goldstein, A.P. (1999). *The PREPARE curriculum: Teaching prosocial competencies.* Champaign, IL: Research Press.
	McGinnis, E. (2012a). *Skillstreaming in early childhood: A guide to teaching prosocial skills* (3rd edn.). Champaign, IL: Research Press.
	McGinnis, E. (2012b). *Skillstreaming the elementary school child: A guide to teaching prosocial skills* (3rd edn.). Champaign, IL: Research Press.
	Glick, B. & Gibbs, J.C. (2012). *Aggression replacement training: A comprehensive intervention for aggressive youth* (3rd edn., rev. & exp.). Champaign, IL: Research Press.
Social Skills Improvement System	Elliott, S.N. & Gresham, F.M. (2007a). *SSIS Performance Screening Guide.* Minneapolis, MN: NCS Pearson.
	Elliott, S.N. & Gresham, F.M. (2008). *SSIS Classwide Intervention Program: Teacher's guide.* Minneapolis, MN: NCS Pearson.
	Elliott, S.N. & Gresham, F.M. (2008). *Social Skills Improvement System intervention guide.* Minneapolis, MN: NCS Pearson.
Strong Kids	Merrell, K.W., Parisi, D. & Whitcomb, S.A. (2007). *Strong Start-Pre-K. A social and emotional learning curriculum for students in Grades K–2.* Baltimore, MD: Brookes.
	Merrell, K.W., Carrizales, D., Feuerborn, L., Gueldner, B.A. & Tran, O.K. (2007). *Strong Kids: A social and emotional learning curriculum for students in Grades 3–5.* Baltimore, MD: Brookes.
	Merrell, K.W., Carrizales, D., Feuerborn, L., Gueldner, B.A. & Tran, O.K. (2007). *Strong Kids: Middle – a social and emotional learning curriculum for students in Grades 6–8.* Baltimore, MD: Brookes.

Otherwise, decision-making falls upon the teaching team to sort through the myriad of potentially useful SEL resources in order to locate material that reconciles student needs with curriculum (including the personal and social capabilities framework) and that matches these choices to the relevant tier for instruction. Time-and-workload difficulties often lead to 'cherry-picking' content and making arbitrary choices from an assortment of SEL skills, tools and strategies (Osher et al., 2010). Some explicit and strategic guidelines can be offered on how to thread SEL skills systematically into tiered learning activities and routines across the teaching cycle. Assessment and planning at the front of this teaching cycle receive particular emphasis because tiered decision-making by a collaborative team during these early phases is critical to school-wide SEL teaching and to SEL outcomes for every student.

Assess

Assessment is a dynamic process in the teaching cycle that 'kick-starts' and feeds into the planning, monitoring and evaluation parts of the teaching cycle. Every interaction at school provides an opportunity to gather some information about student capabilities and the goodness of fit between student skills and the school's SEL program. 'Information about what a child can and cannot do provides the fabric for strengths-based teaching and learning, and for curriculum content to be broadened or reduced' (Beamish & Saggers, 2013, p. 246). Proactive use of screening tools is recommended in order to identify specific student skills and gaps relevant to year level and social context. For example, the SSIS Performance Screening Guide identifies learners requiring additional support and informs SEL instruction, prevention and intervention.

It is important to know every student. To know is to be sensitive to how a student connects thoughts and behaviours to emotions, to recognise individual preferences and favourite things, and to understand the effects of cultural identity and family circumstances on learning. Teachers need to consider which skills can bring about desirable changes in the child's life, and they need to avoid making assumptions based on school performance, problem behaviour and personality traits, and socio-cultural background. A positive focus on student needs means that assessment for planning can be responsive and solution-focused.

For example, Roffey (2011) provides a very simple problem-based checklist for assessing students' engagement in their social world. Questions for rating on a five-point scale include: What does a student view as her/his positive qualities and strengths? Which people support this student at school and at home? Who does this student view as a role model? Which peers positively influence the student? A variety of informal and formal checklists are freely available on the internet (see examples of websites below) and can be used to informally gather information about students. On the other hand, a school can base student assessment on direct observation and use these data to monitor progress and report to parents on SEL priorities established for year level and social context. For example, Elias, Ferrito and Moceri (2016; see also www.edutopia.org/blogs/how-do-we-measure-sel-maurice-elias) outline a step-by-step protocol that uses direct observation to appraise the presence or absence of specific CASEL skills, character strengths, and behavioural indicators; these skills, strengths and indicators then provide a framework for teacher planning and parent reporting.

Examples of websites for SEL assessment tools include:

- California Department of Education, Desired Results Developmental Profile – Preschool (2015) and Desired Results Developmental Profile – School Age (2011). Locate Self and Social Development domain search using Desired Results Developmental Profile for Preschool or School Age: www.cde.ca.gov
- Australian Council of Educational Research, The Social-Emotional Wellbeing (SEW) Survey for students aged 3–18 years – sample questions only: www.acer.org/sew

- Strong Kids Tests for Grades 3–8. Student self-reports of negative symptoms and positive SEL knowledge about SK curriculum: http://strongkids.uoregon.edu/unittests/strongkids.pdf

Plan

Some interactions in the classroom warrant specific planning to embed SEL goals and strategies into existing units of work and other curriculum documents. From knowing student strengths and reflecting on their individual profiles based on assessment information, the teacher can set goals and determine strategies that suit the class as a whole and foster general wellbeing. This whole-class planning can focus on promoting new skills, consolidating emerging skills, or integrating related skills. Planning of this kind, however, will fall short of meeting the SEL needs of all students. Some students will need more opportunity to practise a skill, while others will need more powerful strategies to learn a skill. These adjustments will not be sufficient for a few students, who will require a more intense program with more extensive supports in order to learn basic SEL skills.

Four practices for effective SEL planning have been recommended by Durlak et al. (2011). The acronym SAFE identifies this suite of practices:

- *Sequenced*. New behaviours and more complicated skills usually need to be broken down into smaller steps and sequentially mastered.
- *Active*. Effective teaching emphasises the importance of active forms of learning.
- *Focused*. Sufficient time and attention needs to be devoted to any task for learning to occur.
- *Explicit*. Clear and specific learning objectives are preferred over general ones.

Table 12.2 shows the use of SAFE practices in relation to an example of lessons for teaching self-management of anger in different commercial packages. Such packages routinely apply SAFE practices to lessons devoted to selected SEL skills. They tend to break down teaching of a skill into multiple lessons and learning steps; they provide learning activities such as role-play, rehearsal, and discussion in which students actively participate; they allocate finite times for each step and activity within a lesson; and they specify explicit objectives for each lesson. The seminal Skillstreaming series developed by Goldstein and maintained by McGinnis provide a comprehensive resource of SEL content, strategies, and assessment ideas across the schooling years.

The most influential international websites for SEL research and resources remain those at CASEL (www.casel.org) and the Center on Social and Emotional Foundations for Early Learning (csefel.vanderbilt.edu). Some websites combine sound scholarship about SEL with useful teacher-friendly professional development for safe and emotionally supportive classrooms and healthy school cultures. Teachers can receive email alerts about SEL blogposts from these websites.

Table 12.2: Application of SAFE to commercially available lessons in managing emotions.

SAFE practices	Skillstreaming Elementary Skill 36: Self-control (alternative to aggression)	SSIS Early Elementary Unit 8: Stay calm with others	Strong Kids 3–5 Lesson 4: Dealing with angeR
Sequence	Four-step skill: Stop and count to 10 Think about body feelings Think about choices Act	Four-step skill: Feel Think Talk Do	Four-step skill: Count backwards Make if–then statements Use self-talk Self-evaluate action
Active	Model Practise Homework	Model and role-play Discuss video clips Homework	Role-play Activities Homework
Focused	Extensive coverage of teaching procedures Three pages of skill outline and two practice sessions Link to relaxing skill	Ten pages on three lessons Timed sequence of activities and scripts: Tell (4 mins), Show (4 mins), Do (7 mins), Monitor (2 mins), Practise (4 mins), Generalise (4 mins)	Sixteen pages of scripts and transparencies on four activities: Define anger, Describe control skills, Apply to negative and positive situations and Generalise
Explicit	Use skill to identify feeling when angry or upset Sometimes delay dealing with problem when upset	Control temper in conflict with peers Identify what triggers anger and use anger-reduction skills	Understand anger (Identify triggers, Think about situation and Recognise emotion) Manage aggression (Choose action, Act, & Review consequence)

Source: McGinnis (2012); Elliot & Gresham (2008); Merrell et al. (2007).

Implement and evaluate

Two facets of SEL planning need to be rechecked prior to implementation and evaluation. First, the procedures for collecting data must be in place in order to monitor student progress and the overall effectiveness of the instruction. Second, staff training must be undertaken in order to ensure consistency of implementation as prescribed in the planning and the accurate use of SEL strategies.

A 10- to 12-week cycle of implementation and evaluation is recommended (Hattie, 2015). For each week, the teaching team aims for the highest frequency of SEL instruction with data-gathering that is sustainable within the setting, in order to maximise outcomes. As implementation proceeds, periodic data review is needed in order to establish how students are progressing and to determine whether strategies need to be modified. Evaluation of student skill changes, together with the observed effectiveness of SEL instruction, occurs at the end of the teaching cycle. Feeding of these data into a school database for analysis and discussion can then target those students in need of more intensive support (Anderson & Borgmeier, 2010; Stormont et al., 2012) and can contribute to a culture of evidence, improvement and capacity building (ACER, 2012; Hattie, 2015). Because SEL, by its nature, requires a long-term commitment to a process of teaching and learning over time and settings (Osher et al., 2010), ongoing plan-implement-evaluate cycling of SEL capacity building needs to continue within each year and across the schooling years.

PAUSE AND REFLECT 12.2: THE TEACHING CYCLE IN ACTION

- Share experiences of viewing the teaching cycle in action across different curriculum domains (learning areas) while engaged in work-integrated learning at schools.

- Share examples of formal and informal SEL instruction observed during these placements.

Conclusion

Community values and curriculum expectations are demanding that Australian schools and staff build capacity to deliver SEL teaching to all students. Actioning the teaching cycle – either individually or collectively – can draw from home-grown and international frameworks and resources. In an already crowded curriculum, the immediate challenge for emerging practice in this country is to add SEL as another essential curriculum domain alongside literacy and numeracy into everyday teaching cycles. One solution to meeting this challenge is to scaffold SEL instruction through a school-wide approach. This approach not only enables the sharing of responsibility for curriculum development, implementation and monitoring in a new domain across staff; it also facilitates instructional supports across the three tiers for better student outcomes.

Summary

SEL is a fundamental part of curriculum because it prepares students to work, live and participate in an increasingly complex and changing world. The key points highlighted in this chapter are:

- SEL is integral to academic achievement, school adjustment and social outcomes.
- Knowing every student and their personal and social capabilities in the classroom is the first step in the assess–plan–implement–evaluate teaching cycle.
- SAFE practices – sequenced, active, focused and explicit – are recommended for planning and implementation.
- Evaluation of SEL outcomes provides information for reporting and feedback for the next teaching cycle.
- Online access to SEL websites gives valuable support to teachers building their capacity within a whole-school approach.

Questions

12.1 How do the CASEL five core competencies align with the four PSC elements in the Australian Curriculum?

12.2 How do you get to know an individual student and assess that student's capabilities, preferences and vulnerabilities?

12.3 How should teachers and schools invest time and effort into thinking about teaching SEL?

12.4 How does a school-wide approach assist an individual teachers' SEL instruction?

References

Anderson, C.M. & Borgmeier, C. (2010). Tier II intervention within the framework of school-wide positive behaviour support: Essential features for design, implementation, and maintenance. *Behavior Analysis in Practice*, 3(1), 33–45.

Australian Council for Educational Research (ACER) (2012). *The National School Improvement Tool*. Retrieved from https://www.acer.edu.au/files/NSIT.pdf

Australian Curriculum, Assessment and Reporting Authority (ACARA) (2013). *Personal and social capability*. Retrieved from http://www.australiancurriculum. edu.au/GeneralCapabilities/Pdf/Personal-and-social-capability

Australian Institute for Teaching and School Leadership Ltd. (2010). *Australian Professional Standards for Teachers*. Retrieved from http://www.aitsl.edu.au/ australian-professional-standards-for-teachers

Beamish, W. & Saggers, B. (2013). Diversity and differentiation. In D. Pendergast & S. Garvis (eds), *Teaching early years: Curriculum, pedagogy, and assessment* (pp. 244–58). Sydney: Allen & Unwin.

Bear, G.G., Whitcomb, S.A. & Elias, M.J. (2015). SEL and schoolwide positive behavioral interventions and supports. In J.A. Durlak, C. Domitrovich, R.P. Weissberg & T.P. Gullotta (eds), *Handbook of social and emotional learning: Research and practice* (pp. 453–467). New York: Guilford.

Davies, M., Cooper, G., Kettler, R.J. & Elliott, S.N. (2015). Developing social skills of students with additional needs within the context of the Australian curriculum. *Australasian Journal of Special Education,* 39(1), 37–55.

Durlak, J.A., Weissberg, R.P., Dymnicki, A.B., Taylor, R.D. & Schellinger, K.B. (2011). The impact of enhancing students' social and emotional learning: A meta-analysis of school-based universal interventions. *Child Development*, 82(1), 405–32.

Dusenbury, L.A., Newman, J.Z., Weissberg, R.P., Goren, P., Domitrovich, C.E. & Mart, A.K. (2015). The case for preschool through high school state learning standards for SEL. In J.A. Durlak, C.E. Domitrovich, R.P. Weissberg & T.P. Gullotta (eds), *Handbook of social and emotional learning: Research and practice* (pp. 532–548). New York: Guilford.

Elias, M.J, Ferrito, J.J. & Moceri, D.C. (2016).*The other side of the report card: Assessing students' social, emotional, and character development.* Thousand Oaks, CA: Corwin.

Elliott, S.N. & Gresham, F.M. (2008). *SSIS Classwide Intervention Program: Teacher's guide.* Minneapolis, MN: NCS Pearson.

Hattie, J. (2015). *What works best in education: The politics of collaborative expertise.* Retrieved from https://www.pearson.com/content/dam/corporate/global/pearson-dot-com/files/hattie/150526_ExpertiseWEB_V1.pdf

KidsMatter. (2014). Australian Early Childhood Mental Health Initiative. *Connections with the National Quality Framework: Developing children's social and emotional skills.* Canberra, ACT: Commonwealth of Australia. Retrieved from https://www.kidsmatter.edu.au/sites/default/files/public/KM%20Linking%20resources%20C2%20Book_web_final.pdf

McGinnis, E. (2012). *Skillstreaming the elementary school child: A guide to teaching prosocial skills* (3rd edn). Champaign, IL: Research Press.

McIntosh, K. & Goodman, S. (2016). *Integrated multi-tiered systems of support: Blending RTI and PBIS.* New York: Guilford Press.

Merrell, K.W., Carrizales, D., Feuerborn, L., Gueldner, B.A. & Tran, O.K. (2007). *Strong Kids: A social and emotional learning curriculum for students in Grades 3–5.* Baltimore, MD: Brookes.

Osher, D., Bear, G.G., Sprague, J.R. & Doyle, W. (2010). How can we improve school discipline? *Educational Researcher,* 39, 48–58.

Roffey, S. (2011). *Changing behaviour in schools: Promoting positive relationships and wellbeing.* London: Sage.

Sanson, A. (2016). What leads to a happy, healthy, and productive life? Looking back over a 32-year longitudinal study and forward to future generations. *InPsych*, 38(1), 24–25.

Stormont, M., Reinke, W.M., Herman, K.C. & Lembke, E.S. (2012). *Academic and behaviour supports for at-risk students: Tier 2 interventions.* New York: Guilford.

UNESCO, Learning Metrics Task Force (2013). *Toward universal learning: What every child should learn.* Report No. 1, Executive Summary. Washington, DC: UNESCO Institute for Statistics and the Center for Universal Education, Brookings Institute.

Zins, J.E., Weissberg, R.P., Wang, M.C. & Walberg, H.J. (eds) (2004). *Building academic success on social and emotional learning: What does the research say?* New York: Teachers College Press.

CHAPTER 13

Talking circles

Jennifer Cartmel, Marilyn Casley and Kerry Smith

Introduction

If we view children as strong, capable individuals who co-construct their own experience, we as children's services educators, in conjunction with parents, are providing children with the skills to deal with society with all its current issues. This chapter explores a concept called 'talking circles', which can be used to build relationships between children and adults, and help children understand their everyday experiences. First, the structure and process of the talking circle is defined. Second, the importance of talking circles to the wellbeing of children is discussed. Finally, it outlines the range of strategies that can be used within talking circles to foster and support children's abilities to engage in conversations with other children and adults. These strategies form the basis of the talking circles and, when used on a regular basis in school classrooms and child-care settings, have a profound influence on children's wellbeing.

Through the process of talking to one another, children become creators of their own future as they collaborate and build relationships. Talking circles are designed to encourage children to ask questions about their lives and how they can make a difference for themselves, each other and their community. This process helps to build the resilience and leadership skills of children. These qualities are important to help children consider day-to-day challenges and further contribute to their sense of wellbeing.

Talking circle process defined

The talking circle process is an effective way to build relationships both between adults and children, and between children. It is a process that helps to develop communication skills (including talking and listening) to build strong and responsive relationships between adults and children.

Talking circles provide children and adults with a safe environment in which to practise their relationship-building. Being provided with opportunities to develop relationships is critical to children's wellbeing. The talking circle process strengthens children's capacity to negotiate, problem-solve and show empathy towards their peers. Further, establishing and maintaining relationships is made possible in the talking circle through the capacity of the adult educator to create a safe space and the necessary time for children and adults to establish a sense of connection with each other.

The talking circle process is underpinned by a children's rights perspective. The process is designed to help adults to uphold the children's rights to participate in matters that affect them. Listening to children gives educators the opportunity to understand children's lived experiences or in fact what their reality is about. Listening to children is linked to the notion of talking. In this context, Lundy (2007) conceptualises four elements to consider: 'children must be given the opportunity to express a view; children must be facilitated to express their views; the view must be listened to; the view must be acted upon, as appropriate' (p. 933). This is particularly evident in the conversations between everyone in a talking circle because there is a willingness to hear and understand each person's experiences, knowledge and perspectives. This is important if each person is to realise who they are and to understand their potential for responsible decision-making. This seems to be the key to developing leadership skills within individual children and their sense of belonging to a group or a community.

How talking circles began

The talking circle (Cartmel & Casley, 2010) was based on a guided conversation process that was mindful of the **socio-cultural developmental** characteristics of children. These circles helped undergraduate university students to 'get to know' children better by using a conversational process. Each semester, students were allocated to child-care services for work-based learning in field education placement. In these settings, they undertook guided conversations – that became known as talking circles – with children aged between 5 and 12 years.

Socio-cultural development is the development of children which occurs through relationships within the family, neighbourhood, community and society.

Each university student was the designated educator of a talking circle conversation, encouraging children to learn to look within themselves to see their inherent capabilities and discuss their everyday experiences. Children learn to organise their world-views through interaction with others (Ulvik, 2014; van Nijnatten, 2013) and these views are supported through the development of trusting relationships between adults and children. The voices of children are heard in the exchange of thoughts if children are given the capacity to present and negotiate their identities. Consequently, in these conversations, children were able to develop a sense of **agency** and take an active role in what happened to them and the decisions made for them. They developed perspectives about their

Agency: children have agency when they have influence over things that happen to them. Their thoughts are heard and they are given the capacity to negotiate.

past and present, and were able to project themselves into the future. The talking circle process encouraged individual children to hear from others so that barriers between them dissolved. It also allowed children to consider and understand new perspectives, enabling them to make connections between each other based on their ideas and capabilities. This self-awareness led the children to make positive changes in their circumstances and enhanced their wellbeing. Furthermore, it encouraged them to think about their role in and responsibilities to their families and the local community, including their school-age care service.

When the authors of this chapter used guided conversation with educators in the children's services sector, these conversations helped educators become self-aware, strengthened their relationships with each other and developed their practices in working with children and their families (Cartmel et al., 2015). In revising the process for use with groups of children, it was necessary to consider what the student educators would need to know. It was agreed that in order to facilitate a talking circle session, they would need to be knowledgeable about children's learning and development, attachment theories, conversational processes and, in particular, the U theory (Scharmer, 2009). These ideas were based on the premise that educators understand that knowledge is socially constructed rather than acquired (Moss & Petrie, 2002, p. 119), and that they see the child as a co-constructor of knowledge in partnership with the adult and the other children. To facilitate conversations, the educators needed to be able to know how to initiate and promote healthy relationships with and between the children. They also needed to consider how to provide a safe space, both physically and psycho-socially. Meeting these expectations allowed for the conversations to occur.

The talking circle format was designed on the U-process (Scharmer, 2009). The U-process was developed through intensive learning-by-doing in a range of settings around the world as a strategy for addressing highly complex challenges, solving complex problems and realising opportunities. The process is based on 'ancient wisdom' and systems thinking, which focuses on the shared learning that occurs between individuals in the group. Every member of the group needs to build relationships with the others, and make the necessary connections to share what each other knows so that together they can act as a whole to co-create new opportunities and innovative ideas that address their most complex challenges (Scharmer, 2009). The U-process afforded the children and the student educator the opportunity to learn more about themselves and each other. The process has three phrases that build on each other. The authors have linked the work of Scharmer (2009) and Yukelson (2008) to describe the process (See Figure 13.1).

Generative listening is an approach to listening that requires deepening connections to the content.

The U-process is based on a special type of listening called **generative listening**, which is defined as listening to oneself, listening to others and listening to what emerges from the group (Scharmer, 2009). Generative listening requires each individual to be focused on the conversation that is emerging from the whole group. For the children, generative listening means thinking about the life experiences of other children – not just about themselves. A feature of generative listening is that it means suspending judgement. It also means being focused on the here and now, and thinking

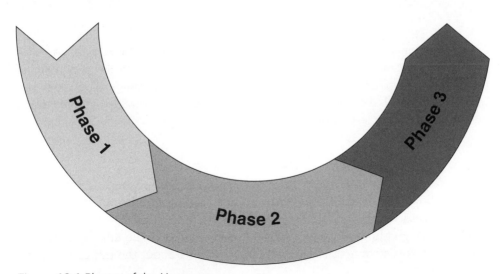

Figure 13.1 Phases of the U-process.

Source: Abridged from Scharmer (2009) and Yukelson (2008).

about what is emerging from the 'whole-group' conversation. It helps children start to consider other children's perspectives and circumstances rather than just their own experiences. Also, children are listening to, and thinking about, the ideas of others and this, in turn, helps them to understand their own situations. Through generative talking and listening, children gain a sense that they are widening their perception, and they are able to feel more connected to the group as a whole. They can move from hearing multiple perspectives to co-creating future possibilities.

> You know that you have been using generative listening when you realize that, at the end of the conversation, you are no longer the same person you were when you started the conversation (Scharmer, 2009).

According to Kahane (2002) children identify themselves as one group rather than a number of individuals; we listen self-reflectively to 'hear ourselves through others' ears' (p. 4). The educator helps the children to listen to each other. The children recognise and respect the diversity of values, ideas and opinions of their peers. The children eventually take ownership of the group processes, relying less on the adult to support them engage in the process of actively exchanging knowledge and ideas, identifying their capabilities and thinking about future possibilities.

CASE STUDY 13.1: ANNA'S STORY

Anna was the educator of the talking circle at Waterdale School-Age Care (SAC) Service. She had facilitated a series of eight talking circles during her field education placement. At the end of the field placement period, she told the children that she would not be able to continue the talking circles. The children expressed their disappointment.

- If you were Anna what would you have done next?

Anna used the process of the talking circle to help the children problem-solve about the situation. The children decided to write a petition to the supervisor of the SAC service to ask whether the talking circles could continue. The supervisor was impressed with the children's enthusiasm and commitment. She assigned a staff member and the process continued.

The talking circle process may not always be a positive experience for all the children; however, the skills of the educator can alter the tone and opportunities of the process for the children. One strategy is for the educator to allow the children the opportunity to have control over the agenda of the talking circle. This situation creates a context in which children can talk about the things that most affected them.

CASE STUDY 13.2: SURVIVING A CHALLENGING SESSION

Millie, aged nine years, and Carly, aged 11 years, asked Ella, their talking circle educator, whether they could take a turn at facilitating a session. Ella agreed, and the children led the group for a session. The experience was disastrous for all concerned. Millie and Carly led the group with language that bullied the rest of the children. Some children started to cry. Millie and Carly were also shouting loudly as they tried to take control of the group. Ella intervened.

• What do you think Ella did next?

Ella stopped the session and the following week, she facilitated the session to debrief with the children. Using a series of carefully planned questions, she helped the children to understand each other's perspectives about what happened. They listened to each other, described their feelings and together made suggestions about how they could lead the group differently in future sessions.

The educators facilitating the talking and listening process between groups of children were inevitably influenced by the conversations. They displayed a genuine interest in the lives of the children through generative listening. Generative listening is fluid rather than static because the children talk and listen with an 'open heart' – which is linked to their ability to think creatively and spontaneously. Moving to generative talking and listening requires us to 'move outside ourselves' (Kahane, 2002, p. 4). The more involved the educators were in using the process, the more skilled they became at providing the opportunities for the children to be self-aware. This self-awareness helps children to experience the sense of agency that contributes to their feelings of resilience and wellbeing. The ability to be actively involved in decision-making is a rite of passage in enabling children to take control of their needs, take healthy risks, build resilience and set out strong pathways for their future (UNICEF Australia, 2014).

A critical aspect of talking circles is the space in which they occur. It needs to be calm enough to allow the children to focus on the communication skills required for sustaining the conversation. One of the talking circles groups met weekly in the Peace Room. After Week 3, the educator was told by school staff that this room was where children were sent during the school day to reflect on inappropriate behaviour. It became apparent that the negative environment impacted on the children's willingness to be involved, and subsequently the talking circles were held in an alternative room with cushions instead of chairs. The children's engagement in the process was markedly different after the room change; their willingness to engage in respectful ways increased dramatically compared with previous weeks. By building a safe space for conversations, as well as attending to the physical environment, the educator carefully created an emotional space in which the children were able to build connections with each other.

Sometimes it was difficult for children to listen to what others were saying and stay connected with the group. This was the case for Tim (aged eight years), who attended the Meadow Park talking circle once a week on Thursday afternoons. Student educator Bree facilitated the group that included Tim and his brother Mitch. The children had decided that if a child did not want to be part of the group anymore, they could leave; or if a child was disruptive, they could be asked to leave the group. Tim was really keen to be part of the group but he could not sit still and listen to what the other children were saying. Bree asked the children what they thought should happen for Tim, and they responded that because there were two educators (a student educator plus the university supervisor), one of them could sit with Tim while the other interacted with the rest of the children. This was not possible because the university supervisor was not going to be in attendance in future weeks. The children then decided that each of them would spend time with Tim because when he had someone with him he would sit quietly and not distract the others. In this way, Tim was able to feel like he could belong to the group and Mitch was able to participate without constantly feeling responsible for Tim's behaviour.

Self-regulation is important to children's wellbeing and this attribute develops during early childhood. The talking circle was an opportunity for the children to learn to self-regulate. The protocols for the talking circles developed by the group meant that children were free to leave the circle if they felt they were unable to focus on the conversation. Children were also able to negotiate to rejoin the group when they felt that they could concentrate. This process allowed children to practise self-regulation, and gave the group an opportunity to assist in this process.

Structure of a talking circle

The format for the talking circle is such that it creates time and space for the children to make connections and build trust with each other and the educator, making the way for open and genuine conversation. The university students started each talking circle session with an activity designated as 'getting connected'. This helped the children get to know each other and build relationships. Each talking circle ended with a closing activity that involved each child and the educator reflecting on what happened for them during the session.

To enable children of different ages and abilities to tell their stories in various ways, play activities, art, music and storytelling can be used to 'create a methodological framework that children fill with their own meaning' (Veale, cited in Christensen & James, 2008, p. 131). The work created by the children was kept as a means of documenting the story of the group's journey using the talking circle process.

Keeping in mind the fact that each individual and group is unique, even though a certain range of activities were recommended, there was no step-by-step plan to be followed routinely. The educator listened for the subtleties of the group and used different activities to increase opportunities for children to tell their story. The process of allowing the children to take the lead gave them the opportunity to take ownership of the talking circle which, in turn, lessened the power imbalance between adults and children and enhanced children's confidence.

Benefits of talking circles

The talking circles program is based on the idea that learning occurs when a cycle of reflection and action takes place, and consequently children and adults can create knowledge and act together out of their individual and common experiences. According to Senge et al. (2005), all learning integrates thinking and doing. Learning is about how we interact with the world and the skills that develop because of our interactions. If we think about learning as a sense of awareness of self and belonging or connection, we have an opportunity to understand more about how we learn and change. If we always think in the same way, we continue to see the world from a place where we are comfortable or from our own world-view, and we disregard other options that are different from what we already know. This hinders the learning process (Senge et al., 2005). The overall framework for talking circles comes from thinking about learning as a process of self-awareness and community-building.

The learning that emerged from the talking circle process accrued benefits for both the children and the educators.

The features of the talking circle that indicated change for the children included each child's ability to self-reflect; develop communication skills through talking and listening; gain social and emotional growth with the ability to have open and questioning relationships with others; develop problem-solving skills and a willingness to negotiate change. The group of children became confident to lead and facilitate the talking circles with their peers. There was a high level of consciousness to ensure everyone in the group had a chance to contribute and work together.

Children's capacity to listen, take notice of others, respect others and be supportive of their peers increased during the talking circle process. They were able to describe the changes they were experiencing. For some children, the talking circles were a place where their emotions felt balanced and in control:

> *It's calm, it's peaceful and I feel less stressed* (Chani, aged 11).
> *We can talk about things that we can't at the oval. We talk about ourselves* (Mitch, aged 9).

For other children, the talking circle was a place where they felt they belonged:

> *People like me here. I have made more friends. I can trust people here* (Tiani, aged 9).
> *I don't get into trouble anymore at school. We can get tips when we are having hard times. We get to share our life* (Zac, aged 10).
> *It's a place to get away from noise and others. We can talk about our problems and we can share our feelings and share about our families* (Manni, aged 8).

There was also a change in the social interactions that occurred in the playground:

> *I don't get bullied anymore* (Reece, aged 9).

Children looked forward to the weekly gatherings to build their confidence and self-esteem.

The student educators indicated that change for them during the talking circles process included an improvement in their ability to self-reflect; they developed skills for communicating with children; they learned to have open and questioning relationships with children; they gained the ability to let go of habitual ways of 'managing' a group of children; and their confidence to help children problem-solve increased.

These student educators often commented that they were not initially confident in their ability to develop relationships with children. Many commented on their fear of letting go of the 'power' and their lack of understanding of how to 'manage' the groups' behaviour. Children were looking to the educator to take control, and when that failed to happen there was often chaos. For the student educators, the opportunity to reflect on the process each week with their peers and lecturers was significant in building their capacity to work with children in a meaningful way. This circumstance gave the students ideas and confidence to try out new things each week, and to include the children in the problem-solving process:

> *Students were not confident in their abilities and understandings about developing relationships with children* (Marilyn, university lecturer).

The children and educators continued to practise building relationships with each other, and a feeling of trust began to emerge. As the sessions progressed, many educators found that the power differential in their relationships between themselves and the children started to diminish. Both the children and educators were gaining skills and confidence in their ability to communicate with each other.

Furthermore, the children were able to open up to the group and talk about things that really mattered to them:

> The children actually listened to each other's stories. The children are very open and they are interested in each other's stories. They have an idea about what is fair and an understanding about what is serious in someone's life. Some faces were shocked when they heard some of the other children's stories. They are able to empathise because they are old enough to understand (Ella, student educator).

Talking circle participants sense a widening of their perception, and can thus be connected to the group as a whole. Further, as shared meaning is developed, there is a shift in power and the ability of the educator to let go of particular ways of thinking about how adults are in relation to children. This shift in power allows children to perceive themselves as contributing equitably to the process. They sense a genuine conversation, where the power base is seen as a more democratic process of guiding rather than telling:

> Adults are different here because they don't talk at us. They are nice (Madison, aged 11).

Subsequently, talking circle participants have a greater sense of trust in each other that has developed through the communication process.

In addition, the educator needs to be aware that eventually children will take ownership of the group. This shift is an indicator of the developing capacities of children. The educator needs to ensure that children have the self-awareness and self-reflection skills to sustain their contribution to the talking circle. The talking circle process is dynamic and fluid, yet it has a significant impact on development of a child's sense of identity and agency which, in turn, influences their capacity for resilience and wellbeing.

The talking circle process uses guided conversations with children and is underpinned by the key principle of practice based on the concept that the child is a strong, powerful, competent and complex individual. Talking circles make a difference for children's wellbeing. These differences in the children are described as the child's ability to self-reflect, develop communication skills, problem-solve and a willingness to negotiate change. In turn, this allows for the development of healthy relationships between adults and children, and children and children, which are essential to children's wellbeing.

How to conduct talking circles

Educators need to plan all aspects of the process when introducing and conducting talking circles. Features to be considered include the creation of the space and time and the communication skills necessary for the process to happen. The communication processes are complex, and the facilitation capacities of the educators involved are important considerations. When children become more aware of the manner in which they develop relationships with each other through talking circles, they are more able to listen and talk to each other about topics that matter to them and to their community. This self-reflection and self-awareness contributes to their overall sense of wellbeing.

First, in order for the talking circle process to be successful, consideration needs to be given to both the physical surroundings and the emotional climate. The space provided for the talking circles needs to be quiet and relaxing, giving children the opportunity to be feel the sense of 'presence'. Presence gives the child and educator the space to notice what is going on within and between individuals. In order to 'listen and talk' to others, all other activities need to be suspended; reducing the distractions means that children are able to solely focus on the conversations in the talking circles.

In one of the talking circles, the educator asked a child, 'Can you listen while you are reading the book?' The child said, 'Yes I can hear you'. The educator responded, 'But can you listen?' The book represented a barrier within the process. This exchange led to the child putting the book away so that she could join the group as a listener who was present in the talking circle, fully aware of all the conversations that were occurring. In turn, this experience created a sense of belonging and community-building which led to an even deeper engagement in the conversation process.

The development of psychological safety requires time for everyone – children and educators – to develop trust in each other. Everyone needs to perceive each other as respecting each person's contribution to the process. Development of group protocols is critical. Protocols initiated by children's ideas provide guidance for everyone about how the group will 'be together'. This discussion leads to the development of trusting relationships.

Second, the educator of the talking circle needs to consider the development of their communication skills. They need a deep understanding of how the process of conversation builds trusting relationships between the children and the adult, and between the children. The critical feature of communication interaction is that it is a three-way process (Stanfield, 2000), as there is a better chance of the meaning of a conversation being understood. Scharmer (2009) describes this three-way process as generative conversation (talking and listening). It is an active process in which all participants exchange thoughts and ideas, gaining a deeper understanding about each other and creating opportunities for future engagement.

PAUSE AND REFLECT 13.1: THREE-WAY PROCESS

Have you ever considered conversation as a three-way process including talking, listening and thinking about where each person is coming from, and their reaction to the information they receive? Think about the most recent conversation you have had with a peer or a colleague. Can you identify the features of the three-way process?

Conclusion

Talking circles use a conversational process to assist in building healthy relationships between adults and children and between children. This process is based on shared learning, where the adults and children get to know each other and share what each person knows so that together they can develop understandings and ideas to respond to life challenges. The process helps children's social and emotional growth and enhances their potential for problem-solving and decision-making.

Talking circles are effective if they are conducted in quiet, safe and relaxing spaces that are considered emotionally safe by the children. Together, the adults and children develop the protocols for being together in that space. Only through safety and trust can the capacity for new ways of thinking about life's challenges be made possible.

The adult facilitator of the talking circle must have the required communication skills that build trusting relationships with children. These are necessary for building trusting relationships between adults and children and require the adult to use generative talking and listening. Evidence suggests the talking circle process has the potential for building relationships and lessening the power imbalance between adults and children, opening up new possibilities for child participation.

Summary

The key messages highlighted in this chapter are:

- Talking circles are a conversational process that builds trusting relationships between adults and children, and between children.
- The process strengthens children's capacity to problem-solve and participate in decision-making, building resilience and enhancing social and emotional growth.
- Consideration needs to be given to building a safe space because physical and emotional safety are essential for building trusting relationships and for open and inquiring conversation to take place.
- Educators need to have generative talking and listening skills, including self-awareness, capacity to suspend judgement and the ability to have open and honest conversations with children.

Questions

13.1 Why is it important for adults and children to be able to converse with each other?

13.2 What characteristics do adults need to display in order to build relationships with children?

13.3 Describe the type of listening skills that are most effective in conversations between adults and children.

13.4 What has changed in your thinking? How might this affect your practice?

References

Cartmel, J. & Casley, M. (2010). *Talking circles: Gathering the wisdom of children.* Brisbane: Early Childhood Australia Queensland Branch.

Cartmel, J., Macfarlane, K., Casley, M. & Smith, K. (2015). *Leading learning circles for educators engaged in study.* Brisbane: Griffith University.

Christensen, P. & James, A. (2008). *Research with children: Perspectives and practices.* London: Routledge.

Kahane, A. (2002). *Changing the world by changing how we talk and listen.* Retrieved 20 December 2013 from http://pioneersofchange.net/ communities/foresight/articles/Kahane%20on%20talking%20and%20 listening.pdf

Lundy, L. (2007). 'Voice' is not enough: conceptualising Article 12 of the United Nations Convention on the Rights of the Child. *British Educational Research Journal*, 33: 927–942. doi:10.1080/01411920701657033

Moss, P. & Petrie, P. (2002). *From children's services to children's spaces.* Abingdon: RoutledgeFalmer.

Scharmer, O. (2009). *Theory U: Leading from the future as it emerges.* San Francisco: Berrett-Koehler.

Senge, P., Scharmer, O., Jaworski J. & Flowers, B. (2005). *Presence.* London: Nicholas Brealey.

Stanfield, B. (2000). *The art of focussed conversation.* Victoria, BC: New Society Publishers.

Ulivk, O. (2014). Talking with children: Professional conversations in a participation perspective, *Qualitative Social Work*, March, 1–16. doi:10.1177/1473325014526923

UNICEF Australia (2014). *Things That Matter Children in Australia share their views.* Sydney, Australia: UNICEF Australia. Retrieved 2 July 2016 from http://www.unicef.org.au/Upload/UNICEF/Media/Documents/UNICEF-Australia-Things-That-Matter.pdf

van Nijnatten, C.(2013). *Children's agency, children's welfare: A dialogical approach to child development, policy and practice.* Bristol: Policy Press.

Yukelson, A. (2008). *Into the wave of life: An exploration of Dreamcatchers' healing work.* Halifax, NS: ALIA Institute.

CHAPTER 14

Partnering with families

Sivanes Phillipson

Acknowledgement

I would like to acknowledge Alison Elliot, who contributed to the ideas and writing that appeared in a similar chapter in the first edition (2014) of this book. While the chapter in this second edition has been updated and revised from the first edition, I acknowledge Alison's earlier contributions that appear in this edition.

Introduction

Nationally and internationally, there is clear recognition that families are central to children's development and wellbeing. This recognition is evident through a growing body of research literature and the inclusion of family partnership as a key consideration in national early years frameworks. For example, the Early Years Learning Framework (EYLF) states, 'From before birth children are connected to family, community, culture and place. Their earliest development and learning takes place through these relationships, particularly within families, who are children's first and most influential educators' (DEEWR, 2009a, p. 7).

Families, being children's first educators, play a major role as children's main support in the ecology of their care and wellbeing (Phillipson, Sullivan & Gervasoni, 2017). Within the ecology of children's development, families are the main carers for children at home and they also act as support systems for children's learning within early childhood environments such as preschools. A disparity in what happens at home and outside of home, in particular in the early childhood education environment, can impact on children's health and wellbeing. Hence, it becomes imperative for early childhood educators to find ways to connect and partner with parents to support children in their early years of development and learning. A warm, caring, consistent and responsive environment underpins a quality care and education experience for early years learners.

This chapter focuses on how to gauge opportunities to partner with families in articulating support systems around child health and wellbeing. In particular, it explores how educators can reach out to families and build the necessary partnerships to successfully support them in their parenting and caring roles, with the aim of impacting positively on children's health and wellbeing.

Families and their children's wellbeing

CASE STUDY 14.1: THE STORY OF MICHAEL AND ANNIE

Michael is a single parent of four-year-old Annie. They live in a regional town in Victoria. Being the sole carer for Annie, Michael has to juggle full-time work and care for Annie. He wants to see his daughter happy and successful in the future and believes that she should have a wholesome upbringing despite his own personal circumstances. Michael makes sure that Annie has healthy food and engages in plenty of physical outdoor activities. He makes an effort to limit her viewing of the 'idiot box' (television) so that she spends more quality time on her educational activities, and with him.

Michael is one of those parents who tries to achieve a holistic development for their children's wellbeing. The **Organization for Economic Cooperation and Development (OECD)** (2015) stresses that **families** have the main role in looking after their children's whole wellbeing including their physical, cognitive and socio-emotional development. In recent years, neuroscience research has provided crucial evidence of the importance of early nurturing and support for early learning and later success (Shonkoff & Phillips, 2000). Shonkoff and Philips noted the importance of children's interaction with their environment, in particular with their family, as a major factor influencing their learning. Their notation assumes that early experiences affect the brain development of young children, and thus the foundation of intelligence, emotional health and educational outcomes (Elliott, 2006).

Shonkoff (2012) also postulated that early experiences are biologically embedded and carried over to adulthood, hence

The Organization for Economic Cooperation and Development (OECD) is a congregation of 34 economies (countries) and 70 non-member economies that work together to promote economic growth, prosperity and sustainable development.

Families may include parents, siblings, grandparents and others in the extended family group. Parents usually are a mother and a father of a child.

highlighting the importance of supporting children's wellbeing from an early age. He argued that for adequate support to be given at an early age, it is crucial for the adults who care for and educate children to have the appropriate mindset to support children's wellbeing. In other words, healthy and nurturing early experiences are enhanced by positive family and other proximal interactional environments such as children's informal and formal educational environments, and these early experiences are the foundation for children's wellbeing.

Wellbeing can be viewed across three interactive dimensions: (1) physical development and health; (2) cognition, encompassing processes of communication, thinking and problem-solving, as well as processes that underpin social relationships with others and healthy lifestyles; and (3) a socio-emotional dimension that encompasses the development of identity, self-concept and self-esteem, and pro-social skills (Zaff et al., 2003). Given the inextricable links between children's physical, cognitive and socio-emotional development, there is a clear need for educators and other professionals to collaborate with families to promote each of these dimensions (Durlak et al., 2011; Sammons et al., 2008), especially in the early years. In the light of evidence of decline in Australian parental involvement in children's formal educational environments, it is important to encourage early years **collaboration** between educators and families before children progress to mid-primary levels (Daniel, 2015).

> **Collaboration** requires people to work together in negotiation of space, time and values that meet a set of goals.

PAUSE AND REFLECT 14.1: FAMILY INVOLVEMENT

Policies of many early childhood centres have been to actively involve parents in their daily routine. This expectation is reflected in the EYLF, especially in the guide for educators (DEEWR, 2009b). Why do we have to start thinking about family involvement in children's wellbeing from the early years?

Partnership concept

Michael's belief in, and trust of, his child's early childhood educator is fundamental to the concept of **partnership** in establishing and maintaining children's wellbeing. Michael's trust in, and involvement with, his child's educator is especially interesting since single parents like Michael are likely not to engage well in

> **Partnership** denotes a collaboration that has shared values and beliefs to achieve target outcomes.

their children's schooling activities, even at early childhood levels (Auger, 2014). Involvement from parents like Michael and others is paramount because family involvement in children's education and care has long been recognised as central to optimising developmental and learning outcomes. Several decades of research show that effective, sustainable school and early childhood contexts – as well as good child outcomes – are achieved when educators, community and families

CASE STUDY 14.2: ANNIE'S TEACHER

Michael raves about Annie's teacher Kathy Lawson. 'Kathy Lawson, you know … she is great! Full of life experience and knows what children need, I have time for her … I know that I can leave my baby with Kathy, knowing that she will be looked after … Annie is full of beans when I pick her up, talking about things she learned, who she played with … and you know what, Kathy has time for me too!'

have a sense of connectedness and work in partnership (Davies, 2000; Elliott, 2006; Epstein & Jansorn, 2004; Hornby, 2011).

Of all the models for educators and families working together, the partnership model has always been seen as the most suitable (Hornby, 2011). The concept of partnership implies mutual or synchronous awareness and understanding within and between members of a group or 'community'. It is more than 'parent involvement'; it signifies a deep level of engagement with caring, teaching and learning. Turnbull et al. (2011) suggest that there are seven elements to partnership: trust, respect, competence, communication, commitment, equality and advocacy. These seven elements form a complex layer of relationship within a collaborative framework. Further to this, Hornby (2011) proposed a parental involvement framework that emphasised the needs of the families and how they would engage in the sphere of their children's education and wellbeing.

No matter which theoretical framework one uses, the fundamental objective of partnership with families must be based on building trust, respect, open communication and shared beliefs, values and goals. Importantly, it must embody mutually respected values about development and learning, shared expectations about the respective roles of family and school, with an articulated vision for each child's developmental journey (Elliott, 2006; Hornby, 2011). Notwithstanding the importance of mutually valuing perspectives on child-rearing and education, there must be concomitant respect for the role and value of learning and education in contemporary society.

PAUSE AND REFLECT 14.2: RESPECTFUL BEHAVIOURS AND ACTIONS

The concept of respect can be simple yet abstract. People who are involved in friendships, relationships or some sort of liaison show respect through many facets of behaviour and action. What are some of these behaviours or actions? Think of them in relation to a conversation you might have with a parent who has little time for you.

Educators' role

Partnership cannot exist without close reciprocal relations between all players. In turn, these are dependent on caring, committed and knowledgeable teachers and inspired education leadership and governance. Internationally, there is strong evidence demonstrating links between students' academic success and school–family relationships. Extensive meta-analysis by researchers such as Hattie (2009) and Sammons et al. (2008) demonstrated that teachers and schools are instrumental in children's academic success. Effective teachers and schools are most likely to impact positively on children's overall wellbeing and their engagement with learning. Schools with a cohesive sense of 'community' have meaningful communications with families, more harmonious climates, better academic results and higher school retention rates than those where families and students are disengaged (Davies, 2000; Epstein, 2001; Jordan & Plank, 2000; Rowe, 2005). Effective and responsive schools have especially positive effects for early years learners who face multiple disadvantages, especially those linked to poverty (Daniel, Wang & Berthelsen, 2016; Melhuish et al., 2008).

Nationally, the importance of school–community involvement and partnerships is widely recognised and accepted. The *Educational Goals for Young Australians in the Melbourne Declaration on National Goals for Schooling in the Twenty-First Century* stress that parents as children's first and continuing educators should be pivotal in curriculum planning, and that all schools should have 'a commitment to collaboration' with families. The Early Years Learning Framework highlights the centrality of 'genuine partnerships' with families who are 'children's first and most influential teachers' (Australian Government, 2008, p. 12). The *Educators' Guide to the Early Years Learning Framework* emphasises that: 'Partnerships are based on the foundations of understanding each other's expectations and attitudes, and building on the strength of each other's knowledge' (DEEWR, 2009b, p. 11).

Established in 2012, the National Quality Framework, or more precisely its key quality guidelines, the National Quality Standards, capture the EYLF model of families' partnership by advocating that educators work closely with families for the benefit of children (Australian Children's Education Care and Quality Authority, 2016). Standard 6 in particular outlines guidelines for educators and professionals in building partnerships with families to support children's overall wellbeing.

The National Professional Standards for Teachers (2012) also highlight the importance of partnerships with families in promoting children's sense of self and wellbeing, valuing diversity and promoting cultural identity. The Standards specify four levels of competence in engaging with families:

1. *Graduate.* Understand the strategies for working effectively, sensitively and confidentially with parents/carers (7.3.1, p. 19).
2. *Proficient.* Establish and maintain respectful collaborative relationships with parents/carers regarding their children's learning and wellbeing (7.3.2, p. 19).
3. *Highly accomplished.* Demonstrate responsiveness in all communications with parents/carers about their children's learning and wellbeing (7.3.3, p. 19).

4. *Lead*. Identify, initiate and build on opportunities that engage parents/carers in both the progress of their children's learning and in the educational priorities of the school (7.3.4, p. 19).

Although the standards for educators and professionals describe ways for educators to collaborate with families to support children's learning, research highlights that a disparity between informal family and formal education settings impacts on children's learning (Hildenbrand et al., 2015), which can extend to their wellbeing. It seems that this disparity may exist due to educators' and professionals' lack of confidence, and perhaps even lack of knowledge of family characteristics and how diverse families engage with their children (Blackmore & Hutchison, 2010; Saltmarsh, Barr & Chapman, 2015; Stacey, 2016).

CASE STUDY 14.3: MICHAEL'S BLENDED FAMILY

Michael has started dating Laila who has two of her own children. Annie loves spending time with her new 'step siblings' and they have started to become a blended family. Annie's kindergarten is having its annual special disco for the year but it happens to fall on the same day she spends with Laila and her children. Michael tried to convince the director of the kindergarten to allow Laila's children to join Annie at the disco along with him. But the kindergarten refused it on the basis that blended families were not part of the kindergarten's concern. Annie was disappointed!

Educational contexts for children – whether they are schools or early learning settings – are diverse. While many have strong, shared cultural ties and affiliations with families, others are characterised by extreme social, cultural and economic diversity. In reaching out and engaging with families, embracing the diverse constellations of families' influences, experiences and beliefs about children and childhood is paramount. Each family is unique and educators must get to know each family on a one-to-one basis to truly facilitate early childhood or school experiences. A one-size-fits-all approach to family partnerships almost never works because of the unique situation of each family – and especially the most vulnerable families. Even within 'named' socio-cultural groupings such as 'Aboriginal' families, or 'Islamic', 'Tongan' or 'middle-class Australian' families, for example, there is dramatic variation. In other words, even within this large socio-cultural grouping diversity exists where no two families are the same. This includes single-parent families, such as Michael's, blended families and same-sex parent families. Most families desire to be included in activities that support their children's health and wellbeing development (Lam, Wu & Fowler 2014) and hence, it is important to find ways to work with these diverse families in promoting their children's health and wellbeing.

Today, most schools and early learning centres implement a range of activities and events to involve families, but with varying degrees of success. Some have high family engagement in numerous activities whereas others struggle to get sufficient response from families. While the National Professional Standards for Teachers, the Early Years Learning Framework, and the National Quality Framework require educators to have a high level of family engagement, the process of engaging families can be a complex matter.

PAUSE AND REFLECT 14.3: DEALING WITH PARENTS

Educators have deal to with parents as part of their daily activities. How can educators do this in a sensitive manner?

Engaging and partnering with families

While the rhetoric for partnering with families is strong, actually building those partnerships is complex – especially where families experience significant economic and educational disadvantages or where there is considerable linguistic and cultural diversity. In early childhood contexts, where children tend to participate on a part-time basis and perhaps for a year or two only, establishing genuine connectedness with families can be challenging. At the same time, parents are usually most interested in their children's development when they are very young. Moving along a continuum from **communication** to involvement, and on to partnerships and connectedness, requires proactive strategies to reach out to individuals and communities in ways that are meaningful, such as the way Kathy Lawson does with Michael (refer to Case Study 14.4) (Elliott, 2006; Hornby, 2011). This is no easy task, given the range of individual families using an early childhood service or school and the demands on personnel and teaching resources.

Communication is the process of using words, actions and gestures to express one's feelings, thoughts and ideas. Communication is very context specific and in relation to parents, the feelings, thoughts and ideas are around their concerns for their children's wellbeing.

Our job as educators and educational leaders is to initiate and sustain an engagement process that suits each family. We must provide support and encouragement on a one-to-one basis so that each family engages in a way that is supportive for their child. Educators sometimes need guidance around this process so a framework, or guiding principles, can help them to partner with families. These principles can be found in works by: Hornby (2011); Phillipson, Sullivan and Gervasoni (2017); Turnbull et al. (2011); and Sukkar, Dunst and Kirkby (2017). They include strategies for clear communication, trust building, non-judgemental liaisons and flexible and culturally relevant responses.

The process of building partnerships requires a team approach that is paved by inspired and dedicated leadership and implemented by committed and competent educators who value and respect each child in their group or class and each child's family. Developing partnerships with families is not a job for the lone educator, nor is it one to be pushed onto the centre director or school executive. It must be a collaborative effort on the part of everyone in a school or early childhood centre.

It is important to remember that for educators to engage with families they need to have an open-minded, generous-spirited view of the classroom, early years learners and families. When our perceptions of children and families are clouded by assumptions based on experiences of previous families, previous school practices or cultural stereotypes, we will either not reach out in a meaningful way or our efforts will fail.

When family events are held at times when most of them can not attend – due to full time employment or lack of opportunities – lack of engagement is inevitable. Also failing to be flexible in response to different family needs – such as the one in Michael and Annie's situation (see Case Studies 14.3 and 14.4) – also requires some rethinking about school rules if families are to be engaged in meaningful ways. While there are industrial, workplace, insurance and occupational health and safety compliance issues that must be considered when planning any family outreach activities, it is also evident that to engage families we need to know them as people, value them as individuals and understand something of their lives. And sometimes we need to 'go the extra mile' to support children; for example, the way Kathy Lawson made a difference in engaging a busy parent like Michael (Case Study 14.4).

Early childhood educators are often the first educational contact for parents since they left school themselves and for some parents, school was not a happy experience. In the early parenting years, when parents are at their most unsure about child-rearing, there are good opportunities to influence attitudes about child development and learning, to learn from parents about their family and their child, and to form enduring partnerships. Ensuring these first interactions are warm, caring, nurturing, respectful and supportive will facilitate longer-term parent engagement. If parents are not involved when children first start school or child care, it is generally difficult to involve them later (Daniel, 2015).

It is acknowledged that parents want the best for their children, and that they want their children to be happy and to succeed (Epstein, 2001; Sarra, 2005; Volk &

SPOTLIGHT 14.3: STRATEGY FOR POSITIVE AND PRACTICAL SUPPORT

Whatever the situation, always start on a positive note when talking with parents. Share something of a child's progress and activities on a weekly – or preferably daily – basis. Provide practical support around wellbeing in small ways: a weekly tip sheet with suggestions for promoting wellbeing at home, such as ideas for positive behaviour guidance, or packing healthy lunches; regular family after-work get-togethers over an early barbecue teamed with a visit from an 'expert' who can informally chat about a relevant parenting or wellbeing issue. A text, short email or note every day or so helps you keep in touch. When parents or caregivers come to collect a child, make sure someone is available to have a conversation about the child's day. Whatever the purpose of the conversation, start and finish on a positive note.

Long, 2005). However, the challenges of contemporary life – with work, social and economic pressures – mean that parents cannot always provide the nurturing that children need. Growing pressures to juggle work and family mean many parents struggle to manage day-to-day life and events, let alone keep abreast of educational developments and the school events calendar. But it does not imply a lack of care; it means they may need support. Where children's families are not able to fully support their wellbeing, it is more important than ever that educators create safe, rich, personalised learning contexts for each child (Hayes et al., 2006).

Conclusion

This chapter sets out how, as educators, we must first connect with families as partners in order to meet the developmental needs of early years learners. The rationale is that children tend to thrive better when educators partner with families to nurture their children and promote their wellbeing. The chapter presents various approaches for educators to connect with families in order to support young children's wellbeing. The main thread of this chapter conveys that getting to know families and partnering with them – especially those who might otherwise be marginalised for various reasons – is the best insurance there is for a child's wellbeing.

Summary

The key messages highlighted in this chapter are:

- Partnering with families acknowledges their central role as children's first teachers.
- Each family is unique, so educators must connect with each family on a one-to-one basis.
- Partnership implies understanding each other's goals and ways of being, knowing and doing, including shared understanding of educational purpose and outcomes.
- Engaging with families means understanding and respecting where they are in their lives.
- Trust and strong interpersonal relationships provide the glue for family partnerships and collaborations with the school or early learning centre.

Questions

14.1 What features should be in an early childhood or school policy to ensure it is family friendly and promotes true connectedness with families?

14.2 Discuss the importance of connectedness in your community. What are some of your connections to your community?

14.3 What steps could you take to develop links with community services and health professionals in your area?

14.4 The mismatch between home and school is usually more pronounced when children participate in an educational program far removed from their home community – for example, one close to their parents' workplace or one where educators' cultural and linguistic background is very different. Often, educators do not live in or near their workplace so have little first-hand knowledge of the community that it serves. Reflect on what this might mean in terms of educators getting to know each family and for families using the centre.

References

Auger, A. (2014). *Child care and community services: Characteristics of service use and effects on parenting and the home environment.* (3669357 Ph.D.). University of California, Irvine.

Australian Children's Education Care and Quality Authority (2016). *National Quality Framework.* Retrieved from http://www.acecqa.gov.au/ national-quality-framework

Australian Government (2008). *The Melbourne Declaration on National Goals for Schooling in the Twenty-First Century.* Canberra: Commonwealth of Australia.

Blackmore, J. & Hutchison, K. (2010). Ambivalent relations: The 'tricky footwork'of parental involvement in school communities. *International Journal of Inclusive Education*, 14, 499–515.

Daniel, G. (2015). Patterns of parent involvement: A longitudinal analysis of family-school partnerships in the early years of school in Australia. *Australasian Journal of Early Childhood*, 40(1), 119–28.

Daniel, G.R., Wang, C. & Berthelsen, D. (2016). Early school-based parent involvement, children's self-regulated learning and academic achievement: An Australian longitudinal study. *Early Childhood Research Quarterly*, 36, 168–177. doi:http://dx.doi.org/10.1016/j.ecresq.2015.12.016

Davies, D. (2000). *Supporting parent, family and community involvement in your school*. Portland, OR: Northwest Regional Educational Laboratory.

Department of Education Employment and Workplace Relations (DEEWR) (2009a). *Belonging, being, becoming: Early Years Learning Framework*. Canberra: Australian Government.

—— (2009b). *Educators belonging, being & becoming: Educators' guide to the Early Learning Framework*. Canberra: Australian Government.

Durlak, J.A., Weissberg, R.P., Dymnicki, A.B., Taylor, R.D. & Schellinger, K.B. (2011). The impact of enhancing students' social and emotional learning: A meta-analysis of school-based universal interventions. *Child Development*, 82(1), 405–32.

Elliott, A. (2006). *Models of school-community connectedness*. Report to ACT Department of Education and Training. Sydney: ACER.

Epstein, J.L. (2001). *School, family and community partnerships: Preparing educators and improving schools*. Boulder, CO: Westview Press.

Epstein, J.L. & Jansorn, N.R. (2004). School, family and community partnerships link the plan. *The Education Digest*, 69(6), 19–23.

Hattie, J. (2009). *Visible learning: A synthesis of over 800 meta-analyses relating to achievement*. Oxford: Routledge.

Hayes, D., Mills, M, Christie, M. & Lingard, B. (2006). *Teachers and schooling: Making a difference*. Sydney: Allen & Unwin.

Hildenbrand, C., Niklas, F., Cohrssen, C. & Tayler, C. (2015). Children's mathematical and verbal competence in different early education and care programmes in Australia. *Journal of Early Childhood Research*. doi:10.1177/1476718X15582096

Hornby, G. (2011). *Parental involvement in childhood education: Building effective school-family partnerships*. doi:978-1-4419-8379-4

Jordan, W. & Plank, S. (2000). Talent loss among high achieving poor students. In M. Sanders (ed.), *Schooling students placed at risk: Policy, research and practice in the education of poor and minority students* (pp. 86–108). Mahwah, NJ: LEA.

Lam, W., Wu, S.T.C. & Fowler, C. (2014). Understanding parental participation in health promotion services for their children. *Issues in Comprehensive Pediatric Nursing*, 37(4), 250–64. doi:10.3109/01460862.2014.95113

Melhuish, E.C., Phan, M.B., Sylva, K., Sammons, P., Siraj-Blatchford, I. & Taggart, B. (2008). Effects of the home learning environment and preschool center experience upon literacy and numeracy development in early primary school. *Journal of Social Issues,* 64(1), 95–114. doi:10.1111/j.1540-4560.2008.00550.x

National Professional Standards for Teachers (2012). Website. Retrieved 20 January 2014 from http://www.aitsl.edu.au.

Organization for Economic Cooperation and Development (OECD) (2015). *Skills for Social Progress: The Power of Social and Emotional Skills,* OECD Skills Studies. Paris: OECD Publishing. doi: http://dx.doi.org.ezproxy.lib.monash.edu.au/10.1787/9789264226159-en

Phillipson, S., Richards, G. & Sullivan, P.A. (2017). Parental perceptions of access to capitals and early mathematical learning: Some early insights from Numeracy@Home project. In S. Phillipson, A. Gervasoni & P.A. Sullivan (eds), *Engaging families as children's first mathematics educators : International perspectives* (pp. 127–145). Singapore: Springer.

Phillipson, S., Sullivan, P.A. & Gervasoni, A. (2017). Families as the first mathematics educators of children. In S. Phillipson, A. Gervasoni & P.A. Sullivan (eds). *Engaging families as children's first mathematics educators: International perspectives* (pp. 3–14). Singapore: Springer.

Rowe, K. (2005). *Report of the National Inquiry into the Teaching of Literacy.* Canberra: DEST.

Saltmarsh, S., Barr, J. & Chapman, A. (2015). Preparing for parents: How Australian teacher education is addressing the question of parent-school engagement. *Asia Pacific Journal of Education,* 35, 69–84.

Sammons, P., Sylva, K., Melhuish, E., Siraj-Blatchford, I., Taggart, B. & Jelicic, H. (2008). *Effective pre-school and primary education 3–11 project (EPPE 3–11): Influences on children's development and progress in Key Stage 2: social/behavioural outcomes in Year 6.* Nottingham: DCSF.

Sarra, C. (2005). Imagine the future by learning from the past. Paper presented at the Communities in Control conference, Melbourne, 7 June.

Sheridan, S. & Kim, E.M. (2015). *Processes and pathways of family-school partnerships across development (Research on family-school partnerships.* doi:978-3-319-16931-6

Shonkoff, J.P. (2012). Leveraging the biology of adversity to address the roots of disparities in health and development. *Proceedings of the National Academy of Sciences,*109 (Sup. 2), 17302–307.

Shonkoff, J.P. & Phillips, D.A. (2000). *From neurons to neighborhoods: The science of early childhood development.* Washington DC: National Academies Press.

Stacey, M. (2016). Middle-class parents' educational work in an academically selective public high school. *Critical Studies in Education,* 57(2), 209–23.

Sukkar, H., Dunst, C.J. & Kirkby, J. (eds). (2017). *Early childhood intervention: Working with families of young children with special needs.* London: Routledge.

Turnbull, A., Turnbull, R., Erwin, E.J., Soodak, L.C. & Shogren, K.A. (2011). *Families, professionals and exceptionality*. Boston: Pearson.

Volk, D. & Long, S. (2005). Challenging myths of the deficit perspective: Honoring children's literacy resources. *Young Children*, 60(6), 12–19.

Zaff, J.F., Smith, D.C., Rogers, M.F., Leavitt, C.H., Helle, T.G. & Bornstein, M.H. (2003). Holistic wellbeing and the developing child. In M.H. Bornstein, L. Davidson, C.L.M. Keyes & K.A. Moore (eds), *Wellbeing: Positive development across the life course*. Mahwah, NJ: Lawrence Erlbaum.

CHAPTER 15

Being a digital image-maker: Young children using the digital camera in learning

Narelle Lemon

Introduction

Young children's social and emotional wellbeing is crucial in the learning context. How they develop their sense of being, their sense of self and their voice are key drivers when it comes to supporting young children and their wellbeing. In this chapter an innovative way to extend learning stories and invite young people to be digital image-makers is explored, using the digital camera as a technology that scaffolds confidence, self-awareness and communication skills.

Seeing young people as capable photographers and documenters of their learning experiences supports their journey of building stable social and emotional approaches to meaning-making and understanding the world (Lemon, 2015; Sairanen & Kumpulainen, 2014). The sense of belonging in the classroom can shift when young people are honoured for their capacity to record what is happening around them, and for the ways in which this can lead to new ways of understanding oneself, seeing others, and developing relationships and leadership qualities in onself. Most importantly, the impact of sharing one's voice enhances the sense of self and wellbeing. This can be especially visible in students and young people, who previously had not had an opportunity to share their perspectives, voice and sense of belonging.

In this chapter, students in the early and primary years share their understandings and meaning-making through their photographs and visual narratives. In doing so, they demonstrate how it is possible to foster the emotional health and wellbeing of all children in a learning environment – especially those individual young people who are more vulnerable due to the presence of multiple risk factors (Coad, 2012; Wall, 2014).

Technology to support learning

In the context of early childhood education, both in early years settings and within the primary school, digital literacy is changing (Hopkins, Green & Brookes, 2013). Young learners are invited to interpret, consider, decode, decipher, transmit, transform and create information visually, verbally and aurally in networked and interlinked ways (Tayler et al., 2008). Before entering formal education, many young children are already immersed in interactive digital environments and engaging with digital devices (Edward-Groves & Langley, 2009). Observation is increasing with regard to early years learners informally developing skills in information navigation, retrieval and creation from their earliest years (Hopkins et al., 2013), which has a significant impact on the formal learning environment. There is no doubt that pressure exists for educators to maintain awareness and skills in being able to rethink the concepts of digital literacy and digital awareness, and how this can inform meaning-making and social and emotional development, while providing opportunities to engage with the new technologies of information and communication (Anstey & Bull, 2006; Baker, 2010; Cloonan, 2010; Cope & Kalantzis, 2000; Pahl & Rowsell, 2005).

In thinking about the place and value of technology in the early years environment, there is a need to extend beyond what Plowman and Stephen

---

PAUSE AND REFLECT 15.1: DIGITAL CAMERA IN THE EARLY YEARS LEARNING ENVIRONMENT AS USED BY CHILDREN

Some of the benefits of integrating a digital camera into the early years learning environment are listed below. Can you think of any other benefits?

Digital cameras are:
- portable
- cost effective
- handheld
- tangible.

Digital cameras:
- provide accessible technology
- allow users to document and record
- promote reflection over time
- support kinesthetic and visual learnings.

Using digital cameras, images:
- can be generated (both still and moving).
- mark a memory in time
- can be repeatedly looked at over time
- thicken ways of seeing.

(2005) acknowledge as practitioners generally referring to 'children playing with the computer' (p. 145). The early years learning space can provide opportunities for meaningful integration of technology to support 'continuity of the learning experience across different scenarios or contexts' that support what emerges from the 'availability of one device or more per student' (Chan et al., 2006, p. 154).

Pedagogically, learning by doing is often the norm when exploring technology (Hopkins et al., 2013). It is clear that 'learners' eager adoption of practices using new technologies presents challenges to traditional school-based teaching and learning relationships, pedagogies and curricula' (Kalantzis, Cope & Cloonan, 2010, p. 62). This chapter shares how the digital device of a mobile handheld **digital camera** can acknowledge both familiar and unfamiliar skills to support the development of digital literacy. It also acknowledges that, while being a student-centred approach that scaffolds young people's sense of self and their emotional and social wellbeing, this meaningful application of a digital technology assists young people to share their meaning-making. The cases presented demonstrate how early years learners can be engaged in their learning settings as they interact with and without technology to negotiate their own understanding of themselves, each other, and of the world around them. The mobile technology becomes not only an example of how the digital camera can be a device for the children to interact with hands-on learning specific to technology, but also an example of interaction to support development in engagement with peers, teachers and other people in their learning community (Barron, 2006; Chan et al., 2006; Lemon, 2015; Looi et al., 2010; Sairanen & Kumpulainen, 2014; Squire & Klopfer, 2007).

Digital camera: a hand-held portable digital device that takes video or still photographs by recording images, still or moving, on an electronic image sensor.

For the young people discussed in this chapter, the digital camera was a way for them to become **digital image-makers**. It allowed them to document and record their learning experiences while also developing their social and emotional skills alongside academic ones, such as literacy. Photographs show fragments that have no specific beginning or ending. The photographer – the generator of the image – captures a moment in time that, in the education field, has the power to allow for ongoing reflective practice, viewing over time and establishing and re-establishing meaning or meanings (Lemon, 2008; 2015). 'Images created with photographs thicken ways of seeing' (Bach, 2001a, p. 1), and assist in marking a memory in our time, a memory around which we 'construct stories' (Clandinin & Connelly, 2000, p. 114). When the photographs are paired with text (spoken or written), a **visual narrative** is formed. Visual narratives produced digitally promote a portable digitised environment that makes for 'anytime' and 'anywhere' teaching and learning possibilities (Groundwater-Smith, Ewing and Le Cornu, 2007; Halverson & Gibbons, 2008; Lemon, 2015; Sairanen & Kumpulainen, 2014; Snyder, 1999; Soep, 2008). The digital technology has the advantage of supporting young children to share their experiences (Burns, Dimock & Martinez, 2000; Dillner, 2001; Leu & Kinzer, 2000; Sairanen & Kumpulainen, 2014). Conversations that occur during and after the creation of images can provide opportunities for young learners that move beyond

Digital image-makers are capturers of lived experiences in the digital format, which can include still photography or moving image (video).

Visual narratives are visuals such as digital images paired with words, written or verbal, to support the communication of a narrative. This acknowledges the needs to highlight the narrative of the visual narrative being told as there is more than one story to be told at any one time or reading.

simply writing about the photograph. Working within a constructivist framework (Denzin & Lincoln, 2000; Guba & Lincoln, 1994; Schwandt, 1994), young children's visual narratives are understood to reveal insights into their lived experiences and their existing schemas of knowledge and understanding. The use of visual narrative as a means for providing opportunities for learners to 'photograph their world inside and outside of school' is discussed in this chapter in relation to working with students in an educational setting (Bach, 2001b, p. 1).

Digital camera in the learning environment: An example in practice

By following the stories of two children aged between five and seven years from an early years setting in Melbourne, insights are gained into the lived experiences of young digital image-makers. The children worked with the author of this chapter, who at the time was the teacher, and were seen as co-researchers inquiring into their being and becoming. The relationship between visual methods to study the classroom and the learning paired with participatory research was a key one in terms of valuing all contributions to studying the lived experiences of the educational environment. The digital camera was introduced to the young children as a technology device for learning – most importantly, a device that they would use to share their stories of learning and teaching.

This chapter shares a study that aimed to show how young children are capable image-makers, and through this can engage productively with portable digital technology and generate digital photographs that share children's lived experiences of teaching and learning. In doing this, careful scaffolding had to occur in order to support safe use of the digital camera (e.g. children had to wear the strap around their wrist in case of an accidental bump), to teach children to take

SPOTLIGHT 15.1: SAFE USE OF THE DIGITAL CAMERA IN THE EARLY YEARS LEARNING ENVIRONMENT AS USED BY CHILDREN

Considerations for safe use of the digital camera in the early years setting can include:

- strap use
- clear instructions
- asking for help
- no running when using
- trying different angles
- charging battery
- taking care not to bump photographer

- holding
- taking of turns
- helping others
- trust
- care of camera
- uploading and saving images
- keeping camera dry and clean.

They have a meaning.

I'm just going to wait.

Until new learning happens.

See, I can turn it off.

And save the battery.

I'm saving the batteries.

So I can make more pictures later.

Figure 15.2

'That's the grade six classroom. I took it because my buddy used to be in it. I'm friends with some grade sixers like Thomas, Jordan and Monty. Do you know Jordan, Miss Lemon? He's good at kicks. He has glasses.'

Figure 15.3

'Joy [learning support aide] gave me silkworms to look after. I have to take them home every day and feed them and care for them. I have to get leaves from the tree outside our room.

One's Spike and he's six centimetres.

This is Delicious cause he eats too much.

This is Fight cause he has a bruise on the back. See. He was fighting with another silkworm. This morning I put new leaves in because they ate so much when I was out. Yesterday they went to bed late because they were sneaky and wouldn't stop eating. We left the light on and then we turned it off. One climbed up the wall and then pushed the leaf down. Now they are lazy because they were so full.'

James' confidence and wellbeing developed when he was able to use the digital camera. His sharing of his photos with others allowed him to realise that he would be listened to, and that he could communicate what he was experiencing. The impact of sharing his voice supported considerable growth in his mental health and overall wellbeing: James moved from being a serial absentee student to an engaged learner; he shifted from being withdrawn in class to realising others would like to work and play with him; and he realised that it was acceptable to share his feelings and perspectives at the time of an event rather than to express frustration or anger at a later date.

For Stan and James, the possibility of being a digital image-maker and of capturing their learning in the classroom seemed to offer many opportunities. It was an opportunity to show who they were as individuals, rather than conforming to their unproductive labels. Being able to see the change in each of these boys over time in relation to their attendance at school, and their enthusiasm for learning, was affirming of the students' engagement in an inclusive classroom environment. It became evident that the generation of digital images, and the corresponding reflection to form visual narratives, was an activity that supported the building of confidence and self-esteem, alongside linguistic and interdisciplinary skills.

Although 'life is not a narrative' (Richardson, 1990, p. 10), we can make sense of our lives, and the lives and stories of children, through narrative construction (Clandinin et al., 2016; Clandinin & Connelly, 1994; Maslin-Ostroski & Ackerman, 2005; Richardson, 1990). In using children's stories to make sense of experiences, insights into their world are acquired. Researchers (Clandinin et al., 2016; Clandinin & Connelly, 1994; Maslin-Ostroski & Ackerman, 2005; Wall, 2014) have identified that stories can be powerful tools that provide real pictures of real situations because stories invite us into someone else's world.

Stan invites us into his world – one of struggle in the classroom, but one of pride where he feels like 'the king of the jungle' when he experiences success (see Case Study 15.2). Stan knew he was different from his peers and he could often be heard saying 'I can't do it'. At times, he could be found sitting by himself at his desk in a state of confusion. Without his round face, rosy red cheeks and cheeky toothy grin on display, he seemed a shadow of himself, distant from his peers and from his learning.

The digital camera ignited an enthusiasm in Stan that was contradictory to past behaviour, where low motivation, tiredness and refusal to participate in learning activities often dominated. With the digital camera in hand, Stan explored his learning experiences with a renewed curiosity for what was happening around him. He shares this in his reflective conversation after using the camera.

Stan's words (like James' in Case Study 15.1) reflect his thinking and enthusiasm for creating visual narratives juxtaposed with one of his visual narratives about learning experiences within the educational learning environment (see Figures 15.4 to 15.7).

The story in Case Study 15.2 shows us Stan's valuing of the positive label 'Stan the Cameraman', as his peers fondly called him. Stan's world had opened up. He could now show us what he saw through the camera lens, and with the words to accompany his photographs he produced visual narratives that flowed and explained his feelings. It was easy to forget that, at seven years of age, Stan had difficulty recognising the letters of the alphabet or basic sounds, and constructing simple sentences to write down his thoughts. It is the photographs that slow the moments in time and, for Stan, these moments invite further exploration as they can be viewed and explored individually or as a collection that makes a mini-narrative series (Bach, 2001a; Spence, 1986).

CASE STUDY 15.2: STAN'S REFLECTION ABOUT BEING A DIGITAL IMAGE-MAKER

Visual narrative produced by Stan

Can I be cameraman?

I think we should have photos of this.

You have to get the right aim to get a good photo.

I love doing different angles.

I can stand and make it look like you are on their shoulders.

Taking photos from a distance.

You have to move.

No, that's not right . . . I can't see everyone.

Some people say I'm good at it.

I like it.

Figure 15.4

'Brad and Mark are working together like a team. They are doing really well and when they finish it maybe Miss Lemon might let them do whatever they want to build?'

Figure 15.5

'They ... Brad's trying to get something out of the box to fix it.'

Figure 15.6

'This one is Max. He's not really helping Cameron. That's not teamwork.'

Figure 15.7

'I put the camera on the table and pushed my hand up a bit higher. I zoomed in a bit closer. Claire is looking down at her pieces. I think it is pretty good. She's trying hard, she's only got one arm. She's a super trier today.'

For Stan the slowing of time through the photographs he generated also supported him to slow down and communicate the story he wished to share. Over time, his language developed and so did his confidence to shift from verbal-only narrative sharing to want to write down his stories. Previously he had difficulty in doing this, and would actively avoid writing activities. Communication extended to emotional and social skills. Stan soon realised peers enjoyed and appreciated his expression of joy during image-making, and this encouraged him to continue to do this during non-camera activities.

Images can represent lived experiences or learning as it happens. They are a form of visual representation similar to that of journal entries, documents and field notes (Bach, 2001a). In using visual narrative in the learning environment, opportunities are provided to evoke memories around which we construct and reconstruct life stories (Bach, 2001a). Importantly, they enable moments in time to be revisited from different perspectives, inviting the possibility of a transformation of fixed memories (Bach, 2001a; Spence, 1986). Photographs can be a tool for learning, reflecting and growing from lived experiences (Barker & Smith, 2012). In the classroom context, photographs can depict celebrations, personal achievements, actions and interactions, and can assist in exploring recurring stories (Spence, 1986; Bach, 2001a).

Inviting the children of this study to use digital cameras to photograph learning that was important to them provided a shared focus for the learning community, whereby individuals are encouraged to be active and construct their identities in relation to these communities. As Wenger (1998) attests, 'such participation shapes not only what we do but also who we are and how we interpret what we do' (p. 4). In integrating the digital camera into the curriculum and the learning community, the children were engaged in meaningful practices where the 'core value and set of practices … support the belief that all students … regardless of their strengths, weaknesses, or labels (and) should be full members of the … community' (Sapon-Shevin, 2007, p. xii). At the heart of this was trust and mutual respect of the children – their voice, their stories and their capacity to use a digital camera and be digital image-makers.

Conclusion

Young children as digital image-makers are capable of exploring their perspectives of teaching and learning through the generation of visual narratives when the digital camera is seen as a valuable mobile learning tool (Barker & Smith, 2012; Egg et al., 2004; Lemon, 2015; MacNaughton, 2005; Sairanen & Kumpulainen, 2014). Still digital photographs and the subsequent visual narratives that they created highlighted the enactment of a research method that was transparent and innovative, and provided a tangible experience with which for young children to engage. As Egg et al. (2004) demonstrate, working in this way involves 'children immediately in collecting, interpreting, and using information without the need for extensive training, understanding of theory or knowledge of the research literature' (p. 11). The visual narratives created by the young children in these case studies communicated new insights into teaching and learning that challenged beliefs and assumptions about their capability to engage with reflective and metacognitive thinking. The integration of technology in the early years learning environment demonstrates how a sense of belonging and self can be enhanced for individuals. The process of generating images, as well as sharing their voice, embodies trust, mutual respect and the valuing of emotional and social development (Barker & Smith, 2012; Lemon, 2015).

Summary

Through scaffolding meaningful integration of a digital camera into learning opportunities, the young people in this chapter were able to become digital image-makers of their lived learning experiences, supporting their social and emotional wellbeing (Coad, 2012; Lemon 2007, 2008, 2013, 2015).

The key messages highlighted in this chapter are:

- Young children are capable digital image-makers. When supported to use the technology, trust underpins this student-centred learning approach to technology integration.
- Digital technology supports communication of ideas through ways that are not just based on text and language and that promote diverse learning styles and a sense of belonging.
- Mobile devices such as digital cameras enhance kinaesthetic and visual ways of learning because they are portable, handheld and easily used within the dynamic early years learning environment.
- Early years children can inquire into their own sense of being, becoming and wellbeing when they are able to explore alternative ways to reflect about their lived experiences and meaning-making.

Questions

15.1   How does being a digital image-maker empower a young child to develop confidence and self-esteem?

15.2   How can handheld mobile technology, such as a digital camera, be utilised in the early years classroom for student-centered learning experiences?

15.3   How can the honouring of voice for young children be supported through being and becoming a digital image-maker?

15.4   What other types of digital devices can be used to support early years learners' emotional and social wellbeing?

References

Anstey, M. & Bull, G. (2006). *Teaching and learning multiliteracies: Changing times, changing literacies*. Adelaide: Australian Literacy Educators Association.

Bach, H. (1998). *A visual narrative concerning curriculum, girls, photography etc.* Edmonton: Qual Institute Press.

—— (2001a). The place of the photography in visual narrative research. *Afterimage*, 29(3), 7.

—— (2001b). *The place of the photograph in visual narrative research – project statement.* Retrieved 4 November 2004 from http://www.findarticles.com/p/articles/mi_m2479/is_3_29/ai_80757500/print.

Baker, E. (ed.) (2010). *The new literacies: Multiple perspectives on research and practice.* New York: Guilford Press.

Barker, J. & Smith, F. (2012). What's in focus? A critical discussion of photography, children and young people. *International Journal of Social Research Methodology*, 15(2), 91–103.

Barron, B. (2006). Interest and self-sustained learning as catalysts of development: A learning ecologies perspective. *Human Development*, 49(4), 193–224.

Berger, J. (1980). *About looking.* London: Writer and Readers Publishing.

Burns, M., Dimock, V. & Martinez, D. (2000). Storytelling in a digital age. *Tap into Learning*, 3(2), 6–9.

Chan, T-W. et al. (2006). One-to-one technology-enhanced learning: An opportunity for global research collaboration. *Research and Practice of Technology Enhanced Learning*, 1(1), 3–29.

Clandinin, D.J., Caine, V., Lessard, S. & Huber, J. (2016). *Engaging in narrative inquiries with children and youth.* London: Routledge.

Clandinin, D.J. & Connelly, M. (1994). Telling teaching stories. *Teacher Education Quarterly*, 21(1), 145–58.

—— (2000). *Narrative inquiry: Experience and story in qualitative research.* San Francisco: Jossey-Bass.

Cloonan, A. (2010). *Multiliteracies, multimodality and teacher professional learning.* Melbourne: Common Ground.

Coad, J. (2012). Involving young people as co-researchers in a photography project. *Nurse Researcher*,19(2), 11–16.

Cope, B. & Kalantzis, M. (eds) (2000). *Multiliteracies: Literacy learning and the design of social futures.* London: Routledge.

Denzin, K. & Lincoln, Y.S. (eds) (2000). *Handbook of qualitative research* (2nd edn). Thousand Oaks, CA: Sage.

Dillner, M. (2001). Using media flexibly to compose and communicate. *Reading Online*, 5(1). Retrieved 30 March 2008 from http://www.readwritethink.org/lessons/lesson_view.asp?id=985.

Edward-Groves, C. & Langley, M. (2009). i-Kindy: Responding to home technoliteracies in the kindergarten classroom. Paper presented at the National Conference for Teachers of English and Literacy, Hobart. Retrieved 6 August 2012 from http://www.englishliteracyconference.com.au/files/documents/hobart/conferencePapers/refereed/Edwards-Groves%20complete.pdf.

Egg, P., Schratz-Hadwich, B., Trubswasser, G. & Walker, R. (2004). *Seeing beyond violence: Children as researchers.* SOS-Kinderdorf: Hermann Gmeiner Akademie.

Groundwater-Smith, S., Ewing, R. & Le Cornu, R. (2007). *Teaching: Challenges and dilemmas.* Melbourne: Thompson.

Guba, E.G. & Lincoln, Y.S. (1994). Competing paradigms in qualitative research. In N.K. Denzin & Y.S. Lincoln (eds), *Handbook of qualitative research* (pp. 105–17). London: Sage.

Halverson, E. & Gibbons, D. (2008). Digital literacy as production: Youth participation in media arts learning environments. *Paper presented at the Annual Conference of American Educational Research Association.* New York, 24–28 March.

Hopkins, L., Green, J. & Brookes, F. (2013). Books, bytes and brains: The implications of new knowledge for children's early literacy learning. *Australasian Journal of Early Childhood*, 38(1). Retrieved 6 September 2013 from http://www.earlychildhoodaustralia.org.au/australian_journal_of_early_childhood/ajec_index_abstracts/books-bytes-and-brains-the-implications-of-new-knowledge-for-childrens-early-literacy-learning-free-full-text-available.html.

Kalantzis, M., Cope, B. & Cloonan, A. (2010). A multiliteracies perspective on the new literacies. In E.A Baker. (ed.), *The new literacies multiple perspectives on research and practice* (pp. 61–87). New York: Guilford Press.

Leitch, R. (2008). Creatively researching children's narratives through image and drawings. In P. Thompson (ed.), *Get the picture: Visual research with children and young people* (pp. 35–58). London: RoutledgeFalmer.

Lemon, N. (2007). Take a photograph: Teacher reflection through narrative. *Journal of Reflective Practice*, 8(2), 177–91.

—— (2008). Looking through the lens of a camera in the early childhood classroom. In J. Moss (ed.), *Research education: Visually–digitally–spatially*, pp. 21–52. Rotterdam: Sense.

—— (2010). Young children as digital photographers: Possibilities for using the digital camera in the primary classroom. *Australian Art Education*, 33(2), 1–27.

—— (2011). Arts and technology. In C. Klopper & S. Garvis (eds), *Tapping into the classroom practice of the arts: From inside out!* (pp. 97–132). Brisbane: Post Pressed.

—— (2013). Digital cameras as renewed technology in a gallery: Young people as photographers of their learning. Refereed paper for 2013 American Educational Research Association (AERA) Annual Meeting, San Francisco, 27 April–1 May.

—— (2015). Narratives by Children. In S. Garvis, E. Eriksen Ødegaard & N. Lemon (eds). *Beyond observation: narrative methods with young children* (pp. 83–104). Rotterdam: Sense Publishing.

Leu, D.J. & Kinzer, C.K. (2000). The convergence of literacy instruction with networked technologies for information and communication. *Reading Research Quarterly*, 35(1), 109–27. Retrieved 30 March 2008 from https://www.catchword.com/ira/00340553/v35n1/contp1-1.htm.

Looi, C-K., Seow, P., Zhang, B., So, H-J., Chen, W. & Wong, L-H. (2010). Leveraging mobile technology for sustainable seamless learning: A research agenda. *British Journal of Educational Technology*, 41, 154–69.

MacNaughton, G. (2005). *Doing Foucault in early childhood studies: Applying poststructural ideas.* London: Routledge.

Maslin-Ostroski, P. & Ackerman, R.H. (2005). Narrative inquiry: The wounded leader story. Paper presentation for the conference of the American Educational Research Association Annual Meeting, Montreal, March.

Pahl K. & Rowsell, J. (2005). *Literacy and education: Understanding the new literacy studies in the classroom.* London: Paul Chapman.

Plowman, L. & Stephen, C. (2005). Children, play and computers in pre-school education. *British Journal of Educational Technology,* 36(2), 145–57.

Prosser, J. (ed.) (1998). *Image-based research: A sourcebook for qualitative researchers.* London: Falmer Press.

Richardson, L. (1990). *Writing strategies: Reaching diverse audiences.* London: Sage.

Sairanen, H. & Kumpulainen, K. (2014). A visual narrative inquiry into children's sense of agency in preschool and first grade. *International Journal of Educational Psychology,* 3(2), 141–74.

Sapon-Shevin, M. (2007). *Widening the circle: The power of inclusive classrooms.* Boston: Beacon Press.

Schirato, T. & Webb, J. (2004). *Reading the visual.* Sydney: Allen & Unwin.

Schwandt, T.A. (1994). Constructivist, interpretativist approaches to human inquiry. In N.K. Denzin & Y.S. Lincoln (eds), *Handbook of qualitative research.* London: Sage.

Snyder, I. (1999). Using information technology in language and literacy education: An introduction. In J. Hancock, (ed.), *Teaching literacy using information technology: A collection of articles from Australian Literacy Educators' Association* (pp. 1–10). Newark, NY: International Reading Association.

Soep, E.M. (2008). Digital literacy as production: Youth participation in media arts learning environments. Paper presented at the conference of the Annual Conference of American Educational Research Association, New York City, America, March.

Spence, J. (1986). *Putting myself in the picture: A political, personal and photographic autobiography.* London: Camden Press.

Squire, K. & Klopfer, E. (2007). Augmented reality simulations on handheld computers. *Journal of the Learning Sciences,* 16(3), 371–413.

Tayler, C., Ure, C., Brown, R., Deans, J. & Cronin, B. (2008). *Victorian Early Years Learning and Development Framework and the Victorian Essential Learning Standards.* Draft discussion paper. Melbourne: University of Melbourne.

Wall, E. (2014). Visualizing risk: Using participatory photography to explore individuals' sense-making of risk. *Journal of Risk Research,* 17(4), 1–17.

Wenger, E. (1998). *Communities of practice: Learning, meaning and identity.* New York: Cambridge University Press.

CHAPTER 16

Promoting wellbeing with educationally disadvantaged children through community partnerships

Susan Whatman

Introduction

In Australia there are many children attending school who are educationally disadvantaged, meaning that they derive the least benefit from the education system. This chapter focuses on the essential role educators play in understanding the relationship between educational benefit and health, physical activity and wellbeing, along with their role in working in partnership with communities to *act upon* educational disadvantage and promote wellbeing in early years learners.

The chapter is organised into sections that provide the background knowledge relevant to the health promotion, physical activity and wellbeing for *all* early years learners, paying particular attention to students with backgrounds that for many reasons can be described as educationally disadvantaged. It reviews policies that should guide educator decision-making across the dimensions of health, physical activity and wellbeing. Insights are given into the relationship between recognition of culture and identity and educational rights, building resilience, safety and pride in the early years and the educator's role in fostering their development. While this discussion does canvass some social and contextual factors underpinning healthy development for children who experience disadvantage, the focus is more on what teachers can do to promote these dimensions from a salutogenic (or strengths-based) approach (Quennerstedt, 2008). The chapter concludes with a case study of how teachers can act locally and in partnership with national and community-level organisations to facilitate health, physical activity and wellbeing in early years learners.

Promoting health, physical activity and wellbeing in education: Some definitions, policies and principles

Health promotion

Health promotion: the World Health Organization's *Ottawa Charter for Health Promotion* (1986) specifies that educators should promote and maintain the health of children and young people and the wider community. Whole-of-community approaches enable an individual or group to realise aspirations, satisfy needs and cope with their environment. Health is therefore a resource for everyday living encompassing personal, social and physical capacities.

The World Health Organization's *Ottawa Charter for* **Health** *Promotion* (WHO, 1986) is an international commitment to improving health through the achievement of eight basic rights or prerequisites: peace, shelter, education, food, income, a stable ecosystem, sustainable resources, and social justice and equity. Health comprises not only a physical state, but spiritual and psychological ones, underpinned by access to and achievement of these basic rights. The relationships between health, education levels, income, home languages and cultural background, and social justice and equity is well discussed in the literature (Lonsdale, 2013). The impacts upon early years learners are equally well documented – for example, the longitudinal study of Indigenous children known as Footprints in Time which is now into its fifth iteration or 'wave' (Department of Social Services [DSS], 2014) and the Australian Council of Social Service (ACOSS) *Poverty Report* (ACOSS, 2014). There is clear evidence that having English as the main home language and living in two-parent, higher income households aligns with better health and education outcomes (ACOSS, 2014). Many early years learners do not live in such conditions, with 18 per cent of children whose main language is not English living in impoverished households (below 50 per cent medium income) compared to 11 per cent of English-speaking households (ACOSS, 2014, p. 23). Many of these factors are systemic in nature, and beyond the immediate control of teachers; these are the responsibilities of governments and communities to address. But improving understanding of the impact of socio-economic circumstances upon health and wellbeing provides a solid basis for deciding what can be done in professional practice to make a difference to a student's health and wellbeing. Educators are an interrelated stakeholder in all systemic measures.

A framework to account for educationally disadvantaged early years learners is suggested in the Australian Health Promoting Schools framework (AHPSA, 2000). Drawing on the *Ottawa Charter* (WHO, 1986), the framework notes that a health-promoting school is one that 'implements policies and practices that respect an individual's well-being and dignity, provides multiple opportunities for success, and acknowledges good efforts and intentions as well as personal achievements' (AHPSA, 2000, p. 8).

The AHPSA framework involves a whole-of-community approach which resonates well with the need to bring parent and community stakeholders into partnership with schools. Culturally safe support of students is highlighted as a key priority outcome in urban, rural and remote schools (AHPSA, 2000, p. 20) so these

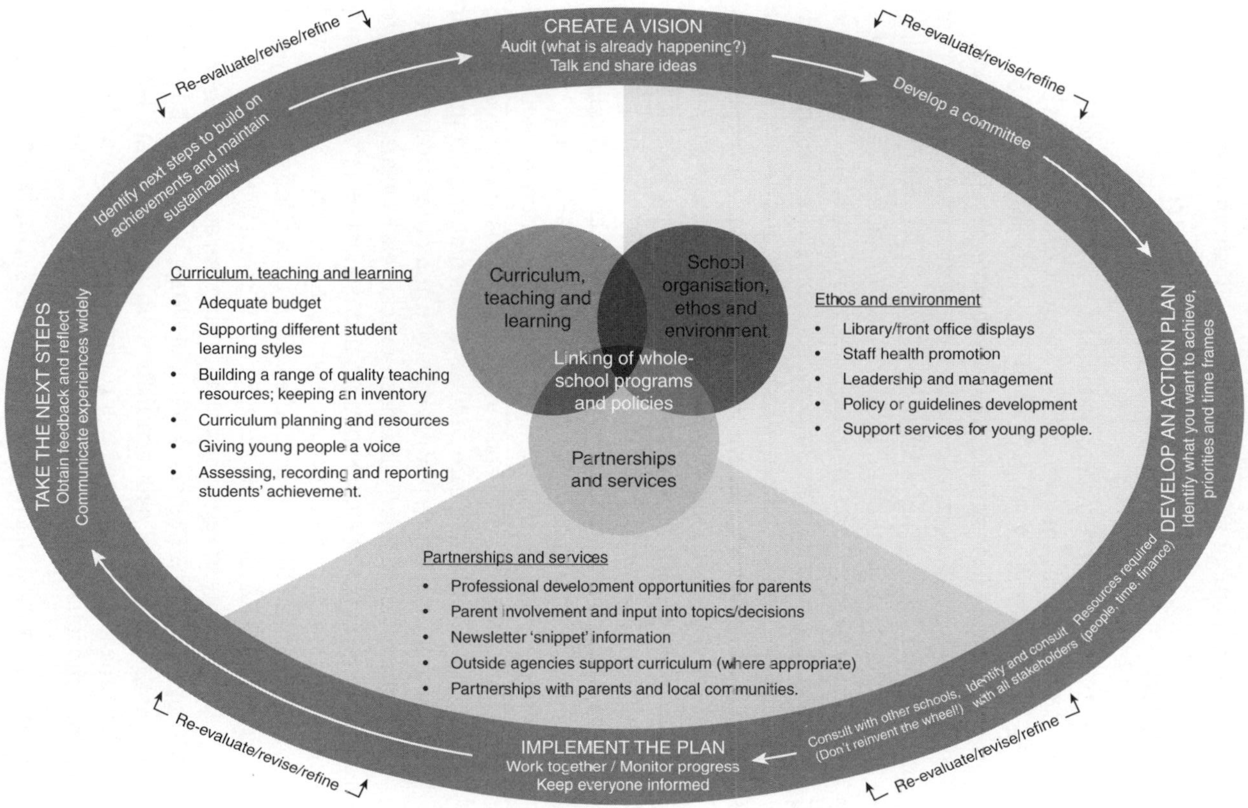

DEVELOP AN ACTION PLAN
Identify what you want to achieve, prioritise and time frames
Resources required (people, time, finance)
Identify and consult with all stakeholders

Re-evaluate/revise/refine
Develop a committee

CREATE A VISION
Audit (what is already happening?)
Talk and share ideas

Ethos and environment
• Library/front office displays
• Staff health promotion
• Leadership and management
• Policy or guidelines development
• Support services for young people.

School organisation, ethos and environment

Linking of whole-school programs and policies

Curriculum, teaching and learning

Partnerships and services

Partnerships and services
• Professional development opportunities for parents
• Parent involvement and input into topics/decisions
• Newsletter 'snippet' information
• Outside agencies support curriculum (where appropriate)
• Partnerships with parents and local communities.

IMPLEMENT THE PLAN
Work together / Monitor progress
Keep everyone informed
Consult with other schools.
(Don't reinvent the wheel!)

Re-evaluate/revise/refine

Curriculum, teaching and learning
• Adequate budget
• Supporting different student learning styles
• Building a range of quality teaching resources; keeping an inventory
• Curriculum planning and resources
• Giving young people a voice
• Assessing, recording and reporting students' achievement.

Re-evaluate/revise/refine

Identify next steps to build on achievements and maintain sustainability

Re-evaluate/revise/refine

TAKE THE NEXT STEPS
Obtain feedback and reflect
Communicate experiences widely

Figure 16.1 The Health Promoting Schools Framework.

Source: WA Health Promotiong Schools Association (WAHPSA) (2016).

community partnerships are essential, no matter where a school is located. The connections between respecting one's culture and identity, building opportunities and partnerships for success and acknowledging different ways of doing things are well argued. Health and wellbeing from a 'health-promoting' approach not only comprises opportunities for early years learners to be physically active, but to 'be' who they are, which is as a member and extension of their community.

Physical activity

Physical activity is body movement produced by skeletal muscles which increases the body's metabolic rate (affecting heart rate, breathing, sweating etc.). Health-related fitness (HRF) can result from physical activity when the movement is designed to improve cardiorespiratory endurance, reduce blood pressure and regulate body fat. Performance-related fitness (PRF) results from physical activity that focuses upon improving muscular strength and power, and cardiorespiratory fitness, usually for application in skilled movement or sports (Bouchard, Blair & Haskell, 2012).

Educational disadvantage can be understood as inequality of educational opportunity, resulting from schooling which fails to account for, or makes assumptions about, socio-cultural and economic contexts and other broader structural inequalities, such as limited access to resources (Lingard, Sellar & Savage, 2014).

The Australian Government established national guidelines for **physical activity** for children in 2004. They note that children between the ages of 5 and 12 years need at least 60 minutes of moderate to vigorous physical activity and should not spend more than two hours a day using electronic media for entertainment (Department of Health, 2014). The Australian Council for Health, Physical Education and Recreation (ACHPER) (2014) notes that teachers should equate moderate physical activity with student 'huffing and puffing'. It is not only their cardiovascular fitness that improves with physical activity; key phases of motor learning and development are facilitated and enhanced via 'affordances' obtained only through such activity. Gross and fine motor skills, coupled with hand–eye coordination, are typically established between the ages of two and eight years (Haywood & Getchell, 2009) and can only be refined in physically active settings; for example, applied as sport skills, once they have been successfully established in the early years.

A key issue for students who experience **educational disadvantage** is that their socio-economic status and/or geographic location and/or family care circumstances may impact upon their ability to pursue sport, physical activity and other motor learning affordances, particularly in these crucial early years. Access to weekend competitive club sport or after-school recreation may be very limited so the chance to develop their motor abilities and therefore their lifelong competence and confidence in physical activity (ACARA, 2015) may only occur *in school time*.

Furthermore, recent research into physical activity in preschool settings (McEvilly, Atencio & Verheul, 2015) notes that educators cannot leave motor skill acquisition up to early years learners' 'play time'. Educators need to structure outdoor play and actually play with the children, modelling the skills:

> … *if you just keep throwing balls at children and letting them lie around, they'll play with them, but they never actually get the skill of catching the ball, because they need an adult to do it with them* … (p. 11).

Educators should also recognise that early years learners develop these skills at different rates for a range of reasons, including affordances. Burrows and Wright

(2001) warned that primary physical education programs often operate from 'a normative, hierarchical trajectory for child development (which) categorises, classifies and marginalises groups of children whose developmental patterns differ from those mapped out in the syllabus' (p. 165). Key requirements for designing physical activity include: to start from *then extend* their existing capabilities, to give as much opportunity as possible to *improve* these capabilities in school time and with school resources, and to make it as *enjoyable* as possible so that students whose developmental rates and interests vary are not marginalised from structured physical activity.

Important policies informing wellbeing in the early years

United Nations declarations

Australia is a signatory to the *United Nations Convention on the Rights of the Child.* Under Article 29.1c:

> … Education of the child shall be directed to … the development of respect for the child's parents, his or her own cultural identity, language and values, for the national values of the country in which the child is living, the country from which he or she may originate and for civilizations different from his or her own …

Similarly, Article 14.1 of the *Permanent Forum and Declaration on the Rights of Indigenous Peoples* argues that:

> … Indigenous peoples have the right to establish and control their educational systems and institutions providing education in their own languages, in a manner appropriate to their cultural methods of teaching and learning.

The key messages here are that home languages and ways of learning should be valued and supported in the early years. This might take the form of bilingual education programs where the student language speaking population is substantial, such as in remote Aboriginal communities or large urban schools with significant migrant populations (Calma, 2008). Or it can be achieved through the inclusion of diverse learners' languages in the material resources of the classroom, through the inclusion of games and typical play activities which can be sourced from their communities – see for example the UNICEF Traditional Games from Around the World (UNICEF, 2016; http://www.recallgames.com/about/unicef-yst) and Yulunga Indigenous Games (Edwards & Meston, 2008).

The Australian Early Years Learning Framework (EYLF)

The EYLF (Department of Education, Employment and Workplace Relations [DEEWR], 2009) states that: 'Children belong first to a family, a cultural group, a neighbourhood and a wider community. Belonging acknowledges children's interdependence with others and the basis of relationships in defining identities. In early childhood, and throughout life, relationships are crucial to a sense of belonging' (p. 7). For Aboriginal and Torres Strait Islander learners, Martin (2012, p. 27) describes such relationships, or 'relatedness', as being the 'ultimate premise of Aboriginal worldview and critical to the formation of identity'. Relatedness sustains ancestral, social, physical and spiritual aspects of a child's family, clan and community, and Martin (2012, p. 28) notes that it is the daily practices and activities of a community with which children engage that relatedness becomes known and enacted.

The EYLF makes reference to the notion that developing children's wellbeing requires sensitivity to their emotional states, their sense of place and belongingness, and provision of safe learning environments, which in turn develop children's sense of self-efficacy, resilience and willingness to learn more.

Melbourne Declaration on Education Goals for Young Australians

The *Melbourne Declaration on Educational Goals for Young Australians* (Ministerial Council on Education, Employment, Training and Youth Affairs [MCEETYA], 2008) is particularly concerned with improving educational outcomes for disadvantaged young Australians, especially those from low socio-economic backgrounds (p. 10). Targeted support for early years learners may take many forms, but in terms of promoting health, physical activity and wellbeing, schools need to invest in providing students with the opportunity to learn how to build upon their individual and community strengths (McCuaig, Quennerstedt & Macdonald, 2013), to participate in physical activity without the financial constraints of commercial sport and recreation provision or cultural insensitivity, and to be nurtured as young learners in safe and supportive environments.

Aboriginal and Torres Strait Islander Education Policy

It is particularly important to become familiar with Indigenous education policies because these extend beyond general appreciation of the impact of socio-economic disadvantage upon Indigenous learners to valuing Aboriginal and Torres Strait Islander knowledges and worldviews as well as community partnership in educational decision-making. The National Aboriginal and Torres Strait Islander Education Strategy (Department of Education and Training [DET], 2015) has been developed after many years of intensive consultation with Aboriginal and Torres Strait Islander educators, communities and education providers. This latest national plan builds upon a long history – since the federal Education Department published the National Aboriginal Education Plan (NAEP) in 1989 – of lobbying by Indigenous communities around Australia for a unified commitment and approach to funding and developing schooling for Indigenous children (Whatman & Duncan, 2012, p. 127).

Figure 16.2 illustrates the priority areas from the National Strategy upon which teachers can focus when designing curriculum and learning experiences for Aboriginal and Torres Strait Islander early years learners.

The central cycles of 'Culture and Identity' and 'Partnerships' gives direction to teachers, school administrators and education departments as to why and how to develop learning experiences for Indigenous Australian and other early years learners. Furthermore, the interdependencies illustrated assist teachers to consider what they could adopt at the local level and those that require institutional support or external partners.

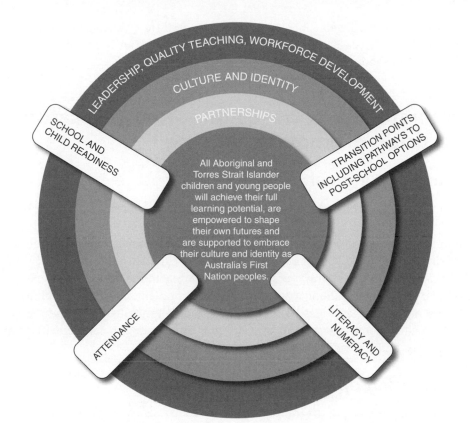

Figure 16.2 Priority areas of the National Aboriginal and Torres Strait Islander Education Strategy 2015 (DET, 2015).

Source: Reproduced with permission from Education Services Australia.[1]

Figure 16.2 shows the complex interplay between stakeholders in Indigenous education, representing not only sites of contrast and often tension between priorities for education, but the opportunities for contrasting perspectives to support common goals. Nakata (2011) described this overlapping space as the 'cultural interface'. For example, literacy and numeracy and attendance may be regarded as the most important outcomes in the plan by school administrators and education department staff, whose daily work consists of collecting data around such outcomes. However, how these outcomes are to be achieved may be conceptualised in a totally different way by someone who believes that engagement and connection are the most important outcomes, from which literacy and numeracy will develop. Figure 16.2 shows that these priority areas are important to Aboriginal and Torres Strait Islander parents and communities

1   © 2015 Education Services Australia Limited as the legal entity for the COAG Education Council (Education Council). Cambridge University Press has reproduced extracts of the National Aboriginal and Torres Strait Islander Education Strategy 2015 in this publication with permission from the copyright owner. Other than as permitted by the *Copyright Act 1968* (Cwlth), no part of this material may be reproduced, stored, published, performed, communicated or adapted by any means without the prior written permission of the copyright owner.

throughout the year levels, but the focus will be on different aspects at different times. In the early years, the focus is most definitely on transitions and building readiness for school.

Understanding how culture, identity, safety and pride promote wellbeing

Understanding culture

Culture comprises many things, including language, daily practices, beliefs, laws, relationships and locality. Culture is neither fixed nor totally fluid – it is enduring yet shifting; culture is developed by the experience of the everyday. It is affirmed by seeing yourself and your family in the everyday experience. Consequently, it is also challenged by not seeing yourself and your family in the everyday experience. It is clear, then, that building a safe learning environment that affirms children's cultures and identities must be achieved through the inclusion of community people in educational decision-making, bringing educators into contact with their perspectives and knowledges.

Recognising epistemological violence

Before examining some of the things that can be done to affirm culture and identity, and build safety and pride in schooling, it is important to consider the consequences if this is not done. School is often the site of early years learners' first experience of epistemological violence. This means that the way they view themselves and the world is challenged and questioned by other early years learners in shocking ways and with real and traumatic consequences. It is often the first time they comprehend that someone else believes there is something 'wrong' with their identity. Acceptance by your peers of your culture, your language and your way of being in the world is essential to childhood wellbeing (Martin, 2012). Case Study 16.1 presents an excerpt from Leesa Watego's blog, which illustrates the impact of epistemological violence on children, their families and the entire education system.

Valuing home languages in the classroom

An essential approach that supports and affirms the cultural identity of early years learners and their sense of belonging is the inclusion of their home languages, wherever feasible, in formal and informal learning settings. Not only do bilingual education programs outperform English-only language instruction, they provide a natural opportunity for community participation and partnership in schools.

> *Bilingual education programs are effective in promoting academic achievement, and … sound educational policy [and] should permit and even encourage the development and implementation of bilingual education programs* (Calma, 2008, p. 1).

CASE STUDY 16.1: I WONDER WHAT JOHNNY'S MUM WAS UP TO TODAY

Yesterday little 'Johnny' (not his real name) told my son that he 'should go back to where he came from' (among other things).

That meant I was up at the office this morning discussing racism with the deputy principal. It wasn't the first time that little Johnny expressed his disgust at my son's apparent Asian-ness (apparently his surname is not Australian enough for little Johnny). The school response was fine. They took little Johnny to the guidance counsellor. But not only does little Johnny have no idea why what he said was racist, turns out there're about five kids who have been saying a whole bunch of racist stuff (rather than Asian-ness being a problem, for them it was his Indigenous-ness) towards my boy for a couple of months.

So it got me thinking …

It occurred to me that after my:

- drive to the school for an emergency conference with the deputy principal
- talking to the Deputy an hour later with an 'I'm sorry but it seems that it's bigger than we imagined' conversation
- an hour or so digesting and absorbing the toxic pit of epistemological violence I send my son to each day
- conference with husband over the phone about 'what this means' and 'what do we do?'
- a few angry tears of frustration
- a quick scroll around the education department's website to look for a fact sheet or two about 'what to do if your child is a victim of racism in our schools' (and finding nothing)
- a call to the education department's Indigenous section who transferred me to a school community liaison officer who quickly suggested that I should simply peruse the bullying resources 'cause racism/bullying: 'it's basically the same'
- a few more angry tears of frustration
- composing a letter to the deputy principal about my course of action
- questioning and doubting myself (am I just being overly sensitive?)
- picking up said son from school early, and
- debriefing him about feelings, ideas, attitudes of Australians and the impact on him and us and Murris in general …

… so after all that, I got to thinking 'I wonder what little Johnny's mum was doing today? I wondered what she had the privilege of having to deal with today. I know I would rather have been doing something else.

Racism sux.

Source: Watego (2010), website no longer active.

Consider how bilingual programs, or programs which encourage the use of home languages in the classroom, involve parent helpers, and are designed to meet EYLF curriculum outcomes, such as Outcome 4: 'Children are confident and involved learners, who develop dispositions for learning through enthusiasm and persistence, transfer learning from one context to another, [and] resource their own learning though connecting with people, place and natural materials' (DEEWR, 2009, p. 34). The privileging of culture and cultural knowledge through language use affirms identity through the inclusion of community members in formal learning, and simultaneously fulfils standard curriculum requirements of all early years learners.

Promoting wellbeing through salutogenic (strengths-based) approaches

The Australian Curriculum has prioritised the inclusion of Asia-Pacific and Indigenous peoples' perspectives and knowledges across every discipline (see ACARA, 2015). However, each discipline is tackling such perspectives and knowledges from 'within' the discipline, shaping its possibilities and therefore placing the limits around its potential. The Australian Curriculum for Health and Physical Education (Version 8.1), endorsed in late 2015, suggests multiple points of access for the inclusion of these knowledges and perspectives, including exploring the importance of extended family and community, **salutogenic** (or strengths-based) approaches to community health development (McCuaig, Quennerstedt & Macdonald, 2013), and games from around the world as choices for physical activity, fitness and motor skill development (Leahy, O'Flynn & Wright, 2013).

Salutogenic: an approach to understanding health and wellbeing that draws attention to the qualities, abilities and knowledge that students already have and can further develop; a perspective on how to teach so that students may learn in ways that enrich their lives and strengthen them as healthy citizens, contributing to sustainable community health development (Quennerstedt, 2008).

The challenges for embedding diverse cultural knowledges in the teaching context are very similar to those facing policy writers determining 'when' and 'where' such knowledges 'fit' in the curriculum. Educators are responsible for developing essential school knowledge in young learners, while validating their existing knowledges as they are introduced to the cultural and discursive practices of the discipline (Nakata, 2007). This requires seeing early years learners as more than empty vessels to be filled.

To develop early years learners' confidence and resilience and to establish important learning dispositions, Armstrong et al. (2010, pp. 6–7) described three strategies that teachers can implement:

- building upon existing capacities in familiar, enjoyable and engaging tasks – such as providing opportunities to demonstrate and develop visual-spatial awareness and fine motor skills with culturally familiar physical activity tasks, as well as 'typical Western' school-based activities such as drawing lines, cutting with scissors, threading pasta and so on;
- employing home language alongside Standard Australian English where possible – such as displaying posters and books and other multimedia resources that feature the home languages of students; and,

- bringing family members into the school learning domain – to contribute to learning experiences, both inside and outside of the classroom.

As do-able as these approaches are, teachers themselves must have the capacity to come to know diverse student capacities, to appreciate what is familiar and enjoyable and to be supported as they develop their own capacity to build solid relationships with parents and community members in order to bring the home and school learning domains closer together. This is where systemic support becomes essential and can take the form of professional development opportunities by employers or professional associations.

A community partnership approach to promoting health, physical activity and wellbeing: Remote Aboriginal Swimming Program (RASP)

In 2005, the Western Australian (WA) government instigated an inquiry to the health benefits of projects providing public swimming pools for remote Aboriginal communities in WA and the Northern Territory (NT). The Education and Health Standing Committee visited the communities of Karalundi, Jigalong, Mugarinya, Burringurrah, Warmun, Balgo and Bidyadanga, the remote townships of Halls Creek and Fitzroy Crossing and the community of Wadeye (Port Keats) in the NT. Associated health, wellbeing, educational and social benefits were considered in the provision of the pools themselves, as well as in conjunction with programs run by the Royal Life Saving Society (RLSS) under a co-funded national scheme to bring swimming pools to remote communities.

Otitis media (a persistent middle-ear infection also known as 'Glue Ear'), and respiratory and skin infections affect significant numbers of children in remote communities, and the effect of the swimming pool programs on such afflictions has been specifically examined. Results indicated that in Jigalong alone there have been reductions of 41 per cent in antibiotic prescriptions, a 44 per cent reduction in the number of cases of ear disease, a 51 per cent reduction in the incidence of skin disease and a 63 per cent reduction in the number of cases involving respiratory disease (Education & Health Standing Committee, 2006, p. xvi).

Six of the remote communities in WA implemented a 'no school, no pool' policy as a part of the Remote Aboriginal Swimming Program (RASP) (Cunningham-Dunlop, 2008; Juniper, Nimmo & Enkel, 2016) which, in some cases, showed increased school attendance, particularly in the 8 to 10 years age range, on school days where pool activities were available (Juniper, Nimmo & Enkel, 2016, p. 41). Clearly, such an approach requires the educational partnership of schools and teachers for it to work, but it aligns very well with Recommendation 4 of the parliamentary report: that schools with access to swimming pools should consider including pool-related educational activities to enhance school attendance (Education & Health Standing Committee, 2006), rather than making access to swimming a reward for school attendance (and, subsequently, prevention of swimming a punishment for non-attendance).

PAUSE AND REFLECT 16.1: REFLECTING ON EDUCATIONAL PROGRAMS

Consider further the impact and benefits to health and wellbeing of educational programs like RASP. Read the Royal Lifesaving Society (2012) report and Juniper, Nimmo and Enkel (2016). Watch the video clip to consider the issue of pool access as reward or punishment for school attendance: http://www.youtube.com/watch?v=uqZtQEe9maY.

(Warning: Aboriginal and Torres Strait Islander viewers are warned that the video may contain images and voices of deceased persons.)

Further data to inform your views are included in Figure 16.3.

If you were an educator at a similar school, would you instigate a 'no school, no pool' access policy, based on the evidence presented in this activity? Why/why not?

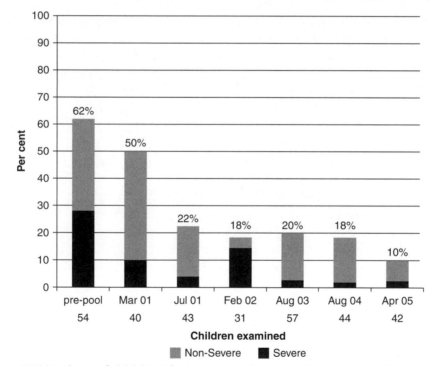

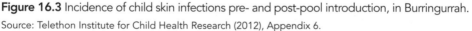

Figure 16.3 Incidence of child skin infections pre- and post-pool introduction, in Burringurrah.
Source: Telethon Institute for Child Health Research (2012), Appendix 6.

Conclusion

Being educationally disadvantaged should not consign young Australians to a lifetime of poor health and wellbeing or physical inactivity. Teachers of early years learners have an essential role and great examples to draw upon from communities around Australia of partnerships that make a real difference in overcoming educational disadvantage to promote wellbeing with early years learners.

Summary

To be an inspiring, motivating, caring and effective educator of educationally disadvantaged children, consider the following recommendations:

- Understand how relevant policies and priorities for early years education should inform your professional practice in designing and delivering curriculum.
- Understand how curriculum and teaching choices you make impact positively on culture and identity.
- Appreciate and *act upon* your important role in preventing epistemological violence against culturally diverse learners to promote their safety and pride in schooling.
- Recognise and cultivate partnerships in educationally disadvantaged communities to contribute to positive systemic change.

Questions

16.1 Which education policies could you consult in developing your teaching and learning approaches for early years learners who experience educational disadvantage and why?

16.2 Explain how providing learning opportunities that affirm culture and identity contribute positively to health and wellbeing.

16.3 What are two teaching and learning approaches that you will adopt in your teaching practice and why?

16.4 What else can you do to continue to understand educational disadvantage and plan curriculum for those early years learners who continue to benefit least from schooling?

References

Armstrong, S., Buckley, S., Lonsdale, M., Milgate, G., Bennetts Kneebone, L., Cook L. et al. (2010). *Starting school: A strengths-based approach towards Aboriginal and Torres Strait Islander children.* Retrieved 3 July 2016 from http://research.acer.edu.au/indigenous_education/27

Australian Council for Health, Physical Education and Recreation (ACHPER) (2014). Website. Retrieved 3 July 2016 from http://www.achper.org.au

Australian Council of Social Service (ACOSS) (2014). *The Poverty Report.* Strawberry Hills, NSW: ACOSS.

Australian Curriculum and Assessment Reporting Authority (ACARA) (2015). *Australian Curriculum: Health and Physical Education/Rationale.* Retrieved 3 July 2016 from http://www.australiancurriculum.edu.au/health-and-physical-education/rationale

Australian Health Promoting Schools Association (AHPSA) (2000). *National Health Promoting Schools Framework 2000–2003*. Melbourne: AHPSA. Retrieved 3 July 2016 from http://www.chpcp.org/resources/health%20promoting%20 schools%20framework.pdf

Bouchard, C., Blaire, S.N. & Haskell, W. (2012*). Physical activity and health* (2nd edn). Champaign, IL: Human Kinetics.

Burrows, L. & Wright, J. (2001). Developing children in New Zealand school physical education. *Sport, Education and Society*, 6, 165–82.

Calma, T. (2008). Keynote Address: Bilingual Education Programs. World Indigenous Peoples Conference, Melbourne Cricket Ground, Melbourne, 9 December 2008. Retrieved 3 July from https://www.humanrights.gov.au/news/speeches/ world-indigenous-peoples-conference-education

Cunningham-Dunlop, E. (2008). No school no pool. Perth: ABC Productions and Film and Television Institute, Western Australia. Retrieved 3 July 2016 from http://www.youtube.com/watch?v=uqZtQEe9maY.

Department of Education (2007). *The Tasmanian curriculum: Health and wellbeing*. Hobart: Author.

Department of Education, Employment and Workplace Relations, Australian Government (DEEWR) (2009). *Belonging, being and becoming: The Early Years Learning Framework for Australia*. Canberra: Commonwealth of Australia. Retrieved 3 July 2016 from http://education.gov.au/ early-years-learning-framework

Department of Education and Training, Australian Government (DET) (2015). *National Aboriginal and Torres Strait Islander Education Strategy 2015*. Canberra: Author. Retrieved 3 July 2016 from https://www.education.gov.au/ national-aboriginal-and-torres-strait-islander-education-strategy

Department of Health, Australian Government (2014). *Physical activity guidelines for children 5–12 years old*. Canberra: Commonwealth of Australia. Retrieved 3 July 2016 from http://www.health.gov.au/internet/main/publishing.nsf/ content/health-pubhlth-strateg-phys-act-guidelines#apa512

Department of Social Services, Australian Government (DSS) (2014). *Stepping Out: Findings from Wave 5 of Footprints in Time: The Longitudinal Study of Indigenous Children (LSIC)*. Canberra: Australian Government. Retrieved 3 July 2016 https://www.dss.gov.au/sites/default/files/documents/02_2015/ wave_5_community_booklet.pdf

Education and Health Standing Committee, Parliament of Western Australia (2006). *Swimming pool program in remote communities*. Perth: Government Printer. Retrieved 3 July 2016 from http://www.parliament.wa.gov. au/parliament/commit.nsf/(Report+Lookup+by+Com+ID)/ A412641A157BE6CD48257831003E9698/$file/Report+on+Swimming+ Pools+Final+Report.pdf

Edwards, K. & Meston, T. (2008). *Yulunga: Traditional Indigenous games*. Canberra, ACT: Australian Sports Commission. Retrieved 3 July 2016

from www.ausport.gov.au/__data/assets/pdf_file/0017/402191/SP_31864_
TIG_resource_FINAL.pdf

Haywood, K. & Getchell, N. (2009). *Lifespan motor development* (5th edn).
Champagne, IL: Human Kinetics.

Juniper, A., Nimmo, L. & Enkel, S. (2016). *The Photovoice Project: Remote
Aboriginal Swimming Pool Research*. Perth: Royal Life Saving Society of
Western Australia.

Leahy, D., O'Flynn, G. & Wright, J. (2013). A critical 'critical inquiry' proposition
in health and physical education. *Asia-Pacific Journal of Health, Sport and
Physical Education,* 4 (2), 175–87.

Lingard, B., Sellar, S. & Savage, G. (2014). Re-articulating social justice as equity
in schooling policy: The effects of testing and data infrastructures. *British
Journal of Sociology of Education,* 35(7), 710–30.

Lonsdale, M. (2013). *Making a difference: Improving outcomes for Indigenous
learners*. Melbourne: Australian Council for Educational Research.
Retrieved 3 July 2016 from http://research.acer.edu.au/indigenous_
education/29/

Martin, K. (2012). Aboriginal early childhood: Past, present and future. In J. Phillips &
J. Lampert (eds), *Introductory Indigenous studies in education: Reflection and
the importance of knowing* (pp. 26–35.) Sydney: Pearson Australia.

McCuaig, L., Quennerstedt, M. & Macdonald, D. (2013). A salutogenic, strengths-
based approach as a theory to guide HPE curriculum change. *Asia Pacific
Journal of Health, Sport and Physical Education,* 4(2), 109–25.

McEvilly, N., Atencio, M. & Verheul, M. (2015). Developing children: Developmental
discourses underpinning physical education at three Scottish preschool
settings. *Sport, Education and Society*. doi:10.1080/13573322.2015.1114917

Ministerial Council on Education, Employment, Training and Youth Affairs
(MCEETYA) (2008). *Melbourne Declaration on Educational Goals for Young
Australians*. Melbourne: MCEETYA. Retrieved 3 July 2016 from http://
www.curriculum.edu.au/verve/_resources/National_Declaration_on_the_
Educational_Goals_for_Young_Australians.pdf

Nakata N.M. (2011). Pathways for Indigenous education in the Australian Curriculum
Framework. *The Australian Journal of Indigenous Education,* 40, 1–8.

—— (2007). *Disciplining the savages: Savaging the disciplines*. Canberra: Aboriginal
Studies Press.

Quennerstedt, M. (2008). Exploring the relation between physical activity and
health—a salutogenic approach to physical education. *Sport, Education and
Society,* 13(3), 267–83.

Royal Life Saving Society, Western Australia Branch (RLSS-WA) (2012). *Remote
Aboriginal Swimming Pool Program*. Mt Claremont, WA: RLSS-WA. Retrieved
3 July 2016 from https://www.lifesavingwa.com.au/programs/remote-pools/
program-benefits

Telethon Institute for Child Health Research (2012). *Healthy Skin, Healthy Lives.* Perth: Telethon Institute. Retrived 3 July 2016 from http://aboriginal. telethonkids.org.au/media/531419/healthy_skin_healty_lives_-_perth_dec_ 2012_-_report.pdf

UNICEF (2016). Traditional Games. Retrieved 3 July 2016 from http://www. recallgames.com/about/unicef-yst

United Nations. (1989). *Convention on the Rights of the Child.* Retrieved from http:// www.ohchr.org/EN/ProfessionalInterest/Pages/CRC.aspx

—— (2007). *Declaration on the Rights of Indigenous Peoples.* Retrieved from http:// www.un.org/esa/socdev/unpfii/documents/DRIPS_en.pdf

WA Health Promoting Schools Association (WAHPSA) (2016). *The Health Promoting Schools Framework.* Retrieved from http://www.wahpsa.org.au

Watego, L. (2010). I wonder what Johnny's mum was up to today… Not Quite Cooked Blogpost, 14 October. Retrieved 3 July 2016 from http://www. notquitecooked.com/2010/10/i-wonder-what-johnnys-mum-was-up-to.html

Whatman, S. & Duncan, P. (2012). Learning from the past: In policy and practice. In J. Phillips & J. Lampert (eds), *Introductory Indigenous studies: Reflection and the importance of knowing (2nd edn*, pp. 114–39). Sydney: Pearson Australia.

World Health Organization (WHO) (1986). *The Ottawa Charter for Health Promotion.* Geneva: WHO. Retrieved 3 July 2016 from http://www.who.int/ healthpromotion/conferences/previous/ottawa/en/index.htm

CHAPTER 17

Supporting resilience

Andrea Nolan, Karen Stagnitti, Ann Taket and Siobhan Casey

Introduction

Resilience is complex and multifaceted, attracting research across a number of disciplines. The focus of this chapter is the importance of teachers' everyday practice in early years settings (preschools and schools) for supporting resilience. Examples are drawn from a longitudinal study funded by the Australian Research Council (ARC) that studied resilience during times of significant transitions in the lives of children and young adults in low socio-economic communities experiencing vulnerability. The conditions and characteristics of resilience were explored with consideration for the educational, health, work-related or leisure interventions that support and foster resilience. Findings from the early years cohort of the study point out the practical approaches and strategies that promote and protect resilience in young children as outlined in this chapter. These strategies relate to the environment, relationships, classroom practices and play skills, and give prominence to aspects such as supportive relationships with adults, developing self-regulation, promoting social-emotional learning and the provision of positive learning environments. Our focus is on the implications for teachers and the classroom environment.

The chapter begins with a brief outline of how resilience is defined, and then moves on to describe ways in which teachers working across the early years promote resilience. The final section of the chapter lists questions that can be useful to help early years teachers reflect on their own practice in relation to resilience.

Nature of resilience

The word 'resilience' conjures up images of confident children with well-developed positive peer relationships, bouncing back from adverse situations and events. In our research we define resilient children as those who thrive and develop despite challenging circumstances. **Resilience** is a dynamic process contingent on a person's personal attributes, caregiver relationships, and psycho-social and socio-cultural environment. An easygoing temperament and the ability for internal **self-regulation** (Benzies & Mychasiuk, 2009), average to high IQ and connections and **attachments** (Alvord & Grados, 2005), and high curiosity about new situations are all associated with resilience (Condly, 2006). Parental behaviour such as displaying warmth and positive attitudes, being more involved with their children, and providing strong guidance are closely linked with a child's social and emotional wellbeing (Kim-Cohen et al., 2004; Sunderland, 2007). Parents being involved in cognitively stimulating activities during a child's preschool years is also a predictor of resilience to more stressful events later in life and favourable behaviour development (Cowen et al., 1995; Serbin & Karp, 2004).

Resilience: thriving and developing despite challenging circumstances.

Self-regulation: understanding your own emotions and the emotions of others, and being able to manage and monitor your feelings, thinking and behaviour.

Attachment: a deep emotional bond that connects one person to another across time and space.

Taking a socio-cultural view of resilience acknowledges the influence of family and significant others, as well as the material situation within a specific location. Children's interactions with schooling, their teachers and peers act to shape resilience in ways that impart – for particular students – a sense of agency, or the capability to analyse, make choices and act to change themselves or their situation. Teachers play an important role in supporting the process and production of resilience in their students; therefore, while there may be personal attributes involved in the construct of resilience, it is more appropriately conceived of as a human capacity that can be developed and strengthened in all people.

Supporting resilience in the early years

Early years settings are important sites where teachers' everyday practices can support, promote and protect resilience. From the research we have conducted into resilience in classrooms, we have been able to identify four aspects for teachers' consideration: the environment, relationships, classroom practices and play skills (see Figure 17.1). Each aspect is discussed in turn.

The environment

The environment impacts on a child in a number of ways. Teachers talk about the need to provide a space for children where they can feel calm and connected to their environment. This calming environment and sense of belonging can be

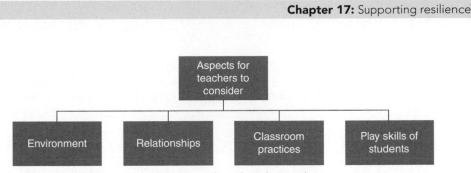

Figure 17.1 Aspects for teachers to consider related to resilience.

fostered by an acceptance of children's feelings and emotions about who they are. Emily (preschool teacher) explained:

> *If someone is crying, you don't say, 'Oh well, you don't miss Mum … don't be silly.' You accept it, and you say, 'Mum will be back' and suggest, 'You can give her a hug when she comes back'.*

Building a positive, supportive classroom environment lets children know that the teacher is there to support them, and this is stated regularly to remind them. Lydia (**Foundation year** teacher) commented:

Foundation year: first year of formal schooling

> *I'll often say to the children in my discussion with them that I am there to support them. I care about them and my role is to help them. 'If I'm going to help you, you need to be able to talk to me and tell me about some of the things that are going wrong.'*

A trusting relationship, which statements like these promote, is considered in the next section.

The psychological and social characteristics of the setting, such as the attitudes, feelings and values of both the students and staff, need consideration. Creating positive learning environments involves fostering a sense of belonging within the children. This can be as simple as providing each child with a pigeonhole, tub or locker that is their own space within the classroom setting. One Foundation year teacher (Jacinta) plays lots of circle games at the beginning of the school year so that the children learn the names of all their peers and features about them, such as their pets, siblings, favourite colours and so on. Well-established routines ensure that expectations are clear for everyone and assist children to build a sense of connection to their environment.

It is particularly important to establish a culture where mistakes are expected and accepted as a normal part of learning. As Finoula (Foundation year teacher) explained:

> *I always try to encourage the children to try new things and develop their learning because they're not going to take their learning further if they're not willing to have a go. So one of my big things is I always say, 'I like you to make mistakes and I don't mind it if it's wrong. I'd much rather see you having a go.'*

This was echoed by a number of teachers across all early years classrooms.

Ideally, the physical environment should be able to be arranged flexibly to allow for social skill-building through partner work, small-group play or larger group engagement. It is often in smaller groupings that young children build confidence in their interactions and interpersonal communication skills with those around them.

Relationships

Numerous studies point to the importance of developing positive, respectful, reciprocal and responsive relationships with the children we teach and their families. Relationships with adults (in this case, teachers) need to be sensitive to, and supportive of, assisting children and their families through critical situations. This means that sensitive and ongoing communication with parents/guardians should be prioritised. This helps teachers to understand the child's home/community situation. In our study, parents – specifically mothers – spoke of the importance of their connection with their child's teacher in supporting resilience. They spoke of mobilising different modes of communication to work collaboratively to counter threats to their child's resilience (Taket, Nolan & Stagnitti, 2014).

Understanding and being aware that young children need time to be listened to and have their feelings acknowledged helps build reciprocal and responsive relationships. As Jacinta (Foundation year teacher) stated:

> We listen a lot to what the children are saying and we develop that relationship with them so they're at this stage ... they're the centre of the universe and everyone else's universe, so we encourage that. We listen to what they have to say. We try and build that connection so it's like a friendship/relationship.

This is even more important during times when difficulties are present in a child's life.

The value placed on listening was reiterated by Pam (preschool teacher), who outlined the two most important roles of the preschool staff as 'keeping the children safe' and 'just really listening'. Showing a genuine interest in each child and what they wish to share with you demonstrates that you value them – who they are and what they experience. As one of the Foundation teachers in our study – Christine – stated, 'We make sure that all of the children are treated as individuals and that their individual voice is heard'.

Building strong relationships with young children provides insight so you can tell when they require extra care when they may be feeling a little more vulnerable. This point was emphasised by Diane (preschool teacher):

> Even my resilient children do occasionally go through sensitive times where they get more fragile and they just need that little bit more extra care.

Part of building relationships is re-emphasising the importance of the caregiver/guardian relationship: 'We reaffirm their relationship with their parent or that person. You know, reminding them about the things that person might do for them' (Diane, preschool teacher). The teachers in our study consciously highlighted the importance of the parent/guardian role in each child's life, as well as their own role of being available for each child when needed. Feeling connected to adults strengthens children's attachment and influences their current and future relationships.

Working with young children is also about helping them to build relationships with each other. In our study, successful strategies noted by the teachers included encouraging children to listen respectfully to each other, providing opportunities for the children to practise this skill, and holding the expectation that everyone will 'get along' within the classroom.

CASE STUDY 17.1: CIRCLE TIME

Christine (Foundation teacher) recounted her 'Circle Time' activity, which she found a useful strategy to encourage individuals to speak out while also listening to their peers:

> One of those strategies I utilise is 'Circle Time'. I have a ball and the only person who's allowed to speak has the ball. Usually I model whatever it might be that we're talking about. Just last week we had a situation outside and something wasn't going so well and so when we came in straight after lunch time I sat them all down and said, 'Okay. We're going to have Circle Time.' Then I had a ball and I started. I said 'I feel … (a certain emotion) when this happens', and then each child had to go around and actually say if there was anything bothering them. So, if there wasn't something bothering them they just passed the ball on and said they had nothing at that time to share. But it gave each individual the opportunity and they all had to either acknowledge that there was something that was bothering them or that there wasn't – they all had an individual turn. I think if they don't have that time … if you just did it haphazardly, it wouldn't happen for some. It would work for the ones who speak out but not for quieter students so you've got to be very aware of your students' individuality.

Classroom practice

Practice needs to be informed by research to ensure that it is mindful and artful, and that each child is provided with the conditions and opportunities to develop to their full potential. Focusing attention on a child's social and emotional learning within the classroom has a demonstrated impact on their mental health and the level of success they experience (Durlak et al., 2011), both cognitively and in terms of wellbeing (Bird & Sultmann, 2010). Being able to collaborate and cooperate with others, show empathy, demonstrate independence, be motivated to set and achieve goals, and be able to self-regulate one's emotions (McCombs, 2004) aids the development of social consciousness (Berman, 1997) and good citizenship (Durlak et al., 2011). However, social and emotional learning is more than acquiring a set of skills; it is a process that takes into account an individual's understandings of their own emotional abilities (Hargreaves, 2000). The teachers we interviewed and observed in our resilience study implemented strategies to reinforce the elements of emotional intelligence (Petrides & Furnham, 2001) to varying degrees, and these practices are outlined next. We have grouped them under the headings of modelling behaviour and language; teaching social skills; supporting self-regulation; and giving choices and providing structure (see Figure 17.2).

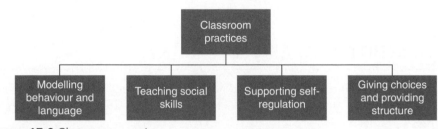

Figure 17.2 Classroom practice.

Modelling behaviour and language

Teachers act as influential role models of desirable behaviours. By accompanying positive role modelling with appropriate language cues and prompts children are able to experience possible ways of acting in particular situations. One strategy employed is when mistakes are deliberately made by teachers when working with the children. These mistakes are then accompanied by statements that use positive language, thereby giving the message that you need to be persistent and persevere with tasks to be successful.

Another strategy is providing prompts to help children consider particular situations and events they may experience. This encourages them to think about possible actions they may take and gives them appropriate words to use. As Diane (preschool teacher) articulated:

> We might say to them 'Well you need to say to Bill, "Bill I'm playing with that. You can play with it in a few more minutes." Or you might say to Bill, "Bill, you need to say can I please have a go of that, or when can it be my turn?"' So that we give them those kinds of … not directions, but cues that they can use in another situation if it were to arise again.

This way of working encourages children to make an initial attempt to deal with situations independently, which can promote a sense of empowerment when successful.

Talking through the options available to children in various situations also provides them with opportunities to make better choices. For example, Lara (Grade 1 teacher) uses scaffolding successfully to prompt and remind children of possible ways forward when faced with difficult situations. This helps the children to make connections to past experiences through guided reflection. In one Foundation classroom we visited, children were encouraged to reflect on what resilience was as a key objective. When they saw others showing resilience, it was highlighted;

PAUSE AND REFLECT 17.1: RECONSIDERING CHOICES

Young children can be encouraged to re-evaluate their choices by the teacher asking questions such as 'I wonder if there was a better choice?', 'I wonder how you could do that differently?' – *without* labelling past choices made as 'wrong' or 'bad'. This way of working encourages the child to reflect and re-evaluate their own behaviour.

Reflect on examples from your own practice when you have or could have used questions like these.

therefore, the children were able to add examples of other people being resilient if something didn't go their own way.

Developing a consistent language and consciously using common phrases and words such as 'persistence', 'having a go', 'trying your best' and 'we all make mistakes to learn more' within and outside of the classroom reinforces notions of resilience.

Teaching social skills

Many teachers are constantly teaching or reinforcing social skills with the children in their classrooms, through discussions relating to what is or is not acceptable behaviour in specific scenarios. All preschool teachers in this study had very clear objectives behind the many and varied experiences they provided within their programs. In this mix of experiences a small group of children worked alongside each other or shared materials. The teachers provided the support and modelling of appropriate social-emotional learning as they moved around the environment, stopping to work with each group of children. This was a deliberate strategy to further develop the children's social and emotional skills. Diane (preschool teacher) noted the importance of having all of the children in one classroom sit down together for group conversations. Conversing with adults or sharing a meal with others were occurences that were becoming scarce in the lives of the children she taught. While this teacher placed importance on these group conversations, any type of small- or large-group event provides opportunities to encourage, support and role model positive social skills in group situations.

Role-play was also used as a strategy to introduce children to acceptable ways of behaving with others. Phillipa (Grade 1 teacher) shared her practice:

> In the classroom we have circle time where we talk about different strategies and role-play how we can just deal with situations.

Most of the role-plays used by teachers dealt with strategies to overcome difficulties in the school playground – for example, when no one will play with a child, or a child is being bullied:

If someone comes in at the end of play time and obviously something has happened, I will get the children involved and we'll role-play what they could have done in a more resilient way. 'What could you have done? Could you have said this? Let's role-play it. Right, someone else get up and do it' (Bianca, Foundation teacher).

This gives children the words they can use and the experience of trying them out in a safe, secure environment.

Explicitly exposing children to the steps to take when they find themselves in confronting situations was valued by the early years teachers:

Basically we ... give them coping strategies in difficult situations. We do a bit of role-playing and if there has been conflict we don't try and move on too quickly where the students are left confused. We talk about it and do the restorative justice stuff, and that positive talk around where they can see both sides of the situation and are able to talk comfortably about it with the different parties and come to an understanding – whether they agree with it or not – but they can see where both sides are coming from and why there was conflict and how to resolve that (Louise, Grade 1 teacher).

One Grade 1 teacher (Pauline) employed a Catastrophe Scale (from 1 to 10) which she finds useful for helping children see the severity – or not – of any given situation. Conversation about this positioning between the teacher and student enables the child to put into perspective (and in words) how they are feeling and, in the process, recognise that there are other things that are far worse.

Supporting self-regulation

Being able to understand your emotions and the emotions of others, and managing and monitoring your feelings, thinking and behaviour (Thompson, 2009) is seen as self-regulation. Caregiver relationships that are both positive and supportive can influence children's self-regulation. Giving feedback about emotions and talking through possible positive solutions to employ in peer interactions can support the development of appropriate and adaptive social behaviours. Children's social participation with peers and adults assists them to become more socially competent and reframe from inappropriate social behaviour (Bronson, 2000).

The sensory-based program Sharon (preschool teacher) incorporated into her preschool program draws from the ideas of the ALERT program (Williams & Shellenberger, 1996), in attempting to assist children to develop strategies to recognise states of alertness, hyperactivity and agitation vs calm. Children have access to fiddle toys in a quiet corner of the room, breathing exercises with music, and a quiet corner that they are free to access at all times, either independently or with teacher guidance. Also in use is a vest (which is weighted). When a child wears this sensory vest it gives the sensation of receiving a hug which can calm and sooth some young children. Sensory experiences such as water trays, slime trays or finger paint have always been incorporated into early childhood programs to calm and foster feelings of reassurance and coping in children.

In early years classrooms in schools, teachers scaffold children to help them become more independent in managing their behaviours in relation to others. As Libby (Foundation teacher) explained:

When a situation occurs we talk about what would be the good option and why we would do it that way. What could be another way? We talk about those kinds of things, especially social issues in the playground at the beginning of the year when you have children trying to find their ground and not mixing well with others.

This strategy was also echoed in responses from Grade 1 teachers, such as 'We involve children in lots of discussing as things happen, asking them how they could deal with things differently', in an attempt to connect past experiences and reflection in the development of peer relationships and self-regulation.

PAUSE AND REFLECT 17.2: THINKING ABOUT OTHERS

When a child says or does something that is likely to hurt another child, he/she can be encouraged to develop empathy and empathic behaviour if the teacher asks questions such as 'How would that make you feel?' (delivered privately).

Reflect on examples from your own practice when you have or could have used a question like this.

Giving choices and providing structure

Providing a predictable routine helps children to settle into the environment because they know what to expect and what will be expected of them. However, children also need to be able to make choices about things that impact on their lives, so assisting them with decision-making processes is important. Teachers tend to begin by offering one or two choices so children don't become overwhelmed by too many decisions that need to be made. For example, Joanne (preschool teacher), suggested: 'You can do this or you can do that'. This can be scaffolded further with 'First you can choose this, then you can do that'. This strategy has been helpful in moving children around the various learning experiences, especially in preschool programs where teachers are mindful that young children need some boundaries; and they also need to know that at times there are things you have to do, whether you want to do them or not.

Taking responsibility for one's actions was something expected by all the teachers in our study. As Diane (preschool teacher) states: 'We all have to share the space. We all have to look after each other'. The teachers generally felt that having high expectations of children about taking responsibility within the classroom was one way to foster their independence. Teachers saw it as important to provide these opportunities because there was a perception that opportunities to take responsibility were lacking in some children's family lives.

Play skills

Play as a child's way of learning and making sense of the world needs to be embraced:

> *Learning in early childhood is not just about pre-set curricula outcomes; it is about child-initiated discovery, children exploring and learning through play and successfully engaging and communicating with a range of people* (Nolan, Kilderry & O'Grady, 2006, p. 1).

Play can be seen as a motivating force in a child's intellectual development – a way of growing and coming to terms with life, and most importantly as a vehicle for learning while still having fun (Johnson, Christie & Wardle, 2005).

While play provides a rich context for learning, it also has the capacity to provide an important medium for teaching (Hedges, 2000). When viewed as active learners, children are involved in the co-construction of knowledge. They are not passive learners; they actively drive their own learning by the choices they make and the experiences they encounter in stimulating environments. Play can advance the aims of early years education in social, emotional, intellectual, creative and physical competencies.

A play-based curriculum, which is common in preschools and is also beginning to be taken up in some early years classrooms in schools, enables children to explore their environment as an active learner. It is set up in a way that allows each child to follow their interests while also promoting independence in choice of activity, interaction within the experience and the opportunity to problem-solve.

Within a play-based curriculum, teachers allow time for children to reflect on the choices they make, and use prompts to assist them in their choices when they are unsure. Through a combination of the provision of resources (activities) and the time and support to make decisions, children are able to direct their own learning. Teachers closely observe each child and then step in to support and extend the learning where and when necessary. Working in this way promotes decision-making, clear thinking and organisational skills. Teachers play an essential role, within play-based programs, as their knowledge and purposeful actions and interactions ensure that each child's learning is further enriched and enhanced (Raban, 2012).

Conclusion

In this chapter, we have presented multiple strategies that teachers can employ to promote resilience in young children in their classrooms. Environmental and social supports coupled with a focus on building respectful, reciprocal and responsive relationships can all facilitate the development of a child's resilience. What is apparent is the importance of the active role a teacher plays in protecting and fostering the development of resilience, through the provision of positive learning environments and being aware of children's social and emotional learning.

It is important to note that the teachers in our study were working in areas where both children and families experience vulnerabilities and complex issues, so their work on resilience with their students could be viewed as even more critical than in classrooms in other geographic locations. If we believe the old adage that it takes a community to raise a child, then the role that schools and individual teachers play in this needs acknowledgement.

Summary

This chapter outlines the importance of:

- building secure relationships and fostering the development of peer relationships
- collaborating with parents
- modelling behaviour and language that could be used in specific situations
- teaching social skills
- providing opportunities for children to practise self-regulation in a safe, supportive environment.

Questions

17.1 In your practice, how conscious are you about protecting and promoting resilience in the children you teach?

17.2 What strategies do you employ in your classroom to support children's resilience? Could the effectiveness of these be strengthened by the addition of more strategies, and if so, which ones and why?

17.3 How do you evaluate the effectiveness of the strategies you currently employ? What criteria do you use to 'assess' a child's level or development of resilience?

17.4 Do you feel confident that you could identify resilient children in your classroom? What makes you think this? Do you think other teachers would identify the same students that you nominate? Why or why not?

Acknowledgements

We would like to acknowledge our industry partners in the research reported in this chapter: the Victorian Department of Education and Training (DET), VicHealth (the statewide health promotion agency) and Community Connections (a statewide NGO). We would also like to acknowledge other team members who worked on the wider study, and the early years teachers who participated in the study, without whom this work would not have been possible.

References

Alvord, K. & Grados, J.J. (2005). Enhancing resilience in children: A proactive approach. *Professional Psychology: Research and Practice*, 36(3), 238–45.

Benzies, K. & Mychasiuk, R. (2009). Fostering family resiliency: A review of the key protective factors. *Child & Family Social Work*, 14(1), 103–14.

Berman, S. (1997). *Children's social consciousness and the development of social responsibility.* New York: State University of New York Press.

Bird, K.A. & Sultmann, W.F. (2010). Social and emotional learning: Reporting a system approach to developing relationships, nurturing well-being and invigorating learning. *Educational & Child Psychology*, 27(1), 143–55.

Bronson, M.B. (2000). *Self-regulation in early childhood: Nature and nurture.* New York: Guilford Press.

Condly, S. (2006). Resilience in children: A review of literature with implications for education. *Urban Education*, 41, 211–36.

Cowen, E., Wyman, P., Work, W. & Iker, M. (1995). A preventive intervention for enhancing resilience among highly stressed urban children. *The Journal of Primary Prevention*, 15, 247–60.

Durlak, J.A., Weissberg, R.P., Dymnicki, A.B., Taylor, R.D. & Schellinger, K. (2011). The impact of enhancing students' social and emotional learning: A meta-analysis of school-based universal interventions. *Child Development*, 82(1), 405–32.

Hargreaves, A. (2000). Mixed emotions: Teachers' perceptions of their interactions with students. *Teaching and Teacher Education*, 16, 811–26.

Hedges, H. (2000). Teaching in early childhood: Time to merge constructivist views so learning through play equals teaching through play. *Australian Journal of Early Childhood*, 25(4), 16–21.

Johnson, J.E., Christie, J.F. & Wardle, F. (2005). *Play, development and early education.* New York: Pearson.

Kim-Cohen, J., Moffitt, T., Caspi, A. & Taylor, A. (2004). Genetic and environmental processes in young children's resilience and vulnerability to socioeconomic deprivation. *Child Development*, 75, 651–68.

McCombs, B.L. (2004). The learner-centered psychological principles: A framework for balancing academic achievement and social-emotional learning outcomes. In J. Zins, R. Weissberg, M. Wang & H.J. Walberg (eds), *Building academic success on social and emotional learning: What does the research say?* (pp. 23–39). New York: Teachers College Press.

Nolan, A., Kilderry, A. & O'Grady, R. (2006). *Children as active learners.* Canberra: Early Childhood Australia.

Petrides, K.V. & Furnham, A. (2001). Trait emotional intelligence: Psychometric investigation with reference to established trait taxonomies. *European Journal of Personality*, 15(6), 425–48.

Raban, B. (2012). Quality area 1: Educational program and practice. In B. Raban (ed.), *The national quality standard: Towards continuous quality improvement – a practical guide for students and professionals* (pp. 16–23). Melbourne: Teaching Solutions.

Serbin, L.A. & Karp, J. (2004). The intergenerational transfer of psychosocial risk: Mediators of vulnerability and resilience. *Annual Review of Psychology*, 55, 333–61.

Sunderland, M. (2007). *What every parent needs to know: The remarkable effects of love, nurture and play on your child's development.* London: Dorling Kindersley.

Taket, A., Nolan, A. & Stagnitti, K. (2014). Family strategies to support and develop resilience in early childhood. *Journal of Early Childhood Research,* 34(3), 289–300.

Thompson, R.A. (2009). Doing what doesn't come naturally: The development of self-regulation. *Zero to Three,* 30(2), 33.

Williams, M.S. & Shellenberger, S. (1996). *How does your engine run? A leader's guide to the ALERT Program for self-regulation.* Albuquerque, NM: TherapyWorks.

CHAPTER 18

Move Well Eat Well: Case study of a successful settings-based approach to health promotion

Janet Dyment, Sherridan Emery, Theresa Doherty and Mary Eckhardt

Acknowledgement

We acknowledge Sue Moir and Sue Frendin, who contributed to the ideas and writing that appeared in a similar chapter in the first edition (2014) of this book. While the chapter in this second edition has been updated and revised from the first edition, we acknowledge their earlier contributions that appear in this edition.

Introduction

Childhood obesity has emerged as a significant global public health issue in the twenty-first century. The World Health Organization's *Report on the Commission on Ending Childhood Obesity* (World Health Organization [WHO], 2016) reports a substantial increase in the proportion of overweight and obese children in the last three decades. The issue is most prevalent in countries with populations in the middle to upper income range including Australia; however, almost all countries are encountering increases in the number of overweight children.

The **International Union for Health Promotion and Education (IUHPE)** and the WHO advocate integrated, holistic and strategic settings-based approaches for promoting children's health. In this chapter, the Tasmanian *Move Well Eat Well* initiative is profiled as one such strategic settings-based intervention implemented to address the overweight and obesity trend in young children. The program is offered to all schools with a primary enrolment and early childhood

International Union for Health Promotion and Education (IUHPE): a worldwide, independent and professional association of individuals and organisations committed to improving the health and wellbeing of the people through education, community action and the development of healthy public policy.

education and care services (ECEC) across the state of Tasmania, Australia, with a view to normalising physical activity and healthy eating for all children in these settings.

This chapter begins with a brief overview of childhood obesity and the settings-based approach to obesity prevention. The *Move Well Eat Well* program is described, highlighting key factors that have been important in establishing and sustaining the program in relation to the IUHPE (2009) guidelines. The chapter concludes with provocations for considering the insights from the *Move Well Eat Well* program in relation to other healthy settings initiatives, and other educational contexts.

Childhood obesity

Childhood obesity is a significant public health issue globally according to the WHO (2016) and we begin by outlining some key aspects of the issue:

- Increasing levels of childhood obesity have been attributed to higher consumption of foods high in salt, sugar and saturated fat and a reduction in the amount of time spent on physical activity (Australian Bureau of Statistics [ABS], 2010).
- The prevalence of obesity and overweight in children aged 5 to 17 years in Tasmania increased steadily between 2007–08, 2011–12 and 2014–2015, from 18.6 to 28.8 to 29.8 per cent.
- In Australia, persistent overweight and obesity is more common among the most disadvantaged children in society, as measured by family socio-economic status and neighbourhood disadvantage (Australian Institute of Health and Welfare [AIHW], 2012).
- High levels of sedentary behaviour have been recognised as risk factors for chronic disease and obesity (ABS, 2015).

Australian Census (ABS, 2011) data reveals that children spend less time engaged in physical activity and more time involved in sedentary activities as they get older. The AIHW (2012) indicates that early childhood education presents an ideal opportunity for health promotion interventions to establish healthy eating and physical activity habits and prevents childhood obesity.

Approaches to childhood obesity prevention

The WHO (2012) outlines the key factors that contribute to the success of childhood obesity prevention approaches; this is based on evaluations of programs conducted in countries around the world. The WHO reports that community-based interventions which are 'culturally and environmentally appropriate are far more likely to be implemented and sustained. Furthermore, interventions which use existing social structures such as school systems reduce barriers to implementation' (2012, p. 35). Early-childhood settings are emerging as important sites for obesity prevention interventions, particularly in high-income countries (WHO, 2012). This has been demonstrated through interventions which have evidenced increased consumption of fruit and vegetables and decreased consumption of energy-rich nutrient-poor food and drink as well as gradual changes in children's knowledge about food (WHO, 2012).

The settings approach

Settings-based approaches to health promotion represent a shift from focusing on the personal competencies of individuals towards creating healthy policies, re-shaping environments to support health, and building partnerships and creating sustainable change through participation, empowerment and ownership of change throughout settings (Whitelaw et al., 2001). This locates public health action and interventions in the social, cultural and physical places in which people live, learn, work and play (WHO, 1986). The approach has been variously applied to schools, hospitals, workplaces, neighbourhoods and cities.

Dooris (2009) identifies three key characteristics of the settings approach: **a socio-ecological model** of health, a systems perspective and a whole system organisation development and change focus. The ecological model understands health to be determined by a complex interplay of environmental, organisational and personal factors largely determined outside of 'health services' (Bronfenbrenner & Morris, 2006).

The **healthy settings** approach provides a comprehensive working framework for systemic change, as depicted in Figure 18.1, to envision community, institutional and policy-level involvement in health promotion. The IUHPE advocates whole setting approaches to health promotion in education, identifying programs that are holistic, integrated and strategic as being 'more likely to produce better health and education outcomes than those which are mainly information-based and implemented only in the classroom' (IUHPE, 2009, p. 2). The principles of health-promoting settings outlined in Table 18.1 demonstrate that all aspects of the life of the school and ECEC community are integral to the promotion of children's health.

> **Settings-based approach** to health promotion: one that involves a holistic and multidisciplinary method for addressing risk factors within the settings where people live, work, learn and play. The settings approach has roots in the *Ottawa Charter for Health Promotion*. Healthy settings key principles include community participation, partnership, empowerment and equity.

> **Socio-ecological models** recognise individuals as embedded within larger social systems and describe the interactive and reinforcing characteristics of individuals and environments that underlie health outcomes.

> **Healthy settings:** places or social contexts in which people engage in daily activities in which environmental, organisational and personal factors interact to affect health and wellbeing.

Move Well Eat Well: A settings approach to health promotion

The remainder of this chapter examines the Tasmanian *Move Well Eat Well* (MWEW) program as an example of a settings-based approach, and draws upon de-identified MWEW membership information (Department of Health and Human Services [DHHS], 2016). MWEW is a Tasmanian Government initiative managed within Public Health Services DHHS, with the objective of making healthy eating and

'Whole-System' Approach

Community development and change management	Top-down political/managerial commitment	Institutional agenda and core business

High-visibility innovative projects	Bottom-up engagement and empowerment	Public health agenda

Methods
e.g. policy, environmental modification, social marketing, peer education, impact assessment

Values
e.g. partnership, equity, participation, empowerment, sustainability

Figure 18.1 A model for understanding a health-promoting setting through a 'Whole-System' Approach.

Source: Dooris (2009, p. 30).

Table 18.1: Principles of health-promoting settings.

- Promotes the health and wellbeing of students.
- Enhances the learning outcomes of students.
- Upholds social justice and equity concepts.
- Provides a safe and supportive environment.
- Involves student participation and empowerment.
- Links health and education issues and systems.
- Addresses the health and wellbeing issues of all school and ECEC staff.
- Collaborates with parents and the local community.
- Integrates health into the setting's ongoing activities, curriculum and assessment standards.
- Sets realistic goals built on accurate data and sound scientific evidence.
- Seeks continuous improvement through ongoing monitoring and evaluation.

Source: IUHPE (2009, p. 1).

physical activity a positive and normal part of every child's day. Initially adapted from the *Kids – 'Go for your life'* Award Program under license from the Victorian government, MWEW was rolled out in the state's primary schools (children 5 to 12 years) in 2008. This was followed in 2012 by an adaption of the program to all early childhood education and care services (ECEC) – that is, long day care, family day care and kindergartens (children birth to five years).

In adopting the IUHPE's principles of health-promoting settings, MWEW uses a framework comprising a range of key messages to establish a sustainable whole school/service approach to increasing fruit and vegetable and water consumption, limiting 'sometimes' foods and drinks as well as promoting physical activity (Figure 18.4). The framework supports, and is supported by, national recommendations for physical activity and healthy eating for children. Central to the MWEW concept is the **Health Promoting School**/Service message. This reflects the IUHPE principle of a 'whole school/service' approach. This means policies,

Health-promoting school: one that constantly strengthens its capacity as a healthy setting in which to live, learn, work and play.

practices, links with families and communities and the curriculum are central to organising, driving and sustaining systems and change. A point of difference that MWEW offers, in contrast to health education programs, is a shift from a reliance on one-off interventions and didactic learning approaches, to integrated and sustained programs which seek to make healthy choices a normal part of life.

Further to promoting these key messages, MWEW offers an award system whereby settings can be awarded status as Health Promoting Schools and Early Childhood Services. At the time of writing, 175 schools had joined the *Move Well Eat Well* Schools program (DHHS, 2016). This represents 79 per cent of eligible Tasmanian schools. Of these, 54 (31 per cent) Member schools have received a *Move Well Eat Well* award in recognition of their organised and sustainable approach to the promotion of healthy eating and physical activity (DHHS, 2016). At this time, 133 eligible ECEC services had joined the Early Childhood program (DHHS, 2016.). This represents 81 per cent of the long day care (of these, 38 per cent have received award status), 38 per cent of the family day care and 11 per cent of the kindergarten sector in Tasmania (DHHS, 2016.).

Figure 18.2 MWEW in the early years context promotes opportunities for active play.
Source: Department of Health and Human Services, Tasmania (2016).

Figure 18.3 MWEW encourages healthy eating in schools.
Source: Department of Health and Human Services, Tasmania (2016).

Figure 18.4 *Move Well Eat Well* messages.

Source: Department of Health and Human Services, Tasmania (2016), icon design © State of Victoria, Australia. Reproduced with permission of the Secretary to the Department of Health.

CASE STUDY 18.1: LAUDERDALE PRIMARY SCHOOL *MOVE WELL EAT WELL* AWARD IS RENEWED

Lauderdale Primary School in southern Tasmania renewed their *Move Well Eat Well* Award for another two years. This means the school has taken an organised and sustainable approach to the promotion of healthy eating and physical activity as a positive, normal part of every day for every student. In doing so, they have made strong links to their families and communities.

Principal Mike Woods said, 'We've seen the benefits of *Move Well Eat Well* over time, as eating and being active has stayed on our school agenda as a consistent and positive theme'. The school is also engaged with the KidsMatter Australian Early Childhood Initiative (2014), a whole-school approach to mental health and wellbeing. This has

Figure 18.5 Lauderdale Primary School's *Move Well Eat Well* award is renewed.

Source: Department of Health and Human Services, Tasmania (2016).

enabled clever connections between positive relationships, eating well and being active – such as students organising innovative physical activities for younger classes.

All classes are actively involved in the school's garden and the promotion of healthy eating is happening across school events, in class breaks and via food sales. Students have an expectation that there will be daily activity, and the school has established connections with the local secondary school in the promotion of dance.

CASE STUDY 18.2: RAILTON KINDERGARTEN IS 'MAD' FOR ITS *MOVE WELL EAT WELL* – EARLY CHILDHOOD AWARD

As one of the first *Move Well Eat Well* – Primary Award schools in Tasmania, Railton Primary is now the first in Tasmania to achieve the MWEW – Early Childhood Award for its Kindergarten and Launching into Learning (birth to five years old) programs.

Extending their existing MWEW Primary School policies, staff and families were involved in embedding age-appropriate healthy eating and active play criteria for children from birth to five years in school policy and curriculum.

What a celebration! The children hosted a 'Mad Hatters Tea Party' and the menu consisted of fruit smoothies, popcorn, 'ants on logs' and fruit salad cups. The sun shone brightly and the children ran, rode bikes and encouraged families and visitors to move *really fast* to the activity song 'Head, shoulders, knees and toes'.

Figure 18.6 Railton Kindergarten is 'mad' for its *Move Well Eat Well* – Early Childhood Award.
Source: Department of Health and Human Services, Tasmania (2016).

Profiling *Move Well Eat Well* against IUHPE guidelines

The IUHPE has identified factors critical to establishing and sustaining settings-based approaches to health promotion and summarised these in the document *Achieving Health Promoting Schools: Guidelines for promoting health in schools*, (IUHPE, 2009). This document brings together key findings from a mounting body of research, evidence and good practice to identify qualities of effective school-based health promotion. The IUHPE's guidelines arise out of the WHO's *Ottawa Charter for Health Promotion* (1986) (see Chapters 1 and 16) and accordingly provide a well-founded framework for assessing the implementation of MWEW in Tasmania.

Establishing *Move Well Eat Well*

The IUHPE identified the elements necessary for establishing effective health promotion education in schools (Table 18.2). Here we discuss some of the elements that have emerged as being the most important in the successful establishment of MWEW (these are indicated with an asterisk in Tables 18.2 and 18.4). Examples from both primary school and ECEC settings are provided to illustrate the elements.

Table 18.2: Establishing health promotion initiatives.

- *Conduct an audit of current health-promoting actions according to the six essential elements (outlined in Table 18.3).
- *Create a small group of people actively engaged in leading and coordinating actions including teachers, non-teaching staff, students, parents and community members.
- *Achieve administrative and senior management support.
- *Ensure appropriate staff and community partners undertake capacity building programmes and that they have opportunities to put their skills into practice.
- *Allow 3–4 years to complete specific goals.
- Establish agreed goals and a strategy to achieve them.
- Develop a Health Promoting School Charter, embedding locally developed principles into the setting's policies.
- Celebrate milestones.

Note: * represents principles discussed in this chapter.

Source: IUHPE (2009, pp. 1–2).

Conducting an audit

As part of the Membership process, schools and services undertake a simple audit of their current policy and practice in relation to each of the *Move Well Eat Well* criteria. This provides an opportunity to take stock; to identify strengths and gaps; and discuss a way forward.

You are a primary school teacher or principal with an interest in health promotion.

1. How might clearly articulating curriculum links with the HPE curriculum help you justify establishing the *Move Well Eat Well* program as a health promotion initiative in your school?
2. Design a professional learning session you could offer to your long day care educators, ensuring that it builds capacity or skills for integrating an aspect of your centre's *Move Well Eat Well* program into teachers' daily program. (For example, a play-based learning plan or a specific MWEW activity.)

Many audit frameworks exist that can serve as useful tools for identifying existing strengths and outstanding needs as they relate to whole school approaches to health promotion. MWEW has reflected on the program using the framework recommended by the IUHPE for audit purposes, the *Ottawa Charter for Health Promotion* (WHO, 1986). The six components in Table 18.3 are useful for enabling the school or service to take a broad settings approach.

A comprehensive and consultative audit that uses the elements of the *Ottawa Charter* allows stakeholders to get a good understanding of their specific setting and assess their current policies and practices against the MWEW criteria. MWEW is not a 'one size fits all model'; the program responds to the socio-cultural context in which it operates and works with existing practices and policies within settings, allowing barriers or characteristics that are unique to each setting to be identified and addressed.

Participation across a range of stakeholders

In introducing MWEW into schools and ECEC services in Tasmania, emphasis has been placed on stakeholder involvement in decision-making and implementation. Relevant stakeholders within these settings include teachers, educators, non-teaching staff, principals, directors, children, cooks and canteen managers. It is also important to highlight the value of including and collaborating with families and community members. This maximises the potential for families and the broader community to support the messages outside the 'school gate'. The desired result is the normalisation of healthy eating and physical activity in children's lives.

Leadership and senior management support

A key element in the successful initiation and sustainability of MWEW is the support and commitment from administrative and senior management (e.g. principals of schools, directors of early childhood services). This leadership allows settings to embrace and enact a socio-ecological model of health promotion

Table 18.3: Framework for reflecting upon settings approaches to health promotion.

Elements	Explanation	Examples relevant to MWEW (Primary and ECEC sector)
Healthy policies	Policies and practices that state expectations and set the scene for a consistent and sustainable whole school/service approach	• provision of a school/service environment that promotes and normalises consumption of fruit and vegetables every day • policies that encourage physical activity as a normal part of every child's day
The physical environment	Buildings, grounds and equipment in and around the setting that limit or enable healthy eating and physical activity	• challenging space for play outside and inside • safe accessible drinking water availability inside and outside
The social environment	Quality of relationships among staff, children, families, broader community	• a whole-school/service approach • involvement of families and broader community in MWEW
Individual health skills and action competencies	Formal and informal curriculum documents that allow children to gain age-related knowledge and skills that allow them to build competencies to improve their health	• links to the Australian HPE Curriculum for primary students • links to Early Years Learning Framework and National Quality Framework for ECEC services • links to relevant Australian dietary and physical activity guidelines
Community links	Connections between the school/service setting and children's families as well as local community groups	• identifying and collaborating with other initiatives working towards similar goals, e.g. Tasmanian School Canteen Association, Active After-school Communities
Health services	Other local, state or federal services that have responsibility for children's health promotion	• working in concert with government and private sector organisations working towards goals of healthy eating and physical activity e.g. oral health services

Source: WHO (1986).

(Dooris, 2009) where the focus is not on the individuals or single issues but on the interplay of people, the environment and organisational factors. Systemic change integrates health 'within the culture, routine life, and core business of a specific setting' (Dooris, 2009, p. 30).

School and ECEC leaders can support a whole-setting approach by making it a priority and by linking it to the core values of the organisation. This can be achieved by establishing policies and procedures that allow MWEW to be embedded across the whole setting; empowering teachers and educators to embed MWEW into their curriculum; and encouraging partnerships with families and the community to support MWEW. Leaders can also prioritise the normalisation of healthy eating and physical activity within the setting and promote their successes to other settings and communities.

Capacity building: Resources plus support

The MWEW model recognises that schools and services require relevant, accessible and tailored resources to maximise their ongoing engagement with the program. MWEW offers a 'resources plus' model to support schools and ECEC settings by providing professional learning to build capacity of those involved through support mechanisms such as frequently asked questions, input from surveys, advisory groups, school/service experiences and access to a support team.

The MWEW support team helps to establish realistic expectations for settings that allow them to work at their own pace within their own context, and to be creatively engaged in the process. An onsite orientation is conducted with teachers, educators and key staff contacts by the MWEW support team and the setting receives access to the program guides, resource templates and implementation ideas. Through MWEW site visits, professional learning opportunities and the MWEW website (www.movewelleatwell.tas.gov.au), Members can build their capacity to participate in a MWEW program that is relevant and appropriate to their context. This responsive partnership can mitigate the challenges of staff turnover, a curriculum-centric approach, and the desire to 'tick the box' on healthy eating and physical activity and move on.

Realistic timeframe

The MWEW program was founded on the understanding that changes to policy and practice take time. A strong emphasis is placed on establishing a starting point, developing a process of continual improvement and maintaining momentum in an environment of competing priorities and changing staff. Most Member schools and services have required 18 months to two years to achieve Award recognition. Awarded Members can retain their status for two years after which they must apply for reassessment, providing a realistic timeframe for policies and practices to be fully implemented, tested in the setting and refreshed with the input of a new parent body and potentially new staff.

Sustaining *Move Well Eat Well*

The IUHPE document outlines important factors for sustaining the efforts and achievements of the first few years of a program to continue over the following five to seven years (Table 18.4). In the next section of this chapter, we explore the factors that are emerging as key to sustaining the MWEW program in Tasmanian schools with a primary enrolment. It should be noted that we only draw on the MWEW primary school experience in this section of the chapter.

The MWEW Primary School program collects data from multiple evaluation activities including post-one-year interviews with the Award schools. This provides valuable information on which to assess the efficacy of the model, and importantly, the sustainability of the approach.

Table 18.4: Sustaining health promotion initiatives in schools.

- *Enable the integration of the health promotion in schools strategy with other relevant strategies relating to the health, welfare and education of young people.
- *Seek and maintain recognition for health promotion actions both within and outside the school.
- *Ensure there is continuous active commitment and support to the ongoing implementation, renewal, monitoring and evaluation of the health-promoting strategy.
- Establish and integrate all the elements and actions of the health-promoting strategy as core components to the working of the school.
- Allocate time and resources for appropriate capacity building of staff and key partners.
- Provide opportunities to promote staff health and wellbeing.
- Review and refresh after each 3–4 years.
- Continue to ensure adequate resources.
- Maintain a coordinating group with a designated leader to oversee and drive the strategy with continuity of some personnel and the addition of new personnel.
- Ensure that most of the new and ongoing initiatives involve most of the staff and students in consultation and implementation.

Note: * represents principles discussed in this chapter.

Source: IUHPE (2009, p. 2).

PAUSE AND REFLECT 18.2: SCENARIO 2

A teacher who has championed the *Move Well Eat Well* program in your school signals at the start of the school year that she/he will be retiring at the end of the year. What can you do to ensure the *Move Well Eat Well* initiative will sustain beyond the departure of that champion teacher?

Integration with other strategies/approaches

The IUHPE recommends integrating and linking strategies such as MWEW within or alongside other relevant strategies that relate to the health, welfare and education of young people. The MWEW framework provides an ideal umbrella to promote and enable integration of policies and practices. MWEW acknowledges and welcomes local, state and federal government and non-government initiatives that reflect the principles of health-promoting settings. The simplicity of the model, credible branding and strong state-wide profile of MWEW provides a structure and framework within the school space for the inclusion of other health-promoting initiatives supported by these organisations. Importantly, the integration of MWEW concepts and ideas into the everyday life of the school works to embed and sustain the program objectives. Evidence of the integration of the MWEW framework includes Member schools that also run breakfast clubs, participate in garden programs (e.g. Stephanie Alexander School Garden Program), work with the Tasmanian School Canteen Association, and regularly participate in the Active After-schools initiative. Several schools have integrated key concepts of MWEW with KidsMatter to promote both physical and mental/emotional health and wellbeing within a whole school approach.

Participation in these initiatives broadens the reach and resources for schools, and brings new ideas and community links while enabling schools to achieve the and MWEW criteria. An important aspect of integration is the strategic alignment between MWEW and the formal curriculum in the primary schooling sector (i.e. Australian Curriculum). Feedback received by the MWEW support team indicates that school educators and administrators are relieved to find that MWEW supports their delivery of the curriculum and this constructive alignment serves to better position MWEW within the education context (DHHS, 2016).

Seek and maintain recognition for health promotion

The IUHPE noted that recognition of milestones and successes both inside and outside settings is an important part of sustaining health-promoting school initiatives. MWEW has embedded this within its structure by building in performance measures that allow settings to work towards, and ultimately achieve, an Award. Schools that receive an Award are seen as health-promoting settings that have successfully changed their policies and practices to meet internationally recognised standards. Feedback received from MWEW Award schools has revealed how this recognition brings with it a sense of accomplishment and pride within the school, as the following principal's comments attest (DHHS, 2016).

> *The Award was an acknowledgement of how far we have come as a school. It means that we focus on sustaining what we have in place. It encourages us to want to do more in terms of health and wellbeing. The real difference for us is that it is more than one teacher doing these health and wellbeing activities – it is everyone all working towards the one goal. MWEW is embedded across many classes and we live it on a day-to-day basis. It is what our school is rather than a separate program. Staff will say that it is 'just the way we work' (Ms Kerry McMinn, Principal, Albuera Street Primary School, Hobart).*

The MWEW Award has enabled schools to receive recognition for their efforts from the wider school community, and has enhanced broader community engagement. The Health Promoting Schools approach, which is designed to inform and support families and the school's parent body, stimulates consideration of factors such as the prevalence of 'occasional' food in fundraising, or how much time will be allocated to physical activity each day. Beyond the school gate, many MWEW schools have raised the profile of healthy eating and physical activity through partnerships with local government (for safe walking to school), with local fruit and vegetable suppliers (for healthy food supplies), with the local shop (for better lunch orders), and with sport and recreation providers (for improved participation in out-of-school-hours activity).

Support ongoing evaluation and renewal

MWEW uses robust evaluation to monitor the issues surrounding school engagement in the program, and to identify areas for growth and renewal. Evaluation measures provide insight into factors such as program reach, the characteristics of Member schools and Award schools, the implications of receiving an Award, sustainability of the program, the extent to which behaviours that promote health are actually normalised through MWEW, and the impact of MWEW outside of schools (e.g. among families and communities) (DHHS, 2016).

Ensuring the ongoing success of MWEW requires a continuous cycle of evaluation and improvements, taking into account the diverse needs and contexts of the ever-growing number of schools and ECEC settings which comprise its membership. Evaluations of the program have highlighted aspects that work well and some areas that need to be strengthened or improved. The issue of maintaining school engagement is new, since Awards have only recently been earned and the program is evolving. Another challenge relates to the children's transition between early childhood and primary school settings. Strategies will need to be developed to best support those transitions. Evaluation findings provide key insights that help to approach such matters strategically.

Conclusion

Increasing consumption of foods high in salt, sugar and saturated fat and reducing levels of physical activity have caused a decline in children's health in recent decades, evidenced in an increasing number of obese and overweight children in Australia. This chapter reports on settings-based approaches to addressing childhood obesity through primary schools and early childhood education and care settings, focusing specifically on a Tasmanian program, *Move Well Eat Well*. This program, which aims at normalising healthy eating and active lifestyles in children, is discussed in relation to the guidelines for establishing and sustaining health-promoting settings developed by the International Union for Health Promotion and Education. Insights from the experience of *Move Well Eat Well* are shared that may be relevant for other regions considering settings-based approaches to children's health promotion.

Summary

The key messages highlighted in this chapter are:

- Childhood obesity and overweight is a serious and increasing problem in contemporary society.
- Settings-based approaches are advocated by the International Union for Health Promotion and Education and include health promotion programs within schools and early childhood education and care settings.
- *Move Well Eat Well* is a settings-based health promotion program that has been introduced into the Tasmanian primary school sector and early childhood education and care sector.
- Key factors that have been critical in establishing effective settings-based health promotion programs in the *Move Well Eat Well* experience include conducting an initial audit of the setting; engaging a range of stakeholders; ensuring support of the setting's leadership team; building staff capacity; and setting realistic timeframes.
- Key factors for sustaining settings-based programs in the case of *Move Well Eat Well* include linking with other synergistic approaches to health promotion; recognising and celebrating milestones along the way; and ongoing evaluation and renewal of the program.

Questions

18.1 Consider a health promotion initiative you are familiar with and evaluate it in light of the IUHPE's guidelines:

  (a) How does it relate to the IUHPE's principles of a health-promoting setting (Table 18.1)?

  (b) Which elements around establishing (Table 18.2) and sustaining (Table 18.4) health-promoting settings resonate with the initiative?

18.2 What other interventions/approaches could be used to normalise healthy eating and physical activity in ECEC settings and primary schools?

18.3 Audit your own educational context in relation to the World Health Organization's *Ottawa Charter for Health Promotion* (Table 18.3). What are your setting's areas of strength and potential growth?

References

Australian Bureau of Statistics (ABS) (2010). *Year Book Australia, 2009–10*. Cat1301.0. Retrieved from http://www.abs.gov.au/AUSSTATS/abs@.nsf/Lookup/ 4266BB1E43756E9FCA25773700169D18?opendocument

—— (2011). *Australian health survey hysical activity, 2011–12*. Retrieved from http//www.abs.gov.au/ausstats/abs@.nsf/Lookup/4364.0.55.004Chapter1002011-12

—— (2015). *National Health Survey: First Results, 2014–2015*. Retrieved from http://www.abs.gov.au/ausstats/abs@.nsf/Lookup/by%20Subject/4364.0.55.001~2014-15~Main%20Features~About%20the%20National%20Health%20Survey~3

Australian Institute of Health and Welfare (2012). *A picture of Australia's children 2012. Cat. no. PHE 167*. Canberra: AIHW.

Bronfenbrenner, U. & Morris, P.A. (2006). The bioecological model of human development. In R.M. Lerner (ed.), *Handbook of Child Psychology* (6th edn, pp. 793–828). Hoboken, NJ: John Wiley & Sons, Inc.

Department of Health and Human Services (DHHS), Tasmania (2016). *Move Well Eat Well [electronic resource]* Retrieved from http://www.movewelleatwell.tas.gov.au/home

Dooris M. (2009). Holistic and sustainable health improvement: The contribution of the settings-based approach to health promotion. *Perspectives in Public Health,*129(1), 29–36.

International Union for Health Promotion and Education (2009). *Achieving Health Promoting Schools: Guidelines for promoting health in school*. Cedex, France: Author.

KidsMatter (2014). Australian Early Childhood Mental Health Initiative. *Connections with the National Quality Framework: Developing children's social and emotional skills*. Canberra, ACT: Commonwealth of Australia. Retrieved from https://www.kidsmatter.edu.au/sites/default/files/public/KM%20Linking%20resources%20C2%20Book_web_final.pdf

Whitelaw, S., Baxendale, A., Bryce C., MacHardy, L., Young, I. & Witney, E. (2001). Settings-based health promotion: A review. *Health Promotion International,* 16(4), 339–53.

World Health Organization (WHO) (1986). *Ottawa Charter for Health Promotion*. Ontario, Canada: Author.

—— (2012). *Population based approaches to childhood obesity prevention*. Geneva, Switzerland: Author.

—— (2016). *Report on the Commission on ending childhood obesity*. Geneva, Switzerland: Author. Retrieved from http://apps.who.int/iris/bitstream/10665/204176/1/9789241510066_eng.pdf?ua=1&ua=1

CHAPTER 19

Fostering children's wellbeing through play opportunities

Marjory Ebbeck, Hoi Yin Bonnie Yim and Lai Wan Maria Lee

Introduction

This chapter proposes that play is fundamental to the holistic development of children and that it is the right of all children to grow through play opportunities. In developing this proposition, ideas and examples are presented which show that wellbeing in children can be fostered through play. The chapter provides information by experts, such as Laevers (1994; Laevers & Heylen, 2004), with his international scale on wellbeing included. This scale is used in many Australian child-care contexts (Department of Education Employment and Workplace Relations [DEEWR], 2009). Other important elements of play central to children's wellbeing are presented with timely examples of how play contexts give children opportunities to grow and play in healthy, self-regulated, confident ways. Some concerns relating to play have come under scrutiny recently and these are examined. These include issues relating to the possible overuse of touchscreen devices and the fact that many young children are spending too many hours on mobile gadgets (Ebbeck et al., 2016). The commercialisation of play is a concern raised by professionals (e.g. Cook, 2013) as they see the huge impact that advertising and film exposure has on the play of children. Other useful content is included about technological toys, war play, and safety criteria for selecting toys and equipment.

Policy development: Wellbeing in young children

The wellbeing of young children has come into sharp focus in the last decade. This is a positive trend, and it is encouraging to see this reflected in curriculum frameworks for early childhood. For example, *Belonging, Being and Becoming*, the Early Years Learning Framework in Australia has, as one of the five developmental learning outcomes, 'Children have a strong sense of wellbeing' as being necessary for early childhood teachers to assess in their work with children (DEEWR, 2009).

Play is seen as the universal right of all children. Policy curriculum statements in some countries are also making provisions for the wellbeing of children in their stated policies and, hopefully, practices. An example is seen in the Scottish curriculum document entitled *Building the Ambition*, which states that 'as the child's keyworker, everything you (educators) do for young children should promote, support and safeguard their wellbeing' (Scottish Government, 2014, p. 15). A further example is seen in *The Guide to the Pre-primary Curriculum* (Curriculum Development Council, 2006, p. 18) adopted in Hong Kong, which notes that the cultivation of children's 'good habits, self-care ability and a healthy lifestyle' should be considered for curriculum planning. The early years curriculum document in Singapore also clearly states that 'play is vital to children's learning. Play is a vehicle for motivating children to explore, discover, take risks, make mistakes and cope with failure' (Ministry of Education, 2003, p. 25). These competencies and skills promote children's sense of wellbeing.

> **Play** includes joyful, engaging, free-flowing and spontaneous activity.

Defining wellbeing as part of policy decision-making

Childhood wellbeing is defined in many different ways. It can be understood as the quality of one's life. It is a dynamic state that is enhanced when one can fulfil his/her personal and social goals (Statham & Chase, 2010, p. 2). Wellbeing also 'includes good physical health, feelings of happiness, satisfaction and successful social functioning. It influences the way children interact in their environments' (DEEWR, 2009, p. 30). A strong sense of wellbeing is fundamentally important for all children, as it enables them to fully participate in, and learn from, the daily routines, play, interactions and experiences in their educational setting (Owens, 2012, p. 1).

As mentioned earlier, the Laevers scale is used widely in Australia and internationally, particularly in educational contexts. The areas assessing children's wellbeing in this scale are shown in Table 19.1.

Table 19.1: Laevers wellbeing scale – domains and indicators.

Domain	Indicators
Domain 1: Happiness and satisfaction	Confidence, self-esteem, sense of self, vitality, enjoyment/sense of humour, ability to rest and relax
Domain 2: Social functioning	Social initiative, assertiveness, coping/flexibility, positive attitude towards warmth and closeness
Domain 3: Dispositions	Openness and receptivity/pleasure in exploring, pleasure in sensory experiences, persistence/robustness

Source: Department of Education and Children's Services (2008, p. 16).

The indicators are used to observe children as they play and, through these, their happiness, social functioning and disposition are gauged.

How do we know when a child has a sense of wellbeing and is happy?

Educators are trained to observe children, and by using the Laevers scale they develop the facility to make objective judgements about children's wellbeing and happiness. Case Study 19.1 shows an example of this.

CASE STUDY 19.1: AN INFANT INTERACTING WITH A CAREGIVER

Tai Koi, a baby of four months, had been attending child care since he was two months old. After some transition visits to the child care centre he formed a bond with his primary caregiver, Leila, who would greet him and his parent each morning. He appeared secure and settled in his behaviours. For example, during the morning he was lying on the floor demonstrating that he could lift his head up steadily for a period of one to two minutes, looking at a bright red rattle placed strategically in front of him. He moved his arms and hands sideways and smiled as he focused his eyes consistently on the rattle. He continued to move his arms and hands more vigorously during the observation, as if he was trying to move closer to the object. When Leila came and sat close to Tai Koi he smiled and focused his gaze on her for several seconds. He listened attentively to Leila's voice when she spoke to him. Both Leila and Tai Koi's parents commented that he appeared to have made the transition to child care in a positive way and did not show any undue distress during his time there or when he returned home.

Reflection

Would one be able to state on the basis of the evidence above, that Tai Koi had a sense of wellbeing based on what was observed?

Refer back to the Laevers domains when answering this question. How many indicators of those domains are evident in Tai Koi's exploratory play and other behaviours?

Although it is difficult to make judgements on the basis of one case study, Tai Koi seems to have a secure attachment to his primary caregiver. According to comments from the caregiver and parents, he has settled into the child care environment and is engaging in activities with his caregiver. He is gaining a sense of physical wellbeing as he gains control over his developing body. The selection of play **materials** for Tai Koi is very important to extend his exploratory play.

Another example of possible wellbeing is presented in Case Study 19.2 where the child is older – five years of age.

Materials are toys, objects or equipment that promote play.

CASE STUDY 19.2: TRANSITION TO PRIMARY SCHOOL

Carla, at five years of age, made the transition to primary school without any major problems according to her mother and teachers. She came to school eagerly each morning and separated without issues from whoever brought her, mother or father. Within three weeks Carla had made two friends and interacted with them in a positive way. She knew their names and greeted them warmly when they arrived at school. Carla was able to interact in a positive way with her teacher and shared at home that she liked her new teacher.

Carla was able to initiate dramatic play in the home corner and invited her friends to take on roles. She was able to negotiate any conflicts that arose in relation to who would be 'mother' and who would be the 'baby'.

At all times during the school day Carla joined any group activities and was able to engage in discussions.

Carla showed resilience by persisting in block play when some boys tried to exclude her even though her friend Millie said, 'There are enough blocks for all of us to share!'

Reflection

On the basis of the evidence above does Carla have a sense of wellbeing based on what was observed?

Are there any dimensions of the child's behaviour, particularly in the play interactions, that could lead us to make the statement that Carla is happy?

Refer back to the Laevers domains when answering this question. How many indicators of those domains are evident in Carla's behaviour?

Carla showed confidence and trust in a new environment and was able to separate from her parents without distress. She had the ability to engage in activities required of the first year of the school curriculum. She was also able to socialise successfully by making friends and engageing in dramatic play, and she formed a positive relationship with her new teacher.

The Australian national curriculum reminds early childhood teachers to take a holistic approach so that they are able to pay attention to children's physical, personal, social, emotional and spiritual wellbeing as well as cognitive aspects of learning (DEEWR, 2009, p. 14). Teachers' knowledge of children's development, health, safety and nutritional needs should be appropriately applied to the educational contents. They can provide children with high-quality learning experiences that encourage a healthy lifestyle.

Play as the foundation of children's wellbeing

Play for children of all ages is central to their sense of identity, confidence and overall wellbeing. Researchers and scholars writing about the value of play have stated that it is universal, is the right of all children occurring across all cultures, is deeply engaging and is intrinsically motivated (Ebbeck & Waniganayake, in press; Hedegaard & Fleer, 2013; Jackson & Forbes, 2014). The wellbeing of children can be seen and measured through their engagement in play.

There is evidence that early exploratory play through to complex abstract play in later years helps children to feel positive about themselves (Figure 19.1) and develop their sense of identity; it assists self-regulation and the ability to feel connected to others and the wider world. From early exploratory play in infancy to formalised games played by older children, physical competencies develop as the child grows and contributes to overall health and wellbeing (see Case Study 19.3).

Figure 19.1 Harry shows confidence after his mastery of bike-riding skills.
Source: Marjory Ebbeck.

CASE STUDY 19.3: DEVELOPING PHYSICAL COMPETENCIES

Crisann is 10 months old and the educarer, Kartini, has placed a small climbing frame near her so that Crisann can pull herself up and use the frame for support. This piece of equipment assists her to develop gross motor control by pulling herself up to a standing position, and ensures that she does not fall over immediately but stands for one to two minutes before sitting down again. Demonstrating her independence, Crisann practises this activity over and over while Kartini stays with her to provide support and encouragement in verbal and non-verbal ways.

Reflection

Refer again to the Laevers wellbeing scale to identify the competencies Crisann shows in relation to wellbeing and health in the above vignette.

Pretend play and wellbeing

Pretend play is variously called dramatic play, role-play and socio-dramatic play. In essence, it is child-initiated, symbolic play which enhances children's ability to think in an abstract way, take on the perspectives of others, learn about the rules and connections with others and increase understanding about the world. Pretend play helps children develop

Pretend play includes dramatic or role-play.

Figure 19.2 Leah and her mother, Claire, engage in pretend play by using unstructured materials.
Source: Marjory Ebbeck.

analytical, critical skills essential for finding problems and solving them. Through pretend play episodes, children may function above their usual intellectual level and develop further cognitive skills. Enabling play experiences can help children to be confident and develop communication skills that are essential for the overall wellbeing of a child of any age (Figure 19.2). Children as young as toddlers also enjoy engaging in pretend play such as 'feeding a dolly' or 'driving a car'.

Bergen (2002), a strong proponent of pretend play, stated:

Pretend play requires the ability to transform objects and actions symbolically; it is furthered by interactive social dialogue and negotiation; and it involves role taking, script knowledge, and improvisation (p. 1).

Bergen also proposed that:

… pretend play engages many areas of the brain including emotion, cognition, language and sensorimotor actions, and thus it may promote the development of dense synaptic connections (2002, p. 1).

Many other researchers endorse the importance of pretend play in developing a range of cognitive and social skills (Gleason, 2016; Robertson, 2016; Russ, 2014).

Carlsson-Paige (2008), an advocate of pretend play, suggested that it emerges in two year olds and can be a source of health and healing throughout childhood. She proposed that the growing sense of autonomy that two-year-olds develop can manifest itself in pretend play. However, she also acknowledged that it is a challenge for parents to support the healthy sense of autonomy in children of this age while still being in charge in a way that supports their security and safety. Similar comments can also be found in some other more recent studies (Connor, 2010; Stonehouse, 2013; Whitebread & O'Sullivan, 2012).

In Case Study 19.4, where three girls are interacting, we can reflect on how older children's pretend play takes into account the many roles they see in real life. Refer back to Bergen's quotes at the beginning of this chapter.

CASE STUDY 19.4: ROLE-PLAY WITH FIVE-YEAR OLDS

Molly (5.4 years), Tina (5.6 years) and Chloe (5.3 years) are playing in the home corner. They have set up a hairdressing salon and have various play items such as a hairdryer, comb and scissors.

The girls have negotiated that Molly is the hairdresser and she is busy 'cutting' Tina's hair. Chloe comes over and asks, 'Would you like your nails done too?'

Tina replies, 'No thank you, I had them done last week'. And she shows her nails to Faith.

After the haircut is completed, Molly says, 'That will be $30, please'. Tina replies, 'That is very expensive, it cost me less the last time. I will not come back here again if you charge so much'. She 'pays' the money and hurries out of the salon. She then returns and the girls discuss who will be the hairdresser next.

Reflection

What understanding about the real world occurred in this play vignette episode? Was any interaction with a teacher necessary in this play episode?

The role of superhero play in children's health and wellbeing

This is undoubtedly a controversial topic for discussion. Superhero play is 'a form of imaginative or dramatic play in which children use figurines, costumes or other props as accessories to imitate the superheroes that they admire' (Barnes, 2008, p. 18). One of the headlines in *Exchange Every Day* read 'Preschool Bans Super Hero Play'. The responses from educators included the following:

> Wow – it's my whole career flashing before my eyes! Star Wars, Ninja Turtles, Spider Man, Power Rangers, He-Man, Star Wars again, Spider Man, Hulk, Batman – it doesn't work to ban this play.

The advice from teachers who responded to this article was to channel this form of play and use it as emergent curriculum (Kelly, 2013).

However, adults occasionally need to intervene if the superhero play becomes random or aggressive in nature. This type of play often manifests itself at about four years of age, and can continue until about seven to eight years of age when more abstract thinking and interest in competitive games develops. Instead of banning this type of play, which may make it even more desirable and may lead to frustration rather than a sense of wellbeing, educators are encouraged to rethink.

Carlsson-Paige (2008) presents an interesting dimension in relation to 'war play'. She wrote that 'many kids need this sort of play, especially when they feel helpless in their lives, as so many children do when having to face scary situations such as separation from home, going to school, and for some, divorce, illness or neighbourhood violence' (p. 98). She further advocates that war play lets children express feelings of hostility and fear towards their imaginary foe and get some inner control over their feelings.

The role of adults is crucial in promoting wellbeing and health through play opportunities in order to extend the learning of children, particularly in the early years – namely, birth to eight years. As an educarer, teacher or other early childhood professional, the adult needs to be intentional in guiding and extending children's play by having an understanding of their developmental needs. Through systematic observation, the adult knows when to intervene or not to intervene, and this requires professional judgement. Sometimes, an adult is needed to share in the child's enjoyment in a play activity. This intervention can enrich the play outcomes and foster the health and wellbeing of children.

Assessing children's play materials for health and safety: Applying criteria

Health and safety as a prime consideration for all play materials

The most important point about play materials is that they must be safe for the age group they are designed for. Babies put everything in their mouth until they are toddlers, and even then small objects should to be avoided as they can be easily swallowed. Also avoidance of small batteries in children's toys is essential as these have caused death by swallowing and can go undetected until it is too late.

Various consumer associations in countries around the world keep a check on toys containing dangerous substances and other health hazards, such as potential for choking. For example, in Singapore some 29 children's toys were recently found to be dangerous due to rough edges and/or small parts that can cause choking (Othman, 2015). Similar toy hazard issues also exist in the Western context (Rood, 2007).

The following criteria apply to toys, equipment and other play materials.

1. Does the toy, object, equipment or other play material comply with health and safety standards? Is it labelled as non-toxic? Is it free of sharp pins, nails or cords which can be dangerous? Avoidance of plastic bags which can be put over heads is essential. Is the toy large enough that it cannot be swallowed by an infant, toddler or young child?
2. Check the toy, object, equipment or other play material carefully to ensure that there are no detachable parts.
3. Avoid including toys with small batteries in play equipment for young children as they can be lethal if swallowed.
4. Is the toy, object, equipment or other play material safe for exploratory and other forms of play?
5. Can the toy, object, equipment or other play material be cleaned easily?
6. Is the toy, object, equipment or other play material well constructed to withstand banging and rough play?
7. Does the object, equipment or other play material have an interest level for the age it is intended for?
8. Can the toy, object, equipment or other play material be used in more than one way?

9. Does the toy, object, equipment or other play material help a child gain some competencies?
10. Does the toy, object, equipment or other play material stimulate exploration, imagination or creativity?
11. Is the cost of the toy justified in terms of what it claims to do?
12. Does the toy, object, equipment or other play material offer opportunities for independent learning?

Play opportunies in the digital age

In any discussion on play opportunities, the issue of technological tools emerges. This issue has always been a hot topic in early childhood education. Nowadays it is common to see toddlers/young children accessing technological devices (e.g. laptop, mobile devices, interactive medias, television) (Figure 19.3), and some guidelines are also made available for adults to support their work with young children (e.g. American Academy of Pediatrics, 2016; Raising Children Network, 2016). Some

Figure 19.3 Leah and Eve play with a touchscreen device.
Source: Marjory Ebbeck.

researchers express concerns that such an early access to technology may negatively impact on their health and wellbeing (Cespedes et al, 2014; French et al, 2013; Hale & Guan, 2015). Nevertheless, technology and interactive media are here to stay. Educators are therefore encouraged to understand the possible teaching and learning opportunities available via technology. Also, they are reminded that technology can never replace children's active learning experience by involving real objects.

There is no doubt that children below the age of two should not be accessing smart phones, tablets or any other ICT gadgets. Such comments are supported by the Australian and American guidelines (National Association for the Education of Young Children and the Fred Rogers Center for Early Learning and Children's Media at Saint Vincent College, 2012; Raising Children Network, 2016). The judicious use of computer programs for children who are three years and older can be appropriate by referring to the aforementioned guidelines. Older children beyond the early childhood years will be using technology in their school and social lives and, in some instances, they will be more familiar with these tools, games and applications than their parents.

So, the issue is not about banning children from accessing technological tools but, rather, considering at what age they should be given access. Further, all screen usage should be closely supervised at home by parents and wise choices made by teachers when deciding which programs/platforms are suitable for use.

Commercialisation of play opportunities

Childhood has become a great source of revenue for the marketing of play toys, equipment and other play materials. The marketing extends to children's clothing, shoe wear, eating utensils and school materials. Sometimes these toys can 'talk' and more often than not, these voices have an American accent. A superhero or an adult-constructed product can be lucrative business for toy manufacturers. If children become 'hooked' on a particular figure, be it a superhero or a harmless dwarf-like small model, clever marketing can make it highly sought after by children of any age upwards of two years.

Parents and family members may become irritated at the pervasive advertising and indeed exploitation of childhood by commercialisation. Parents and educators need to be vigilant in making wise choices about these toys and equipment. The right kinds of open-ended toys will foster children's development and provide hours of learning, cooperation, social interaction and, above all, enjoyment.

Children beyond the early childhood years may outgrow some commercialisation marketing ploys targeted at the younger age group but they may subsequently become addicted to electronic games instead. Parents need to be aware for health and safety reasons which games and programs are being used by their children and for what duration.

A study of Hong Kong parents' spending patterns on toys purchases revealed that 19 per cent bought toys from chain stores and 15 per cent from fast-food chains (Yim, Lee & Ng, 2012). The toys were mostly selected for their branding of superheroes or cartoon characters which appeared on television programs, movies or commercials.

An indoor play centre is an emerging play trend. Such a space is named differently in different contexts, such as play café, playhouse or playground. This type of play space is commercially designed for both parents and children, featuring some purpose-built indoor adventure playground facilities and eateries (Figure 19.4). However, the development of such play spaces can be an entrepreneurial strategy to attract new customers (i.e. children) based on the concept of 'implosion' (i.e.

Figure 19.4 Indoor adventure playground facilities.
Source: Bonnie Yim.

the erosion of boundaries) (Ritzer, 1999). This type of play space reduces the boundaries between drinking, eating and playing. Research also indicates that children may become an important market for entrepreneurs of this type of commercial play space (i.e. process of commercialisation of childhood) (Karstena, Kamphuisb & Remeijnseb, 2015). Parents are advised to re-think the need and purpose of visiting such a space with their children as compared to using some natural settings (e.g. a park or beach).

Reducing culture and gender stereotyping and gender role conformity in play

In any discussion on play, gender stereotyping and gender role conformity, health issues arise, particularly in relation to social and emotional development.

As children grow in age and development, they become strongly aware of gender and other stereotypes. Berk and Meyers (2016, p. 299) noted that biology channels boys towards higher activity level and greater impulsivity in play, while girls tend to seek out quieter and more intimate interactions. However, adults can be influential in encouraging children to take on different roles in their play based on interests rather than gender stereotyping.

CASE STUDY 19.5: GENDER STEREOTYPING SO EARLY IN PLAY

Carl and three other four-year old boys are playing in the sand pit digging drains, making tunnels and using water from a hose to expand their play. Matilda, a girl of 3.8 years approaches the sand pit. Carl immediately raises his hand and says in a loud voice, 'Men only!' Matilda stops and looks uncertainly at the group of boys. Her teacher, Patricia, who has witnessed the incident, moves forwards quickly and says, 'Of course, Matilda can join in. Both men and women can dig in the sand pit'. Patricia sits on the side of the sand pit and helps Matilda join in the group play.

The choice of a range of dolls representing different ethnic groups including Indigenous groups can facilitate play. A cultural diversity pretend play corner in an educational setting can also help to break down prejudice. Some teachers' careful provision of play materials (e.g. persona dolls) can support children's development of cultural awareness and sensitivity (Srinivasana & Cruza, 2015). Very young children are able to show empathy for others (Yim, Lee & Ebbeck, 2013) and research has shown that this can occur under two years of age (Ebbeck, Tan & Teo-Zuzarte, 2013).

Helping children express their emotions and increase their sense of wellbeing can be facilitated by the type of social interactions in play, which occur in the centre or school. The use of persona dolls, pictures and story books, games and materials can foster respect and empathy for others, leading to increased positive self-esteem in the children. This can extend a child's understanding of other people and respect for their culture.

Conclusion

This chapter deals with many important issues related to health and wellbeing in childhood. Discussion ranged from wellbeing policies, to a definition and examination of play as the foundation of children's wellbeing, to criteria for assessing children's play materials. Then, finally, other important issues were presented – play in the digital age, commercialisation of play opportunities and gender and play.

Summary

The key messages highlighted in this chapter are:

- Play continues to be the foundation of development as children experience childhood.
- Wellbeing in children includes good physical health and feelings of happiness, satisfaction and positive social functioning and is demonstrated through their interactions in the environment.
- Adults need to help the children feel positive about themselves and aim to develop their resilience and self-awareness. This is facilitated through play.
- Bergen's 2002 work is summarised in that *pretend play* engages many areas of the brain including emotion, cognition, language and sensorimotor actions, and as such it may promote the development of dense synaptic connections essential for healthy brain development.
- The prime consideration of all play materials is that they are safe and in some way promote children's wellbeing and health.

Questions

19.1   How can parents be helped to understand that touch screen usage for young children needs to be monitored?

19.2   What play materials do you see as essential for infants and toddlers?

19.3   How can these be expanded for preschool-aged children?

19.4   What play opportunities would you hope to provide for six- to eight-year-old children in primary school?

References

American Academy of Pediatrics (2016). Media and young minds. Retrieved 21 October 2016 from http://pediatrics.aappublications.org/content/pediatrics/early/2016/10/19/peds.2016-2591.full.pdf

Barnes, H. (2008). The value of superhero play. *Putting Children First*. Retrieved 15 May 2016 from file://cifs-g.its.deakin.edu.au/yim/UserData/Desktop/The_value_of%20_superhero_play_Sep08.pdf

Bergen, D. (2002). The role of pretend play in children's cognitive development. *Early Childhood Research and Practice*, 4(1), 1–8.

Berk, L.E. & Meyers, A.B. (2016). *Infants and children: prenatal through middle childhood* (8th edn). Boston: Pearson.

Carlsson-Paige, N. (2008). *Taking back childhood: Helping your kids thrive in a fast-paced, media-saturated, violence-filled world*. USA: Penguin Group.

Cespedes, E.M., Gillman, M.W., Kleinman, K., Rifas-Shiman, S.L., Redline, S. & Taveras, E.M. (2014). Television viewing, bedroom television and sleep duration from infancy to mid-childhood. *Pediatrics*, 133(5), e1163–71.

Connor, J. (2010). Thinking about play. *The Early Years Learning Framework-Professional Learning Program*. Retrieved 18 October 2015 from http://www.earlychildhoodaustralia.org.au/nqsplp/wp-content/uploads/2012/05/EYLFPLP_E-Newsletter_No3.pdf

Cook, D.T. (2013). Commercialisation of play and the toy industry. In L. Brooker & M. Woodhead (eds), *The Right to Play. Early Childhood in Focus, 9* (pp. 42–43). Milton Keynes: The Open University with the support of Bernard van Leer Foundation.

Curriculum Development Council (2006). *Guide to the pre-primary curriculum (consultation)*. Hong Kong: Curriculum Development Council (CDC) of Hong Kong.

Department of Education and Children's Services (2008). *Assessing for Learning and Development in the Early Years using Observation Scales: Reflect Respect Relate*. Adelaide, SA: DECS Publishing.

Department of Education Employment and Workplace Relations (DEEWR) (2009). Belonging, being & becoming: The Early Years Learning Framework for Australia. Retrieved 3 September 2015 from https://docs.education.gov.au/system/files/doc/other/belonging_being_and_becomin_the_early_years_learning_framework_for_australia.pdf

Ebbeck, M., Tan, C. & Teo-Zuzarte, G. (2013). Showing empathy for others during transition: A Singapore example. *Every Child*, 19(1), 28–29.

Ebbeck, M. & Waniganayake, M. (eds) (in press). *Play in early childhood education: Learning in diverse contexts* (2nd edn). South Melbourne, Vic.: Oxford University Press.

Ebbeck, M., Yim, H.Y.B., Chan, Y.Y.Y. & Goh, M. (2016). Singaporean parents' views of their young children's access and use of technological devices. *Early Childhood Education Journal*, 44(2), 127–34. doi:10.1007/s10643-015-0695-4

French, A.N., Morgan, I.G., Burlutsky, G., Mitchell, P. & Rose, K.A. (2013). Prevalence and 5- to 6-year incidence and progression of myopia and hyperopia in Australian school children. *Ophthalmology*, 120(7), 1482–91.

Gleason, T. (2016). Why make-believe play is an important part of childhood development. Retrieved 6 April 2016 from https://theconversation.com/why-make-believe-play-is-an-important-part-of-childhood-development-49693

Hale, L. & Guan, S. (2015). Screen time and sleep among school-aged children and adolescents: A systematic literature review. *Sleep Medicine Reviews*, 21, 50–58.

Hedegaard, M. & Fleer, M. (2013). *Play, learning and children's development: everyday life in families and transition to school.* Cambridge: Cambridge University Press.

Jackson, S. & Forbes, R. (2014). *People under three: Play, work and learning in a childcare setting.* Hoboken: Taylor and Francis.

Karstena, L., Kamphuisb, A. & Remeijnseb, C. (2015). 'Time-out' with the family: the shaping of family leisure in the new urban consumption spaces of cafes, bars and restaurants. *Leisure Studies, 34*(2), 166–81.

Kelly, T. (2013). Super hero play controversy: Preschool bans super hero play. *ExchangeEveryDay.* May/June. Retrieved 3 March 2016 from http://www.childcareexchange.com/eed/news_print.php?news_id=3366

Laevers, F. (ed.). (1994). *Defining and assessing quality in early childhood education.* Leuven, Belgium: Leuven University Press.

Laevers, F. & Heylen, L. (eds). (2004). *Involvement of children and teacher style: Insights from an international study on experiential education.* Leuven, Belgium: Leuven University Press.

Ministry of Education (2003). Nurturing early learners: A framework for a kindergarten curriculum in Singapore. Retrieved 16 March 2016 from http://ncm.gu.se/media/kursplaner/andralander/singaporeforskola.pdf

National Association for the Education of Young Children & Fred Rogers Center for Early Learning and Children's Media at Saint Vincent College (2012). Technology and interactive media as tools in early childhood programs serving children from birth through age 8. Retrieved 11 December 2015 from http://www.naeyc.org/files/naeyc/file/positions/PS_technology_WEB2.pdf

Othman, L. (2015). Exercise caution when choosing toys for children: SPRING Singapore. Retrieved 18 May 2016 from http://www.channelnewsasia.com/news/singapore/exercise-caution-when/2342330.html

Owens, A. (2012). Health, safety and wellbeing. *National Quality Standard-Professional Learning Program.* Retrieved 23 May 2016 from http://www.earlychildhoodaustralia.org.au/nqsplp/wp-content/uploads/2012/05/NQS_PLP_E-Newsletter_No29.pdf

Raising Children Network (2016). Screen time and children. Retrieved 7 January 2016 from http://raisingchildren.net.au/articles/screen_time.html/context/1112

Ritzer, G. (1999). *Enchanting a disenchanted world: Revolutionizing the means of consumption.* Thousand Oaks, CA: Pine Forge Press.

Robertson, N. (2016). The complexity of preschool children's dramatic play behaviour and play styles in Australia: A mixed methods study. *Asia-Pacific Journal of Research in Early Childhood Education, 10*(2), 71–92.

Rood, D. (2007). Recall ordered for toy that turns into drug. *The Age.* Retrieved 24 May 2016 from http://www.theage.com.au/news/national/recall-for-toy-that-turns-into-drug/2007/11/06/1194329225773.html

Russ, S.W. (2014). Pretend play and creativity: An overview. In *Pretend play in childhood: Foundation of adult creativity* (pp. 7–28). Washington, DC: American Psychological Association.

Scottish Government (2014). Building the ambition: National practice guidance on early learning and childcare children and young people (Scotland) Act 2014. Retrieved 4 May 2016 from http://www.gov.scot/Resource/0045/00458455.pdf

Srinivasana, P. & Cruza, M. (2015). Children colouring: Speaking 'colour difference' with diversity dolls. *Pedagogy,Culture & Society*, 23(1), 21–43.

Statham, J. & Chase, E. (2010). Childhood wellbeing: A brief overview. Retrieved 24 April 2016 from http://www.cwrc.ac.uk/documents/CWRC_Briefing_paper.pdf

Stonehouse, A. (2013). Supporting babies' social and emotional wellbeing. *National Quality Standard-Professional Development Program*. Retrieved 14 December 2015 from http://www.earlychildhoodaustralia.org.au/nqsplp/wp-content/uploads/2013/08/NQS_PLP_E-Newsletter_No61.pdf

Whitebread, D. & O'Sullivan, L. (2012). Preschool children's social pretend play: Supporting the development of metacommunication, metacognition and self-regulation. *International Journal of Play*, 1(2), 197–213.

Yim, H.Y.B., Lee, L.W.M. & Ebbeck, M. (2013). Preservation of Confucian values in early childhood education: A study of experts' and educators' views. *Asia-Pacific Journal of Research in Early Childhood Education*, 7(1), 51–68.

Yim, H.Y.B., Lee, L.W.M. & Ng, K.Y.C. (2012, 20–22 July). *Toy selection for young children: A study of caregivers' views*. Paper presented at the Pacific Early Childhood Education Research Association 13th Annual Conference 'Building a Community of Researchers: Children at the Heart of Research', Singapore.

CHAPTER 20

Bullying and social emotional wellbeing in children

Cathrine Neilsen-Hewett and Kay Bussey

Introduction

Research both within Australia and around the world underscores the short- and long-term negative effects of bullying on children's socio-emotional health and wellbeing. While there has been a significant increase in the number of studies conducted with upper primary and secondary students, comparatively fewer studies have focused on the prior-to-school and early school contexts. The few studies that have examined the impact of bullying in the early years underscore its negative effects, with victims and bullies exhibiting psycho-social maladjustment and psychosomatic problems similar to outcomes reported with older samples (see Neilsen-Hewett, Bussey & Fitzpatrick, 2017). Bullying poses a significant risk to children's socio-emotional wellbeing and mental health. A growing awareness of how bullying manifests itself in early peer contexts is therefore critical in the development of effective preventative anti-bullying initiatives. The goal of this chapter is to provide a synthesis of this research including an overview of the causes and correlates of bullying and its effects on children's socio-emotional wellbeing.

What is bullying?

Bullying typically refers to physically or psychologically aggressive behaviours that intentionally cause harm to another child, are repeated over time, evolve from a position of power and are frequently used to establish dominance within the peer group (Olweus, 1993). Direct bullying involves face-to-face encounters

Bullying: verbal, physical, social or psychological behaviour that is harmful, perpetrated by a more powerful (or perceived powerful) individual or group towards a less powerful individual, which is repeated (or has the potential to be repeated) over time.

between the bully and the victim. This includes physical aggression such as punching, shoving or breaking of belongings. Direct bullying also includes direct verbal aggression such as name-calling. Indirect bullying or relational bullying involves more covert behaviours and includes harm caused through the damaging of social relationships, manifesting through social exclusion, withdrawing friendships or spreading rumours (Hawker & Boulton, 2000).

Cyberbullying

Cyberbullying, a comparatively new form of bullying, involves using information and communication technology (ICT) to intentionally hurt or harm another child. The proliferation of electronic media has provided a new platform for bullies to threaten, harass and humiliate their victims; the multi-contextual nature of this form of bullying means children are potentially at risk 24/7, with few avenues for escape (Kowalski, Limber & Agatston, 2012). Cyberbullying can occur anywhere at anytime; it is not limited to the schoolyard as with most traditional bullying. It is also less subject to monitoring by others, particularly by adults, than is traditional bullying. Children who are cyberbullied are often reluctant to report it to their parents for fear of losing access to the cyber world, a major avenue for social interaction among youth. Even when children do disclose cyberbullying to their parents, parents often do not know how to respond (Tokunaga, 2010). Cyberbullying differs from traditional bullying in that bullies are able to conceal their identity, thereby allowing them to be even more vicious towards their victim than they may be in face-to-face bullying (Runions & Bak, 2015). Cyberbullies justify their bullying by downplaying its effects on the target. These justifications are part of the moral disengagement process which enables bullies to engage in bullying behaviour without feeling any remorse (Bussey, Fitzpatrick & Raman, 2015). Moral disengagement is one of factors most strongly associated with cyberbullying (see Kowalski et al., 2014). Cyberbullying also differs from traditional bullying in that the bully is able to send messages not only to the victim, but to an audience of thousands and even millions. Therefore, not surprisingly, the impact on those who are victimised can be even more severe than for traditional bullying (Bonanno & Hymel, 2013). Those who witness the bullying can also be affected, with some trying to defend the victim and others joining in the bullying (see Allison & Bussey, 2016). Although there are distinct features of cyberbullying and traditional bullying, there are many similarities and they are highly inter-related. Most children involved in one form of bullying are also involved in the other (Cross, Lester & Barnes, 2015).

PAUSE AND REFLECT 20.1: CYBERBULLYING AND THE RESPONSIBILITY OF THE SCHOOL

A parent brings a cyberbullying incident to your attention and asks for your assistance in resolving the issue. What responsibility or authority does the school have to regulate or sanction inappropriate cyber behaviour?

Developmental trends

While there has been considerable debate surrounding whether young children are in fact capable of bullying, research focused on younger samples reveals that physical bullying is the most prevalent form of bullying in the early years. This is not surprising as physical aggression is often regarded as relatively normative among early years learners. However, even at this stage, children are beginning to replace physical aggression with relational aggression (Swit, McMaugh & Warburton, 2016). Children have been observed engaging in relational aggression (e.g. 'the child tells a peer they won't be invited to their birthday party unless she/he does what the child wants') during the preschool years (Murray-Close & Ostrov, 2009) and it may well occur earlier (Vaillancourt et al., 2007). Longitudinal studies show the percentage of children reporting victimisation decreases as children age, although children's risk for experiencing bullying shifts at various transitional points – such as moving from primary to high school – when issues of identity surface and children are seeking to re-establish their position in the peer group.

The age-related pattern of cyberbullying differs from that of traditional bullying, with the highest rates occurring in the later high school years. Younger children are much less likely to have been cyberbullied than older children. One of the reasons for this age difference is that younger children have more restricted access to cyber space than their older counterparts.

Who bullies and who is bullied?

Although there is general consensus within the literature regarding the negative effects of bullying, there is less agreement concerning the actual causes of bullying and the most effective means of reducing it. Research indicates that children's characteristics along with environmental factors work together to affect their risk of being bullied or bullying others. Social-ecological systems theory provides a comprehensive framework for understanding the complex array of individual, familial and contextual factors at play in the bullying context (see Neilsen-Hewett, Bussey & Fitzpatrick, 2017). Individuals also bring with them a complex array of characteristics that either place them at risk or protect them from bullying.

SPOTLIGHT 20.1: FACTORS PREDICTING INDIVIDUAL DIFFERENCES IN BULLYING AND VICTIMISATION AMONG YOUNG CHILDREN

Bullying is an ecological phenomenon, established and propagated over time as a result of a complex interplay between individual, family, peer, community (i.e. media) and educational contexts (Yoon & Barton, 2008). Effective interventions designed to reduce bullying need to consider these multiple forms of influence.

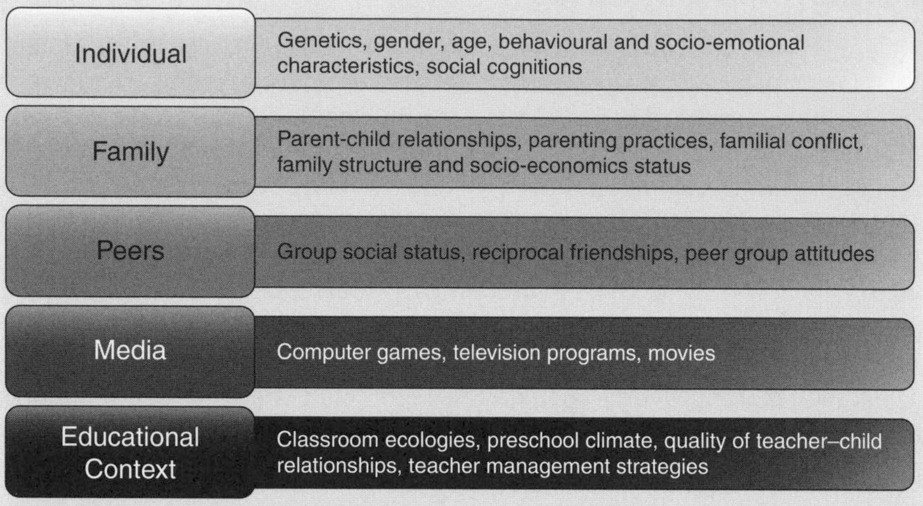

Figure 20.1 Social and personal influences on bullying.

Perpetrators of bullying

Research in the early years has focused mainly on children's aggressive behaviour rather than their bullying. However, as new measures of bullying are developed, there is an increasing focus on bullying (Camodeca, Caravita & Coppola, 2015) in the preschool age group. Drawing on the well-established research on aggression, it is evident that aggressive behaviour is relatively stable from as early as two years of age (Vaillancourt et al., 2007). Much of the aggression literature paints a picture of the aggressive preschooler and first-grade child as evidencing behavioural maladjustment, hyperactivty, externalising problems, and being socially rejected by their peers. For those children whose aggressive behaviour leads to peer rejection, this experience leads to further aggressive responding, thereby perpetuating a cyclical relationship between peer-rejection and aggression.

In contrast to children who experience peer rejection, popular children are more sociable with peers, engage in less aggressive behaviour and spend more time in hierarchical play (Braza et al., 2007). These findings have been found to extend to relational aggression. That is, in contrast to their popular peers, relationally aggressive children tend to be socially rejected by their peers.

Not all children who use aggressive strategies are rejected by their peers; some are popular. Observational research has shown that children who selectively use both aggressive and pro-social strategies when interacting with their peers in different situations do not incur the typical rejection experienced by aggressive children. These children who use a combination of strategies when interacting with peers behave in more socially skilled aggressive ways than peer-rejected children (Roseth et al., 2007). It is these children who may later develop into bullies.

Bullies were once cast as oafs and socially unskilled children who could only obtain what they wanted and settle disputes with aggressive behaviour. More recent characterisations of these children show little support for this view. Instead, bullies are often dominant members of the peer group and use aggression to achieve and maintain their status within the peer group. Rather than possessing social deficits that lead them to resolve conflicts aggressively, these children learn during the early preschool years that they can achieve their goals through aggression and social manipulation of their peers. It is important to identify children who are bullying others to achieve social dominance so that they can learn other more acceptable and pro-social ways of achieving their goals during the early years.

Victims of bullying

Children's behaviour often places them at risk for being the targets of bullying. However, there is less stability in those children identified as victims in the early years than later in development. Some of the reasons for this lack of stability are related to the perpetrator rather than to the victim. Young perpetrators may be more indiscriminate in their selection of victims until they are more able to anticipate the reactions of specific victims to bullying. Identifying certain reactions such as timidity and withdrawn behaviours with specific children may take time to develop. The dominance hierarchies among peers are less firmly established during the preschool years which may enable children to escape identification as a 'victim'. Increasingly, as children enter school and dominance hierarchies are more clearly established and behavioural patterns formed, some children become the targets of bullying. In the early years, overt social behaviour such as submissiveness, withdrawal and aggression make children susceptible to **victimisation**. As children enter primary school, low self-esteem is one of the most robust predictors of victimisation (Guerra, Williams & Sadek, 2011). Emotional reactivity and poor emotional regulation have also been linked to poor peer relationships including peer rejection and victimisation (Iyer et al., 2010). There is also evidence that psycho-social problems, including internalising difficulties, are not only an outcome of peer victimisation, but are also an antecedent to it (Arseneault, Bowes & Shakoor, 2010).

Victmisation: the experience of being the target of physical, verbal, social or psychological harm.

As already discussed, social status in the peer group is related to children's aggression; however, it is less strongly related to their victimisation, at least in the early years (Monks, Smith & Swettenham, 2005). Status within the peer group, however, has been associated with loneliness among preschoolers with some being anxious and others being aggressive (Coplan, Closson & Arbeau, 2007). Most importantly, pro-socialness has been associated with social acceptance in the peer group and high-quality friendships (Sebanc, 2003). It therefore seems that children's standing in the peer group affords protection from bullying and victimisation by enabling them to develop high-quality friendships and pro-social concern for others. Across the school years, high-quality friendships play a major protective factor against peer victimisation.

Peer group involvement in bullying

Bullying rarely occurs in isolation, with most incidents being witnessed or even supported. How the peer group responds to acts of bullying may either contribute to the problem or help stop it. Olweus (2001) described the different roles and modes of reaction of the peer group to bullying incidences in his oft-cited 'bullying circle', in which eight distinct bystander roles are identified and characterised with respect to their support for the bully (positive–neutral–indifferent–negative) and the assistance they provide the victim (not intervening-intervening).

A significant number of peers are involved in the bullying process, with the role of bully, bully-assistant or reinforcer adopted by up to 40 per cent of school-aged children and the role of onlooker by a further 30 per cent (Salmivalli, 2010).

Bystanders' active involvement and support of bullying has been shown to result in significant increases in bullying, while challenging the bully's actions and defending the victim results in significant decreases in bullying behaviours (Salmivalli, 2010). The social context, particularly the peer group, also influences bystander responses. The more that witnesses perceive that their classmates justify the acceptability of bullying, the less likely they are to defend victims (Gini,

Students' Modes of Reaction/Roles in an Acute Bullying Situation

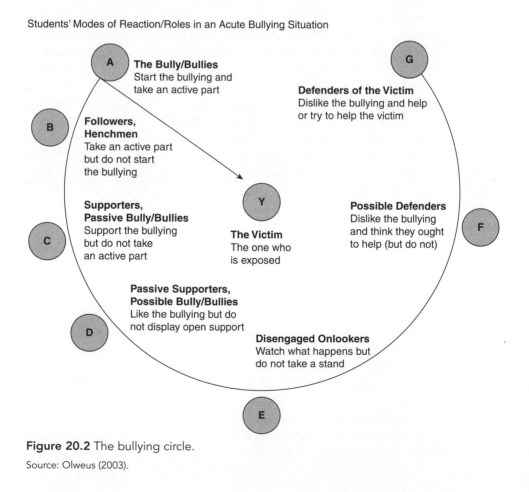

Figure 20.2 The bullying circle.

Source: Olweus (2003).

Pozzoli & Bussey, 2015), highlighting the importance of peer group involvement in all intervention efforts.

Familial factors associated with bullying

Family characteristics such as low parental involvement, low levels of parental warmth, low family cohesion and high levels of conflict have all been associated with increased risk of childhood bullying. Parental use of harsh and power-assertive disciplinary strategies with five- to six-year-old children has been linked to their child's externalising difficulties and physical aggression, especially among temperamentally inflexible children. Whereas the use of psychological control techniques, in which parents threaten their child with loss of love, has been associated with children's relational aggression (see Neilsen-Hewett, Bussey & Fitzpatrick, 2017).

Parenting styles have also been related to children's victimisation. Maternal overprotectiveness, maternal enmeshment, harsh discipline, and parental control have all been associated with vulnerability to peer victimisation (Finnegan, Hodges & Perry, 1998; Lereya, Smaara & Wolke, 2013). In addition, longitudinal research has pointed to the predictive role of child maltreatment, parental depression, and familial domestic violence with increased rates of bullying and victimisation among children (see Arseneault et al., 2010).

Social ecology of the school and classroom environment

The amount of bullying that occurs in schools and classrooms varies. Classrooms that are well managed in terms of competent teaching, monitoring of homework and behaviour, and caring for students have less bullying (Olweus, 1993). Apart from teachers' management strategies, how they intervene in bullying episodes also contributes to the level of school bullying (Leadbeater et al., 2015; Sokol, Bussey & Rapee, 2016). Schools in which there is teacher supervision outside the classroom tend to have lower levels of bullying in comparison with 'bully-friendly schools' that involve little teacher supervision, inconsistent handling of bullying and no serious consequences for it.

How does bullying impact children's health and socio-emotional wellbeing?

All forms of bullying have been associated with negative sequelae among both boys and girls of all ages. Perpetrators and victims of bullying are at risk of experiencing a range of short- and long-term negative psychological (e.g. feelings of loneliness, anxiety, shame, fear, guilt and depression) and physical (e.g. poor health) issues. A review by Arseneault and colleagues (2010) shows bullying has long-lasting effects that can extend into adolescence, with victimisation associated with a wide range of serious mental health problems including psychotic symptoms and self-harm. Individual differences in children's responses to bullying underscore the need for researchers to examine both characteristics of the individual and situational factors that heighten the risk of maladaptive outcomes. The following sections examine the consequences of bullying for both victims and bullies.

Victims of bullying

Victims of bullying in the early years display psycho-social maladjustment in adolescence and adulthood. In particular, school-aged children who are the victims of bullying have increased incidence of continued depression, loneliness, low self-esteem, poor academic performance, early school drop-out, delinquency, later involvement in crime, physical health issues, sleep disturbances and suicidal ideation (Arseneault et al., 2010; Gini & Pozzoli, 2013; Hawker & Boulton, 2000; Reijntjes et al., 2010). Longitudinal research conducted with children in Grades 3 to 6 showed the negative impact of victimisation on their self-perception and depressive cognitions, with children describing themselves as a failure, physically unattractive, socially incompetent and angry. Both relational and physical victimisation were associated with increases in negative cognitions and decreases in positive cognitions, with strongest effects being experienced by boys and children experiencing relational acts of bullying (see Gini & Pozzoli, 2013).

Internalising difficulties resulting from peer victimisation become most evident during the middle childhood years. Goodman, Stormshak and Dishion (2001) showed that peer victimisation in fifth grade predicted internalising behaviours in sixth, seventh and eighth grades after controlling for initial levels of internalising behaviours. In addition, peer victimisation in Grade 2 and increasing victimisation across Grades 2 to 5 were associated with depressive symptoms and overt aggression for both boys and girls, and with relational aggression for girls in Grade 5 (Rudolph et al., 2011).

As noted above, the consequences of peer victimisation are well documented. Increasingly, however, it has been shown that the impact of peer victimisation on children's adjustment is quite variable (Kochenderfer-Ladd & Skinner, 2002). Therefore, a major agenda for the research on peer victimisation has been to identify the factors that moderate the impact of peer victimisation on children's **socio-emotional wellbeing**. Some of these potential moderating variables include the child's attributional style, quality of their friendships, and coping styles.

Socio-emotional wellbeing refers to the way an individual perceives (thinks and feels) him or herself. It encompasses mental health, resilience and coping, and cultural and social wellbeing.

SPOTLIGHT 20.2: VICTIM RESPONSES

Although it is imperative that teachers focus on reducing bullying behaviour, it is also important that they provide advice to children about possible strategies for responding to bullying. The strategies provided in Figure 20.3 are part of the WITS program in Canada, which is a comprehensive anti-bullying program for handling bullying in schools (www.witsprogram.ca).

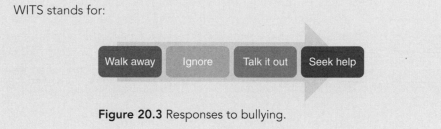

WITS stands for:

Walk away | Ignore | Talk it out | Seek help

Figure 20.3 Responses to bullying.

Children's attributions and links to adjustment

Research by Visconti, Kochenderfer Ladd and Clifford (2013) with 8- to 11-year-old children suggests children's beliefs about why they are bullied may help explain individual differences in socio-emotional adjustment and mental health. Children who believed they were victimised for their 'uncool' behaviour (e.g. *I don't wear cool clothes*) reported greater loneliness and lower self-esteem, whereas those who believed their victimisation was motivated by jealousy (e.g. *because I am smart, because I have something other kids want*) reported lower levels of loneliness and greater peer acceptance. These findings complement those of Prinstein, Cheah and Guyer (2005) showing that the more children made critical, or negative, self-referent attributions for their victimisation, the worse were their mental health (anxiety and depression) and social (loneliness) outcomes compared with children who provided neutral attributions for their victimisation. Not only does low self-regard contribute to victimisation, but the experience of victimisation leads to a further diminution in self-regard over time. Negative views of the self appear to contribute to the cycle of peer victimisation with poor self-regard occupying a central role in the process.

Children who are relationally victimised are at risk of forming negative peer beliefs, which places them in further jeopardy in their future peer interactions. In a study involving 10-year-old children, Rudolph, Troop-Gordon and Flynn (2009) found that the more children were relationally victimised, the more likely they were to develop negative beliefs about the peer they were playing with, especially if the interaction was challenging and involved conflict. Although negative beliefs about **peers** have the potential for leading to the development of poor peer relationships, it is important to note that relationally victimised children who experienced more positive peer interactions while playing with a peer did not develop such negative beliefs about peers. Providing children with positive peer interactions that promote peer relationships may offer children some protection from peer victimisation.

Peers: people who are of similar age or social standing (i.e. a class of preschoolers would be considered 'peers').

Links between children's responses and socio-emotional adjustment

In examining the effects of bullying, researchers have also shown individual differences in children's adjustment depending on their coping mechanisms or response to peer provocation. Behavioural avoidance strategies, whereby victims walk away or ignore acts of bullying, are typically found to be associated with increased risk of maladaptive outcomes (Kochenderfer-Ladd, 2004). Studies comparing boys and girls reveal that avoidant strategies are particularly problematic for girls. Girls who use these avoidant strategies show increased maladjustment while greater use of these strategies by boys was associated with increased levels of pro-social behaviour (Visconti & Troop-Gordon, 2010). Further highlighting the potential negative effects of avoidant-responses, Troop-Gordon and Quennette (2010) showed that girls and victimised boys reported more emotional distress in response to bullying when their teacher advised them to either avoid or stand up to bullying.

The potential for coping strategies to moderate the effects of bullying is further highlighted in research comparing problem-focused (i.e. seeking help from a teacher or friend) and emotion-focused (i.e. eliciting sympathy or discussion of feelings) responses. Emotionally focused support that is elicited from an emotional response to bullying tends to heighten negative outcomes and potential maladjustment among victims (Visconti & Troop-Gordon, 2010). In contrast, a problem-based response draws on the support of others in an attempt to combat the stressor and minimise the perception of threat.

Perpetrators and victims of bullying

Bullies experience a range of negative psychological sequelae including increased risk for psychiatric maladjustment, substance abuse problems, and criminal convictions as adults. Children who are chronic victims show increased risk of internalising difficulties and bullying others when they become adolescents (Barker et al., 2008). Because of their dual role, the risk for adversity is even greater for bully–victims than either victims or bullies, with children showing symptoms of both internalising and externalising problems and worse mental health problems in childhood (Arseneault et al., 2010). Research conducted by Sourander and colleagues (2007) attests to the long-term impact of increased risk of engaging in criminal behaviours between the ages of 16 and 20 for boys who were classified as bully–victims in childhood. While the combination of being bullied and bullying others is less well understood and less common than either being a victim or a bully, the significant mental health implications for this group of children highlights the need for targeted interventions for this group.

Cycle of bullying: Importance of early intervention

Research reviewed in this chapter attests to the early origins of bullying, while highlighting the need for intervention and preventative efforts which target children during the preschool and early school years, before negative patterns of peer interaction are established. The need for early intervention is further reinforced by the limited success experienced by school-based intervention and

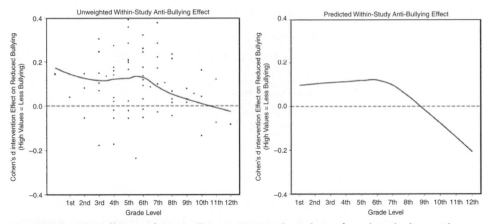

Figure 20.4 The efficacy of anti-bullying initiatives have been found to decline with age.

Source: Yeager et al. (2015).

prevention efforts (Yeager et al., 2015), with some adolescent groups reporting *increases* rather than decreases in bullying following high-quality interventions (Finkelhor et al., 2014).

What can preschools and schools do?

Findings from studies examining the effectiveness of a range of bullying interventions clearly demonstrate that bullying is significantly reduced when confronted with a caring and responsive community, which includes the whole-school community of students and teachers (see Neilsen-Hewett, Bussey & Fitzpatrick, 2017). This research highlights, among other factors, the importance of teacher understanding and knowledge within the context of a systemic approach to intervention, which is grounded within a bullying policy. Anti-bullying policies that directly address bullying behaviours, the accountability of the offenders, and the role of peers, teachers and other school personnel are critical for establishing and maintaining a positive school climate and for reducing bullying in schools.

A **whole-school approach** to bullying intervention highlights the importance of classroom-level intervention strategies that include regular weekly meetings between students and teachers to discuss bullying and peer relational difficulties (Dupper, 2013). These classroom meetings illustrate to students that the teacher cares and is engaged while helping teachers stay on top of what is happening both inside and outside the classroom. Additional classroom-level strategies that have been identified as effective in combating bullying include incorporation and integration of anti-bullying themes across the curriculum as well as the modelling of positive interpersonal skills by teachers, coupled with the fostering of positive bystander responses.

Whole-school approach: one that encompasses all aspects of the school community – students, teachers, administrators, parents, policies and the physical environment. Intervention approaches ensure a cohesive and collaborative approach targeted at all levels of the school curriculum.

To prevent peer victimisation it is crucial that even in early learning contexts evidence-based anti-bullying policies and programs are part of the school

Table 20.1: Essential components of a whole-school approach to bullying intervention.

School-management level strategies	• Effective school leadership in countering bullying • Establishment of policies that are widely disseminated • Commitment to professional development for all staff • Increased adult supervision • Understanding of context (which incorporates data-driven decision-making) • Commitment to ongoing evaluation
Classroom-level components	• Regular classroom discussion and clear expectations • Anti-bullying themes are integrated throughout the curriculum • Teachers encourage the reporting of bullying incidents • Teachers recognise some children are at greater risk of being bullied than others • Interventions are consistent and appropriate • Effective classroom management and modelling of appropriate behaviours • Actively support effective bystander behaviour and provide intervention for children who are bullied or who bully
Individual-level initiatives	• Children learn to intervene and how to support others • Interventions for different types of victims and bullies • Fostering of high-quality relationships between students and adults
Connections with the home context	• Effective communication with parents • Parents are involved in dealing with cases (where appropriate) • Intervention efforts incorporate parents and extend to the home environment

curriculum. One such program that has been trialled in Australia is the Friendly School Friendly Families Programme (Cross et al., 2012). This whole-school multilevel program targets three main levels for intervention and prevention: the school level where pastoral care staff receive training and resources in how to prevent bullying; the family level where parents are provided with resources and information about communicating with their children; and the classroom level where children are provided with 8 to 10 hours of classroom instruction about anti-bullying. Resources and training material have been developed for children from 5 to 14 years of age. A randomised control trial with children in Grades 4 and 6 showed that this program was effective in reducing peer victimisation. Anti-bullying programs that provide training for personnel to implement the program, provide resources for students, and involve parents offer a promising direction for reducing bullying in schools. In future it is important to implement whole-school programs with younger children before bullying patterns are firmly established. In this way, we may be able to provide safe and caring schools in which young learners can maximise their potential free of harassment and the negative socio-emotional sequeale that accompanies victimisation and bullying.

Conclusion

In this chapter it has been shown that even in the early years children bully each other in school contexts. They engage in a broad array of bullying behaviours including physical, verbal and relational bullying. The increasing reliance on social media for communication has led to an increase in cyberbullying starting in the primary school years. The socio-emotional wellbeing of those who bully and those who are the victims of bullying is negatively impacted. As bullying typically occurs in the peer group in the presence of other children, the social-emotional wellbeing of those who witness bullying is also negatively impacted. Both parents and teachers can play an important role in reducing bullying and victimisation in schools. Bullying in schools is most likely to be reduced by teachers, parents, children and the school working together in the implementation of anti-bullying programs. The earlier these programs are introduced in the school curriculum, the more effective they will be.

Summary

The key messages highlighted in this chapter are:

- Leaving out other children and making up stories about them constitutes bullying. All forms of bullying are wrong, not just physical bullying.
- Young children who bully will not 'grow' out of it unless they receive help and guidance in how to do this.
- The causes of bullying are multi-contextual, incorporating individual and familial factors, peers, teachers and the school context.
- Teachers who do nothing about bullying are part of the problem, not part of the solution.
- Children's socio-emotional wellbeing is affected by bullying as well as their physical health (e.g. sleeping problems, bed wetting, headaches, poor appetite).
- Bullying is everyone's problem, not just the victim's. A whole-school solution is necessary to stop bullying.

Questions

20.1 The causes of bullying are multi-contextual, extending beyond individual children to encompass both the familial and classroom contexts. What is your role and responsibility as an individual teacher with respect to working with parents and the broader educational community in reducing the incidence of bullying among early years learners?

20.2 The extent to which victims of bullying suffer negative outcomes is partly determined by how they cope with being bullied. What role can teachers play in shaping the perceptions of, and providing strategies for, early years learners to deal with bullying?

20.3 Imagine you were given the task of developing an anti-bullying policy for your centre or school. What do you consider to be essential components of this policy and would this differ depending on the age of the child?

20.4 What can you do as a teacher to stop bullying in your classroom?

References

Allison, K.R. & Bussey, K. (2016). Cyber-bystanding in context: A review of the literature on witnesses' responses to cyberbullying. *Children and Youth Services Review, 65*, 183–84. doi:10.1016/j.childyouth.2016.03.026

Arseneault, L., Bowes, L. & Shakoor, S. (2010). Bullying victimization in youths and mental health problems: 'Much ado about nothing'? *Psychological Medicine, 40*, 717–29.

Barker, E.D., Arseneault, L., Brendgen, M., Fontaine, N. & Maughan, B. (2008). Joint development of bullying and victimization in adolescence: Relation to delinquency and self-harm. *Journal of the American Academy of Child and Adolescent Psychiatry,* 47, 1030–38.

Bonanno, R.A. & Hymel, S. (2013). Cyber bullying and internalizing difficulties: Above and beyond the impact of traditional forms of bullying. *Journal of Youth and Adolescence,* 42, 685–97. doi:10.1007/s10964-013-9937-1

Braza, F., Braza, P., Carreras, M.R., Muñoz, J.M., Sánchez-Marín, J. R., Azurmendi, A. et al. (2007). Behavioral profiles of different types of social status in preschool children: An observational approach. *Social Behavior and Personality,* 35, 195–212.

Bussey, K., Fitzpatrick, S. & Raman, A. (2015). The role of moral disengagement and self-efficacy in cyberbullying. *Journal of School Violence,* 14, 30–46 doi:10.1080/15388220.2014.954045.

Camodeca, M., Caravita, S.C.S. & Coppola, G. (2015). Bullying in preschool: The associations between participant roles, social competence, and social preference. *Aggressive Behavior,* 41, 310–21. doi:10.1002/ab.21541.

Coplan, R.J., Closson, L. & Arbeau, K. (2007). Gender differences in the behavioral associates of loneliness and social dissatisfaction in kindergarten. *Journal of Child Psychology and Psychiatry* (Special Issue on Preschool Mental Health), 48, 988–95.

Cross, D., Lester, L. & Barnes, A. (2015). A longitudinal study of the social and emotional predictors and consequences of cyber and traditional bullying victimisation. *International Journal of Public Health,* 60, 207–217. doi:10.1007/s00038-015-0655-1

Cross, D., Watres, S., Pearce, N. Shaw, T., Hall, M., Erceg, E. et al. (2012). The friendly schools friendly families programme: Three-year bullying behaviour outcomes in primary school. *International Journal of Educational Research,* 53, 394–406.

Dupper, D.R. (2013). *School bullying. New perspectives on a growing problem.* Oxford workshop series: School Social Work Association of America.

Finkelhor, D., Vanderminden, J., Turner, H., Shattuck, A. & Hamby, S. (2014). Youth exposure to violence prevention programs in a national sample. *Child Abuse and Neglect,* 38, 677–86. http://dx.doi.org/10.1016/j.chiabu.2014.01.010

Finnegan, R.A., Hodges, E.V. & Perry, D.G. (1998). Victimization by peers: Associations with children's reports of mother–child interaction. *Journal of Personal and Social Psychology,* 75(4), 1076–86.

Gini, G. & Pozzoli, T. (2013). Bullied children and psychosomatic problems: A meta-analysis. *Pediatrics,*132, 720–29.

Gini, G., Pozzoli, T. & Bussey, K. (2015). The role of individual and collective moral disengagement in peer aggression and bystanding: A multilevel analysis. *Journal of Abnormal Child Psychology,* 43, 441–52.

Goodman, M.R., Stormshak, E.A. & Dishion, T.J. (2001). The significance of peer victimization at two points in development. *Journal of Applied Developmental Psychology*, 22(5), 507–26. doi: 10.1016/S0193-3973(01)00091-0

Guerra, N.G., Williams, K.R. and Sadek, S. (2011). Understanding bullying and victimization during childhood and adolescence: A mixed methods study. *Child Development,* 82, 295–310. doi:10.1111/j.1467-8624.2010.01556.x

Hawker, D.S.J. & Boulton, M.J. (2000). Twenty years' research on peer victimization and psychosocial maladjustment: A meta-analytic review of cross-sectional studies. *Journal of Child Psychology and Psychiatry,* 41(4), 441–55.

Iyer, R.V., Kochenderfer-Ladd, B., Eisenberg, N. & Thompson, M. (2010). Peer victimization and effortful control: Relations to school engagement and academic achievement. *Merrill-Palmer Quarterly,* 56, 361–387.

Kochenderfer-Ladd, B. (2004). Peer victimization: The role of emotions in adaptive and maladaptive coping. *Social Development,* 13, 329–49. doi: 10.1111/j.1467-9507.2004.00271.x

Kochenderfer-Ladd, B. & Skinner, K. (2002). Children's coping strategies: Moderators of the effects of peer victimization? *Developmental Psychology,* 38, 267–78.

Kowalski, R.M., Giumetti, G.W., Schroeder, A.N. & Lattanner, M.R. (2014). Bullying in the digital age: A critical review and meta-analysis of cyberbullying research among youth. *Psychological Bulletin*, 140, 1073–137. doi:10.1037/a0035618

Kowalski, R.M., Limber, S.P. & Agatston, P.W. (2012). *Cyberbullying: Bullying in the digital age* (2nd edn). Malden, MA: Wiley-Blackwell.

Leadbeater B., Sukhawathanakul P., Smith D. & Bowen F. (2015). Reciprocal associations between interpersonal and values dimensions of school climate and peer victimization in elementary school children. *Journal of Clinical Child and Adolescent Psychology,* 44(3), 480–93. doi:10.1080/15374416.2013.873985.

Lereya, S.T., Smaara, M. & Wolke, D. (2013) Parenting behavior and the risk of becoming a victim and a bully/victim: A meta-analysis study. *Child Abuse & Neglect,* 37, 1091–108. doi:10.1016/j.chiabu.2013.03.001.

Monks, C.P., Smith, P.K. & Swettenham, J. (2005). Psychological correlates of peer victimization in preschool: Social cognitive skills, executive function and attachment profiles. *Aggressive Behavior*, 31, 571–88.

Murray-Close, D. & Ostrov, J.M. (2009). A longitudinal study of forms and functions of aggressive behavior in early childhood. *Child Development,* 80, 828–42.

Neilsen-Hewett C., Bussey, K. & Fitzpatrick, S. (2017). Relationships with peers. In J. Grace, K. Hodge & C. McMahon (eds). *Children, families and communities: contexts and consequences* (5th edn). South Melbourne, Vic: Oxford University Press,

Olweus, D. (1993). *Bullying in school: What we know and what we can do.* Oxford: UK: Blackwell.

—— (2001). Peer harassment: A critical analysis and some important issues. In J. Juvonen & S. Graham (eds), *Peer harassment in school: The plight of the vulnerable and victimized* (pp. 1–20). New York: Guilford.

—— (2003). A profile of bullying at school. *Educational Leadership*, 60(6), 12–17.

Prinstein, M.J., Cheah, C.S.L. & Guyer, A.E. (2005). Peer Victimization, Cue Interpretation and Internalizing Symptoms: Preliminary Concurrent and Longitudinal Findings for Children and Adolescents. *Journal of Clinical Child & Adolescent Psychology*, 34, 11–24.

Reijntjes, A.H.A., Kamphuis, J.H., Prinzie, P. & Telch, M.J. (2010). Peer victimization and internalizing problems in children: A meta-analysis of longitudinal studies. *Child Abuse & Neglect*, 34, 244–252. doi:10.1016/j.chiabu.2009.07.009.

Roseth, C.J., Pellegrini, A.D., Bohn, C.M., Van Ryzin, M. & Vance, N. (2007). Preschoolers' aggression, affiliation and social dominance relationships: An observational, longitudinal study. *Journal of School Psychology*, 45(5), 479–97. doi: 10.1016/j.jsp.2007.02.008

Rudolph, K.D., Troop-Gordon, W. & Flynn, M. (2009). Relational victimization predicts children's social-cognitive and self-regulatory responses in a challenging peer context. *Developmental Psychology*, 45, 1444–54.

Rudolph, K.D., Troop-Gordon, W., Hessel E.T. & Schmidt, J.D. (2011). A latent growth curve analysis of early and increasing peer victimization as predictors of mental health across elementary school. *Journal of Clinical Child Adolescent Psychology*, 40, 111–22.

Runions, K.C. & Bak, M. (2015). Online moral disengagement, cyberbullying, and cyberaggression. *Cyberpsychology,Behaviour,and Social Networking*, 18(7), 400–405. doi:10.1089/cyber.2014.0670.

Salmivalli, C. (2010). Bullying and the peer group: A review. *Aggression and Violent Behavior*, 15, 112–20.

Sebanc, A.M. (2003). The friendship features of preschool children: Links with prosocial behavior and aggression. *Social Development*, 12, 249–68.

Sokol, N., Bussey, K. & Rapee, R. (2016). The impact of victims' responses on teacher reactions to bullying. *Teaching and Teacher Education*, 55, 78–87. doi:10.1016/j.tate.2015.11.002.

Sourander, A., Jensen, P., Ronning, J.A., Elonheimo, H., Niemela, S., Helenius, H. et al. (2007). Childhood bullies and victims and their risk of criminality in late adolescence: The Finnish from a boy to a man study. *Archives of Pediatrics and Adolescent Medicine*, 161, 546–52.

Swit, C.S., McMaugh, A., Warburton, W.A. (2016). Preschool children's beliefs about the acceptability of relational and physical aggression. *International Journal of Early Childhood*, 48, 111–27. doi:10.1007/s13158-016-0155-3.

Tokunaga, R.S. (2010). Following you home from school: A critical review and synthesis of research on cyberbullying victimization. *Computers in Human Behavior*, 26, 277–87. doi: 10.1016/j.chb.2009.11.014

Troop-Gordon, W. & Quenette, A. (2010). Children's perceptions of their teacher's responses to students' peer harassment: Moderators of victimization-adjustment linkages. *Merrill-Palmer Quarterly*, 56, 333–60.

Vaillancourt, T., Miller, J.L., Fagbemi, J., Cote, S. & Tremblay, R.E. (2007). Trajectories and predictors of indirect aggression: Results from a nationally representative longitudinal study of Canadian children aged 2–10. *Aggressive Behavior, 33,* 314–26.

Visconti, K.J., Kochenderfer-Ladd, B. & Clifford, C. (2013). Children's attributions for peer victimization: A social comparison approach. *Journal of Applied Developmental Psychology, 34,* 277–87.

Visconti, K.J. & Troop-Gordon, W. (2010). Prospective relations between children's responses to peer victimization and their socioemotional adjustment. *Journal of Applied Developmental Psychology, 31,* 261–72.

Yeager, D.S., Fong, C.J., Lee, H.Y. & Espelage, D.L. (2015). Declines in efficacy of anti-bullying programs among older adolescents: Theory and a three-level meta-analysis. *Journal of Applied Developmental Psychology, 37,* 36–51. http://dx.doi.org/10.1016/j.appdev.2014.11.005

Yoon, J.S. & Barton , E. (2008). The role of teachers in school violence and bullying prevention. In T. Miller (ed.), *School violence violence and primary prevention* (pp. 249–275). New York, NY: Springer.

CHAPTER 21

Strengthening social and emotional learning in children with special needs

Wendi Beamish and Beth Saggers

Introduction

Research undertaken over the last 20 years provides compelling evidence that early and ongoing development of socio-emotional skills contributes to an individual's overall health, wellbeing and competence throughout life. Moreover, competence in this domain is now recognised as fundamental to school readiness, school adjustment and academic achievement. As a consequence, social and emotional learning (SEL) is an important theme in current educational policy, curriculum frameworks and classroom practice.

This chapter focuses on a particular group of vulnerable learners – children with special needs. These children are at high risk of developing social and emotional problems because their presenting conditions negatively influence growth in two critical areas of functioning: attention, planning and problem-solving; and language and communication (Stormont, 2007). It follows that delays in these areas routinely put in place the conditions not only for reduced opportunities to engage, interact and learn with others, but also the increased likelihood of developing challenging, unsafe and socially inappropriate behaviours.

In this chapter we introduce the Teaching Pyramid (Fox et al., 2003), a validated, multi-level model for promoting children's social-emotional development while preventing problem behaviour. Next, we discuss aspects related to making decisions about 1. what to teach and 2. how to teach. We then highlight the critical importance of social understanding for children with special needs and provide key evidence-informed strategies for teachers to use in their everyday classroom practices to strengthen SEL from early years through to the end of primary school. Finally, we argue the case for partnering families in order to strengthen SEL outcomes for these learners across school, home, and community environments.

Recommended teaching model for SEL

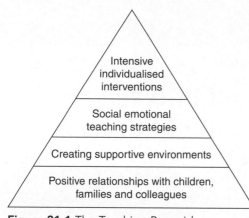

Figure 21.1 The Teaching Pyramid.
Source: Fox et al. (2003, p. 49); CSEFEL (2006).
Copyright © 2003 NAEYC. Reprinted with permission.

The Teaching Pyramid model (Fox et al., 2003) provides a strong framework for supporting SEL, particularly in the earlier years of learning. Its level of effectiveness in building social-emotional competence and preventing problems has been demonstrated not only with toddlers, but also with school-age children. The model is both educative and preventative. It comprises four hierarchal and interrelated levels of practice, with each level providing the foundation for the next (see Figure 21.1). Within this framework, behavioural intervention is viewed as a consequence of insufficient consideration given by teachers to the lower levels of the model – that is, to building positive relationships, providing supportive learning environments and the explicit teaching of social-emotional skills. Hence, the first three levels of practice in this model provide a sound structure for teachers seeking to strengthen SEL in all children, including those with **special needs** Each level of practice is now described with examples to illustrate how practices can be implemented in inclusive settings.

Special needs: a team used to describe children (0–12 years) on the autism spectrum; with intellectual and other developmental disabilities; with sensory impairments including hearing, vision and physical; with communication, emotional or behaviour disorders; and with learning difficulties.

Building positive relationships

The quality and reliability of relationships with important 'others' has a significant influence on children's wellbeing, development, academic success and future life outcomes. From birth, responsive relationships and shared interactions between carers and young children promote the development of secure attachments, the confidence to explore and learn, and a framework for moral behaviour and emotional regulation. From the early years of formal schooling, and extending through the primary years, successful interactions with peers are a strong predictor of positive mental health and school success. For these reasons, building secure, respectful and reciprocal relationships with and around all children is vital.

Many children with special needs experience substantial difficulties in establishing and maintaining positive relationships and interactions with both adults and peers. Personal attributes, competencies and actions often set them apart, and prevent them from being connected and belonging to the group

(Beamish & Saggers, 2013). Because interaction is a two-way process, and positive interactions are the building blocks for rapport and relationships, teachers need to interact positively and frequently with this group of learners, and be a role model for other staff and peers.

Responding sensitively and promptly to any communication attempts (verbal and non-verbal), inserting exchanges with the child across classroom routines and activities, and acknowledging children's efforts are examples of everyday strategies that need to be employed in order to show all children that they are valued and contributing members of classroom communities.

Bullying and students with special needs

Bullying is one issue that can often be a barrier to children with special needs being accepted by peers as valued members within the classroom context and larger school community. Children with special needs are at greater risk of being bullied, and compared to peers, may experience increased verbal abuse, social exclusion and physical aggression. Children who are on the autism spectrum are particularly prone to having difficulty with communication and social interaction. Bullying can have a significant impact on a child's self-esteem, mental health, socialisation, and academic achievement, SEL can help strengthen protective factors and minimise vulnerability to bullying.

It may be difficult to identify if a child is being bullied because his/her reactions can vary; however, physical signs (e.g. feeling sick, bruising), changes in behaviour (e.g. not wanting to come to school) and emotional responses (e.g. mood swings, crying) can often be evident. When you suspect that bullying is occurring, it is important to gather information to help you determine the best way to address the issues. This information is best gained from other staff, the child, peers and the families of the children involved.

Some examples of children with special needs experiencing incidents of bullying are given below.

- Jimmy is 11 years old and has a diagnosis of autism spectrum disorder. He has started catching public transport home from school in preparation for the transition to high school and is constantly teased by a group of boys from his school. They wait for him to leave the school in the afternoon and follow him to the bus stop where they call him names, and try to trip and push him over.
- Emily is nine years old and has a speech language impairment. She is desperate to communicate with other girls in her class and build friendships. Recently, some of the girls in Emily's grade have told her at lunchtimes they will be her friend if she buys them ice blocks from the tuckshop with her lunch money. Emily is not sure what to do.
- Amon is five years old and has an intellectual disability. He is having trouble fitting in at Prep, the other boys in his class keep calling him names and telling him they don't want him to play with them because he is ugly and smells funny.

Bullying prevention is most effectively implemented within a school-wide approach. Examples of practice include:

- a strict 'no bullying' zero tolerance policy reinforced throughout the school
- supervised options for children at lunchtime to give the choice of a safe haven (e.g. library activities, or computer, chess, music or gardening club)
- a designated supervised safe place in the school that children know they can access if they need help
- a designated member of staff who children know they can report bullying to, or a bully box to use if they don't want to speak to a person
- recognition and acknowledgement of peer support across the whole school
- a structured peer buddy/mentoring support system across the whole school for all children.

PAUSE AND REFLECT 21.1: BULLYING

- How can strengthening social and emotional learning in children with special needs help prevent bullying occurring?
- What additional social and emotional learning strategies could you put in place in your everyday practice to minimise the incidents of bullying children with special needs?

Providing supportive and safe learning environments

Supportive and safe learning environments are accepting, interactive and responsive environments in which positive relationships are developed, communication is promoted and self-esteem and confidence are fostered.

Supportive and safe learning environments foster the healthy growth, wellbeing and SEL of all children within them. Simply put, they are places where children want to be. Providing an environment to actively support SEL for children with special needs, however, is no easy matter. It demands careful consideration, planning, management and monitoring.

First, the learning environment needs to be warm, accepting and responsive, so that the child has meaningful, formal and informal opportunities to not only interact positively with staff and selected peers but also listen to, model and learn new communication, social-emotional skills and behaviours from them. Over time, these ongoing interactions and exchanges provide a starting point for the child to develop a sense of belonging, building positive relationships with peers, and ultimately establishing and maintaining friendships.

Second, the learning environment needs to be sensitively structured so that the child feels safe and secure, engages in classroom activity and develops independence and self-direction. Structuring involves preparing and adjusting the physical environment in relation to the management of time, space, furnishings, materials and equipment. Time management is a crucial factor to be considered when teaching children with special needs. The majority of these children feel safe and learn best when they are provided with a predictable routine and follow a regular schedule of activities. Visual schedules can be used to prepare them ahead of time for transitioning to the next activity or to changes in the regular schedule. Spaces also can be creatively adjusted to serve a multitude of purposes.

Third, the learning environment needs to be managed carefully so that the child progressively learns to monitor his/her own behaviour and emotions. If careful attention is given to fostering self-management skills, these children can become more self-determined learners who, in the long term, can take control of many aspects of their lives. Unfortunately, many children continue to respond impulsively to social situations without pausing to appreciate the perspectives of others, or connecting consequences to their actions.

Adherence to classroom rules and codes of acceptable behaviour is fostered when clear and fair behavioural expectations and consequences are consistently put into effect. Gaining the child's attention before giving directions, individualising the directions and giving the child sufficient time to respond to directions increases the likelihood of compliance. Noticing and reinforcing instances of good behaviour by providing acknowledgement, access to a favourite activity or earning a special job frequently increases coping, tolerance and engagement across daily routines and activities. Finally, spending time understanding, preventing and responding effectively to low levels of problem behaviour can often alleviate the need for intense behavioural intervention at a later date.

However, despite teacher care, organisation and responsiveness, behaviours requiring additional support still occur. In today's busy world, anxiety is of increasing concern globally for teachers and parents.

Anxiety and children with special needs

Students with special needs, particularly those with autism and learning difficulties, are at greater risk of exhibiting **anxiety**-related symptoms. Social-behavioural difficulties generally tend to present in one of two ways:

1. through externalising behaviour such as anger and aggression, which is outwardly directed and creates discomfort and conflict in the surrounding environment, or
2. through internalising behaviour such as anxiety and depression, which is inwardly directed and generates distress within the individual.

Anxiety is a social-behavioural internalising problem that takes many forms. Separation anxiety, social phobia, generalised anxiety and obsessive compulsive disorder are among the most commonly identified anxiety-related disorders in school-aged children. More extreme examples include selective mutism, panic attacks and school refusal.

Children experiencing anxiety difficulties frequently display signs of fatigue, restlessness and irritability, and routinely have concentration difficulties. They may also complain of experiencing headaches or stomach-aches. Further, as anxiety affects our ability to think, many children living with anxiety become more anxious, worried and tense when required to complete particular cognitive and/ or socially oriented tasks. It follows that children dealing with anxiety are more likely to experience difficulties with peer relations and have low self-esteem, poor academic achievement, and future social-emotional adjustment problems.

It is important that teachers recognise when children are not coping and are in an anxious state. In order to do this effectively, teachers need to know each child well, especially in terms of temperament, individual and typical response patterns, ways of expressing emotions, and family circumstances. Recognising observable signs of anxiety enables each child to be supported as quickly as possible before the anxiety increases. Some examples of children with special needs experiencing anxiety are described below.

- Jacob is 12 years old and has a diagnosis of autism spectrum disorder. Although he can competently read his personalised timetable and follow maps, he is experiencing difficulties getting to class on time at his new secondary school. Moreover, he is reluctant to have any staff assist him; when offered assistance, he shouts 'I can do it, I can do it!'
- Jessica is 10 years old, has a diagnosed learning difficulty and is well below her age group in reading. Whenever it's time for reading groups, she either requests to go to the toilet or remains at her desk sorting slowly through her books.
- Cameron is seven years old and considered to have ADHD. In addition to being generally restless and inattentive in the classroom, he frequently tries to avoid activities requiring sustained concentration and thinking by complaining of a stomach-ache.

SEL can help strengthen social-emotional regulation, coping skills and resilience in children with anxiety difficulties. Support should be provided at two levels.

Level 1: Immediate response to signs of anxiety and not coping

Focus is on communicating with the child and assisting him/her to return to a more positive emotional state. Examples of practice include: sensitive questioning, genuine requests for information, and responding to the need within the child's message.

Level 2: Assessment and skills building

Focus is on undertaking an early assessment, team problem-solving, and the design, implementation and evaluation of a plan of action that will deliver meaningful outcomes for the child and family over time. Examples of practice include:

- recording observations of behaviour(s) of concern for a number of days
- communicating with the school guidance officer or psychologist before discussing matters with the family or intervening in any way
- teaming with other professionals and the family to develop a plan for teaching the child coping thoughts and behaviours through explicit instruction and real-life experiences.

- Why is communication with parents/caregivers critical in instances of child anxiety? Identify some effective modes of communicating with parents/caregivers in these situations.
- What additional social-emotional learning strategies could you put in place within the classroom to help all children – including those with special needs – to feel emotionally secure, accepted and supported?

Teaching critical social-emotional skills

Teaching critical social-emotional skills to children with special needs involves making decisions about what to teach and how to teach. The what refers to individually targeted SEL content that needs to be referenced to the curriculum and specified in terms of the scope of knowledge and the skill or behaviour to be learnt. The how refers to the key learning arrangements through which the targeted content will be delivered (e.g. teaching strategies, equipment and materials, pace of instruction, embedded learning opportunity).

Determining what to teach

Critical social-emotional skills need to be acquired in a structured and sequenced way across the years of schooling. Curriculum frameworks, areas, content descriptions and achievement standards typically provide the anchors for skill scoping and sequencing. For many years, the internationally recognised SEL framework developed by the Collaborative for Academic, Social and Emotional Learning (CASEL) has provided key areas for guiding what to teach (2003). These areas are:

- *self-awareness* – identifying and recognising emotions; accurate self-perception, recognising strengths, needs and values; and self-efficacy
- *self-management* – impulse-control and stress-management; self-motivation and discipline; goal-setting and organisational skills
- *social awareness* – perspective-taking; empathy; difference-recognition; respect for others
- *relationship management* – communication, social engagement and relationship-building; working cooperatively; negotiation, refusal; conflict management; help-seeking
- *responsible decision-making* – problem-identification and situation-analysis; problem-solving; evaluation and reflection; personal, social and ethical responsibility.

At the curriculum level, the Australian Curriculum, Assessment and Reporting Authority (ACARA), in common with educational institutions in many other countries, has drawn upon the CASEL framework for structuring SEL content. In the Australian Curriculum, SEL is embedded in the General Capabilities dimension under the label of Personal and Social Capabilities. Importantly, personal and social capability skills are specifically equated to social-emotional skills, and referenced to SEL. They are also recognised as foundational supports to student learning across the curriculum:

> Personal and social capability skills are addressed in all learning areas and at every stage of a student's schooling. This enables teachers to plan for the teaching of targeted skills specific to an individual's learning needs to provide access to and engagement with the learning areas (ACARA, 2013, p. 2).

Hence, the progressive levels of skills detailed in the Personal and Social Capability Learning Continuum within the Australian Curriculum provides content relevant to children with special needs under the elements of self-awareness, self-management, social awareness and social management. In general, determining what to teach requires initial and thoughtful consideration on the goodness of fit between the child's age, ability, curriculum demands and classroom activities with peers. SEL content then needs to be selected carefully according to the child's assessed social-emotional need and cultural background. Family involvement in this decision-making is recommended, together with increased input from the child over time. In addition, SEL content should target only one or two specific skills or behaviours for a particular period of time. When making these decisions, a number of factors should be considered – for example, the social significance of the skill, the number of years left for schooling, the level of home–school cooperation and the learning diversity in the class.

Determining how to teach

Social-emotional skills need to be taught within the security of positive relationships and supportive learning environments. In common with academic learning, SEL for children with special needs requires explicit teaching, practice and reinforcement across a range of activities and settings, to ensure that skill generalisation and maintenance take place. Moreover, skills need to be not only taught to mastery but also consolidated through motivational activities that ensure frequent use of skills.

Furthermore, teaching social-emotional skills should be anchored by SAFE practices (Durlak et al., 2011). SAFE-recommended practices are:

- *sequenced* – new and more complicated skills are frequently broken down into smaller steps and sequentially mastered by the child
- *active* – teaching activities are focused on actively engaging the child in learning
- *focused* – sufficient time and attention are devoted to each activity task so that learning occurs
- *explicit* – a clear and specific learning objective is set for the teaching and assessment of each skill.

In addition, determining how to teach requires a responsive pairing of a systematic and intentional teaching approach with the child's interests, preferences and learning style. When activities and materials have a goodness of fit with these inclinations, learning is promoted through increased motivation and engagement. It is important to remember that children with special needs are typically poorly motivated because they repeatedly experience failure.

Increasing social understanding

Social understanding is a crucial component of SEL because it is commonly viewed as the root of our social behaviour. Acquiring this understanding permits us to navigate our social world, interact effectively with each other, form successful relationships and become members of a community. Social understanding has both social and cognitive aspects. It stems from being aware of self and evolves over time through communicative interactions with others and one's cognitive interpretation of these experiences, beliefs and emotions (Carpendale & Lewis, 2004). The complex process involves becoming aware of one's ideas, inferring these ideas on others, becoming aware that others have ideas and reflecting on the ideas of others in relation to self (Kostelnik et al., 2012).

From a curriculum perspective, and using the personal and social capabilities elements, good social understanding comprises adequate self-awareness, efficient self-management, appropriate social awareness and effective social management. Within this framework, self-awareness provides the child with the ability to effectively understand self, as well as the skills to recognise emotions. Self-management and self-regulation allow the child to exercise control over personal actions, thoughts and emotions. Social awareness provides the child with the ability to cultivate a sense of self and understand the perspective of others, while skills in social management allow the child to maintain social rules, interact effectively and successfully work with others. It is also important to recognise that increased social understanding and related skill acquisition also contribute to aspects that make a positive difference to children's learning and children's lives – namely self-identity, self-confidence, self-discipline and resilience.

Children with special needs typically have very poor social understanding. Taken as a group, language and cognitive delays coupled with difficulties in attending to others and the environment often contribute to these children experiencing problems in developing an awareness of self as an independent being and an awareness of feelings and emotions. They also experience difficulties in differentiating between feelings and behaviours. This group in general lacks the ability to adequately reflect on feelings, control impulses, monitor behaviours and deal with stress. It follows that incidental and structured class SEL activities are not sufficient to promote adequate social understanding in this group of learners. In most cases, strategic small-group and/or individualised SEL interventions are warranted to build social knowledge, interactions and skills from early years through to the end of primary schooling. While typically developing children construct social understanding through a process of observation, self-reflection and imagination, children with special needs require a more teacher-directed approach to gradually acquire these understandings. Increasingly, interventions are becoming multi-modal in nature, and feature promising strategies such as video priming and self-modelling, social stories and specialised visual supports. The strategies that follow provide additional ideas to support SEL instruction.

Core strategies suited to all age groups

Strategies to strengthen social and emotional learning for students with special needs include opportunities for learning that:

- practise and rehearse new skills regularly
- receive feedback and praise on new skills
- offer problem-solving opportunities and encourage alternative solution-generation
- encourage independence and calculated risk-taking.

Age-specific strategies to support social understanding

0–5 years

- Strengthen basic social rules with adult modelling and support of skill development (e.g. sharing, using your words, being gentle).
- Engage in simple turn-taking games, card games and board games.
- Encourage use of language to express emotions by labelling emotions (e.g. 'You look like you are feeling happy').
- Engage in active listening to get the child's version of what happened and what they are experiencing.
- Help the child to identify activities or things that are calming or promote relaxation.

5–8 years

- Strengthen social rules for greetings, everyday interactions at school and home, and joining a group.
- Identify, express and label emotions using language.
- Provide opportunities to practise simple role-play and modelling activities to solve social situations.
- Give children roles and responsibilities to support group activities.
- Use video priming and self-modelling, social stories and visual supports to reinforce the understanding of key concepts associated with a skill.
- Share concerns so children realise it is normal to feel worried.

8–12 years

- Strengthen social rules for engaging socially with others.
- Engage and take responsibility in problem-solving activities in teams or groups.

- Practise skills of negotiation and compromise, dealing with compliments, competition, and winning and losing.
- Encourage practice of social skills in co-educational groups.
- Rehearse calming activities and routines.
- Use role-play to act out positive ways to deal with emotions and stress.

Partnering with families

SEL for children with special needs is substantially boosted through partnering with families. When families are supported, the home can provide the best conditions for fostering emotional security and the natural conditions for learning many social skills. Moreover, when there is strong alignment and consistency in support across environments, optimum conditions are provided for the repeated practice, consolidation and generalisation of critical social-emotional skills.

Partnering with families often requires teachers to take the lead in building a trusting relationship with parents/caregivers and actively striving to understand the family and the home ecology. Learning about family structure, culture, values and child-rearing practices often provides insight into parent–child relationships and the day-to-day challenges faced by both the family and the child. Research confirms that the burden of raising a child with special needs results in many parents having significantly elevated levels of stress and reduced marital satisfaction compared with parents of typically developing children. Moreover, as children with special needs are more prone to experience both anxiety and bullying, partnering with parents/caregivers in these circumstances is not an option; it is essential.

Supporting families to strengthen SEL in the home involves not only sharing specific information about the child and the targeted learning, but also making connections to explicit practices at home. While much of this information can be provided on an individual basis, school-wide family engagement activities and workshops, the creation of a SEL lending library or resource centre, and even a SEL advisory board can be used to promote SEL and partnering with families.

Once SEL partnering has been established, maintaining effective communication with families is essential. The following strategies provide effective ways to support ongoing communication and partnerships with families:

- child-centred communication that is specific to the child
- constructive information that is meaningful and useful because it provides families with clear and concrete suggestions
- specific information about classroom and school-wide policies and practices
- a back-and-forth journal or folder for parents and teachers
- invitations for families to actively participate in SEL classroom activities
- regular newsletters to keep parents informed and involved.

Conclusion

Locally and globally, social-emotional wellbeing is viewed as the passport to success at school and in life. Guiding children's social and emotional learning therefore is no longer optional for teachers. As a consequence, teachers are being pressed to provide quality SEL experiences to all children in their classrooms, including children with special needs. Teachers need to not only promote SEL at school but also support families in fostering SEL at home.

Summary

The key messages highlighted in this chapter are:

- Children with special needs are at high risk of developing social-emotional problems because they experience difficulties in: (1) attention, planning and problem-solving; and (2) language and communication. These difficulties often result in these children having reduced opportunities to engage, interact and learn with others.
- The Teaching Pyramid model provides a strong framework for strengthening SEL in children with special needs. The model recommends building positive relationships, providing supportive learning environments and teaching critical social-emotional skills in order to reduce the likelihood of developing challenging, unsafe and socially inappropriate behaviours.
- SEL content for this group of learners should be drawn predominately from relevant content in the personal and social capabilities section of the General Capabilities dimension of the Australian Curriculum.
- SEL instruction for this group of learners should be guided by the *SAFE* practices (sequenced, active, focused and explicit), and focus on the repeated practice, consolidation and reinforcement of specific skills across a range of activities and settings.

Questions

21.1   Why is it important for an educator to have positive beliefs about children with special needs?

21.2   What can be done to build positive relationships with and around children with special needs?

21.3   How can the classroom environment be adjusted so that it is more responsive to children with special needs and their SEL?

21.4   Consider why is it important for teachers to encourage and support families of children with special needs to partner in SEL.

References

Australian Curriculum, Assessment and Reporting Authority (ACARA) (2013). *General capabilities in the Australian Curriculum.* Retrieved from http://www.australiancurriculum.edu.au/GeneralCapabilities/ Personal-and-social-capability.

Beamish, W. & Saggers, B. (2013). Diversity and differentiation. In D. Pendergast & S. Garvis (eds) *Teaching early years: Curriculum, pedagogy and assessment* (pp. 244–58). Sydney: Allen & Unwin.

Carpendale, J.M. & Lewis, C. (2004). Constructing an understanding of mind: The development of children's social understanding within social interaction. *Behavioral and Brain Sciences, 27,* 79–151.

Center on the Social and Emotional Foundations for Early Learning (CSEFEL) (2006). *Promoting the social emotional competence of young children: Facilitator's Guide.* Retrieved from http://csefel.vanderbilt.edu/modules/facilitators-guide.pdf

Collaborative for Academic, Social and Emotional Learning (CASEL) (2003). *Safe and sound: An educational leader's guide to evidenced-based social and emotional learning (SEL) programs.* Retrieved from http://www.casel.org.

Durlak, J.A., Weissberg, R.P., Dymnicki, A.B., Taylor, R.D. & Schellinger, K.B. (2011). The impact of enhancing students' social and emotional learning: A meta-analysis of school-based universal interventions. *Child Development, 82*(1), 405–32.

Fox, L., Dunlap, G., Hemmeter, M.L., Joseph, G.E. & Strain, P.S. (2003). The Teaching Pyramid: A model for supporting social competence and preventing challenging behavior in young children. *Young Children,* 58(4), 48–52.

Kostelnik, M.J., Gregory, K.M., Soderman, A.K. & Whiren, A.P. (2012). *Guiding children's social development and learning* (7th edn). Belmont, CA: Wadsworth Cengage Learning.

Stormont, M. (2007). *Fostering resilience in young children at risk of failure: Strategies for Grades K–3.* Columbus, OH: Pearson.

PART 4

Leadership and innovations

CHAPTER 22

Teachers' roles in building girls' leadership identity

Nicole Archard, Romana Morda and Manjula Waniganayake

Introduction

Continuing gender disparity among leaders in Australia today highlights the necessity of developing girls for future leadership roles, and this begins with early years learners. Not only do women in Australia hold a significantly smaller number of leadership positions than men; they are also poorly represented in domains such as politics, mathematics, science and information technology. Increasing women's representation in leadership roles is a necessary aspect of establishing gender equity in leadership decision-making in society, so that both women and men can contribute to the evolution of social change.

Research suggests that leadership identity, as well as self-concept with regard to particular skills and attributes in becoming a leader, emerges during early childhood (Morda, 2011). It has also been found that the formation of a girl's leadership identity is an important prerequisite for her development as a future leader (Archard, 2013b). However, in order for girls to be able to establish a strong sense of readiness to lead, a variety of factors must be taken into consideration. These include cultural and social influences on women and girls, which in turn can impact their confidence, self-efficacy and resilience, as well as their overall wellbeing and capacity to perform as effective leaders.

The extent to which the early formation of leadership potential can create or reinforce gendered assumptions is strongly aligned with the values, beliefs and attitudes towards women in a given society. Moreover, these societal 'norms' can impact on girls' ability to fulfil leadership roles during their childhood as well as throughout their lives. Based on research into leadership with young female learners, this chapter examines the personal, social and cultural influences that can shape leadership attainment by girls, and subsequently as women. We focus on the role of teachers as being able to make a difference by actively influencing the advancement of girls' leadership potential, beginning from early-childhood settings.

Social and cultural influences on women and girls

Social and cultural influences play a significant function in determining the place and role of women and girls in contemporary society, as they have done throughout time. Typically, the beliefs and values of a society prescribe the attributes of each sex and, as a consequence, the roles that are available to them are often defined by stereotypical norms. This has meant that the feminine schemata attributed to women and girls – such as being emotional, nurturing and communal – not only prescribe what women and girls can and cannot do, but also define the roles they are expected to perform within a particular society or a community (Eagly & Karau, 2002).

In applying schemata to social functions, leadership is one role that may cause tension in relation to the application of leadership attributes and behaviours towards women and girls. The feminine schema is not always congruent with the traditional view of leadership that is often associated with more masculine attributes such as power, authority and control. Therefore, based on the attribute of gender, women may be seen as never having the necessary prerequisites for leadership. Essentially, gender stereotypes can influence women and girls' leadership enactment not only by how women and girls view themselves as leaders, but also by how they are viewed by others (Carli & Eagly, 2007; Eagly & Karau, 2002; Paustian-Underdahl, Slattery Walker & Woehr, 2014).

Additionally, the same masculine schemata that define leadership may also define associated areas of social participation, particularly in areas most often aligned with male leadership – for example, what has become commonly known as 'STEM' which refers to science, technology, engineering and mathematics. Within each of these domains, girls/women are under-represented and given their importance in advancing societal growth, governments, both local and global, are investing heavily to increase women's participation in these fields of study and employment, as seen in Australia through the National STEM School Education Strategy 2016–2026 (Education Council, 2015).

In addressing areas where the social and cultural paradigms influence gendered roles for women and men, as well as girls and boys, the role that education plays in either perpetuating or challenging these social and cultural influences warrants closer examination. While gender stereotypes are well established and self-perpetuating within societies, educational experiences can be used as opportunities to confront gendered assumptions and better prepare girls for different types of leadership roles, thereby increasing their influence in non-traditional arenas. Importantly, both formal and informal teaching that takes place within early years classrooms has the potential to impact on girls' behaviour (performance) as well as their thinking (perceptions). Therefore, in order to address broader social issues concerning women and leadership, it is important to gain a greater understanding of leadership in relation to girls – especially during the period from birth to 12 years.

Defining leadership: Distinguishing between leadership and dominance

Traditionally, **leadership** research has focused on adult males within business settings while education scholars have explored leadership in schools. In comparison, relatively little is known about leadership in child and adolescent peer groups (Ayman-Nolley, 2004; Edwards, 1994; Murphy & Reichard, 2011). In particular, there is a lack of research examining leadership enactment and development in girls (Archard, 2013a; Edwards, 1994). Reviews of leadership research with children and adolescents (Ayman-Nolley, 2004; Murphy & Johnson, 2011; Roach et al., 1999) have indicated that leadership

> **Leadership** involves actively building relationships with children, families and staff and this contributes to building girls' leadership identities. Leaders play a pivotal role in shaping the vision, pedagogy and organisational cultures of educational organisations.

has been defined primarily in terms of the personality traits and behaviours of those who lead activities within small-group contexts. However, research examining the traits and behaviours of young leaders is somewhat inconclusive.

One area of debate is the relationship between leadership and dominance in children. Early researchers, such as Coie and Dodge (1983), have argued that dominance and ascendancy were indices of leadership in young children. Other researchers (such as Bohlin, 2000; Choi, Johnson & Johnson, 2011; LaFreniere & Sroufe, 1985) have contended that dominance is distinct from leadership. LaFreniere and Sroufe (1985) for instance, found that dominance was not significantly related to social competence or leadership. In contrast, leadership was significantly related to measures of social competence.

Trawick-Smith (1992) investigated strategies employed by preschool children to direct the activities of other children. He argued that persuasive children could be distinguished from dominant children in that they possessed a broader range of strategies, and were more skilful in their application of them. This reinforces his earlier findings (Trawick-Smith, 1988) that effective leaders were assertive, but also diplomatic and pro-social, in their persuasive attempts. In contrast, children who were categorised as bullies, in that they displayed domineering and aggressive behaviours, were perceived as ineffective leaders.

The interplay between dominance and leadership perception becomes even more complex in research that has examined gender differences in dominance and leadership (Bohlin, 2000; Williams & Tiedens, 2016). Bohlin (2000) investigated predictors of young children's use of leadership and dominance strategies when interacting with peers. She found that girls were more likely to use pro-social and organisational leadership strategies than boys. This finding was consistent with past research that found that girls tend to use indirect and cooperative persuasive strategies. In comparison, boys were more likely to use assertive and aggressive strategies. Therefore, explicit dominance strategies appear to be more acceptable for boys rather than girls.

Research undertaken with children reveals that there may indeed be a cost in engaging in leadership behaviour that violates traditional gender role expectations (Davies, 1989; Madrid, 2013; Marsh, 2000). Researchers (Davies, 1989; Kane 2012) have argued that children are active agents in the social construction of gender and gender roles and that children explore and negotiate their gendered identities through play. Studies (Davies, 1989; Madrid, 2013; Marsh, 2000) have investigated the challenges faced by girls in asserting themselves and taking the lead in play that seemingly disrupts traditional **gender role expectations**. In an early study by Davies (1989) it was found that 'rough tough princesses' had more status than 'home corner girls'. That is, 'rough tough princesses' were able to powerfully assert themselves, and were perceived to have control over others. However, Davies argued that although the 'rough tough princesses' in some ways challenged gender role expectations; this challenge was enacted within the gendered role of a princess. Consistent with Davies' (1989) findings, Madrid (2013) and Marsh (2000) have also found that girls challenged gender role expectations in their play scenarios.

> **Gender role expectations** are characteristics and behaviours associated with, and considered appropriate for, males and females.

To assist readers to reflect on these research findings, we introduce four-year-old Arabel, the assertive princess, and her peers from an early learning centre in Melbourne, Australia, and discuss the potential learnings reflected in three play excerpts described in Case Study 22.1.

CASE STUDY 22.1: ARABEL: THE ASSERTIVE PRINCESS

PLAY EXCERPT 1

Arabel is in a group of five preschool-aged children. She is standing and the other children are sitting down on some stairs. She says to her peers, 'Put your hand up if you have stairs in your house'. All five children put their hands up. She points to three of them and says, 'You, you and you can come to my house to play Barbies'. John, who was not selected by Arabel, says 'but I put my hand up'. Arabel repeats, 'I said you, you and you can come to my house'. John protests again as the other children start to crowd around Arabel. Arabel walks off but Sienna starts to follow her. Arabel turns to Sienna and says, 'I said I want to be alone'.

PLAY EXCERPT 2

Arabel has been playing with Anna in the sandpit, building castles and being the princess. She then notices that Sienna has arrived for the day and yells out, 'Hi hi'. Arabel waves her arms and yells, 'Come here, come here'. Sienna walks over to the two girls. Arabel says to Anna, 'Sienna is here and you have to go'. Anna replies, 'Why?' and does not move. Sienna is standing behind the group with hands clasped as Arabel says to Anna, 'Go away right now Sienna is here' and shoves Anna. Anna does not budge. Arabel shoves Anna again and says loudly, 'Go away'. Anna still does not move. Arabel repeats, 'Go away, I always play with Sienna and you are playing with me'. Sienna has wandered away from the group. Anna angrily replies, 'I'm never going to play with you first ever again' and walks off to sit with the other girls who are also playing in the sandpit. Arabel calls out 'Sienna' in a happy voice and Sienna runs back to sit next to her. Anna repeats, 'I will never start playing with you again'. Arabel ignores her.

PLAY EXCERPT 3

Arabel is lying on a slide and yells out, 'I'm dying, I'm dying'. She then lays her head on the slide and pretends to be dead. A girl runs over and asks her, 'Can I also be a princess?' Arabel moves over slightly to give the girl room to lie down on the slide. She then yells out, 'We're dying, we're dying'. She yells out to the girls who are running to her (Sienna is first), 'No you are still being the witch'. Sienna then says to Arabel and the girl on the slide, 'We put on a spell for you to be alive'. The girl sits up but Arabel does not. The girl says, 'Only one thing can wake me up, a kiss from a prince'. Arabel gets up and says, 'No I have to kiss you' and pretends to kiss her.

Reflections

Arabel actively embraced the role of leading play experiences and her peers, such as Sienna, were aware of this. For example, when the researcher asked Arabel, 'Do you like it when Kathy is the leader?' Arabel firmly replied 'No'. Sienna, who was listening, added 'She likes herself being it'. It also reinforces that Arabel was very confident and highly assertive. Observations of Arabel's behaviour during free play also indicated that she was very popular with other girls. At times her behaviour could have been interpreted as bossiness and even bullying, as she engaged in physically and verbally aggressive acts to control the actions of others. As can be seen in Play Excerpt 2, other girls seemed to mostly accept Arabel's leadership. One reason for this may be that Arabel's play scenarios (Play Excerpt 1 and Play Excerpt 3) were attractive to the other girls.

It could be argued that Arabel's style of leadership seems to be reminiscent of Maccoby's (1990) description of boys' interactional style of 'competition and dominance' rather than girls 'acting nice'. Arabel's actions also appeared to challenge Davies' (1989) argument that even 'rough tough princesses' accepted traditional narratives of the power of the central male hero. In Play Excerpt 3, the prince traditionally has the central role of kissing princesses back to life but it was Arabel who did the kissing. Therefore, Arabel seemed to both challenge and conform to gender role expectations regarding how girls should behave. In terms of her leadership style, Arabel did not seem to be conforming to gender role expectations. Her leadership was, however, at times enacted within a gendered narrative of a princess play.

PAUSE AND REFLECT 22.1: PROMOTING LEADERSHIP POTENTIAL

As a teacher, how would you promote the leadership potential of girls such as Arabel and her peers in Case Study 22.1 to ensure that every girl has opportunities to enact leadership within your classroom?

Girls and leadership: Confidence and self-efficacy

Research about girls' leadership is not extensive, but available research indicates that girls have a good understanding of the concept of leadership as it applies to them, and when given the opportunity to enact leadership they can perform leadership roles effectively (Archard, 2013a). However, the translation of this success into the acquisition of leadership positions as adults and the breaking into leadership roles in non-traditional areas such as STEM continues to be problematic in Australia. It has been suggested that by exploring the relationship between women's leadership achievement and girls' leadership behaviour, a better understanding can be developed regarding how early childhood centres and schools can enhance girls' leadership development.

Confidence is an individual's view of their ability to undertake tasks (Archard, 2012).

Self-efficacy is the view an individual has in relation to their capacity to achieve the desired task (Archard, 2012).

In developing girls for leadership roles which might conflict with traditional social and cultural paradigms of gender, it is essential to develop girls' levels of **confidence** and **self-efficacy** in relation to these roles. Confidence and self-efficacy are also important indicators of social and emotional wellbeing that can influence early years learning outcomes. The concepts of confidence and self-efficacy are also often associated with gender differences. It is in understanding these differences that strategies might be crafted in order to assist the development of girls for leadership and non-stereotypical participation.

In understanding how to best prepare girls for leadership and non-stereotypical participation, performance attribution theories have been used to explain the varying levels of confidence in girls (Archard, 2012). Inferences that an individual makes in order to attribute their success and failures have been shown to influence notions of confidence and self-efficacy and thus can impact on girls' levels of participation and performance, particularly in non-traditional roles. The foundation for this thinking can often be formed in the early years of learning, and then manifest in adolescence and into adulthood.

Research has found that boys are more likely to attribute success to their skills and abilities, whereas girls are more likely to link failures (rather than successes) with their personal attributes (Meece, Glienke & Burg, 2006). While these mindsets can impact levels of confidence, it is a girl's ability to manage failure that leads to higher levels of confidence and consequently self-efficacy, which in-turn has an impact on girls' sense of wellbeing. Girls' levels of confidence and self-efficacy are formed at a young age; thus the early years of learning are a pivotal time for implementing strategies to assist girls' development in this area.

Developing a female leadership identity in STEM

Of interest is how girls' levels of confidence and self-efficacy impact on their identity as a leader, particularly when acting in professional domains such as science, technology, engineering and mathematics (STEM) dominated by male leaders. The formation of a leadership identity has been established as an important step in preparing girls for leadership in adult life and specifically in non-gendered roles (Archard, 2013b). It has also been suggested that by actively addressing the social and cultural assumptions underpinning gender stereotypes, girls' leadership identity can be strengthened. However, it has been noted through research that breaking gender stereotypes in STEM occupations, such as engineering, is met with many challenges:

> Barriers and opportunities relating to women's participation in engineering occurs at all points along people's education and work pathways, from early engagement with STEM activities and interests in early years and primary school through educational experiences in secondary school leading to subject choices, to the experiences of women in university engineering courses and then in the workplace (Sarkar, Tytler & Palmer, 2014, p. iv).

Addressing gender stereotypes must therefore commence from a young age, prior to school settings such as preschool centres. Consequently, it is essential that teachers are intentional in observing, reflecting and addressing these concerns within their teaching and learning environments, and beginning in early childhood.

The construction of leadership identity as either feminine or masculine can provide or deny access to girls wishing to fulfil leadership roles. The importance of forming a female leadership identity lies in providing girls with an understanding of themselves as leaders in both stereotypical and non-stereotypical domains. Thus, girls can envisage themselves in these roles with the aim of not feeling excluded from leadership and other stereotypical male roles in the future. Leadership identity is subject to diverse influences, including historical, geographical, political, religious and economic contexts of a society as well as from a girl's family and community backgrounds and educational experiences.

In order to engage readers more directly with the implications for practice and policy, we present observations of Jessica, a Grade 6 learner, made by her

Conclusion

This chapter highlights the fact that there is sufficient research to demonstrate that girls and women can be effective leaders. Research also shows that leadership identity can emerge during early childhood and is observable in young children's play. The challenges of excluding or including women from leadership positions are inextricably tied with overcoming barriers that are socially and culturally constructed. The constructions of leadership in relation to gender can impact on how others view women and girls as leaders, and reciprocally, how they perceive themselves as leaders. Being able to see yourself as a leader and fulfilling leadership roles is vital in fostering women's identification as leaders.

Summary

This chapter also shows that teachers can play an important role in shaping girls' leadership potential in a variety of ways. This includes the teacher's role in:

- Strategically nurturing girls' leadership potential from childhood through observation, documentation, and analysis of patterns of behaviour against prevailing gender norms to inform the reformulation of future policy and practice and thereby halting the continuation of prevailing biases towards women's engagement in leadership positions.
- Planning and implementing play-based learning experiences to explore the nature of leadership and thereby offering opportunities to explore, enact and practise leadership roles commencing in the early years of education.
- Providing mentoring and coaching, and thereby enabling girls to develop their self-confidence, self-efficacy and hence resilience to take on leadership roles at school and later in life as women.

Questions

22.1 Watch the YouTube video of Julia Gillard's 'misogyny speech' made in 2012 in which she highlights entrenched sexism against women in Australia. Reflect on the key barriers to women's leadership achievement in Australian society today. To what extent are these barriers difficult to eliminate? Why?

22.2 If you were Lauren, the teacher depicted in Case Study 22.2, what strategies would you put in place to enable Jessica to transfer her leadership capabilities from playing with the robotics into other areas in the classroom?

22.3 Sheryl Sandberg, the chief operating officer for Facebook, stated: 'I want every little girl who's told she's bossy, to be told instead she has leadership skills' (Facebook, 6 April 2013). Do you agree or disagree? Give your reasons. Play the CBS *60 Minutes* video of the Sandberg interview from YouTube. Reflect on how you would discuss taking on leadership roles with early years learners – both girls and boys – and their families.

22.4 How might the research findings presented in this chapter influence your approach to leadership development in early years learning settings? Consider how you might adjust both organisational policy and teaching practice.

References

Archard, N. (2012). Adolescent girls and leadership: The impact of confidence, competition, and failure. *International Journal of Adolescence and Youth*, 17(4), 189–203.

—— (2013a). Women's participation as leaders in society: An adolescent girls' perspective. *Journal of Youth Studies*, 16(6), 759–75.

—— (2013b). Female leadership framework: Developing adolescent girls as future women leaders through the formation of a female leadership identity. *Leading and Managing*, 19(1), 51–71.

Ayman-Nolley, S. (2004). Trends in the study of leadership in children. In G.R. Goethals, G.J. Sorenson & J.M. Burns (eds), *Encyclopedia of leadership* (pp. 171–7). Thousand Oaks, CA: Sage.

Bohlin, L.C. (2000). Determinants of young children's leadership and dominance strategies during play. PhD Thesis, Indiana University.

Carli, L.L. & Eagly, A.H. (2007). Overcoming resistance to women leaders: The importance of leadership style. In B. Kellerman & D.L. Rhode (eds), *Women and leadership: The state of play and strategies for change* (pp. 127–48). San Francisco, CA: Jossey-Bass.

Choi, J., Johnson, D.W. & Johnson, R. (2011). The roots of social dominance: Aggression, prosocial behavior, and social interdependence. *The Journal of Educational Research*, 104, 442–54.

Coie, J.D. & Dodge, K.A. (1983). Continuities and changes in children's social status. A five-year longitudinal study. *Merrill-Palmer Quarterly*, 29, 261–82.

Davies, B. (1989). *Frogs and snails and feminist tales: Preschool children and gender.* Sydney: Allen & Unwin.

Eagly, A.H. & Karau, S.J. (2002). Role congruity theory of prejudice toward female leaders. *Psychological Bulletin*, 109(3), 573–98.

Education Council (2015) *National STEM School Education Strategy: A Comprehensive Plan for Science, Technology, Engineering and Mathematics Education in Australia.* Retrieved 23 May 2016 from www. educationcoucil.edu.au

Edwards, C.A. (1994). Leadership in school-age girls. *Developmental Psychology*, 30(6), 920–7.

Kane, E.W. (2012). *Rethinking gender and sexuality in childhood.* London: Bloomsbury.

LaFreniere, P.J. & Sroufe, L.A. (1985). Profiles of peer competence in the preschool. Interrelations between measures, influence of social ecology, and relation to attachment history. *Developmental Psychology*, 21(1), 56–69.

Maccoby, E.E. (1990). Gender and relationships: A developmental account. *American Psychologist*, 45(4), 513–20.

Madrid, S. (2013). Playing aggression: The social construction of the 'sassy girl' in a peer culture peer routine. *Contemporary Issues in Early Childhood*, 14(3), 241–254.

Marsh, J. (2000). 'But I want to fly too!': Girls and superhero play in the infant classroom. *Gender and Education*, 12(2), 209–20.

Meece, J., Glienke, B.B. & Burg, S. (2006). Gender and motivation. *Journal of School Psychology*, 44(5), 351–73.

Morda, R. (2011). Examining the role of intelligence in leadership emergence and enactment in young children's groups. PhD thesis, University of Melbourne.

Murphy, S.E. & Johnson, S.K. (2011). The benefits of a long-lens approach to leader development: Understanding the seeds of leadership. *The Leadership Quarterly*, 22, 459–70.

Murphy, S.E. & Reichard, R.J. (eds.) (2011). *Early development and leadership. Building the next generation of leaders*. New York: Routledge.

Paustian-Underdahl, S.C., Slatery Walker, L. & Woehr, D.J. (2014). Gender and perceptions of leadership effectiveness: A meta-analysis of contextual moderators. *Journal of Applied Psychology*, 99(6), 1129–45.

Roach, A.A., Wyman, L.T., Brookes, H., Chavez, C., Heath, S.B. & Valdes, G. (1999). Leadership giftedness: Models revisited. *Gifted Child Quarterly*, 43(1), 13–24.

Sarkar, M., Tytler, R. & Palmer, S. (2014). *Participation of women in engineering: challenges and productive interventions*. Melbourne: Deakin University.

Trawick-Smith, J. (1988). 'Let's say you're the baby OK?' Play leadership and following behaviour of young children. *Young Children*, 43(5), 51–9.

—— (1992). A descriptive study of persuasive preschool children: How they get others to do what they want. *Early Childhood Research Quarterly*, 7(1), 95–114.

Williams, M.J. & Tiedens, L.Z. (2016). The subtle suspension of backlash; A meta-analysis of penalties for women's implicit and explicit dominance behaviour. *Psychological Bulletin*, 142(2), 165–97.

CHAPTER 23

Building the capacity of early childhood educators to promote children's mental health: Learnings from three new programs

Sarah Cavanagh, Jo Cole, Judy Kynaston, Kim-Michelle Gilson, Elise Davis and Gavin Hazel

Acknowledgement

The authors would like to acknowledge Jo Cole, who contributed to the ideas and writing that appeared in a similar chapter in the first edition of this book. While the chapter in this second edition has been updated and revised from the first edition, we acknowledge Jo's earlier contributions that appear here.

Introduction

Early childhood is a critical time for children's brain development. The experiences children are exposed to shape brain development, and the skills and capacities developed during this time provide the foundation for lifelong learning and mental health and wellbeing. While children's primary caregivers and the family environment have the most significant impact on children's early development, children learn within the context of all their relationships and, increasingly, children experience significant relationships with early childhood educators. The number of children attending an early childhood education and care (ECEC) service is growing in Australia, as is the amount of time each child spends in the service. This provides an opportunity to influence ECEC services and educator knowledge and skills to support positive social and emotional development and good mental health. Educators can build the 'social and emotional capacities of infants and children by supporting predictably available, adequately sensitive and responsive care giving' (Australian Association for Infant Mental Health and Australian Research Alliance for Children & Youth, 2013, p. 3). Educators who are consistently engaged with children and families can also assist in preventing or mitigating the consequences of mental health problems by buffering young children from serious threats to their wellbeing (National Scientific Council on the Developing Child, 2007).

ECEC sector reform in Australia has led to a National Quality Framework (NQF), which is the result of an agreement between state and Commonwealth governments, to improve the quality of early childhood education and care. This framework comprises the *Early Years Learning Framework* (EYLF) (Council of Australian Government [COAG], 2009) and *National Quality Standard* (NQS) (Australian Children's Education and Care Quality Authority [ACECQA], 2013), and applies to most long day care, family day care and preschools/kindergartens in Australia. Quality in early childhood education has been shown to lead to better outcomes in learning, health and wellbeing for children. In this context, Response Ability, Thrive and KidsMatter Early Childhood are three Australian initiatives that focus on fostering the knowledge, confidence and competence of early childhood educators and providing support to the sector to enable ECEC services to become promoters of good mental health in children and families, and to respond early and effectively to mental health problems. Each initiative targets a different segment of the ECEC sector and provides a range of resources and support for fostering children's mental health. Response Ability targets pre-service educators, Thrive was implemented in family day care and KidsMatter Early Childhood has, to date, largely focused on long day care and preschool settings (with the increasing inclusion of family day care settings). This chapter provides information about each initiative in turn.

Response Ability

Response Ability National Mental Health Education Initiative (Response Ability) is an initiative of the Australian Government Department of Health, implemented by the Hunter Institute of Mental Health (2010). It is an evidence-based intervention for pre-service preparation of education and care professionals to contribute, through their daily practice, to children and young people's mental health. By targeting a common core of capabilities (Center on the Developing Child at Harvard University, 2012) that are essential to support vulnerable children and families, Response Ability aims to simultaneously strengthen both the workforce and the community.

One of the fundamental principles of Response Ability is that appropriately prepared early childhood professionals can actively work to strengthen children and families so that they are more likely to possess the skills they need to achieve self-sufficiency, as well as healthy, secure lives (Center on the Developing Child at Harvard University, 2010). To do this in the most effective, efficient and sustainable way, professionals must have targeted evidence-based preparation for this role during their basic training and ongoing professional development opportunities.

the pre-service environment. This is both an enabler and a barrier to uptake by students and instructors.

- *Graduates don't need to be experts.* Graduates need experience to mature in their capabilities and progress towards mastery. It is important to build skills and then link with ongoing professional development and reflection.
- *Implementation and fidelity is the key.* Fidelity during implementation is an important factor in achieving consistent outcomes. It is important that resources are used in a way that is consistent with their intent. Response Ability is flexible but modifications need to be a balanced against the current evidence base supports/recommendations.
- *Mental health promotion, prevention and early intervention are not always intuitive.* Although health promotion messages often target reasonably simple behaviours and easily remembered messages, this disguises the deeper theoretical and methodological sophistication behind this work. Accessible material and frameworks like CHILD are important for scaffolding learning.
- *Educators can learn about and champion mental health and wellbeing.* Even considering the practical, conceptual and cultural challenges in fostering professional learning and ensuring dissemination occurred independently of direct onsite input from project staff, Response Ability has demonstrated that this approach can bring about change.

SPOTLIGHT 23.1: TIPS FOR THE VET SECTOR IN PREPARING PRE-SERVICE EDUCATORS TO SUPPORT CHILDREN'S MENTAL HEALTH

Examine mental health as a positive idea associated with the social and emotional wellbeing of individuals and communities (World Health Organization, 2004). Mental health and wellbeing is essential to people's quality of life, health and productivity. A range of components, including **risk factors**, protective factors and the wider social determinants of health, can influence mental health and wellbeing both positively and negatively, throughout people's lives.

Risk factors are things in a child's life that are associated with a higher risk of mental health difficulties, mental illness or a neurodevelopmental disorder.

Build understanding of how the early environment, brain development, stress, attachment, social and emotional skills, self-regulation and relationships all influence the development of the child. These factors simultaneously effect social and emotional wellbeing and people's mental health in childhood, as well as into adolescence and adulthood.

Increased awareness and knowledge of children's developmental needs and of the risk and protective factors for mental health and social and emotional development is an important responsibility of primary caregivers, families and children's services staff (Hazel, 2014).

Thrive

Thrive was the first program that aimed to build the knowledge, confidence and skills of family day care (FDC) educators in the area of childhood mental health in Australia and internationally (Davis et al., 2011).

FDC is an approved child care scheme in which family day care educators provide both care and education in their own homes for children from birth to five years of age, although primary school children can also attend outside of their school hours (Productivity Commission, 2011). Family day care educators are managed by a locally based family day care service called a coordination unit where professional staff (family day care coordinators) support and advise the educators. Family day care operates under the NQF, the same as other forms of child care. More information on family day care in Australia can be found at http://www.familydaycare.com.au.

There are large numbers of children accessing FDC services in Australia, which means there is a significant opportunity for the FDC scheme to promote children's social and emotional wellbeing through the care that is provided. However, to date, there is neither a requirement to study mental health in the training to become a registered educator nor any professional development program specifically designed for educators to build their capacity to promote children's social and emotional wellbeing. As such, Thrive was developed to address the need and opportunity within FDC to promote mental health, which may ultimately foster better identification of the children who are at risk of mental health problems and prevent these problems from developing in adolescent and adult years.

Thrive focused on capacity building, which is an essential element of effective health promotion (Hawe et al., 1997). It involved actions aimed at strengthening the skills and capabilities of individuals but also at the broader levels of organisations and communities, and was heavily dependent on collaboration and partnership. Full details of the design of Thrive are given in the previously published protocol paper by Davis et al. (2011). Thrive comprised a number of core activities (summarised in Table 23.2) that were developed in partnership with FDC educators and coordinators within one FDC service. These activities were rolled out across a 12-month period (2011–2012) and involved the participation of four field workers and 24 educators.

Thrive activities

1. *Workshops* – two-hour interactive workshops on child social and emotional wellbeing (major topics included development, promoting resilience, infant and child mental health problems and partnering with parents).
2. *Activity/experience exchanges* – educators connected by their coordinator to facilitate the weekly sharing of information on ways to promote children's social and emotional wellbeing.
3. *Focused discussion during coordinator monthly visits* – dedicated time given to focused discussion about the social and emotional wellbeing of children in care.

Table 23.2: Summary of core activities in Thrive.

Thrive component	Description of contents
Workshops – for educators and/or field workers	Workshop formats include PowerPoint presentations, discussions, video clips and role-play activities. Topics included: • Overview of child and infant mental health • Activities to support social emotional wellbeing • Responding to children's behaviour issues • Working in partnership with educators/sharing information • Relationships with children • Resilience: risk and protective factors • Recognising and responding to mental health problems, including early signs.
Activity exchanges – for educators	Activities were those that help children express feelings, master and achieve. These could include dress-up and role-playing games. The process for conducting the activity exchange was: • Email all educators to introduce the activity exchange • Set up a roster so that a different educator sends in a new activity each week • Remind each rostered educator to send in an activity during their week; remind them of due date • Email the activity to all educators.
Enhanced family day care monthly visits – for coordinators	Focused discussions on promoting children's social and emotional wellbeing regarded a number of topics such as: • Knowing when there are problems with a child • Responding to behaviour • Talking with parents about problems • Avoiding negative labelling of children.
Resource provision – for educators and coordinators	Resources covered a wide variety of topics related to child social and emotional wellbeing, reference guides and content on where to find additional information or seek further support. Websites for this information include: www.responseability.org and www.kidsmatter.edu.au.

4. *Resource provision* – evidence-based information recently developed in the area of child mental health, including those developed by the KidsMatter Early Childhood team and the Response Ability team, provided at the end of workshops.

Thrive activities were considered essential to educators' learning on promoting children's mental health and intended to build their knowledge, confidence and skills. The educators received many of them positively and they were most interested in the practical topics (as opposed to theoretical background information on children's mental health); these included responding to challenging behaviours, building relationships and connections with children and communicating with parents (Davis et al., 2011).

Other successful elements of Thrive include the resources provided, which educators found useful throughout the duration of the program. They described them as good reference material should issues arise and also a reminder to promote children's wellbeing. Both of these findings may be useful for other FDC schemes (Davis et al., 2011). The monthly visit from coordinators to educators' homes focusing on discussions about mental health was also valued, especially when they involved active components such as problem solving. Furthermore, evidence of promising practice change was observed at a 12-month follow up, where coordinators continued to discuss children's social and emotional wellbeing at their monthly visits to educators' homes. This is in contrast to a time before Thrive existed, where coordinators reported not having time allocated for this discussion.

Thrive provided a solid understanding about the challenges FDC educators face, including their limited time for involvement in additional learning activities and their need for information about promoting children's mental health. These can be applied to other FDC contexts and include: more practical advice on strategies to increase children's social and emotional wellbeing, particularly with children who express behavioural and emotional difficulties, and accessible resources that can enhance support and awareness about children's social and emotional wellbeing.

Conversations with educators revealed a number of issues at play, which may have prevented them from being involved. These included the following:

- they were uncomfortable with home visits and assessment
- they did not have the mental space to take on one more 'extra' thing
- they were unable to commit to training at night
- they were nervous about being involved in research.

These issues are important for other FDC services to consider (Davis et al., 2011).

Although the Thrive program was developed in collaboration with FDC educators and based on a strong partnership with the FDC service, it was difficult for educators to participate in some of the activities, particularly the workshops and activity exchanges that involved a lot of their unpaid time. For educators to be more willing to engage in mental health promotion programs, and thereby have an increased awareness of children's mental health, there needs to be stronger support at the overall FDC scheme level.

SPOTLIGHT 23.2: TIPS FOR FDC COORDINATORS AND SCHEMES ON SUPPORTING CHILDREN'S MENTAL HEALTH

- FDC educators are looking for *practical advice on strategies* for increasing children's social and emotional wellbeing and in responding to children with social and emotional difficulties.
- FDC services can enhance educators' engagement in mental health promotion, prevention and early intervention by *providing access to high-quality resources* on children's mental health.
- A *stronger framework* for supporting professional developmental activities, which enhance knowledge about children's social and emotional wellbeing at the FDC organisational and scheme level, might be warranted.

KidsMatter Early Childhood

KidsMatter Early Childhood (KMEC) is a national mental health promotion, prevention and early intervention initiative, jointly developed by Early Childhood Australia, beyondblue, and the Australian Psychological Society (APS), with funding from the Australian Government Department of Health and beyondblue.

Early childhood mental health is related to thoughts, feelings and behaviour, and is viewed within the context of the child's development.

KMEC was based on the model developed for and piloted successfully in primary schools, KidsMatter Primary (Graetz et al. 2008; Slee et al. 2012) and adapted for the ECEC sector, using research about **early childhood mental health** and linking to the NQS. The KidsMatter Primary model was modified to meet the different needs of the ECEC sector and content was tailored to the age range covered by the initiative (generally birth to five years), taking into account the developmental context. KMEC was piloted between 2010 and 2011 with 106 long day care centres and preschools across Australia. There are now over 480 services participating in KMEC.

KidsMatter Early Childhood provides a continuous improvement framework for ECEC services to review their practice under four key areas, known as Components (Figure 23.2).

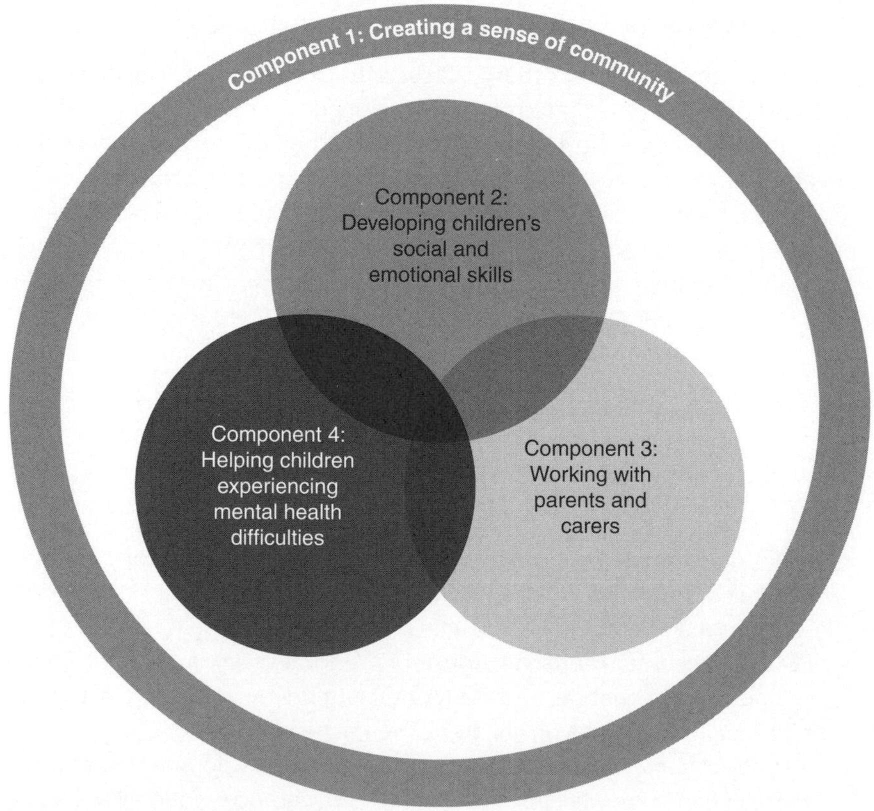

Figure 23.2 The KidsMatter Early Childhood Components.
Source: KidsMatter Early Childhood (2012).

Each Component has key target areas and goals, and ECEC services implement Action Plans to address each Component according to the priorities of their service. KidsMatter provides a range of implementation tools and resources to assist services with understanding children's mental health and wellbeing and with the implementation of evidenced-based strategies to support positive child development. All of these resources are available at www.kidsmatter.edu.au.

KidsMatter implementation at each service is led by a service Leadership Team. The Leadership Team can include the service Director or Coordinator, members of the management committee, and service staff. It can also include parents and representatives from the broader community. The Leadership Team is responsible for driving the implementation of the initiative, but consults with and engages the whole ECEC service community. KidsMatter recommends Leadership Teams meet regularly to PLAN, DO and REVIEW their actions under each of the four Components and provides tools as part of the KidsMatter implementation resources to assist this process.

In addition to a range of written and online tools and resources, ECEC services also have access to online professional learning about how to implement KidsMatter and about children's mental health, through the lens of each of the four Components. The aim of the professional learning is to increase staff understanding about children's mental health and wellbeing and the actions services can take to support wellbeing, as well as to facilitate increased staff competence and confidence through personal reflection, skill-based and discussion activities to practise and embed learning. KMEC services also receive support from a KidsMatter Facilitator who has extensive knowledge about KidsMatter and experience of children's mental health promotion, prevention and early intervention. Facilitators provide support to services through telephone, videoconferences, webinars and through established online collaborative learning communities.

Each ECEC service and Leadership Team are assisted by their Facilitator to implement the PLAN, DO, REVIEW process for each Component, which can then form part of their Quality Improvement Plan (QIP) which is required under the NQS. The KMEC Implementation Flowchart (Figure 23.3) outlines the process that services undertake to implement a Component.

Some of the Component 2 strategies implemented by KMEC services have included:

- changing the way families and children are greeted and welcomed into the service and farewelled each day
- accessing more resources for staff to continuing learning and supporting staff in developing their own social and emotional skills
- expanding the range of activities available to children in the service with development of specific social and emotional skills in mind (e.g. increasing the opportunities for children to work together on an activity and supporting them with planning, problem-solving, decision-making and communicating with each other)
- explicitly noticing and verbalising emotions during everyday interactions with children to further develop their ability to understand, recognise and express emotions

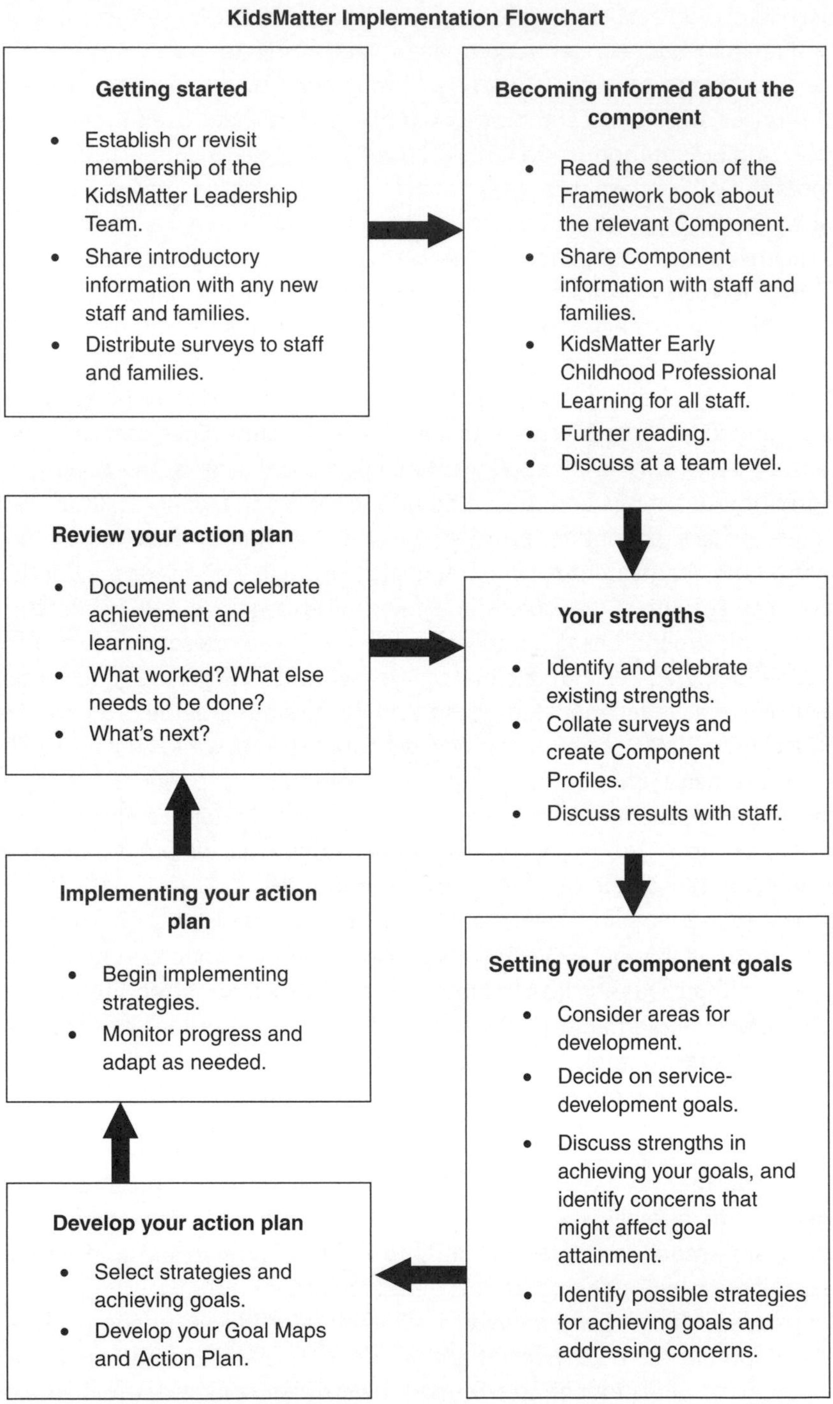

KidsMatter Implementation Flowchart

Getting started

- Establish or revisit membership of the KidsMatter Leadership Team.
- Share introductory information with any new staff and families.
- Distribute surveys to staff and families.

Becoming informed about the component

- Read the section of the Framework book about the relevant Component.
- Share Component information with staff and families.
- KidsMatter Early Childhood Professional Learning for all staff.
- Further reading.
- Discuss at a team level.

Review your action plan

- Document and celebrate achievement and learning.
- What worked? What else needs to be done?
- What's next?

Your strengths

- Identify and celebrate existing strengths.
- Collate surveys and create Component Profiles.
- Discuss results with staff.

Implementing your action plan

- Begin implementing strategies.
- Monitor progress and adapt as needed.

Setting your component goals

- Consider areas for development.
- Decide on service-development goals.
- Discuss strengths in achieving your goals, and identify concerns that might affect goal attainment.
- Identify possible strategies for achieving goals and addressing concerns.

Develop your action plan

- Select strategies and achieving goals.
- Develop your Goal Maps and Action Plan.

Figure 23.3 KidsMatter Early Childhood Implementation Flowchart.
Source: KidsMatter Early Childhood (2012).

- providing more information to families about the social and emotional skills of their child and how they demonstrated those during the day
- providing families with information about child development.

Further information about KidsMatter and free downloadable resources for ECEC services, schools and families is available at www.kidsmatter.edu.au. The resources include:

- information and tools to support KidsMatter implementation in schools and ECEC services, including information about how KMEC and the NQS complement each other, a blog, stories about how other services and schools have implemented KidsMatter, action plan templates, suggestions for staff meetings and reflection tools
- a programs guide that provides information on more than 80 different programs that can be implemented within schools and ECEC services to improve children's mental health
- a portal with links to more than 200 resources about the social and emotional wellbeing of Aboriginal and Torres Strait Islander people
- factsheets on more than 40 different topics with information about the topic, tips about what parents, schools and ECEC staff can do to support children's mental health and wellbeing, and links to further resources – topics include cultural diversity, play, friendships, relationships, separation, problem-solving, good decision-making, curiosity, confidence, conflict, anger, discipline, fears and worries, anxiety, praise, managing emotions, mental health difficulties, ADHD, anxiety, depression, behaviour problems, trauma, knowing where to get help, managing the transition to school
- e-learning for school and ECEC staff about connecting with families and managing difficult conversations
- short videos and accompanying factsheets on topics such as resilience, bullying, student voice and schools and ECEC services working in partnership with health and community agencies
- tools to support schools, ECEC services and health and community agencies to work together to support children's mental health
- e-newsletters, and social media such as Facebook and Twitter, for keeping up to date with the latest news on KidsMatter and children's mental health more broadly.

The KMEC pilot was independently evaluated by Flinders University Research Centre for Student Wellbeing and Prevention of Violence (Slee et al., 2012). The evaluation examined the quality of implementing KidsMatter and how this influenced ECEC services' capacity to achieve positive outcomes for children's mental health. KMEC was associated with improvements in children's mental health, educator's knowledge, competence and confidence and family engagement with the services. There were also significant benefits for educators (as highlighted in the quote overleaf) who reported an increase in their understanding and ability to support mental health in early childhood and to respond to children experiencing difficulties.

To me, KidsMatter Early Childhood has meant OPPORTUNITY. An opportunity to re-think the way we interact with children and families. An opportunity to broaden our knowledge on social and emotional wellbeing. An opportunity to develop strategies to improve the Centre, the staff relationships and the relationships between staff and parents and staff and children … (an early childhood educator, quoted in Slee, et al. 2012, p. 16).

Qualitative data from educators also indicated that involvement in KidsMatter resulted in increased levels of job satisfaction, and improved communication and connection between educators which enhanced relationships and contibutions to their service.

SPOTLIGHT 23.3: KIDSMATTER TIPS FOR ECEC SERVICES ON SUPPORTING CHILDREN'S MENTAL HEALTH

Educators interested in implementing KidsMatter at their school or service should consider the following factors that can assist with effective implementation:

- *Commitment of leadership* is critical to ensuring KidsMatter can be made a priority. The *involvement* of all staff and families is also important. One way to get leaders interested is to show them the website and great resources available or put them in touch with another service that is achieving great outcomes with KidsMatter. Involving everyone helps to ensure KMEC does not become one person's sole responsibility and that it can continue even if the service experiences staffing changes.
- *Be systematic.* The KMEC Framework consists of the four Components, with 16 professional learning topics and the PLAN, DO, REVIEW process. Services implementing KMEC achieve greater outcomes when they systematically implement all four Components across the *whole service*, rather than doing bits and pieces, or only doing KidsMatter in one classroom. However, it is possible to identify a topic that is assessed to be of greatest need in the service as a starting point.
- *Get informed.* Professional learning for all staff in each of the four KMEC Components provides the opportunity for developing a shared understanding and vision for children's mental health and wellbeing among all staff and provides a catalyst for change. There are also a lot of other resources, professional learning and tools available via KidsMatter and other reputable organisations.
- *Access support* by implementating the tools and resources on the website, the social media sites and the skilled and experienced KidsMatter Facilitators who can assist services and schools to critically reflect on their own practice, to create innovative strategies and to keep going with the initiative despite challenges.

Challenges to bringing about change

There are significant challenges within the ECEC sector, including the current funding and policy environment, that can hinder the effective implementation of mental health promotion, prevention and early intervention initiatives like Response Ability, Thrive and KidsMatter. These include the following:

- Diversity in the sector of educators' knowledge, experience and training means that any professional learning needs to be flexible and provide layered content to enable educators to access the materials at a depth appropriate to their prior knowledge and experience.
- Limited time and funding for professional learning means that innovative solutions to providing access to professional learning need to be implemented. KidsMatter implemented solutions such as: professional learning after-hours; undertaking learning in small chunks – such as 30-minute blocks during staff meetings; combining sessions with staff from nearby centres; using peer discussions during everyday practice to facilitate learning; and closing the service for a day to hold professional learning. However, without an organisational commitment to support professional development, these solutions can be difficult to implement, as was found during the implementation of Thrive.
- High levels of staff turnover can also make it difficult for initiatives to be sustained within a service. Commitment from leadership and engagement of all staff, with a planned approach to making time for implementation, can help to overcome the inevitable faltering in implementation that occurs when key staff leave. Online professional learning resources can help support new staff to 'catch up' with the others in their team, or provide a way to refresh knowledge and learning.
- Community-level factors such as high levels of disadvantage, parental unemployment, family stress and distress, and children with social, emotional and behavioural problems coupled with a lack of community services can also impact upon the time and resourcing available to implement initiatives within services. However, focusing on mental health and wellbeing in these communities also provides the opportunity to make the greatest difference.
- Services also need to consider the socio-cultural context of the community and individual families within it, tailoring the initiative accordingly. For example, services may need to cater for different child-rearing practices, beliefs about mental health, and the needs of groups who may have experienced trauma – such as refugees.
- Changing policy and regulatory context for the ECEC sector means that services already have a range of mandatory changes to implement and any new initiative needs to dovetail into existing practices and legal obligations, rather than be seen as an extra burden requiring significant resources to implement.

While challenging for the sector, the current policy drivers such as the NQS and the EYLF provide substantial leverage for improving mental health outcomes for children. ECEC service engagement in service-wide mental health initiatives can be enhanced where services clearly identify the links with meeting the requirements of the NQS. For example, KMEC tools and resources explicitly reference the EYLF and NQS and KidsMatter supports services to understand how KMEC helps services meet the NQS requirements. ECEC services are also actively identifying children's mental health and support for managing challenging behaviours as critical issues. Early childhood advocates also continue to argue for systemic changes to the health promotion, early childhood and education systems that recognise and respond to the solid body of evidence that now exists. It is clear that creating environments for optimal early childhood development has significant long-term benefits for individuals and the community as a whole.

Moving forward

In the face of these challenges, educators and services can draw on the Response Ability, Thrive and KidsMatter resources and focus on improving their own practice to support children's mental health and wellbeing by:

- learning more about children's social and emotional development and the risk and protective factors for mental health and wellbeing
- advocating within their service for a whole-of-service approach to supporting children's mental health
- developing warm and responsive relationships with children in their care, and their families
- acknowledging each child's strengths and interests and supporting them to try new things and practise new skills, including by arranging a variety of developmentally appropriate experiences, routines and interactions
- helping children understand and manage their emotions by describing and labelling emotions, telling and reading stories about emotions and social situations, and teaching and modelling coping and problem-solving strategies for strong emotions (such as taking quiet time away, slow breathing, talking about feelings)
- giving children control over their environments and routines; for example, giving choices at meal times and over different activities, and talking to them about what is happening
- noticing when children need additional support; for example: if they are not meeting developmental milestones; if they have difficulty settling or calming themselves; if they have difficulty interacting with other children or are acting aggressively towards others; if they appear sad or lacking enjoyment in activities; if they regularly appear worried, anxious or fearful; and, in particular, by paying attention to the pervasiveness, frequency, persistence and severity of difficulties across different settings and contexts and over time

- being alert to changes in a child's behaviour and seeking to understand what is happening
- taking action if concerned by talking to the child's family and to colleagues to gather a full picture, and working collaboratively to support the child.

Conclusion

Early child education and care services and educators have a significant opportunity to contribute to the mental health and wellbeing of children. The three initiatives outlined in this chapter demonstrate the ways in which ECEC services can be empowered to promote good health as part of a national quality agenda. By fostering knowledge, confidence and competence we can build the capability of early childhood educators, working in partnership with families and the community, to promote wellbeing and to respond early and effectively to mental health problems.

Summary

The key messages highghted in this chapter are:

- Early childhood mental health can be addressed in early-childhood settings.
- Awareness of risk and protective factors can aid educators in putting measures into place or seeking appropriate support for children and families.
- Many Australian resources are available to support your work in this area.
- Mental health promotion, prevention and early intervention during the early years can make a significant difference to wellbeing in the long term.

Questions

23.1 What are the characteristics of warm and responsive relationships between educators and children? How can educators actively foster a warm and responsive relationship with each child in their care?

23.2 What are some activities and routines that you could build into a program or curriculum for children that explicitly teach social and emotional skills?

23.3 How might educators find out more about the needs of families in their ECEC service community?

23.4 If you were worried about the mental health and wellbeing of a child, what would your first step be? Who could you consult with?

References

Australian Association for Infant Mental Health and Australian Research Alliance for Children & Youth (2013). Halving rates of mental illness in Australia – by starting at birth. Retrieved 10 December 2013 from http://www.iecsewc2013. net.au/downloads/IECSEW-Conference-2013-Communique.pdf

Australian Children's Education and Care Quality Authority (ACECQA) (2013). *A guide to the National Quality Standard*. Retrieved from http://files.acecqa. gov.au/files/National-Quality-Framework-Resources-Kit/NQF03-Guide-to-NQS-130902.pdf

Center on the Developing Child at Harvard University (2012). In Brief – Executive function: Skills for life and learning [Video file]. Retrieved from http://www. developingchild.harvard.edu

—— (2010). The foundations of lifelong health are built in early childhood. Retrieved 10 December 2013 from http://www.developingchild.harvard.edu

Council of Australian Governments (COAG) (2009). *Belonging, being and becoming: The early years learning framework for Australia*. Canberra: Department of Education, Employment and Workplace Relations.

Davis, E., Williamson, L., Mackinnon, A., Cook, K., Waters, E., Herrman, H.et al. (2011). Building the capacity of family day care educators to promote children's social and emotional wellbeing: An exploratory cluster randomised controlled trial. *BMC Public Health* 11, 842.

Graetz, B., Littlefield, L., Trinder, M., Dobia, B., Souter, M., Champion, C. et al. (2008). KidsMatter: A population health model to support student mental health and well-being in primary schools. *International Journal of Mental Health Promotion*, 10(4), 13–20.

Hawe, P., Noort, M., King, L. & Jordens, C. (1997). Multiplying health gains: The critical role of capacity-building within health promotion programmes. *Health Policy*, 39, 29–42.

Hazel, G. (2014). *Submission to Australian Government Productivity Commission Public Inquiry: Childcare and Early Learning*. Newcastle: Hunter Institute of Mental Health.

Hunter Institute of Mental Health (2010), *Response Ability Vocational Education and Training Resources: Children's Services Background Reading for Teachers*. Newcastle: Hunter Institute of Mental Health.

KidsMatter Early Childhood (2012). *Tools and guidelines for implementation*. Canberra: Department of Health and Ageing.

National Scientific Council on the Developing Child (2007). The science of early childhood development. Retrieved 10 December 2013 from http://www.developingchild.net

Productivity Commission (2011). *Early Childhood Development Workforce Research Report, June 2011*. Melbourne: Commonwealth of Australia.

Slee, P.T., Murray-Harvey, R., Dix, K.L., Skrzypiec, G., Askell-Williams, H., Lawson, M. et al. (2012). *Kids Matter Early Childhood Evaluation Report*. Adelaide: Shannon Research Press.

World Health Organization (WHO) (2004). *Promoting mental health: Concepts, emerging evidence and practice. Summary Report*. Geneva: World Health Organization.

CHAPTER 24

Loose parts on the school playground: A playful approach to promoting health and wellbeing for children of all abilities

Shirley Wyver, Anita Bundy, Lina Engelen, Geraldine Naughton and Anita Nelson Niehues

Introduction

School playgrounds offer many opportunities for children to connect with others, improve their conflict resolution skills, become physically active and use imaginative play. Nonetheless, it is known that individual characteristics can predict the extent to which children have opportunities to enjoy the benefits of the school playground. This chapter, focuses on a school-based intervention to promote playfulness, known as the Sydney Playground Project. This project was developed by a multidisciplinary team, including the authors of this chapter. The key principles of the Sydney Playground Project were to find ways to enable children to engage in better quality play and have the intervention accessible to *all* children, families and teachers. Recently, we have seen a particular focus on children with disabilities for whom goals include development in areas promoted through play; however, a range of barriers often prevents this group from full participation.

Playfulness

Play is difficult to define, so it is important to be clear about what we mean by the word 'play'. Skard and Bundy (2008) have identified four elements of **playfulness** (internal control, intrinsic motivation, freedom to suspend reality and framing) which we believe are important in any definition of play. With these elements in mind, it is clear that many environments promote playfulness, not just those specifically

Playfulness includes the elements of internal control, intrinsic motivation, freedom to suspend reality and framing.

designed for early years learners. It is also clear that playfulness can be enhanced by lack of structure in an environment. Structure and equipment with a specific purpose can inhibit children's creativity. It is important to note that our definition does not include some activities that broader definitions of play capture.

Before describing the Sydney Playground Project in detail, we briefly review some of the changes in the social and physical contexts of early years learners that are now understood to have a negative impact on mental and physical wellbeing.

Compelling international research provides evidence of direct relationships between play of early years learners and wellbeing. There is also international consensus that historically recent lifestyle changes have had the unintended consequence of reducing the quality and quantity of opportunities for play. Decline in opportunities for early years learners to participate in playful experiences has been linked to increases in a range of physical and mental health problems (see Bundy et al, 2011). Changes include inadequate provision of appropriate environments for play and excessive concerns about safety. In Australia, for example, the outdoor play space regulatory requirement for early years learners in long day care is seven square metres (horizontal space) with limitations to height of equipment (vertical space) (Ministerial Council for Education, Early Childhood Development and Youth Affairs, 2011). Numerous authors have argued that these provisions are not adequate for high-quality play involving physical activity or learning through **risk-taking** (see Little & Wyver, 2014). Opportunities for play have also been compromised by an excessive concern for safety, sometimes referred to as 'surplus safety'. Unfortunately, an unintended consequence of protecting children from injury has been a denial of opportunity for early years learners to engage in activities that promote wellbeing by allowing children to master their bodies and the environment. Concerns about tragic but extremely rare events are magnified and are not rationally balanced against the negative consequences that overprotection can have on wellbeing (Wyver et al., 2010).

> **Risk-taking** involves challenging limits, allowing for uncertainty and risking potential injury (especially scrapes and bruises) during play.

Issues related to early years learners' playfulness and wellbeing are best considered using a systems approach, such as the ecological systems theory or the dynamic systems theory (Bundy et al., 2009). Too often, stereotypes are invoked to blame individuals within the system (e.g. children hooked on computers, helicopter parents) which lead to individually focused solutions that are generally ineffective and can lead to feelings of guilt and disempowerment. In our research, we have found that adults are quite often aware that their practices are restricting early years learners' freedom to play, yet they are concerned about the repercussions of relaxing acknowledged excesses in safety that stymie high-quality play. A perceived neglect of 'duty of care' by a teacher, for example, may have significant personal and career implications. Success is therefore more likely achieved when addressed within systems to ensure shared understanding of stakeholders. We will return to this issue in our discussion of Sydney Playground Project's **risk-reframing** component.

> **Risk-reframing:** a process by which an individual's or group's perceptions of the risks related to a behaviour or event are changed.

For children with disabilities, play is often valued for its therapeutic role rather than being based on children's interests and explorations. Indeed, it has been argued that exploiting play for its therapeutic value may lead to negative associations as it becomes associated with areas of difficulty (Gielen, 2005). It was noted 25 years ago that barriers to free play for children with disabilities can lead to secondary impairments such as lower self-esteem, greater dependence on adults and problems with social skills (Missiuna & Pollock, 1991). The barriers that lead to secondary impairments continue to be in place and, as Bundy et al. (2015) have noted, recent government reforms in Australia – such as the National Disability Scheme – assume people with disabilities have the skills and self-confidence to exercise autonomous decision-making. The current focus of the Sydney Playground Project specifically examines whether changes on the playground lead to better coping skills (see Case Study 24.1).

CASE STUDY 24.1: KATIE WON'T UNDERSTAND HOW TO PLAY WITH THE OBJECTS

Katie has autism. Her play with objects is solitary and tends to be repetitive. She enjoys lining up cars, dolls and other small objects. There was concern at her school that the large loose objects introduced by the Sydney Playground Project team would require a level of abstraction beyond her existing abilities and might exacerbate her repetitive play tendencies. Staff at the school decided to observe Katie's play when the new materials were introduced. During the two-week observation period, they noticed that although she didn't play with the materials, she stayed close by and watched what other children were doing.

Early years learners' risk-taking and wellbeing

Although risk is usually considered in terms of potential negative outcomes, in recent years, researchers have started to examine the positive role of risk in early years learning. Removing barriers to risk-taking in play has been an important element of the Sydney Playground Project. The following are two examples that demonstrate the links between risk-taking and wellbeing.

A range of international studies show that early years learners benefit from environments that allow risk-taking. From infancy, early years learners respond to environments that offer challenge. Work by Adolph et al. (2012), for example, demonstrates that infants problem-solve in the process of learning to walk, which includes variations in gait to adjust to changes in surface. Infants' walking occurs most often during their spontaneous free play and they fall regularly when learning to walk (an average of 17 falls per hour for 12- to 19-month-olds). Clearly, a very basic skill such as early walking requires early years learners to take risks.

It is difficult to elicit the experience of risk during the period when early years learners cannot express their emotions verbally. However, by the preschool years, early years learners start to describe the complexity of mixed emotions. Participants in Sandseter's (2009) study used terms such as 'scary-funny' to describe the shift between negative and positive emotions experienced during risky play. In this sense, risk-taking in the context of play can provide important opportunities to develop emotional awareness and resilience, especially as early years learners are generally able to revisit play episodes to re-experience challenges.

Physical activity and wellbeing

The rise in overweight and obesity in young children has drawn attention to the negative impact of modern lifestyle changes on early years learners. Estimates of prevalence of early learner overweight/obesity in countries such as Australia, UK and the USA range from 20 to 30 per cent. Thus, even the lowest, most conservative estimates are cause for concern. Attempts to reduce children's weight by introducing programs to increase physical activity have largely been unsuccessful. The EarlyBird researchers have found from their longitudinal study of 7- to 10-year-olds that most interventions have been based on the wrong assumption about the direction of causality. Their longitudinal data suggest that overweight/obesity seems to be the cause of low levels of physical activity rather than the consequence (Metcalf et al., 2011). Importantly, the EarlyBird findings considered in conjunction with the difficulties in finding successful interventions for weight reduction suggest that a stronger emphasis needs to be placed on prevention of overweight/obesity. Ensuring adequate or better levels of physical activity from infancy is an important component of any effective prevention strategy.

The focus on overweight/obesity has also masked a somewhat more significant problem, namely that many early years learners do not achieve recommended levels of physical activity, regardless of weight status. In the EarlyBird study, only 42 per cent of boys and 11 per cent of girls met government guidelines for physical activity (namely $\geq$ 60 minutes of activity with a metabolic equivalent of $\geq$ 3 per day). This study found improved metabolic health for the early years learners who engaged in more physical activity than the government-specified minimum physical activity per day. Metabolic health was estimated from measures of triglycerides, insulin resistance, cholesterol/HDL ratio and mean arterial blood pressure (Metcalf et al., 2008). These metabolic health indicators are predictors of chronic health problems such as cardiovascular disease and type 2 diabetes, both of which are known to be on the rise and affecting early years learners, not just the adult population.

The EarlyBird study is not unique in identifying low levels of physical activity in the majority of children studied. Nor is it unique in finding a gender difference in physical activity levels. In the Sydney Playground Project, for example, we found that boys engaged in more physical activity than girls (Engelen et al., 2013). So, although attention has been directed to the concerning number of early years learners who are overweight/obese, numerous studies have made it clear that many more, perhaps the majority, are detectably at risk of chronic health problems, and that girls are potentially at greater risk than boys. Additionally, children with intellectual disabilities are almost twice as likely to become obese as children without intellectual disabilities, and this appears to be partly attributable to lower levels of physical activity (Segal et al., 2016).

To provide interventions for all early years learners with low levels of physical activity, or other indicators of potential chronic health problems, would be impractical and expensive. It would involve large-scale, individualised behavioural and physiological measurement of children to detect potential problems, coupled with targeted behavioural interventions that capture early years learners' interests in order to ensure sustainability. Even if the necessary resources were available, most likely there would be many false positives and negatives in detecting children at risk. Interventions offered are unlikely to be of the type that we discussed in our opening paragraph; namely, building on behaviours early years learners want to do more often and involving all friends and peers. A more reasonable approach is to find a preventive strategy that can benefit all early years learners. This is the approach taken in the Sydney Playground Project, which is discussed next.

The Sydney Playground Project

The Sydney Playground Project (SPP) was developed as an inexpensive school playground intervention available to all early years learners regardless of ability. SPP has two main components: introduction of large, loose, recycled objects onto the school playground; and risk-reframing for parents and teachers. Although the two components are conceptually separable, they have not been offered or evaluated separately. We consider the two components to have a synergistic relationship. The full protocol of SPP is described in Bundy et al. (2011) and detailed content of the risk-reframing workshops can be found at Niehues et al. (2013).

Some important aspects of SPP are:

Loose parts: in the context of play, these are any objects or materials not classified as fixed equipment. In this chapter, we refer specifically to loose parts that are large and have no obvious play purpose (e.g. a car tyre).

- The changes made to playgrounds by introducing **loose parts** lead to a change in early years learners' play behaviours. There is no requirement for specialist staff to teach children new skills or encourage physical activity. Changes emerge during free play. Many interventions require specialist personnel for implementation, which involves costs to schools that usually experience budgetary constraints as well as being a barrier to sustainability and widespread implementation since the intervention cannot occur when the specialists are not available.

- Although specialist staff are not required for implementation, teachers conduct their regular playground duty. Teachers have the opportunity to learn more about early years learners' social interactions and creativity by observing them in an active play context.
- Loose parts used are large, heavy objects that have been recycled. We have included car tyres, packing boxes, barrels, pool noodles and other similar items. An important principle when selecting items is that the items have no obvious play objective. Children use their imaginations to construct their own play scenarios with these objects. Play using this equipment has ranged from simple short-duration episodes to complex games with rules, extended over many episodes.
- Because the materials are large and heavy, they are difficult for children to manage. Consequently, play becomes more social since more children are needed to move the materials. Play also becomes more physically active. Although a child's primary purpose may be to engage in imaginative play, the child needs to be physically active to do so with the loose objects we provide. Children who would not usually engage in activity that is purely physical (e.g. jumping rope) and who are therefore likely to be inactive on the school playground, find themselves engaged in physical activity in order to achieve their imaginative play goals.

Figure 24.1 A typical collection of large loose parts used in the Sydney Playground Project.

CASE STUDY 24.2: BEN DOESN'T KNOW THE ENGLISH WORDS NEEDED FOR PRETEND PLAY

When Ben lived in Shanghai he loved playing pretend games at school. He has just moved to Sydney and the children at his new school are friendly, but he doesn't understand the words they use for play. He hears children say things and then run off excitedly. He tries to join in but has trouble contributing to the play and tends to watch rather than interact. Last week a teacher organised for some large loose objects such as car tyres and barrels to be left on the playground. Some of his classmates signalled for his help to move the objects to build 'the big castle' and he had a great time jumping from the high platform they built.

- The materials are inexpensive which means schools can extend the collection we provide or initiate their own collection. The use of recycled materials is consistent with sustainability policies of many schools and local authorities and supports early years learners' thinking about reuse of limited resources. It must be noted that we checked materials and removed potential hazards before placing them on the playground.

- Although none of the items are hazardous and they do comply with Australian Safety Standards for playground equipment, early years learners have used materials in ways that increase the physical-emotional challenge of play by increasing the element of risk. For example, play equipment was observed to be used to increase height for jumping and propel children forwards when jumping. Increasing the risk component was intentional. We have argued elsewhere that most playgrounds in Western countries lack challenge for early years learners because the element of risk has been removed (Wyver et al., 2012). Importantly, we can report that none of the schools in which our research took place reported an increase in injury rates when the materials were available for children. This suggests that risks did not become hazards or dangers and could be managed by the early years learners without need for additional staffing resources.

- Increased risk-taking on the playground occurred in a context where parents and teachers had been involved in a workshop to examine the positive role of risk-taking in early learners' development. Thus, the adults were encouraged to view play from a different perspective and value risk-taking rather than giving disproportionate consideration to potentially negative outcomes such as injuries.

Figure 24.2 Large loose parts promote imaginary play, cooperation and physical activity during school recess and lunch breaks.

- An important component of the risk-reframing workshop was that teachers and parents were together. In our pilot study, teachers had expressed concern about risky play, noting their duty of care and potential disciplinary or legal action that may be taken against them if a child was injured. At the same time, teachers understood the potential of risk-taking to enhance children's development. Parents also expressed concerns such as not wanting to be seen as negligent if they allowed their child to take more risks. The risk-reframing workshop provided an important forum for parents and teachers to see each others' perspectives (Niehues et al., 2013).

To date, SPP has been evaluated in a single school pilot study and later in a cluster randomised controlled trial (CRCT). An evaluation in schools for children with disabilities is currently in progress. As the CRCT is the most scientifically rigorous of the two completed projects, we will confine our discussion to this part of the project. The CRCT was conducted in 12 Sydney Catholic schools with children in Kindergarten and first year (five to seven years of age). Each school was randomly allocated to an experimental condition or a control condition. The six schools in the experimental condition received the interventions (i.e. loose materials and risk-reframing) and those in the control condition did not have access to either intervention during our evaluation phase, but were offered the interventions after our evaluation was concluded.

We visited the schools during the intervention to check whether any equipment needed to be replaced, to resolve any problems that may have arisen and to check compliance and conduct observations. In some schools we observed children hoarding the equipment during the initial period of the intervention. Although the items we used could otherwise have been destined for the scrap-heap, these were valuable play resources for many of the early years learners.

The intervention group experienced a statistically significant increase in physical activity. Retesting in one of the schools two years later revealed that the increase was maintained (Engelen et al., 2013). Although the increase was significant, it was smaller than expected. We used accelerometers to measure physical activity and while this was a useful method of capturing movements such as walking and running, it did not capture some of the changes in physical activity that accompanied the intervention, particularly lifting, pushing and pulling. We collected data on a randomly selected group of early years learners aged five to seven years from each school. Nonetheless, it is important to note that use of the intervention materials was not confined to the participants; they were accessed by children of all ages within the schools.

Changed attitudes to risk-taking were revealed through comments in risk-reframing workshops (Niehues et al., 2013). Parents and teachers acknowledged that some of their protective behaviours towards early years learners may have a basis in self-protection. They also reminisced about their own early experiences and the importance risk-taking had played. Importantly, parents and teachers were together in sharing their changing perspectives. Together they reconstructed risk to deepen their awareness of its positive contribution to early years learners' experience and development. Playground materials introduced to the school were reappraised through these new frames. At the three-month follow-up, participants continued to reflect on the workshop and indicated that their beliefs and practices had changed. Unfortunately, not all parents and teachers participated in the risk-reframing workshops. It is unclear whether participants shared their new frames with parents and teachers who did not participate or indeed, children in their care.

In general, the SPP was successful and some schools have continued to use the materials. Although we experienced only positive feedback from children, we encountered some unexpected negativity from some adults. For example, some schools or staff within schools found that the materials looked messy and did not want to continue using them. We also discovered that some teachers were placing limits on access to the materials, such as making access contingent upon good behaviour or only allowing access on certain days per week in order to make access to the materials 'fair'. The intention was for children to have free access to the materials during all free play periods and it is likely that rationing of material in some schools weakened the overall impact of the intervention for early years learners in those schools.

PAUSE AND REFLECT 24.1: SAM'S TEACHER

Sam enjoys rough and tumble play with his friends. His teacher knows he loves rough games and his style of play makes him popular with other children. Sam's parents have made it clear that they won't tolerate injuries, even small cuts and bruises. While his teacher is aware that rough play is promoting Sam's socio-emotional and physical development, she sometimes redirects him to quieter play due to fear of the consequences if an injury occurs. She has noticed that when his play is redirected he sometimes engages in covert teasing of other children.

Do you consider that risk-reframing might change Sam's parents' attitudes to rough play?

Conclusion

School playgrounds offer many opportunities for children to enjoy themselves while at the same time enhancing their health and wellbeing. As demonstrated in the Sydney Playground Project (SPP) and other research, introducing elements to the playground that challenge children and add to risk and uncertainty can promote playfulness. It is important to couple these strategies with risk-reframing for adults involved. Changes on the playground that promote playfulness do not need to be expensive or elaborate and, as in SPP, can involve materials that would otherwise become landfill.

Summary

Play has an important role in health and wellbeing. In this chapter we have identified the following:

- Opportunities for outdoor play, particularly play that involves risk, is known to be diminishing.
- Reduction in opportunities for high-quality play is now being realised in a range of mental and physical health problems.
- Use of loose parts on school playgrounds coupled with risk-reframing is a low-cost intervention for promoting health and wellbeing.
- Children with disabilities experience greater barriers to participation on school playgrounds and are therefore less likely to receive the benefits of outdoor play.
- Playground interventions should be designed for children of *all* abilities.

Questions

24.1 The core business of schools is education, including that of early years learners. In this chapter, and particularly through our discussion of the Sydney Playground Project, we have attempted to show that schools can be sites for opportunities beyond traditional learning. Do you think the recent increased emphasis on national testing of a limited range of academic outcomes may have a negative impact on the broader role schools play within communities?

24.2 When adults think about changing environments for early years learners, they often draw upon their own childhood experiences to capture what they valued or found burdensome. In the Sydney Playground Project risk-reframing workshops, we worked with adult memory for childhood experiences to provide a cognitive-emotional scaffold for adult understanding of risk-taking for early years learners. What do you see as the benefits of adults reminiscing about their own childhoods when considering opportunities for early years learners? Do you see any problems that may arise?

24.3 When you think about your own childhood play, can you remember a time when you took a risk that turned out to be a valuable learning opportunity? Do you have any regrets about risks you have taken? What benefits did you gain? How would the presence of parents have influenced the risks you took?

24.4 Do you believe that risk-taking of children with disabilities should be closely controlled by adults or do you believe children can mostly make reasonable judgements to avoid real danger when engaging in risky play?

References

Adolph, K.E., Cole, W.G., Komati, M., Garciaguirre, J.S., Badaly, D., Lingeman, J.M. et al. (2012). How do you learn to walk? Thousands of steps and dozens of falls per day. *Psychological Science*, 23(11), 1387–94.

Bundy, A.C., Naughton, G., Tranter, P., Wyver, S., Baur, L., Schiller, W. et al. (2011). The Sydney Playground Project: Popping the bubblewrap – unleashing the power of play: A cluster randomized controlled trial of a primary school playground-based intervention aiming to increase children's physical activity and social skills. *BMC Public Health*, 11, 680. doi:10.1186/1471-2458-11-680

Bundy, A., Tranter, P., Naughton, G., Wyver, S. & Luckett, T. (2009). Playfulness: Interactions between play contexts and child development. In J. Bowes & R. Grace (eds), *Children, families and communities: Contexts and consequences* (3rd edn, pp. 76–88). Melbourne: Oxford University Press.

Bundy, A.C., Wyver, S., Beetham, K.S., Ragen, J., Naughton, G., Tranter, P. et al. (2015). The Sydney playground project – levelling the playing field: A cluster trial of a primary school-based intervention aiming to promote manageable risk-taking in children with disability. *BMC Public Health,* 15, 1125.

Engelen, L., Bundy, A.C., Naughton, G., Simpson, J.M., Bauman, A., Ragen, J. et al. (2013). Increasing physical activity in young primary school children - it's child's play: A cluster randomised controlled trial. *Preventive Medicine*, 56, 319–25. doi:10.1016/j.ypmed.2013.02.007

Gielen, M.A. (2005). Play, toys and disabilities: The Bio-approach to designing play objects for children with various abilities. *Proceedings of the 4th International Toy Research Association World Congress, Alicante, Spain.* Retrieved from https://www.researchgate.net/publication/242685578_Play_toys_and_disabilities_The_Bio-approach_to_designing_play_objects_for_children_with_various_abilities

Little, H. & Wyver, S. (2014). Outdoor play in Australia. In T. Maynard & J. Waters (eds), *Exploring outdoor play in the early years* (pp. 141–56). Berkshire: Open University Press.

Metcalf, B.S., Hosking, J. Jeffery, A.N., Voss, L.D., Henley, W. & Wilkin, T.J. (2011). Fatness leads to inactivity, but inactivity does not lead to fatness: A longitudinal study in children (EarlyBird 45). *Archives of Disease in Childhood*, 96, 942–47. doi:10.1136/adc.2009.175927

Metcalf, B.S., Voss, L.D., Hosking, J. Jeffery, A.N. & Wilkin, T.J. (2008). Physical activity at the government-recommended level and obesity-related health outcomes: a longitudinal study (Early Bird 37). *Archives of Disease in Childhood*, 93, 772–77. doi:10.1136/adc.2007.135012

Ministerial Council for Education, Early Childhood Development and Youth Affairs (2011). *Education and Care Services National Regulations.* Retrieved from http://www.legislation.nsw.gov.au/sessionalview/sessional/subordleg/2011-653.pdf

Missiuna, C. & Pollock, N. (1991). Play deprivation in children with physical disabilities: The role of the occupational therapist in preventing secondary disability. *American Journal of Occupational Therapy, 45*, 882–88.

Niehues, A.N., Bundy, A., Broom, A., Tranter, P., Ragen, J. & Engelen, L. (2013). Everyday uncertainties: Reframing perceptions of risk in outdoor free play. *Journal of Adventure Education and Outdoor Learning, 13*(3), 223–37. doi:10.1080/14729679.2013.798588

Sandseter, E.B.H. (2009). Affordances for risky play in preschool: The importance of features in the play environment. *Early Childhood Education Journal, 36*, 439–46. doi:10.1007/s10643-009-0307-2

Segal, M., Eliasziw, M., Phillips, S., Bandini, L., Curtin, C., Kral, T.V.E., et al. (2016). Intellectual disability is associated with increased risk for obesity in a nationally representative sample of US children. *Disability and Health Journal, 9,3*, 392–98.

Skard, G. & Bundy, A.C. (2008). Test of Playfulness. In L.D. Parham & L.S. Fazio (eds), *Play in Occupational Therapy for Children* (2nd edn, pp. 71–93.) Missouri, Mosby Elsevier.

Wyver, S., Tranter, P., Naughton, G., Little, H., Sandseter, E.B.H. & Bundy, A. (2010). Ten ways to restrict children's freedom to play: The problem of surplus safety. *Contemporary Issues in Early Childhood, 11*(3), 263–77. doi:10.2304/ciec.2010.11.3.263

Wyver, S., Tranter, P., Sandseter, E.B.H., Naughton, G., Little, H., Bundy, A., et al. (2012). Places to play outdoors: Sedentary and safe or active and risky? In P. Whiteman & K. De Gioia (eds), *Children and childhoods 1: Contemporary perspectives, places and practices* (pp. 85–107). Newcastle upon Tyne: Cambridge Scholars Publishing.

CHAPTER 25

Using contemplative practices to enhance teaching, leadership and wellbeing

Alison Black, Gillian Busch and Christine Woodrow

Introduction

Teaching is a multidimensional undertaking that calls on educators to engage in responsive interactions and decision-making as they navigate complex and ambiguous contexts, examine deeply held beliefs and values, and integrate personal and professional knowledge. Such an undertaking requires personal integrity and ongoing reflective practice. This chapter considers how the concept of mindfulness might become an integral part of reflective practice – supporting more holistic understandings of interactions, contexts and experiences. Mindful and contemplative ways of paying attention to the current moment are important strategies for negotiating the multi-faceted and relational challenges of teaching, learning and leadership. Mindfulness can help us attend to the personal, emotional and interactive dimensions of our work, and to the implications of actions for the longer term. Mindfulness can support our ability to connect with and respond to young children and make a positive difference to *their* learning, health and wellbeing. Bringing ourselves fully and purposefully to teaching and leadership practices requires self-understanding and appreciation of our personal histories, identities, strengths and experiences, as well as awareness of our values and aspirations. Working mindfully supports the development of interpersonal relationship and ethics. Heightening our abilities to listen and bring caring and compassion to our collaborative interactions contributes to leaderful practice and sustainable professionalism. To support the application of this knowledge, this chapter offers some everyday resources and specific practices to support the development of mindfulness through self-study and self-reflection. Incorporating these into daily practice will encourage authenticity, intentionality and agency and facilitate meaning, wellbeing and purpose.

Contemplation.

Mindfulness is important.

In the activity of my life,

I take time to stop, listen, and reflect.

I slow my pace. I do not rush.

Throughout the day I pause …

and engage mindfully

with stillness.

I re-establish serenity.

I am led in the way of focused productivity,

through the art of awareness and attention in the present moment.

Even though I have so much to undertake and complete each day,

I will not worry, for I know who I am and what gives meaning to my work.

Practising mindfulness keeps me balanced,

and fully conscious in my experiences.

Contemplative practices refresh and renew.

They support my wellbeing and my learning to see.

I watch how children experience the world. I tap into their sense of wonder,

curiosity and playfulness. I look with children's eyes to see the magic

in everyday things. I appreciate my relationships and employ an ethic of care.

Inspiration and purpose flow into all that I do. Harmony and effectiveness are

the products of my efforts as I engage consciously, deliberately, intentionally

and meaningfully. I work leaderfully, collaboratively and compassionately.

My work is fulfilling and rewarding. I am where I want to be.

(Authors' original work inspired by Toki Miyashina, 'Psalm 23 for busy people'.)

'Being': A foundation for inquiry

This chapter invites reflection on personal ways of knowing. As part of being and becoming effective educators and leaders, we need to know how our human self is interwoven into our work and practice. **Reflection** – on issues of self and identity, on who we are, and the personal and intellectual characteristics and personal/professional knowledge we bring to our work – is important.

Reflection is a 'meaning-making' process. When we reflect we are thinking, we are engaged in inquiry, we are interacting with ideas and with others.

It is widely acknowledged that teaching is a caring profession, and the nature of teachers' work is ambiguous, demanding, sometimes overwhelming and often stressful. Educators manage many expectations and responsibilities. Currently, holistic views of teachers and teaching are being challenged by wider social, economic and political contexts. Often, human, personal and relational domains seem overshadowed by the increased emphasis on accountability, performativity and empirically measurable outcomes.

In this chapter, we offer a reverse discourse to value the pivotal role of teachers and the human dimensions of teaching. Rather than focusing on technical skills for *doing* the work of a teacher, we consider the relevance of *being* in our work. Human **relationships** loom large in teaching, and it is suggested that we teach who we are (Palmer, 1997). Self-reflection and self-understanding are essential for the educator engaged in negotiating complex environments and expectations, and striving to be innovative, responsive, authentic and balanced. Emerging in the latest research is the idea of 'being mindful in leadership' – putting value on how we live and lead, and the importance of 'wellbeing', 'being' and 'contemplative practices' that promote awareness, curiosity, open-mindedness and mindfulness (Sinclair, 2015).

> **Relationships** underpin everything that we do as early childhood educators. For children, relationships are the foundation for the construction of identity. When we think about relationships we are thinking about characteristics like responsiveness, being connected, listening, and nurturing interactions.

> **Mindfulness** is about awareness and the effort to be fully present in the moment. It is about giving our full attention to our experience and the people and environments we are interacting with.

Mindfulness works alongside the action of leadership. It enables us to do our leadership work differently – with more joy and love, and less judgement of self and others. By focusing attention on the interactions and relationships of leadership in action – of working alongside and with others, being connected to others and appreciative of their efforts, and being reflective about ourselves – leadership becomes a collective practice rather than an individual role (Harris, 2014; Sinclair, 2015).

Viewing teaching and leadership as a mindful, relational practice linked to self-understanding and action provides us with a foundation for inquiry.

Ways of knowing and experiencing our work

There are many ways that we know and experience our work. Paying attention to emotional and relational qualities supports the caring orientation that we have towards our work. Our ways of *knowing* and *being* are interconnected and creative, and have personal, emotional and relational dimensions that involve artistry and story (Lessard et al., 2015). They are also often *tacit*, which means that we need to actively and deliberately engage in reflective practices. Understanding our ways of knowing contributes greatly to achieving meaningful goals and vibrant relationships, which in turn support wellbeing.

Wellbeing is closely linked to our personal and professional identities, to emotional and social capabilities, and to mental, physical and spiritual health.

Wellbeing is a state where we have a sense of self-worth, where we feel we are managing the normal stresses of work and life, and are living to our potential with optimism, a sense of purpose and contribution to community. When we experience wellbeing and purpose, we are more able to navigate difficulty and complexity, and more likely to experience longevity and productivity in the teaching profession.

However, the daily work of teaching, the constant interactions and the many ongoing demands and accountabilities can challenge wellbeing and leave little opportunity or space for reflection on our knowledge or the values that drive what we do. We can lose connection with the teacher we want to be and the difference we want to make. We can lose heart. In these situations, opportunities to engage with practices that support reflection and self-understanding are all the more important.

Contemplative practices can contribute to a wellbeing strategy for us *and* for the children we teach (see Spotlight 25.1). Well teachers are more able to influence and enable the wellbeing of children in their care (Cumming, 2016; McCallum & Price, 2010). We influence children not only by how and what we teach, but by how we relate, listen and respond to them – through the quality of our relationships with them. Contemplative practices support our abilities to relate, listen and respond.

SPOTLIGHT 25.1: WHAT ARE CONTEMPLATIVE PRACTICES?

Contemplative practices encompass a wide assortment of approaches that value reflection, awareness, ways of knowing and self-study. Rituals such as journaling, storytelling, creative expression, movement, yoga, dance, enjoying friends and family, volunteering, spending time in nature, meditation and prayer are all ways of cultivating connections with who we are and what gives us meaning. These are everyday practices that serve to renew and replenish.

Mindfulness is probably the most well-known contemplative approach. Research shows that the benefits of practising mindfulness are many, including improved mental focus and attention, self-monitoring and self-awareness, resilience and creativity, and the reduction of stress. Mindfulness is an approach to being present in the moment and fully aware of attitudes and interactions. It has been described as a 'particular way of paying attention' that can be learned and practised; a 'way of looking deeply into oneself in the spirit of self-inquiry and self-understanding' (Kabat-Zinn, 2009, p. 12). It is achieved by focusing attention on our thoughts and emotions, noticing and observing thoughts and emotions as they arise, and refocusing attention to the present moment. In the state of being mindful, we are aware of ourselves and our thoughts; we are aware of our surroundings; we are fully present in our interactions and focused on the information we are giving and receiving. This isn't easy to do in the fast-paced multi-tasking world in which we operate – often on auto-pilot. So while we might appear to be engaged in an interaction, our mind can drift to the next pressing task to which we need to attend.

A feature of mindfulness is that it involves noticing what is happening, and noticing how we are thinking about what is happening, but without judging, evaluating or reacting. Employing this type of noticing helps us see more in our experiences and nurtures more intentional responses. Mindfulness often involves 'slowing down' to pay attention to what is happening, but this isn't always necessary. The essential component is 'focusing' attention on the present moment rather than thinking about the past or the future. We acknowledge that bringing this kind of mindful approach to our observations and interactions is not easy, particularly when we have been taught in teacher education to be on the lookout for teachable moments, and interpret and analyse learning situations.

Mindfulness is also about our interpersonal relationships and ethics. It includes being aware of our behaviour and the quality of our relationships. It is about bringing caring and compassion to our interactions, bringing consciousness and appreciation into our listening, into our speaking, into our relationships and into our thoughts and actions. When our work is with children, mindfulness enables us to be open, receptive and responsive to their ideas and who they are as people. Mindfulness helps us see the world like children do: curiously, playfully, as if for the very first time (Kolbe, 2007). As we engage in the art of awareness we are present in the moment, and more able to listen to and observe children's perspectives. (Curtis & Carter, 2012). When we are working in mindful ways, we are less likely to respond in reactive, judgemental or automatic ways to internal and external circumstances.

A recent shift in conceptualisations of leadership in education contexts resonates with these views about mindfulness, interpersonal relationships and ethics. Contemporary Australian frameworks of leadership are recognising the importance of self-knowledge and self-management (including attending to personal wellbeing) as central to successful leadership practices. This shift has been informed by research that highlights the shared, distributed and relational dimensions of effective leadership, and the recognition of leadership as an empowering practice that can be exercised within and across organisations by all participants. The key message is that we are all capable of working together in leadership, and leadership is not a role, but rather a social practice that is fundamentally about relationships and interactions (Harris, 2014).

PAUSE AND REFLECT 25.1: LEADERSHIP

We are now looking at leadership not so much as role responsibility but leadership as the practice, the enactment of leadership (Harris, 2014).

Watch this video where Alma Harris talks about education leadership in a changing environment: https://www.youtube.com/watch?v=rn8tFU8hQ60.

As you watch, reflect on the question Alma Harris poses and your experiences of leadership: What forms of leadership actually make the difference to organisational improvement and change?

> If leadership exists in the interactions between individuals, if it is a practice, or the 'enactment' of leadership, how will you share and build the collective leadership through your daily interactions with others?

Related to these discussions about leadership is the idea of a **leaderful practice** (Raelin, 2010). Leaderful practice emerges during negotiation of shared understandings and in the everyday activities of what people do together to accomplish a shared purpose. In leaderful practice, there is a commitment to collaborate and offer leadership collectively at the same time for the common good. And there is recognition of the views of others, of how values are interconnected with leadership and participation. Ultimately, opportunities to co-create with like-minded people (including children) in collaborative endeavours supports active participation and the development of connected and productive learning communities (Woodrow & Busch, 2008).

> **Leaderful practice** redefines leadership from something individual to something collective. Leaderful practice is about being collaborative and compassionate and showing deep consideration and care for others.

'**Sustainable professionalism**' is a useful framework that aligns with and supports the concepts of mindfulness, shared or distributed leadership, and leaderful practice (Fasoli, Scrivens & Woodrow, 2007). This framework values personal and professional renewal and collaboration and care. This type of leadership is action-oriented, connected, caring, collaborative and located in everyday practice. (For a full elaboration of the conceptual components of the framework and its usefulness for leadership practice, see Fasoli, Scrivens & Woodrow, 2007).

> '**Sustainable professionalism**' is a framework for leadership comprised of ethical entrepreneurship, futures orientation, collaboration, activism and care.

An ethic of care, including caring, is a core value of the teaching profession, and it is also a key component of mindfulness and this sustainable professional framework. Together, these help us to consider the reciprocal and collaborative nature of care and how taking care of ourselves supports our ethical practice.

Looking at these new understandings and frameworks for leadership as practice, we can see the importance of self-knowledge, self-awareness and presence of mind. We can see how bringing self-understandings and mindful approaches to interactions and practices can support the building of meaningful and productive relationships where we are ethically connected within and across our work contexts and communities.

Lifelong practices and commitments

The process of being and becoming a mindful educator is lifelong. Ongoing processes of reflection and daily intrapersonal and interpersonal mindfulness practice are needed. Mindfulness as a regular core practice will help us become self-reflective and conscious of our interactions and relationships with children and with others. Becoming self-reflective will support self-management, and empower us to be architects of our own wellbeing development and leaderful leadership practice.

As we recognise the links between our wellbeing and the wellbeing of the children in our care (Cumming, 2016), we can see the crucial contribution of contemplative practices. If we are to have a positive impact on children's wellbeing, we must be well ourselves – a great incentive for engaging regularly with mindfulness strategies. When we are mindful and responsive in our interactions and relationships with children, they are also more likely to experience a sense of trust, connectedness, security and community – all of which are necessary for children to experience wellbeing, and to thrive socially, emotionally and academically.

The remainder of the chapter is devoted to supporting the development of mindfulness, wellbeing and leadership practice through self-study and self-reflection. A series of everyday resources and specific practices to support contemplation and mindfulness follow. These resources and activities are aimed at heightening understanding of your personal history, identities, strengths and experiences. They will help you become more alert to your ways of knowing, and your values and aspirations. They will support clarity about what matters in your work, remind you of your purpose and passions, and enrich your experience of connectedness and wellbeing. They will also enhance the quality of your relationships with children and with others.

Because we sometimes need support in accessing the knowledge that we have and bring to our work, it is helpful to engage with a range of processes, approaches and representations. You will discover there are many useful approaches for representing knowledge and experience, supporting attention on practice and encouraging reflection and creative inquiry. We include some possible strategies in Spotlight 25.2, but there are many others and we encourage you to engage in as part of your own research. Using internet search terms such as 'mindfulness', 'meditation', 'character strengths' and 'contemplative practices' will support initial investigations.

SPOTLIGHT 25.2: HELPFUL BOOKS AND WEBSITES TO GET YOU STARTED

There are many wonderful books and websites available to support your inquiry and self-reflection. Some of our favourites include:

- Mark Bryan with Julia Cameron and Catherine Allen, *The Artist's Way at Work: Riding the Dragon*; and http://juliacameronlive.com/
- *Parker Palmer, The Courage to Teach: Exploring the Inner Landscape of a Teacher's Life*; and http://www.couragerenewal.org
- Ken Robinson, *The Element: How Finding your Passion Changes Everything*; and http://sirkenrobinson.com/
- Ian Gawler and Paul Bedson, *Meditation: An In-depth Guide*.

Attending conferences is also a great way to engage in professional learning. There are many annual conferences for educators. In terms of conferences in Australia aimed at mindfulness and wellbeing, consideration could be given to: Happiness and Its Causes. Often, the internet sites for these conferences have videos and resources from past speakers and presenters, for example: http://www.happinessanditscauses.com.au/resources-talks.html

TED talks – 'TED Ideas Worth Spreading' – are also sources of inspiration, and can be accessed via the internet.

Practising mindfulness strategies

When you are practising mindfulness, you are intentionally anchoring your mind and your awareness to the present moment. You can practise mindfulness anywhere, but it does require a level of discipline and application. One strategy is to experience the present by *anchoring attention through the five senses*. Paying attention to sights, sounds and physical sensations helps us live more fully and with greater awareness of our experience and interactions. You can practise anchoring your attention through your senses as you take a shower, as you eat a meal, as you have a conversation with a friend or walk along the beach. For one of the authors of this chapter, mindfulness was developed during the process of learning Ikebana, the Japanese art of flower arrangement. During the process of flower arranging, she began to focus more and more on the visual and the colours and the shapes of the flowers. She then gave attention to her other senses. Noticing and observing and attending to the flowers using all of her senses helped her be fully present in the moment.

Another mindfulness strategy is to *focus your attention on the breath and on the act of breathing*. A focus on the breath has been found to promote awareness and reflection. To begin this practice, you will find it helpful to take a few deep breaths and then relax and be calmly attentive to your breathing. Notice your diaphragm expanding and contracting. Notice the feeling of your breath as it flows through your nostrils. Spend a few minutes just focusing on your breathing. If you notice your mind wandering, just bring your attention back to your breath. Focusing on your breathing can help you develop greater control over your internal and emotional responses, and support emotional balance, empathy and compassion. This kind of mindfulness practice supports the development of a positive state of mind and reduces stress.

As a way of developing your relationships with others (and with children), make a commitment to practising *mindful listening*. Choose at least one person (a child?) a day to practise mindful listening with (they don't need to know you have chosen them). As that person speaks to you, 'really listen' to them. Listen intently. Give time to listening closely. Avoid the temptation to rush conversation. Notice and be curious about the words they are using. Watch their facial expressions and their body language closely. Consider the tone and sound of their voice and the way they are speaking. See if you can read their emotional state. Pay attention to every detail of their face. Notice the colour and shape and movement of their eyes, the colour and shape and movement of their eyebrows. Listen without thinking about your own reply. Bring your full attention to what they are saying, feeling and communicating. If you feel your mind wandering, just bring your attention back to the other person. Notice what you have become aware of during this interaction. Pay attention to your own reactions, body language and physical sensations. How has empathy and understanding been supported? Did you become consciously aware of emotions or meanings that would otherwise have remained unseen due to rushing, inattention or business? How might engaging in mindful listening with children support their sense that they can trust you and that they are respected, listened to and cared for?

Engaging with such mindfulness strategies for even one minute per day has benefits. Bringing mindfulness into your life and your workplace can help you be more empathetic and compassionate. It can support your listening skills, your social and emotional skills, and your leadership practice. It can support the development of skills like responding to difficult conversations and building trusting relationships and teamwork. Deeper thinking and heightened awareness about situations and interactions improve ethical decision-making, understanding of the bigger picture, connection-making and responsiveness. Mindful listening and respectful communication contribute to supportive, responsive and encouraging relationships. Daily mindfulness strategies support our relationships with children and the development of optimal social and emotional environments. They support smoother transitions, lower levels of conflict, more respectful communication and problem-solving to encourage positive learning outcomes and wellbeing experiences. In short, mindfulness strategies promote high-quality teacher–child relationships, and support effective social and emotional learning, health and wellbeing for both teacher and child. You, as teacher, are an important contributor to the development of supportive relationships and healthy learning environments. Healthy learning environments directly contribute to children's social, emotional and academic outcomes. Children learn best when they have trusting relationships with responsive adults, and when they feel happy, heard, respected and cared for. Healthy learning environments also reinforce your enjoyment and love of teaching, your commitment to the profession and your overall sense of wellbeing and efficacy.

Reflective writing

Engaging in reflection through writing provides opportunities to explore the knowledge and beliefs that form the underpinnings of our work, and encourages awareness and analysis of daily experiences. Writing for personal and professional learning is a well-established practice in teacher education. The power of this type of writing emerges when it moves beyond the telling or description of life experiences to become an active way of constructing, representing and interpreting identity.

You might like to buy a visual diary to record and revisit your reflections and stories. You might use images and drawings, concept maps, magazine pictures or poetry alongside your writing. These arts-based forms can help to access and illustrate feelings, relationships and meaning-making. One of the authors keeps a visual diary where she includes drawings, images and sources of inspiration. She reflects on experiences using stories and poetry. Her visual diary is a tool for recording and identifying what is important, what is troubling her, what is motivating her. It helps her galvanise a sense of agency over her life. It helps her recognise, express and understand her emotions and experiences. Like her, you might write about a range of things such as:

- specific situations or specific dilemmas or conflicts; situations where you feel you 'don't know' enough and can identify knowledge needs
- the influence of your life history (childhood, family, schooling experiences) and past experiences on your current decisions, understandings and everyday actions
- the influence of university, reading, research and relationships on your ideas and everyday actions
- your emotions, feelings, images of self, images of teaching
- your guiding philosophy and values for working with young children, what you hope for your relationships with children, what you hope for their learning and wellbeing, and for their futures
- whatever is on your mind. Sometimes engaging in writing an unedited stream of consciousness is helpful. This type of writing – a loose internal monologue – can help siphon off the thoughts on the mind's surface and help you get to the deeper thoughts and meanings that lie beneath daily mind-chatter and voice-over. It can connect you to emotions, feelings, points of view and intuitions, and help you metabolise your life.

Of most importance is that you make the time and opportunity to reflect in ways and on things that have *relevance for you*.

You will find that upon reflecting on experiences, insights will emerge in terms of how past experiences influence and colour current actions. For example, you might reflect on experiences that you had as a child. You might remember a teacher who made you feel stupid or invisible, or one who touched your life, cared for you and captivated you with their passion. Memories like these might bring to the surface values and practices that influence and shape your teaching approaches now. You might consider how you are influencing the wellbeing of young children through your daily interactions and practices. As you reflect, you are supporting your own personal and professional learning, and exploring connections between your inner life as an educator, your daily interactions and the legacy you hope to leave.

PAUSE AND REFLECT 25.2: STARTER QUESTIONS

You may find you need some starter questions to help you begin. You may find you want to talk out loud first, sharing your thoughts with a friend or colleague, before putting pen to paper. Holly's work on journal writing, 'Keeping a personal-professional journal' and particularly her section 'Journal keeping – a writer's manual' (Holly, 1984) offers some really useful suggestions. She suggests (pp. 42–3) engaging with these sorts of questions:

- Why, when and how did you decide to become a teacher?
- Was there anyone or anything that influenced you?
- As you look back, even to your early years of schooling, what feelings and images remain?
- Which teachers do you remember, and why do you remember them? What do you remember about them? What feelings do you associate with them?
- What would you like to change or work on to improve your own teaching and leadership practice?

You might want to direct your reflection specifically to wellness and wellbeing with questions like:

- How might my wellbeing influence children's wellbeing?
- How important is it that I care for myself?
- How *do* I care for and replenish myself?
- What are my personal rituals for letting go of stress and for cultivating contemplation?
- What rituals and mindfulness strategies can I build into my daily routine?
- How do I express my care and compassion for others and for children?
- How am I promoting their wellbeing?
- What aspects of my work inspire me and give me meaning?

Here is an example of an early childhood teacher's reflections, as she responded to Holly's questions and engaged in some life-history writing:

My childhood experiences have certainly shaped who I am. The values that drive my practice are clearly connected to memories from my early years – memories of relationships and interactions and discovery. My childhood was filled with happy memories … of regular trips to the beach; of riding my bike to visit my friends; of constructing cubbies in the backyard; of floating on my back in the ocean; of visiting my grandparents and the delights we shared like drinking tea, playing board games, searching for strawberries, and feeding the chooks.

Some memories are less positive, and strangely enough are linked to school or learning experiences. I remember how my dance teacher disciplined me for being late to class and how bad that felt. I remember another teacher who made me feel afraid. I was humiliated by this teacher, and so was my friend. Later, as a young adult, gainfully employed as a teacher myself, I saw that teacher in the distance and immediately a sense of fear ran through my body.

Recording these memories has made me think about a number of things. I think of Henry, a child I know. Henry doesn't want to go to school. His schooling experiences haven't been positive.

My commitment to relationships and genuine intergenerational relationships is sharpened. What I knew intuitively was that the adults in my home life were fully present with me and interested in me. I am reminded again why mindful and compassionate interactions are so important. I can also see how important being connected to the outdoors and to nature was in my childhood. And this is still important for me now. I recognise how just walking along the beach serves to refresh me after a long stressful day. Being in nature calms me and nourishes me. Being in nature supports my goal to be fully present. I notice the changes in the colour of the water as the sun goes down. I feel the wind and salt on my skin. I feel the sand between my toes. I feel calmer, more grounded. I know that in my work as a teacher, I want to find ways for children to have a real connection with the earth. I want them to have opportunities to plant things and see them grow. I want them to have an opportunity to care for animals. I want to give them time to just be.

As this teacher looked over her reflection, she could connect again with what mattered to her as child and to what mattered to her as an educator. She could identify the important role of responsive interactions, caring relationships and experiences in the natural world in supporting wellbeing. She could see the importance of her role as a teacher in terms of creating warm and nurturing learning environments, being emotionally responsive and forming caring and supportive relationships with children. Articulating these things renewed her awareness and commitment to promoting her own wellbeing and, in turn, the wellbeing of children.

Give time to writing your own life reflections. Once you have written your reflection, look over it again. What common issues, keywords or enduring themes are emerging? What connections or ideas keep popping up in your writing? Can you identify words or phrases that sum up your experiences or your feelings? What have you connected with? Dreams? Realities? Dilemmas? Possibilities? Interests? Passions? Relationships? What does your writing suggest you need to do more of or less of?

Using metaphor and drawing

Metaphors are another useful reflective tool. Metaphors can help us describe what our work is like, and what being an early years' educator involves (Black, 2013). Metaphors capture the experiential ways in which we know and feel about our work. They can also bring to light unexplored and unexamined tensions. Can you identify a metaphor that captures what your work has been like for you this year?

PAUSE AND REFLECT 25.3: PLAY WITH METAPHOR

Have some fun engaging with some multiple-choice options. As you engage with the following questions, imagine there is only one choice. Explain why the metaphor you have chosen is the right one for you:

1. Being a teacher is like:
   (a) white water rafting
   (b) working in a garden
   (c) putting a puzzle together

(d) training for a marathon
(e) juggling
(f) playing a game of strategy such as chess.

2. Managing the relationships of my work is like:
    (a) building a house
    (b) knitting a jumper
    (c) surfing
    (d) bush walking
    (e) creating an art work.

You might find it helpful to find some images or create some drawings as you explore your chosen metaphor. In the example in Figure 25.1, early years educator Debbie identified 'juggling' as a metaphor for her work (Black, 2000). Debbie felt that at university she had focused on just one ball. That ball was studying. Now, in her real work of teaching, there were so many more dimensions and so many more balls to juggle. Her drawing illustrated this for her.

After identifying her juggling metaphor and representing it in a drawing, Debbie engaged in some written reflection. This is an excerpt from her reflection:

This representation of 'my teacher self as juggler' has helped me clarify what I was feeling, and address these feelings. After seeing myself as a juggler, and the ball representing my needs being significantly smaller than the rest, I became more deliberate in terms of my self-care. I carefully reflected on my needs and feelings as part of decision-making processes. An important step for me!

Figure 25.1 Being a teacher is like juggling – Debbie's metaphor and drawing.

Metaphors are useful because they have a natural ability to make visible and bring to awareness the emotional, sensory and complex dimensions of our experiences. They encourage us to review experiences and examine feelings and tensions. They can also encourage exploration of alternatives and intentions. What insights do your metaphors offer you?

Conclusion

Teaching is an important but demanding undertaking that requires navigation of complex and ambiguous contexts and attention to personal, emotional and interactive dimensions. Learning how to *be* in our work, more than *doing* the work, is perhaps the real work of teaching. This requires personal integrity and ongoing reflective practice. Self-reflection and self-understanding are vital, particularly as we teach who we are. Being and becoming a mindful educator is a lifelong process. Preparing for any kind of 'becoming' requires the cultivation of practices and knowledge. Mindfulness, as an integral and everyday part of reflective and contemplative practice, supports self-reflection and the conscious development of knowledge, relationships and ethics. It supports wellbeing strategies and sustainable professionalism by connecting us to our values, and heightening our ability to engage in leaderful leadership practices to bring authenticity, caring and compassion to our collaborative interactions and relationships with children and others.

Summary

This chapter offers a rationale and a range of resources for cultivating contemplative practices and mindful approaches in teaching and leadership. It highlights the links between our wellbeing and children's wellbeing. The key messages highlighted in this chapter are:

- Mindful and contemplative ways of paying attention to the current moment are important for educator wellbeing and renewal, and teaching and leadership practice.
- Effective leadership encompasses mindful relational and reflective practices, and holistic understandings of ourselves and our work.
- Because our ways of knowing are often tacit, we need to actively engage in reflection in order to become conscious of, and make sense of, who we are and what and how we know.
- Incorporating contemplative and wellness strategies and rituals into our daily life supports our relationships with others and enables us to engage positively and productively with complex work demands.
- When we know and experience wellbeing for ourselves, we are better able to support the wellbeing of children.

Questions

25.1   What do you know about mindfulness after engaging with this chapter?

25.2   What ideas have resonated with you the most? How will you incorporate these into your future teaching and leadership practices?

25.3   What relationships can you see between your own wellbeing and your ability to promote children's health and wellbeing?

25.4   What practices or rituals will you build into your daily routines and interactions to cultivate mindfulness, reflection, knowledge, and compassionate relationships with children?

References

Black, A.L. (2000). *Who am I as teacher? Promoting the active positioning of self within teaching realities.* (Ph.D), Queensland University of Technology, Brisbane.

—— (2013). Picturing experience: Metaphor as method, data and pedagogical resource. In W. Midgley, K. Trimmer & A. Davies (eds), *Metaphors for, in and of education research.* Newcastle upon Tyne: Cambridge Scholars Publishing.

Cumming, T. (2016). Early childhood educators' well-being: An updated review of the literature. *Early Childhood Education Journal*, 1–11. doi:10.1007/s10643-016-0818-6

Curtis, D. & Carter, M. (2012). *The art of awareness: How observation can transform your teaching* (2nd edn). St Paul, MN: Redleaf Press.

Fasoli, M., Scrivens, C. & Woodrow, C. (2007). Challenges for leadership in New Zealand and Australian early childhood contexts. In L. Keesing-Styles & H. Hedges (eds), *Theorising early childhood practice: Emerging dialogues*. Sydney: Pademelon Press.

Harris, A. (2014). *Distributed leadership matters: Perspectives, practicalities, and potential*. Thousand Oaks, California: Corwin

Holly, M.L. (1984). *Keeping a personal-professional journal*. Geelong: Deakin University.

Kabat-Zinn, J. (2009). *Wherever you go, there you are: Mindfulness meditation in everyday life*. New York: Hyperion.

Kolbe, U. (2007). *Rapunzel's supermarket: All about young children and their art* (2nd edn). Byron Bay: Peppinot Press.

Lessard, S., Schaefer, L., Huber, J., Murphy, S., Clandinin, J. (2015). Composing a Life as a Teacher Educator. In C. J. Craig, & L. Orland-Barak (eds), *International Teacher Education: Promising Pedagogies (Part C) (Advances in Research on Teaching, Volume 22C)* (pp. 235–52). Emerald Group Publishing Limited.

McCallum, F. & Price, D. (2010). Well teachers, well students. *Journal of Student Wellbeing*, 4(1), 19–34.

Palmer, P.J. (1997). The heart of a teacher: Identity and integrity in teaching. *Change Magazine*, 29(6), 14–21.

Raelin, J.A. (2010). *The leaderful fieldbook: Strategies and activities for developing leadership in everyone*. Boston: Davies-Black.

Sinclair, A. (2015). Possibilities, purpose and pitfalls: Insights from introducing mindfulness to leaders. *Journal of Spirituality, Leadership and Management*. 8(1), 3–11.

Woodrow, C. & Busch, G. (2008). Repositioning early childhood leadership as action and activism. *European Early Childhood Education Research Journal*, 16(1), 83–93.

Index